THE BOURGEOIS EPOCH

THE

Bourgeois Epoch

MARX AND ENGELS ON BRITAIN, FRANCE, AND GERMANY

Richard F. Hamilton

The University of North Carolina Press

Chapel Hill and London

© 1991 The University of North Carolina Press

Manufactured in the United States of America

The paper in this book meets the guidelines for perma-
nence and durability of the Committee on Production
Guidelines for Book Longevity of the Council on
Library Resources.

95 94 93 92 91   5 4 3 2 1

Library of Congress Cataloging-in-Publication Data

Hamilton, Richard F.
    The bourgeois epoch : Marx and Engels on Britain,
France, and Germany / Richard F. Hamilton.
        p.   cm.
    Includes bibliographical references (p.   ) and index.
    ISBN 0-8078-1976-X (cloth : alk. paper). —
ISBN 0-8078-4325-3 (pbk. : alk. paper)
    1. Social classes—Europe—History—19th
century.   2. Europe—Social conditions—1789–
1900.   3. Marx, Karl, 1818–1883.   4. Engels,
Friedrich, 1820–1895.   I. Title.
HN380.Z9S64365   1991
305.5'094—dc20   91-50252
                                                        CIP

To Henry Ashby Turner, Jr.

CONTENTS

PREFACE

My first extensive reading of Marx and Engels occurred in the early 1950s when I was a graduate student in sociology at Columbia University. Apart from the second and third volumes of *Capital*, I read all that was available in English (including some of the then hard-to-find early writings). As was expected of us, I read widely in the work of Max Weber and Emile Durkheim. I also read, among others, all of the works of Thorstein Veblen and all of Talcott Parsons's writings up to and including his 1951 opus, *The Social System*. In my spare time, what little there was of it, I read widely in literature, in the work of Dostoevsky, Conrad, and Thomas Mann, among others.

My reading of the academic literature had to be rapid and, a necessary correlate, without much depth or understanding. One had to cover a lot of ground for the sake of forthcoming examinations. While reading Marx's *Eighteenth Brumaire*, I wondered about his portrait of Louis Napoleon Bonaparte. How would other authors treat the man and his policies? What facts would be included or excluded? What factors would be emphasized? What framework would be used? In short, how would other treatments differ from Marx's portrayal? I found a biography of Louis Napoleon in Butler Library and read it quickly. But the welter of material was all too complicated. There was no time for a detailed comparison of the texts. There was no time for critique or assessment. I made a mental note: it was something to be done, a task for some future research.

One evening, after a hasty supper in the Lion's Den, I overheard a conversation between some history graduate students. One of them said: "Those sociologists don't know any history." I recognized the truth of the conclusion. It took me some time, more than I care to think about, to remedy the problem in my own mind and work.

Of all the reading done back then, I most regret the time spent on the work of Talcott Parsons. It was, as Herbert Marcuse once pointed out to me, empty formalism. C. Wright Mills translated some of those formalisms and showed the commonplace observations lying behind the portentous language. Not many years later, other writers and schools appeared offering new baroque theoretical systems. And again, many otherwise intelligent students went to work learning the intricacies of that new filigree discourse. The pathology, the predilection for exotic language and exotic logics, seems most prevalent in the social sciences, although in recent decades it has appeared also in the literary sciences. As a countering measure, should anyone be interested, I recommend the reading of solid narrative histories. A knowledge of those histories will provide a much better guide to one's understanding of human affairs than all of Parsons's abstract and general formulations or those contained in any of the more recent systems.

Marx and Marxism effectively disappeared from the social sciences of the 1950s and 1960s, making at best a ritual appearance. But then, unexpectedly, in the early 1970s, Marxism gained a significant following and, for better or worse, has received more attention since. That statement, to be sure, needs specification: Marxism gained attention and favor in the United States, in Canada, in Britain, in the Federal Republic of Germany, and in some other minor outposts of the capitalist world. One writer has noted that the attraction of Marxism, of Marxist thought, appears to increase with distance from Marxist practice. That revival, ultimately, in a dialectical process, led to the writing of this book. Like many others, I was led to reread the texts and to think once again about the basic claims. On this occasion, however, I found the time for an assessment. While not dealing specifically with *The Eighteenth Brumaire*, this book does pursue the basic intent of that research task noted some forty years ago.

Accountants have provided us with a useful notion, that of zero-based budgeting. Until recently, the general practice was to judge budgetary allocations against the previous year's experience. But that assumes the wisdom of the previous experience. Zero-based budgeting requires justification of the entire effort. That new budgeting principle may be applied in the scholarly effort. It is useful to think in terms of zero-based theorizing. Many texts treat favored theories as sacrosanct. Students in sociology, for example, are introduced to the classical theories and, in effect, are told that respect and proper obeisance are in order. Those theories (and their authors) are canonized. They are, by general agreement, set above the common run of scholarly achievements. Many accounts, for example, make reference to Weber's Protestant ethic, treating the ethic as an obvious explanation for economic development (or the lack thereof). But the linking of a thesis with an esteemed author is no substitute for actual investigation. The practice avoids the question of validity: has the thesis been supported? Zero-based theorizing focuses on this question of support, of empirical adequacy. What the canonization assumes, basic adequacy, is thereby put to the test.

This strict requirement is entirely in keeping with the expressed rules of scholarship, with the regular calls for doubt, skepticism, and fundamental criticism of received views. The requirement seems so obvious as to need no justification. Should there be any lingering anxiety, should some justifying authority be needed, one might note that the requirement was vouched for by Descartes, the eminent philosopher. Or, to cite another eminent figure, Karl Marx (as will be seen) once declared his motto to be *de omnibus dubitandum*, which may be translated as an elemental command—"doubt everything."

Many people have helped in the various stages of development of this work. Although in some instances the specific contributions made were to chapters that do not appear here, I nevertheless wish to express my appreciation to all who have given of their time and wisdom. I also wish to thank the Ohio State University for the financial support it has provided.

Henry A. Turner, Jr., friend and co-worker, to whom the book is dedicated, has been extremely generous with his time and effort. Others who have read, commented, and advised on all chapters are Chandler Davidson, G. William Domhoff, William Form, Williamson Murray, Rick Ogmundson, and Michael Smith.

For expert advice and counsel on specific chapters, I wish to thank the following: on Britain, Martha Garland, Michael P. Maxwell, and Clayton Roberts; on France, Peter Amann, Frederick de Luna, David H. Pinkney, and Mark Traugott; on Germany, Jeffry M. Diefendorf, Raymond Dominick, W. O. Henderson, Peter Hoffmann, Paul A. Rahe, and Helmut Smith.

For general assistance, in matters big and small, I wish to thank Micheline Besnard, Lewis Coser, Irene Hamilton, James M. Laux, Maurice Pinard, Axel van den Berg, Donald Von Eschen, Robert Wesson, and James D. Wright.

Some anonymous reviewers of the manuscript also provided invaluable assistance. I am deeply appreciative of the efforts provided by Yuhui Li and Dianne Small.

Many persons listed here wrote ten, twenty, and more pages of comment on the chapters sent them. Friends, as a matter of course, give generously of their time and counsel. Several persons who were exceptionally generous with their assistance were approached out of the blue. If the scholarly world gave out medals, Peter Amann, Frederick de Luna, and Mark Traugott would each deserve a *pour le mérite*.

Upper Arlington
28 August 1990

THE BOURGEOIS EPOCH

1

INTRODUCTION:

THE MARXIAN

THEORY

Objectives

Beginning in the mid-1840s Karl Marx and Friedrich Engels developed a general social theory which, supposedly, provided the key to the world's historical development. In subsequent decades they elaborated their position and, in the process, applied it to the experience of many countries. Three nations, however, stood at the forefront of their attention: Great Britain, France, and Germany. Developing in the sequence indicated, they were the first of the modern capitalist societies. Their experience, so it was argued, showed the paths that would be followed by other capitalist nations. This work will review and assess Marx and Engels's analyses of those three nations, the forerunners of the bourgeois epoch.

Any assessment of Marx and Engels's work must, of necessity, be selective, since their writings covered such a vast range of topics. Much of their early effort focused on philosophy, although, in the same period, Engels produced an important work of social history. Two general theoretical statements stand out among their writings: the jointly written *Communist Manifesto* and Engels's *Socialism: Utopian and Scientific.* Both men produced historical monographs, the most important of these dealing with France and Germany. Marx, of course, wrote on the economy, publishing *The Critique of Political Economy* and *Capital.* The two men produced hundreds of journalistic articles dealing

I

with events in major, middling, and minor nations. For obvious reasons, therefore, delimitation is necessary. This work will focus on the major claims contained in their treatments of the social and political history of the three forerunner nations. These are, basically, claims about class and class dynamics. They are central propositions in the theory as applied in the key supporting cases. Even with this restricted focus, again because of the extent of their work, some further selection is required.[1]

The attention Marx and Engels paid to those three nations differed significantly, both in quality and quantity. Engels wrote an important book about the British working class, *The Condition of the Working Class in England* (1845). Marx's *Das Kapital* (1867) was based largely on British experience. England, he wrote, "is used as the chief illustration in the development of my theoretical ideas." The "natural laws of capitalist production," he declared, work "with iron necessity towards inevitable results. The country that is more developed industrially only shows, to the less developed, the image of its own future." Given that announcement, and given the centrality of the British experience, it is remarkable that neither man wrote even a brief monograph dealing with Britain's social and political development in the years after 1850. After Engels's early effort, there was no extended study of that nation's social and political history. No monograph treats the linkage of classes to the political parties. There is no detailed account of the bourgeoisie in power, ruling the nation and the empire. Since there was no proletarian revolution, no positive contribution was possible on that theme. It is an important gap.

Another omission is even more remarkable: the bourgeois epoch begins with the bourgeoisie taking power; the epoch begins with the bourgeoisie's overthrow of its predecessor, the aristocracy. Marx and Engels declared, on many occasions, that in England this takeover occurred in the seventeenth century. But they provided no detailed study to support their claim. A central proposition, a cornerstone assumption of their system, in short, was never adequately established. The analysis of their position, accordingly, must be assembled from scattered articles and passing references. For this reason, the review in Chapter 2 will be rather brief. It focuses on this central claim: the occurrence of a bourgeois revolution in the seventeenth century.[2]

The next assessment deals with Marx's discussion of events in France from 1848 to 1851. The focus is on Marx's first major historical monograph, *The Class Struggles in France*. The February Revolution of 1848 overthrew the regime of

Louis Philippe, that spark then igniting conflagrations across the continent. The Second Republic was proclaimed with a legislature and a president to be elected by "universal suffrage." A series of demonstrations and riots occurred throughout the spring, these culminating in the June Days, described by Marx as the first of the modern proletarian risings. That insurgency was put down in a brief—and bloody—conflict. Many complicated machinations followed in the struggle for control of the new regime. Louis Napoleon, a nephew of the great Napoleon, was elected president of the republic and swore to uphold its institutions. The complicated events of the period posed a first challenge and opportunity for Marx's theory of history. It was necessary to show how that complexity was to be explained in terms of the theory. Marx had to show the underlying class formations and indicate their development in the course of the unfolding events.[3]

The third assessment deals with German history from roughly 1840 to 1875, a period reviewed and discussed repeatedly by Marx and Engels. It was out of that experience that they, or more precisely, that Engels formulated interpretations intended to demonstrate the merits of their mode of analysis. One might wonder about their focus on Germany. They saw that country playing an exceptional role in the imminent revolutionary struggles. As early as 1848, in the *Manifesto*, a final paragraph declared that "the Communists turn their attention chiefly to Germany, because that country is on the eve of a bourgeois revolution that is bound to be carried out under more advanced conditions of European civilization, and with a much more developed proletariat, than that of England was in the seventeenth, and of France in the eighteenth century, and because the bourgeois revolution in Germany will be but the prelude to an immediately following proletarian revolution."[4]

That early declaration of Germany's centrality was not an idle or passing comment. Although not quite "on the eve of" a bourgeois revolution, at least not a successful one, Germany was destined, some decades later, to overtake both Britain and France in its industrial development. Germany also proved to be different both in terms of the early development and the success of its socialist party. Even in Marx and Engels's lifetimes that party's membership was the largest in the world. Its share of the vote, until well into the twentieth century, was also the largest of the world's socialist parties. In terms of its organization, it was the strongest and most capable of the world's socialist parties. Its theory, as seen by most partisans, was the most developed, the most advanced in the world. It is not surprising, therefore, that both Marx and Engels, amidst all of their other interests and concerns, should have given special attention to events in Germany.

The work of the two men differs in focus (or emphasis), this being the product of an informal division of labor with respect to their subject matter. Marx's task was *die Wirtschaft* (the economy), while Engels dealt with politics and, among other things, military affairs. They had also worked out a division by territory, Marx writing on France, Engels on Germany. From 1847 to 1874, Engels produced several summary accounts dealing with developments in Germany, analyses intended to show the utility of their theoretical framework. Chapter 4 provides an exposition, analysis, and assessment of four of those discussions of the German experience.[5]

As will be seen, a remarkable lack of consistency appears in the various Marx and Engels accounts. Many formulations prove to be ad hoc efforts, responses to the needs of the moment, and aim to support some practical goal or to account for some recent development. Consistency appears only in the predictions made about the proletariat: it is always moving (or being moved) toward revolution. The accounts of the bourgeoisie are not consistent. The original, the most frequent or standard account of that class portrays it as revolutionary, as driven to gain exclusive control of the state. In the later Engels works, one finds a significant deviation from that original—the bourgeoisie neglects its historical task. About that intervening class, the petty bourgeoisie (or, as it is also termed, the lower middle class), one finds an extraordinary range of predictions.

The final chapter will summarize and discuss the lessons drawn from the previous analyses. These are lessons about the adequacy of the Marxist theory. The chapter will address both substantive and methodological questions. It will consider the adequacy of the claims as given in the original texts and will ask about the methods or procedures required to generate the evidence needed to support those claims.

Central Issues

To provide the background for the subsequent discussions, some key elements of the Marx-Engels position will be reviewed.

Marx and Engels saw history as divided into sharply differentiated epochs, each possessing a distinctive set of dominant and subordinate classes. The dominant classes were defined by their ownership of "the means of production." Rather than having a continuous history, one involving gradual or incremental changes (as, for example, a series of legislative reforms), the transformations were said to be abrupt and, in most cases, revolutionary in character. A new class, after all, was displacing its predecessor, taking power, transforming property relationships, and arranging laws and institutions, so far as possible, in its own interest. One could not expect such a transformation to occur without a serious struggle.

The Marx-Engels analyses generally begin with a delineation of the classes present in a given historical epoch. That account of the class nomenclature is then, typically, followed by a description of the historic task, mission, or fate of those classes. The nomenclature provides only a static picture. But the classes are in continuous movement; their relative positions change, this following a largely predetermined course. It is this fate or mission of the classes, driven by economic developments, that provides the all-important dynamic.

Although well known to most readers, *The Communist Manifesto* is a useful starting point. This brief work provides the best overview of the Marx-Engels historical system. With the possible exception of Engels's *Socialism: Utopian and Scientific*, there is nothing like it anywhere in the entire Marx-Engels writings.

The class nomenclature offered in the *Manifesto* is highly simplified; essentially it is an account of three classes: bourgeoisie, petty bourgeoisie, and proletariat. Two others, the nobility and the *Lumpenproletariat*, figure only peripherally. Since the petty bourgeoisie is in process of disappearance— falling into the proletariat—most attention is given to the two major contenders. The first of the four major sections of the work, it will be remembered, is entitled simply "Bourgeois and Proletarians." That simplicity is not merely editorial in character, that is, aiming at economy of presentation. It reflects Marx and Engels's interpretation of the actual historical tendency of the capitalist epoch. As the authors put it: "Our epoch, the epoch of the bourgeoisie, possesses . . . this distinctive feature: it has simplified the class antagonisms. Society as a whole is more and more splitting up into two great hostile camps, into two great classes directly facing each other: Bourgeoisie and Proletariat." In the preceding epoch, they report, one found "almost everywhere a complicated arrangement of society into various orders, a manifold gradation of social rank, . . . [and] in almost all of these classes, again, subordinate gradations."[6] Some examples of this complication will be seen in later chapters.

In that initial discussion, Marx and Engels review the achievements of the bourgeoisie. It has, they report, "played a most revolutionary part." It has transformed the feudal economy, restructuring virtually all social relationships in the process. The property relationships typical of the feudal regime, it is said, were experienced by the bourgeoisie as "so many fetters," as restraints to be removed so that its affairs could flourish. The bourgeoisie, therefore, was driven to take power, to replace the previous ruling class, and to govern for the first time in its own interest.[7]

Once power is achieved, however, the position of the bourgeoisie changes dramatically. Although still forced to undertake "revolutionary" tasks, although still required to institute changes that, ultimately, would prove detrimental to its own interests, the class now becomes conservative in orientation. Its members now seek to preserve their social order.

The bourgeoisie is forced to create the proletariat, to increase its numbers, and to bring its members together in large cities and giant factories. The bourgeoisie does things—it is forced to do things—that erode the traditional outlooks of the workers, thus unveiling the hitherto obscure processes of the society. The bourgeoisie, in summary, itself creates both the class and the class awareness that will bring about its own overthrow.

An important correlated development occurs within the ranks of the bourgeoisie itself. "Entire sections of the ruling classes" are "precipitated" into the proletariat or at least threatened with that fate. And some of them "supply the proletariat with fresh elements of enlightenment and progress." As in the last stage of the previous era, when some nobles went over to the bourgeoisie, "so now a portion of the bourgeoisie goes over to the proletariat." In a passage that describes their own situation, Marx and Engels declare that this involves "a portion of the bourgeois ideologists, who have raised themselves to the level of comprehending theoretically the historical movement as a whole."[8] It is a statement of the role to be played by socialist intellectuals. They will accelerate the historical movement by providing workers with that larger understanding.

The third class, the petty bourgeoisie (or lower middle class), is also transformed in this process. Competition with the larger, capital-intensive, and more efficient bourgeois producers threatens their independent existence, or worse, eliminates it, forcing them into bankruptcy. The first relevant passage reads: "The lower strata of the middle class—the small tradespeople, shopkeepers, and retired tradesmen generally, the handicraftsmen and peasants—all these sink gradually into the proletariat, partly because their diminutive capital does not suffice for the scale on which Modern Industry is carried on, and is swamped in the competition with the large capitalists, partly because their specialised skill is rendered worthless by new methods of production. Thus the proletariat is recruited from all classes of the population."[9]

The major consequence of this sinking into the proletariat (a process our contemporaries call downward mobility) is simple: it reduces the size of the bourgeoisie while simultaneously increasing that of the proletariat. Although not stated explicitly, one implication of the argument is eminently clear. When those petty bourgeois individuals have fallen, when engaged as wage workers, they will adopt the values and outlooks of their new class. The end result is a polar confrontation, a struggle between the dwindling minority class and the overwhelming majority class. The historical process, for this reason, is inherently democratic; the end result is rule by the previously oppressed majority. That majority then takes up the progressive mission abandoned by the bourgeoisie when it gained power.

Prior to the fall of the petty bourgeoisie, the basic prediction of *The Manifesto* is unambiguous; that class will be reactionary. The key statement of the claim follows: "The lower middle class, the small manufacturer, the shopkeeper, the artisan, the peasant, all these fight against the bourgeoisie, to save from extinction their existence as fractions of the middle class. They are therefore not revolutionary, but conservative. Nay more, they are reactionary, for they try to roll back the wheel of history." A second possibility, a subordinate option, is also indicated there. Some members of the lower middle class may— by chance—be revolutionary. The passage reads: "If by chance they are revolutionary, they are so only in view of their impending transfer into the proletariat, they thus defend not their present, but their future interests, they desert their own standpoint to place themselves at that of the proletariat."[10]

A significant difference in the predictions should be noted. Defections from the *grande* bourgeoisie mean "fresh elements of enlightenment and progress" for the proletariat. Defections from the petty (*petite*) bourgeoisie mean only added numbers for the proletariat. As will be seen repeatedly, apart from this chance (and self-interested) addition to proletarian numbers, nothing good, nothing progressive, and nothing worthwhile issues from the petty bourgeoisie. Its members are generally portrayed as small-minded, as persons with no wider "theoretical comprehension."

Marx and Engels's analysis of the lower middle class is rather spare, giving rise to several problems. First, there is no specification of the conditions that might determine the outcome—whether reactionary or revolutionary. One could proceed with a priori speculation, but since the character of lower-middle-class responses is an empirical question, it is a task best left for research. As will be seen in the final chapter, the lower middle class has remained a problem for the speculative commentators down to the present day.

A second problem with the Marx-Engels discussion of the petty bourgeoisie involves the basic prediction: that they are reactionary, fighting to maintain their class position. But later, one is supposed to assume, having fallen, they will assimilate to their new circumstances and become part of the working class. Given the previous logic, this seems rather implausible. Having engaged in a desperate struggle to retain their bourgeois status, would they then, with no apparent difficulty, adjust to their new condition? It is again one of those questions best left for research. For the moment, it is sufficient to note that Marx and Engels have glossed over a serious problem. It assumes an unusual psychology; on the surface at least, such a dramatic shift of commitments, of loyalties, and of life goals seems an unlikely possibility.

A third problem is contained in the two passages quoted above. The authors use a procedure that has been followed in scores of later analyses: the lower middle class is illustrated rather than defined. One is provided with examples of the kinds of occupations found there. The usage, moreover, is categorical, suggesting sharp boundaries and discrete experience when, in fact, one is obviously dealing with a continuum of experience. Tradespeople, shopkeepers, handicraftsmen, and peasants operate with varying amounts and kinds of capital. They do varying amounts of business (that is, gross sales). Their businesses yield different amounts of return, of profit. The entire process generates—presumably—varying degrees of security or satisfaction. The division of the bourgeoisie into two segments, upper and lower (or *grande* and *petite*) amounts to an arbitrary and undefined division of a continuum.[11]

The use of illustration rather than definition allowed Marx and Engels to avoid a key question: What is the basis for the distinction between the two segments? In practice, the division depends on the amount of capital possessed and the closely linked consequence, the amount of return received. The key consideration, the basic distinguishing circumstance, in short, is the amount of money available to them. Engels makes this clear when, at a later point, he describes the petty bourgeoisie as "possessed of small means, the insecurity of the possession of which is in the inverse ratio of the amount."[12] That, however, is but a fugitive recognition of the basic problem. In the most frequent formulation, the imagery is one of category-versus-category confrontations and of categorical shifts in outlooks or loyalties. The existence of a continuum, however, would entail more diffuse expectations or predictions. A continuum, after all, means differences in degree.

It is remarkable that this crude dichotomy has been so widely accepted for so many decades. If one followed an analogous procedure in any other context, it would normally be rejected as simplistic. If, for example, one were to treat height as the basis for class divisions and proceeded to analysis in terms of the short and the tall, a demand for definition (where is the dividing line?) and a call for finer divisions (beginning with short, medium, and tall) would instantly follow. But where definition and specification are demanded in other contexts, here much of the intellectual world has remained satisfied with the crude dichotomy—one in which the line of separation has remained unspecified.

A fourth class is given brief attention at this point. In the German original it is referred to as the *Lumpenproletariat*—the rags or riff-raff proletariat. The English translation reads: "The 'dangerous class', the social scum, that passively rotting mass thrown off by the lowest layers of old society may, here and there, be swept into the movement by a proletarian revolution; its conditions of life, however, prepare it far more for the part of a bribed tool of reactionary intrigue." More a statement of invective than of analysis, one element is constant in later treatments: the claim of ready availability for reactionary purposes.[13]

The *Manifesto*, as indicated, provides a general summary overview of the development in the modern era. But the proof of the general case depends on validation in the individual cases.[14]

Methodology

Alvin Gouldner pointed to the existence of two Marxisms. Marxism, he wrote, is both "science and ideology; rational understanding and political practice; 'reports' about the world and a 'command' to do something to change it."

Unless otherwise indicated, I have treated the Marx-Engels texts as science, that is, as reports about the world. It is always possible, in any given instance, that the authors' intentions were rhetorical rather than scientific. Since we cannot know their intentions with regard to each and every claim, I have chosen to treat their statements as scientific claims, as "reports about the world." This procedure is in keeping with Marx and Engels's methodological principle expressed in their early work, *The German Ideology*, that "empirical observation must in each separate instance bring out empirically, and without any mystification and speculation, the connection of the social and political structure with production." Assessment of the rhetorical value of those same claims (e.g., their success in moving people to action) would require an entirely different kind of study.[15]

A basic unity to the Marx-Engels corpus is assumed throughout. That unity was the product of the aforementioned division of labor, each of the partners specializing in the agreed-upon area. Their efforts, from the 1840s to Marx's death in 1883, involved a remarkable collaboration; there was an extensive correspondence, continuous discussion, and much exchange of ideas, information, and documents. Marx wrote that "we both work according to a common plan and after prior agreement." Engels, in a letter to Bernstein, referred to some special questions which "in our division of labor" fall into Marx's territory. It is difficult to see their effort as anything else but close, mutually supportive, and symbiotic.[16]

There is a contrary position, however, one that argues divergences and differences. Engels's contribution is systematically denigrated. He is alleged to be less gifted intellectually, a junior partner in the enterprise. His contributions, moreover, are said to have had nefarious (in one formulation, tragic) consequences. All of the bad things associated with Marxism in subsequent history are ascribed to Engels's directions and influence.[17]

The argument is not plausible. Against the separate positions hypothesis, one must reckon with the existence of their sustained collaboration. The two worked closely, for example, on an extended critique of left Hegelian philosophy, this resulting in *The German Ideology*. *The Communist Manifesto* was also a collaborative effort, with Marx writing the final version based on Engels's draft. One of the works to be considered here, *Germany: Revolution and Counter-Revolution*, a collection of articles, was written by Engels but published under Marx's name. The work disappeared for several decades and was only rediscovered, after Engels's death, by Karl Kautsky (Germany's leading Marxist theoretician) and Marx's daughter Eleanor. Not recognizing any differences in content or style, they reissued the work, again indicating Marx as the author.

As for the "lesser partner" claim, we have Marx's own statement in a letter to Engels: "You know that, first of all, I arrive at things slowly, and, secondly, I always follow in your footsteps." Humility and deference were rare behaviors for Marx. In this case, his judgments have a firm base in reality. It is striking the extent to which elements of the later Marxism appear in Engels's *Condition of the Working Class in England* (1845). In February 1845, moreover, at a time when Marx was attacking the errors of German philosophy, Engels gave two public lectures (later published) on Communism. Both of Engels's contributions, the book and the lectures, provide a better match or a more accurate foreshadowing of *The Communist Manifesto* than anything Marx was doing at the time.[18]

Marx's magnum opus deals, of course, with the dynamics of capitalist economies. In that respect too, he was following in Engels's footsteps. Marx's first major work on economics is entitled *A Contribution to the Critique of Political Economy* (1859). The key phrase also appears as the subtitle to his *Capital*. Engels had made his first contribution on that subject in 1844, fifteen years earlier, in an essay entitled "Outlines of a Critique of Political Economy." It was Engels's influence that convinced Marx to turn from his philosophical concerns to this much more important topic, the economy. In the preface to his *Contribution*, Marx referred to the Engels essay as a "brilliant sketch on the critique of economic categories."

Much of the anti-Engels effort focuses on his *Anti-Dühring* (1877) and *Dialectics of Nature* (not published in his lifetime). The basic objection is to Engels's deterministic materialism, the complaint being that Engels had made Marxism more mechanistic and deterministic than Marx ever intended. The subject matter of that discussion, it should be noted, is natural science. The question at issue is whether Marx shared and approved of Engels's position or whether he disapproved but, for tactical reasons, did not express his disagreement. I am not sure about the resolution of this particular dispute. That controversy, however, does not bear on the discussion here. The assessments made here focus on a sample of historical writings. My sense is that, in terms of method, Engels's historical works are of the same character as those of Marx.

As will be seen in Chapter 4, Engels was much less deterministic than his detractors assert.[19]

Perry Anderson has provided reviews of two discussions of Prussian history, one by Engels, one by Marx. It was Marx, he reports, who "reduce[d] the emergence of the Hohenzollern State . . . to a virtual caricature of merely economic necessity." The comparison, he notes, serves as "a reminder of the dangers of assuming any general superiority of Marx over Engels in the historical field." Anderson adds that "the balance of insight between the two was perhaps, if anything, usually the opposite."[20]

We turn now to Marx and Engels's treatments of class and class dynamics in the British, French, and German experience. The major task is to see how the general claims were used in the analyses of those three nations. The logic of their presentations will be explored. Some assessment will be made of the empirical adequacy, of the historical validity of their major claims.

One last observation: as will be seen, serious problems appear in connection with all three historical analyses. Many of the claims, in short, must be rejected or, at minimum, reconsidered and revised. The rejection of a claim is often deprecated as a purely negative contribution. But such a view is one-sided; the rejection of a hypothesis is positive in two respects. It is a step forward in our understanding; the disproved claim, we now know, was mistaken, a misleading option. And if the first option proves mistaken, that fact in itself constitutes an invitation to consider other options. That the butler "did *not* do it" is a negative finding but, at the same time, one that significantly advances the case by requiring consideration of other positive options. That positive direction has been signaled already in the above discussion—in the notion that a continuum might be a more appropriate image of the bourgeoisie than that of two sharply differentiated categories. Positive alternatives to rejected options will be indicated, albeit briefly, throughout the following chapters. They will be developed at greater length in the concluding chapter.

2

THE BOURGEOIS

REVOLUTION

IN ENGLAND

Marx and Engels, we have seen, portray history as divided into discrete epochs, each characterized by a distinctive set of classes. The dominant class of a given epoch owns and controls the means of production, those central to the economy of the era. The principal subordinate class works for and is exploited for the benefit of the owners. There are, at most times, a range of other classes present. Some are remnants from the previous epoch; others, those just emerging, are destined to play central roles in the next epoch. The modern era, described by the two in writings beginning in the 1840s, is dominated by the bourgeoisie, by the capitalist class, the owners of the new rapidly growing manufacturing establishments. That class, they said, had conquered power; it had taken control of governments in the economically advanced nations. The rule of the previously dominant class, the aristocracy, had been an obstacle for the rising bourgeoisie. Aristocratic institutions and policies were a fetter hindering capitalist development.

The hereditary monarchs and aristocrats were seen as involved in the same system. Marx posed—and answered—a basic question about that arrangement in an 1849 article: "Does history provide a single example showing that under a king imposed by the grace of God, the bourgeoisie ever succeeded in achieving a political system in keeping with its material interests? In order to establish a constitutional monarchy it was twice compelled to get rid of the Stuarts in Britain, and the hereditary Bourbons in France, and to expel

William of Orange from Belgium." The interests of the two classes, he declared, were sharply opposed: "State power in the hands of a king by the grace of God is state power in the hands of the old society existing now merely as a ruin; it is state power in the hands of the feudal social estates, whose interests are profoundly antagonistic to those of the bourgeoisie."[1]

There was no room for compromise, for reconciliation or adjustment of differences. The bourgeoisie took power from the previously dominant class. The result, as expressed in *The Communist Manifesto*, was that "the bourgeoisie has at last, since the establishment of Modern Industry and of the world market, conquered for itself, in the modern representative State, exclusive political sway. The executive of the modern State is but a committee for managing the common affairs of the whole bourgeoisie." In this passage, it will be noted, the bourgeoisie is linked to and, in effect, defined as the owners and controllers of Modern Industry.[2]

Marx and Engels's writings, as noted, focus on the experience of three nations: Britain, France, and Germany. At mid-nineteenth century, they declared, Britain and France had already experienced their bourgeois revolutions. In Germany that revolution was imminent. Given the central position of these epochal claims in the theory, it is striking that the documentation, the evidence offered in support of these propositions, is so limited, being best described as sketchy. Neither man, as indicated previously, produced so much as an introductory essay on the bourgeois revolution in Britain or France. Given the centrality of the claims, it is useful to review the scattered comments provided by them to see how the subject was actually treated.[3] Given the basic assumption of history divided into epochs characterized by distinct modes of production and dominant classes, some conclusions follow, so to speak, as the night the day. One should be able to point to those transitions and, with relative ease, be able to date them. One should be able to state precisely when, in the terms of the *Manifesto*, "the ruins of feudal society" gave way to "the epoch of the bourgeoisie."[4]

The Seventeenth Century

Marx and Engels's writings show some uncertainty as to the date of the bourgeois revolution in England. While always placed in the seventeenth century, the years vary. In a letter from 1846, Marx declares: "Indeed, two thunderclaps occurred, the revolutions of 1640 and of 1688. In England, all the earlier economic forms, the social relations corresponding to them, and the political system which was the official expression of the old civil society, were destroyed." In a *Neue Rheinische Zeitung* article, he refers to "the revolutions of 1648 and [the French revolution of] 1789" declaring that the "bourgeoisie was victorious in these revolutions. . . . [It was] the victory of bourgeois ownership over feudal ownership." This third option, 1648, was the year of Parliament's final victory over King Charles I. At a later point, in the same publication, Marx refers again to "the English revolution of 1640." Engels, initially at least, settled on the third date, referring to "that political supremacy which the English bourgeoisie has enjoyed ever since 1688."[5] The bourgeois revolution in England occurred in 1640, 1648, or 1688. Some simple questions arise: Why the discrepancies? Why the evident uncertainty? Why was there no attempt at reconciliation?

A brief review of the history is in order. Charles I, the second of the Stuart monarchs, was king from 1625 to 1649. Seeking to enhance royal power, he soon clashed with Parliament and, from 1629 to 1640, ruled without that body. Two remarkably obtuse policy decisions, however, generated a rebellion in Scotland and led to the entry of a Scottish army into northern England. To obtain the funds needed to counter that threat, Charles was forced to summon Parliament in 1640, the earliest of Marx's dates. Faced with unexpected recalcitrance, the first assembly, later called the Short Parliament, was quickly dismissed. The second, called the Long Parliament, was even more defiant; it was to last until 1653. One text refers to it as "a workshop of revolution. . . . It dictated that the king must summon parliament at least every three years. It outlawed all nonparliamentary taxation. It abolished the special royal law courts, the Court of Star Chamber and the Court of High Commission. . . . In less than a year, (1640–41) parliament destroyed absolute monarchy in England."[6] This first episode, 1640–41, was basically political in character. The king and the Long Parliament fought over the question of sovereignty; the basic issue was that of exclusive versus shared rule. The property question, whether feudal or bourgeois, was not at issue, and property relationships remained unchanged.

A civil war followed, one generally portrayed as a struggle between the king and Parliament (with strong Puritan support). The dates are generally given as

1642–48. The king was defeated in 1645, but the struggle was renewed in 1648, this time with Scottish forces on the king's side. Charles was again defeated, and in January 1649, he was tried and executed. The monarchy was abolished and a republic of sorts was established. Oliver Cromwell, the leader of the insurgent forces, dismissed the Rump Parliament in 1653 and, with army backing, became the nation's ruler, assuming the title of lord protector.

Of the three dates under review, the changes brought about in 1648–49 are most appropriately termed a revolution. The monarchy, the House of Lords, and the Anglican episcopacy, the core institutions of the old regime, had been abolished and replaced with other arrangements. The second of the Marx-Engels dates, 1648, thus marks the end of the civil war, a struggle that was clearly social in character, involving large segments of the general populace. It pitted the monarch and his supporters against the forces aligned with Parliament. The outcome in this case, unambiguously, was a revolution: the old regime was overthrown and replaced.[7]

Anyone familiar with those events knows that religion was a significant factor in both struggles. The king's religious policies in Scotland precipitated the rising that forced him to recall Parliament. Puritanism was a driving force in the civil war, some even placing it at the center of the insurgency. One key institutional change in the new commonwealth, it will be remembered, was the disestablishment of the Church of England. It is difficult, however, to see those events as class struggles. Even more problematic, it is difficult to see any central role for a rising bourgeoisie such as would be required to make it a "bourgeois" revolution.

One way that history might be made consistent with the Marxian framework is through a transformation. It might be argued that parliamentary supremacy and Puritanism were mere covers for the real struggle; religion was a front for the rising bourgeoisie. That is in fact the argument used by Marx. In *The Eighteenth Brumaire of Louis Bonaparte*, he writes: "Cromwell and the English people had borrowed speech, passions and illusions from the Old Testament for their bourgeois revolution. When the real aim had been achieved, when the bourgeois transformation of English society had been accomplished, Locke supplanted Habakkuk."[8]

Those knowing something of the history might be led to ask some basic questions: What is meant by that key term, "bourgeoisie"? How large was the bourgeoisie at that time? How did that class stand in numbers and resources vis-à-vis the aristocracy? What power did it have at that early point? And, last but not least, what was its position in the civil war? The problem of limited bourgeois numbers can be handled very easily—it was others who did the fighting. This is stated with eminent clarity by Engels:

> The second great bourgeois upheaval . . . took place in England. The middle-class of the towns brought it on, and the yeomanry of the country districts fought it out. Curiously enough, in all the three great bourgeois risings, the peasantry furnishes the army that has to do the fighting; and the peasantry is just the class that, the victory once gained, is most surely ruined by the economic consequences of that victory. A hundred years after Cromwell, the yeomanry of England had almost disappeared. Anyhow, had it not been for that yeomanry and for the *plebeian* element in the towns, the bourgeoisie alone would never have fought the matter out to the bitter end, and would never have brought Charles I to the scaffold.[9]

That revolution, in short, is said to have been the work of a coalition of forces. As such, the dynamics involved are only imperfectly captured with that summary expression, "the bourgeois revolution." To establish the point, one must define "bourgeoisie," one must show that class to have been insurgent, and furthermore one must establish that it provided the leadership of the insurgent forces. It, the bourgeoisie, mobilized the yeomanry and plebeian elements and moved them into combat against Charles and his forces. The composition of the contending coalitions in the civil war will be discussed later in this chapter.

The Marx-Engels listings of dates generally fail to mention the Restoration. The Commonwealth lasted only a little more than a decade. In 1660–61, the Convention Parliament brought back the monarchy, the House of Lords, and the Anglican establishment. Charles II, the eldest son of the executed king, was invited to take the throne, and he reigned without interruption to his death in 1685. The change should not be seen as a counterrevolution, since Parliament established its own powers before restoring the monarchy. Through the powers of the purse, Parliament severely limited the king's independence. The prerogative courts (the Star Chamber and several others), pivotal instruments for the arbitrary rule of the early Stuarts, were not restored. The new arrangement, in short, involved divided sovereignty; it created a balance between king and Parliament.[10]

Charles's brother, James II, had only a brief rule, being deposed in the Glorious Revolution in 1688. The nutshell summary would note that this revolution also had both a religious and a political basis. James was thought to be seeking a Catholic restoration and, like other European monarchs of the age, to be striving for absolute power. The revolution was precipitated by the birth of a son to the royal couple. Given the succession rules, the child was heir to the throne, and given the couple's religion, Roman Catholic, the entire religious settlement appeared threatened. A small group, later called the Immortal Seven, a half-dozen aristocrats and an Anglican bishop, invited William and Mary to assume the throne. William and his army landed in the south of England and moved toward London, carefully leaving an easy escape route for his opponent. James's limited support quickly disappeared. He used the opportunity created for him and went into exile in France. The victorious forces in Parliament then wrote laws guaranteeing its supremacy and its control over finances and assuring Anglican dominance in all matters of any importance. It is difficult to see the bourgeoisie as decisive in any of these events.[11]

From one perspective at least, it is not surprising that Engels later, in 1892, revised his judgment of this episode. He refers to the subsequent parliamentary activity as the "compromise of 1689," something that was "easily accomplished." The events of the previous year were then referred to as "the comparatively puny event entitled by Liberal historians 'the Glorious Revolution.'"[12] That would, as a consequence, make 1648 the most likely date for England's bourgeois revolution. If that were the final position on the subject, it would leave two problems unresolved: it does not account for the restoration, nor does it explain the need for that puny event of 1688.

Marx and Engels's brief accounts of the Glorious Revolution misrepresent some of the key underlying dynamics. The achievement is treated as a brief episode; the deposition, the installation of the new royal couple, and the passing of laws stipulating the terms of the new arrangement were all achieved by 1689. In fact, however, many of acts that formed the ultimate settlement were passed in the course of the next two decades. The new constitutional guarantees were secured in the context of the war with France. William was continuing the struggle against the ambitions of Louis XIV. Parliament authorized the involvement and the necessary funds. But, at the same time, it sought and gained concessions that could not have happened otherwise. Marx and Engels treat the constitutional changes as stemming from purely internal pressures, from the class struggle. In great measure, however, those changes were made possible by the international conflict.[13]

Some questions about evidence are in order. If the English civil war was a struggle in which the bourgeoisie overthrew (or at least subordinated) the aristocracy, one should find persons with unassailable bourgeois credentials on the side of Cromwell (and later on the side of the 1688 insurgents). And one should find members of the aristocracy clearly aligned on the other side, as the defenders of Charles I (and later of James II). A simple question: Was that the case? If so, in what sources has the point been established? If the point has not been documented, then the claim, even now, 130 years after its first exposition, must be counted as unsupported.

A second question regarding evidence needs consideration. The previous paragraph focuses on the social characteristics of the contenders. One ought also to consider the consciousness of the aspiring class. If the Puritans are actually only the bourgeoisie in disguise, that ought to be indicated at least in their private writings. If what was being passed off as a religious revolution was actually social and economic, they would have had to discuss their real purposes, the details of their insurgency, and the maintenance of the religious disguise or cover for their activities. If they were driven by a concern with fetters on their capitalist activities, discussion of those problems should be writ large in their private papers. Such concerns should all be indicated in surviving letters, diaries, memoirs, and histories. There should be no problem in documenting the case. Again a simple question: Where is that documentation to be found?[14]

Was there a bourgeois revolution in 1640? or in 1648? or in 1688? The first of those dates, as indicated, involved a political revolution; to gain funds needed to suppress the Scottish uprising, Charles was forced to convene Parliament. The famous Long Parliament used the occasion to alter the balance of power, severely limiting the prerogatives of the crown and guaranteeing itself important elements of control, most notably those involving taxation. This struggle occurred at the top of the society; it was a conflict between the monarch and Parliament, with little involvement of the masses. Given the composition of Lords and Commons at that point, both houses representing landholders (and with many in the Commons being sons or retainers of noble families), the conflict cannot be counted as a bourgeois revolution—at least not as Marx and Engels generally define that term.

The king only grudgingly accepted the 1640–41 reforms, and a civil war, a social conflict, followed. A vast literature aiming to establish the character of the division has appeared in recent decades. The following paragraphs report Lawrence Stone's summary of those findings:

> More and more the tensions within the society are seen to take the traditional forms of a political conflict between a series of local power élites and the central government, and a religious conflict between Puritans and Anglicans. What has begun to emerge is the social basis for these tensions in the transfer of power and property and prestige to groups of local landed élite, increasingly organized on both a national and a county basis to resist the political, fiscal and religious policies of the Crown; and the parallel shift to new mercantile interests in London, organized to challenge the economic monopoly and political control of the entrenched commercial oligarchy.

Stone reviews several problems with the handed-down accounts. One of the most serious is an assumption of constancy about the sides present in the conflict. But like many other wars, this also involved coalitions of forces, and over an extended period, with incentives changing, some groups were led to change position, some to join the fray, some to defect.

> The English Revolution, like all others we know of, tended to devour its own children. The alignment of forces of 1640 was quite different from that of 1642, by which time a large block of former Parliamentarians had moved over to reluctant Royalism; it was different again in 1648, when the conservative elements among the Parliamentarians, misleadingly known as the Presbyterians, swung back to the side of the King. In 1640 or 1642 virtually no one was republican; in 1649 England was a republic. In 1640 or 1642 virtually no one favoured religious toleration; by 1649 wide toleration for Protestants was achieved. One of the major causes of the muddled thinking about the causes of the English Revolution has arisen from the failure to establish precisely which stage of the Revolution is being discussed. Since each stage was triggered off by different immediate issues, since each was made possible by different long-term movements of society

and ideology, and since each was directed by a different section of society, these distinctions are vitally important.[15]

Were property relations dramatically changed as a result of the revolution? Apart from the usual war-end penalties, Stone says no: "Such attempts to change the distribution of property as were made, notably by the confiscation and sale of the estates of important Royalists, are now known to have been largely unsuccessful, and in terms of the spread of wealth between social groups, and even between individual families, England at the end of the revolution in 1660 was barely distinguishable from England at the beginning in 1640."[16]

Addressing the questions issuing from the Marxist position, Stone summarizes the impacts of the revolution as follows:

> Those who, following Engels, see the upheaval as the first bourgeois revolution, argue that it opened the way for laissez-faire capitalism and middle-class influence in government. In fact, however, there is little evidence to suggest that it did more than accelerate and consolidate trends that were already apparent long before the Revolution began. . . . The only possible conclusion is that the first Revolution did almost nothing positive to encourage economic laissez-faire and almost nothing to stimulate a more capitalistic and market-oriented approach to agriculture, industry, or trade. Previous, muddled trends continued, astonishingly unaffected by the political turmoil of the middle of the century.[17]

Stone provides a brief account of all major segments of the society. Here too, a review of his conclusions proves useful. Possibly the largest collectivity in the nation at the time would be the rural poor. One of the "most striking features" of the revolution, Stone reports, was "the almost total passivity of the rural masses, the copyholders and agricultural labourers." The rural poor, he indicates, "were almost entirely neutral during the 1640s and 1650s." There were "a few pathetic and easily crushed" attempts to retrieve lost common lands. Late in the war there were some other "desperate attempts by the rural poor to protect their fields, crops, cattle and women from the depredations of both armies, and themselves from the clutches of the recruiting officers of both sides." Wage earners in the towns, Stone writes, "were equally passive, even in London." One "stage up the social ladder," however, a clear division has been discovered. There "can be no doubt," Stone reports, that "among the apprentices, artisans and small shop-keepers in the towns, there was a definite tendency to side with Parliament."

The claim of a distinctively bourgeois revolution hinges on the behavior of the members of "the bourgeoisie." In the seventeenth century, the group closest to Marx and Engels's usage would have been the "rich merchant oligarchies in the cities." But they, Stone writes, "were either cautiously and selfishly neutral or sided with the King as the protector and patron of their political and economic privileges. The only exceptions to this rule were when religious convictions or resentment at previous ill-treatment triumphed over the calculations of interest. *The bourgeoisie, therefore, was either neutral or divided.*" The point is reiterated later: "It is not possible . . . to support claims that the entrepreneurial classes, industrialists and merchants, supported Parliament. There is no evidence whatever that the alignment of forces in 1642 split the country along these lines."[18]

One important line of argument, a major controversy in fact, involved the gentry. These were well-off landowners who were not of the nobility. Unlike the yeomen, these gentlemen presumably never put hand to plow. Unlike the nobility, they, supposedly, were market-oriented commercial farmers making use of modern technology. Some writers identified this landed segment as the rising bourgeoisie and put it at the center of Parliament's coalition of forces. But, apart from the definitional problem (to be considered below), this claim also has not stood up well in the face of evidence. Stone's summary reads: "The gentry were equally neutral or divided, without any clearly marked division on lines of wealth. There were plenty of rich gentry who were active Parliamentarians, especially in the early stages, and an analysis of the political affiliations of the richer gentry M.P.s in the Long Parliament reveals an almost even split on either side. Nor can the poorer parish gentry legitimately be identified with either side."

A minority of the "small gentry" played a prominent role late in the struggle when they "thrust themselves to the fore, both in the local county committees and in national politics." But, arguing against the "class explanation" was the fact of regional differentiation: "In the north and west these [men of small gentry origin] . . . formed the backbone of the Royalist army and party in the 1640s, and were to be the most fanatical of Church and King men in the post-revolution era." Stone reports a variation put forth by R. H. Tawney, who saw "the money-minded, enterprising, entrepreneurial (i.e. bourgeois) gentry [on the side of] Parliament, and the paternalistic, conservative, rentier (i.e. feudal) gentry . . . with the King." Although "an attractive notion," Stone reports "there is at present not a shred of evidence to support it."[19]

Stone's major summary conclusions differ significantly from the Marx-Engels reading of the subject: "To sum up, therefore, the only sociological conclusions which seem plausible for the early stages of the war are that there was a clearly marked tendency for the yeomen in the countryside and middling groups in the towns and industrial areas to side with Parliament, and a much less marked tendency for the aristocracy and the merchant oligarchies to side with the King. None of the polarities of feudal-bourgeois, employer-employee, rich-poor, rising-declining, county-parish gentry seem to have much relevance to what actually happened in the early 1640s." Turning to a larger issue, Stone indicates that "what has to be explained in the first place is not a crisis within the society, but rather a crisis within the regime, the alienation of very large segments of the élites from the established political and religious institutions. . . . The war began as a power struggle *between competing elements of the pre-existing structure of authority.*"[20]

The civil war ended with major revolutionary changes. Key institutions of the old order, beginning with the monarchy itself, were abolished, and a new regime, the Commonwealth, was instituted. Marx and Engels provide only skimpy details about the next episode of the history. Engels, for example, provides only a few brief sentences on the counterrevolution, combining lessons of the English civil war, of France in 1793, and of Germany in 1848: "Upon this excess of revolutionary activity there necessarily followed the inevitable reaction which in its turn went beyond the point where it might have maintained itself. After a series of oscillations, the new centre of gravity was at last attained and became a new starting-point." There is not a word on the class dynamics that made the Restoration possible. It is in this connection that Engels describes "the Glorious Revolution" as a "puny event."[21]

The Glorious Revolution, as indicated above, was basically a revolution from above. James II had lost almost all his aristocratic support, most nobles having been driven into opposition. The basic issues, as indicated, were religious (the possibility of Catholic restoration) and political (again the question of power, the king's versus that of Parliament). Again, it is difficult to see the revolution as the work of a rising bourgeoisie.[22] If members of that class were, somehow or other, the key planners of the overthrow, it is a fact that has remained well hidden during the subsequent three centuries. The claim is, at best, an unsupported hypothesis. More plausible hypotheses are available, however, ones that are well supported. It was a revolution led by the nobility, Whig and Tory alike. The aim was to prevent alteration of the existing religious and political settlement.

The Nineteenth Century

The problem, the dating of the bourgeois revolution, may be approached from another direction. If the bourgeoisie took power in the seventeenth century, in 1688 at the latest, one should find bourgeois rule evident in the eighteenth and nineteenth centuries. This matter, too, poses some difficulty, as may be seen in the writings, private and public, of the principal authors. We have, for example, a note of puzzlement expressed by Marx in an 1852 letter to Engels: "It is remarkable how army, navy, colonies, fortifications and the whole administration has rotted under this extraordinary regime of aristocratic cliques which the English bourgeois has, since 1688, traditionally dragged along with them at the peak of executive power."[23] This statement indicates, at the very least, an appearance-reality discrepancy. It says that the aristocracy, somehow, is still present at the centers of government. If the original claim, that of a seventeenth-century revolution, were valid, one would have to show the ruling bourgeoisie operating behind the scenes.

The problem, bourgeois revolution but continued aristocratic rule, was so patently obvious that it had to be addressed also in Marx and Engels's public writings. Those accounts betray the same perplexity shown in their private discussions. Engels, in an overview article discussing developments in 1847, writes of Britain's parliamentary election and its consequences: "In *Britain* a new parliament has assembled, a parliament which, in the words of John Bright the Quaker, is the most bourgeois ever convened. John Bright is the best authority in the matter, seeing that he himself is the most determined bourgeois in the whole of Britain. . . . When John Bright speaks of a bourgeois he means a manufacturer. Ever since 1688, separate sections of the bourgeois class have been ruling in England. But, in order to facilitate their seizure of power, the bourgeoisie has allowed the aristocrats, its dependent debtors, to retain their rule in name."

It is a remarkable glissade. The bourgeois "seizure of power" claim is again affirmed, but, to deal with manifestly contrary evidence, Engels provides the off-the-cuff arguments of facilitation and debt-dependency. A rising class defeated its opponent but then, showing remarkable indifference (or generosity), allowed that class to retain the offices of government for almost eightscore years. As of 1847, however, Engels reports: "The manufacturers have no interest in maintaining the appearance of government by the aristocracy. . . . They have a great interest in destroying this appearance. . . . The present bourgeois or manufacturers' parliament will see to this. It will change the old feudal-looking England into a more or less modern country of bourgeois organisation. It will bring the British constitution nearer to those of France and of Belgium. It will complete the victory of the English industrial bourgeoisie."[24]

The same problem gained public expression in an 1854 article by Marx analyzing Britain's involvement in the Crimean War. It contains an unqualified reference to the ruling aristocracy. This group, called the oligarchy, is said to have "led the English people into the great war with France which began in the last century." The reference, should it be at all unclear, was to "the great anti-Jacobin war." In 1854, the aristocracy was still in power, but at this point, even more surprisingly, "the people . . . forced the English oligarchy into the current war with Russia." The war, it seems, threatened to upset the handed-down political arrangements: "And here we come to the crucial point. For the English aristocracy *war with Russia* is equivalent to the *loss of its monopoly of government*. Forced since 1830 to conduct its internal policy exclusively in the interests of the industrial and commercial middle classes, the English aristocracy has nevertheless retained possession of all government posts, because it has retained the monopoly of *foreign* policy and of the army." That monopoly, however, was secure "only as long as there was no people's war—and such a war was possible *only against Russia*—which would make foreign policy the concern of the people." Knowing this, the "whole of English diplomacy," from 1830 to 1854, was based on one principle—"to avoid war with Russia at *all* costs."[25]

Here, long after the decisive bourgeois victory of 1688, one finds the English aristocracy having a monopoly of government. But then, inexplicably, despite their control of the army (and, one might add, of navies, colonies, fortifications, and the whole administration), they are forced to follow middle-class interests—exclusively—in domestic affairs. Here Marx is having it both ways. He is recognizing the perplexing fact, aristocrats in control of most government positions, but still arguing the validity of his bourgeois revolution thesis.

Again there is an easy possibility for validation: if Marx and Engels were correct about 1648 and 1688 bringing the bourgeois revolution, that should be easily demonstrated in the nineteenth-century documentary record. There should be a plethora of documents—letters, memoranda, position papers, etc., telling prime ministers (ministers of the exchequer, home office, colonies, etc.) what is expected of them—attesting to the bourgeoisie's control over political affairs. If the oligarchy were forced to institute middle-class domestic policies since 1830, that should be indicated with great clarity in the documentary record. Again there is a simple question: Where is that established?

Another recognition of this same problem, one which overlooks Marx's 1854 revisionism, appears in a comment by Engels written in 1870: "In England, the bourgeoisie could place its real representative, Bright, into the government only by extending the franchise." The suffrage extension referred to is that of 1867, it being introduced and carried by Disraeli's Tory government. Contrary to Disraeli's expectation, the Liberals, presumably *the* party of the bourgeoisie, won the subsequent election and formed the government. Gladstone, a man of unquestionable bourgeois antecedents, pressed Bright to join the new government, and despite personal reluctance, the reformer became president of the Board of Trade. Bright, it should be noted, had entered Parliament in 1847 (first representing Manchester, later Birmingham) and, with only brief interruption, was a member until his death in 1889. If in power, the bourgeoisie could have placed him into the government at any time in the two decades prior to the 1867 reform. But two other considerations proved decisive. Palmerston, the prime minister during much of that period, disliked him; there were major policy differences, a problem compounded by "violent language and boorish manners." Bright, nevertheless, had been sounded out about joining the government, but he refused the opportunity. Even when yielding to Gladstone's persuasion, he recognized a personal limitation: he did not feel comfortable dealing with the everyday routines of government.[26]

A basic question remains: Why should the English bourgeoisie prove so helpless, two-thirds of the way through the nineteenth century, if they had gained political supremacy in 1688? Engels's 1870 formulation suggests a clear alternative: the bourgeoisie had *not* gained supremacy in the Glorious Revolution.

A useful summary statement describing the social backgrounds of British cabinet members just before the 1867 reform is provided by the historian Norman Gash: "What seemed to have changed least was the position of the traditional governing classes. The county families that sent MPs to Westminster in 1865 would have been familiar to George III in 1765, though their members wore top hats and trousers instead of cocked hats and breeches and travelled by train instead of coach. Palmerston's cabinet of 1859 was composed of seven peers, two sons of peers, three baronets and only three untitled commoners. This was a slightly more aristocratic body than Liverpool's cabinet of 1825 which had five commoners in a membership of thirteen."[27] The Palmerston government, a Liberal one incidentally, was clearly dominated by aristocrats. One can readily understand Marx and Engels's perplexity. That result, which they could hardly have ignored, does not conform with their image of the English bourgeoisie being in power.

Hippolyte Taine, the eminent French historian, made several trips to England, in 1859, 1862, and 1871, and wrote an impressive book reporting his observations and experiences there. He tells, among other things, of a conversation with "one of the greatest industrialists in England," a person who, unfortunately, goes unnamed. The man, described as "a radical and a supporter of [the just-discussed] Mr. Bright," announced: "It is not our aim to overthrow the aristocracy: we are ready to leave the government and high offices in their hands. For we believe, we men of the middle class, that the conduct of national business calls for special men, men born and bred to the work for generations, and who enjoy an independent and commanding situation." The crux of the statement, clearly, is that this leading bourgeois, speaking for his class, indicated no interest in taking power. Contrary to Marx and Engels's unquestioned conclusions, he was satisfied to leave the management of government to the aristocracy. His only stipulation was "that all positions of power be filled by able men. No mediocrities and no nepotism. Let them govern, but let them be fit to govern." "To sum up," Taine declares, "England is becoming a republic wherein the aristocratic institution is engaged in turning out the requisite supply of Ministers, Members of Parliament, Generals and Diplomats."[28]

A century later, John Vincent, in a leading scholarly account of the period, came to a similar conclusion:

> There was in no sense in the mid-nineteenth century, a real middle-class alternative to aristocratic government, as is occasionally supposed. On this point such observers as Mill, Arnold, Cobden, and Gladstone were fully agreed. Nor was there an insurrection of "bourgeois" ideas against the old ways of thought. The middle class did exist, socially, in the sense of "broadcloth-wearing" inhabitants of the towns: but it could not be identified with any particular set of social or political ideas. . . . The limited education and the still small businesses of such people restricted their competence to take part in public life.

Elaborating on the point, Vincent discusses some other factors that made any concentrated bourgeois political effort impossible: "The large capitalists . . . were initially only a fractional part of the middle class: of this fraction, only amongst one subdivision, that of the textile masters, was there anything like a general feeling of alienation from the conventions of aristocratic government: and even amongst the textile masters, the attempt of the Manchester School to turn this feeling into a collective support of a distinctively bourgeois policy was a resounding failure."

The northern textile masters, Vincent points out, were "an isolated occupational group even in the business world." The point, basically, is that small numbers and diversity of outlooks were nearly insurmountable obstacles to political efforts. "The Liberal mill owners of Lancashire," he adds, "may be guessed at 500 families (from the trade directories): not enough to batter at the English constitution very effectively. Cobden's daughter wrote a novel suggesting they are unlikely to do anything very effectively: and she knew every one of them."[29]

Taine's informant and Cobden's daughter touch on a consideration rarely mentioned in Marx and Engels's writings: ability or competence. For Marx and Engels, the capability of the bourgeoisie was simply assumed. That assumption is clearly indicated with respect to John Bright, the leading advocate of bourgeois interests. Vincent, however, offers some important comments on Gladstone's 1868 cabinet and Bright's position in it. The new bourgeois prime minister, one learns, "was prone to appoint Whigs [in this context, aristocrats] over the heads of better men, in order to carry out his theory of aristocracy." It meant a difference in the average age at which they began their careers, the aristocrats, Vincent reports, having a twenty-year advantage over the bourgeois representatives. But "once in office, the same standard of competence was expected from all. The cabinet carried few passengers or cronies."

In his initial discussion of Gladstone's expectations, Vincent gives a single sentence to the bourgeoisie's supposed spokesman, declaring that Bright was the "great exception" to this demand for competence: "What Bright brought to the Cabinet was not weight in counsel or departmental ability, but political support." Later, the point is discussed at length. "Bright's lack of capacity," Vincent writes, "showed how little the university men had to fear for their monopoly of government in this age." Bright found it necessary to delegate the writing of an important reform measure, one with which he was closely identified. On the suspension of the Bank Charter in the crisis of 1857, he wrote his collaborator Cobden that "I don't understand this question and . . . so I never speak on it." A Bradford merchant, described as "an ardent Cobdenite," wrote of Bright as the "most incapable President of the Board of Trade who ever took office." Because Bright's term there was so brief, essentially only one year, Vincent feels that specific judgment might not be entirely fair. The general point remains, however: "Bright strikingly indicated the lack of a middle-class alternative to aristocratic rule, and the large share that education had in sustaining aristocratic monopoly." Bright lacked "the capacity for detail and bulk needed for Parliamentary success." Vincent notes also that he was "naturally indolent except when excited."[30]

There is no paradox here: Bright was one of the leading nineteenth-century reformers. He was also "a representative of business interests," although that phrase needs some qualification. While lacking administrative skills, he did have talents in another area: he was a brilliant public speaker. He was able to formulate, to argue (somewhat demagogically), and to inspire followers; in those respects he had exceptional capacities. It was his co-worker Cobden who attended to the bureaucratic details. Given Bright's unique abilities and limitations, no astute bourgeois would wish to place "its real representative" (Engels's phrase) into the government. What is remarkable is that Engels was unaware of the problem. Bright represented Manchester in Parliament for ten years, until his defeat in 1857. At that point, Engels had lived in that city for some seven years. Given Engels's position in society, it is curious that he had not picked up some information on the reformer's limitations. Even in Manchester, Bright was viewed as a controversial figure. One writer, describing the 1857 loss, reports: "He had never deferred to the views of his constituents. . . . His outspoken advocacy of a more democratic system and his criticism of the aristocracy became increasingly uncongenial."[31]

Given the evidence of aristocratic dominance in Palmerston's last cabinet, in 1865, one may ask: When did the bourgeoisie gain power in Britain? Did it come, as Engels suggested, with the extension of suffrage in 1867? Or did it come sometime later? W. L. Guttsman's researches provide a useful first approach to this issue. He has given us a portrait of the class structure of cabinets from 1868 to 1955. Gladstone was the first prime minister to hold office after the 1867 reform. His cabinet was distinctive in that it had a bourgeois majority, eight middle-class members as against seven aristocrats. It appeared to be a sharp break vis-à-vis the Palmerston cabinet. In addition to the change in class composition, there was a marked change in personnel, with only five members of the earlier cabinet serving in the new government.[32]

For the uninitiated, it would be easy to assume that the Gladstone's 1868 cabinet was only the beginning. But that was not the case: all of the next six administrations, which included three Gladstone cabinets, had aristocratic majorities. The most striking instance of aristocratic persistence involves Lord Salisbury, the Conservative prime minister who formed governments in 1885, 1886, and 1895. He was a member of one of England's oldest aristocratic families, the Cecils. One ancestor, William Cecil, was a minister to Queen Elizabeth; another was the favorite minister of James I. Salisbury's successor as prime minister in 1902 was his nephew, Arthur Balfour.[33]

Judged in terms of cabinet composition—a very crude measure—the transition to bourgeois rule occurred in the last decade of the nineteenth century.[34] The basic findings (recalculated from Guttsman's data) are shown in Table 1.

Britain's last aristocratic majority served under the bourgeois Gladstone. The first decisive bourgeois majority of modern times, it would appear, served under the aristocrat Salisbury. But even that appearance, as will be seen, is deceptive.

These tabulations make an unrealistic simplification in that all cabinet posts are treated as equal. But some posts involved major powers; some were minor, bordering on insignificance. Guttsman provides some important details about the transition:

Table 1. Aristocratic Presence in British Cabinets

Administration	Percent Aristocrats	N
Five administrations, 1868–86	55	49
Salisbury, 1886	67	17
Gladstone, 1892	53	19
Salisbury, 1895	42	19
Three administrations, 1902–14	40	55

Source: Guttsman, *Political Elite,* p. 78.

The entry of the middle-class representatives in the Cabinet is paralleled by a process of diffusion of office-holding among a widening range of political functions. Governments have their own hierarchy of posts, and the representatives of the *new* middle class tended, at first, to hold offices with less prestige, such as the Presidency of the Board of Trade, the Chancellorship of the Duchy of Lancaster, the Poor Law Board or, later, Local Government Board. Men of affairs tended to be put at the head of departments, which had large administrative functions, while the sinecure posts in the Government went almost invariably to elderly politicians of long aristocratic lineage. Foreign and empire affairs were likewise the prerogatives of the traditional politicians from the aristocracy. The first non-aristocrat to hold the office of Foreign Secretary was James Ramsay MacDonald who combined it with the Premiership in 1923.[35]

Until late in the nineteenth century, the aristocratic cabinet members held the key positions in government. They were, to borrow Marx's language, "at the peak of executive power," and they brought in—or were "dragging along"— those bourgeois figures. The relationship, in short, was diametrically opposite to that put forth by Marx and Engels.[36]

An important review of the same evidence by Walter L. Arnstein puts the transformation at an even later date. His categories are different from those of Guttsman (there is an unavoidable judgmental element in such research).

He finds only a third of Salisbury's 1895 cabinet to be commoners, roughly half being themselves peers, with the remainder classified as "lesser aristocrats." Barbara Tuchman describes this cabinet as "the last government in the Western world to possess all the attributes of aristocracy in working condition." The "only true commoner" in the cabinet, Arnstein writes, was Joseph Chamberlain, formerly a "screw manufacturer," later a radical mayor of Birmingham.[37]

Some writers have pointed to three nineteenth-century prime ministers—Robert Peel, Benjamin Disraeli, and William Gladstone—as examples of the bourgeois arrival. They were, respectively, the sons of "a cotton manufacturer, a Jewish literary critic, and a Scottish businessman." The fathers of Peel and Gladstone had purchased estates. All three sons sought aristocratic connections and all three acquired estates. Gladstone left some seven thousand acres of land with twenty-five hundred tenants. None of the three, initially at least, was welcomed by the leaders of his party; if anything, disdain or open hostility was more often the case.[38]

The first decisively middle-class government would be that of Campbell-Bannerman in 1906. He was succeeded by Herbert Henry Asquith in 1908. Apart from Disraeli, Asquith was "the first prime minister who did not come from a landed family."[39] Asquith continued the new pattern of middle-class dominance in the cabinet, in both 1908 and 1914. An even greater middle-class dominance came with Lloyd George's cabinet of 1919: Guttsman reports three aristocrats, seventeen members from the middle class, and one from the working class. It had the strongest middle-class representation of any British government in the period from Gladstone (1868) to Churchill (1951). The arrival of the British bourgeoisie at the peak of executive power came only in the early years of the twentieth century. Even then, bourgeois possession of that power proved remarkably tenuous. Arnstein describes the history as follows:

> Who, after all, were the businessmen prime ministers of Great Britain? A case might be made for Sir Henry Campbell-Bannerman (1905–8), for Stanley Baldwin (1923–24, 1924–29, 1935–37), and for Neville Chamberlain (1937–40), though in all three cases involvement with business took up a very brief portion of a lengthy public career, and according to A. J. P. Taylor, Baldwin was "the only industrial capitalist who has ever been prime minister." Yet before either Baldwin or Chamberlain ever

reached the pinnacle, the prime ministership had gone to David Lloyd George (1916–22), the nephew of a Welsh shoemaker, and before Baldwin had completed two years as head of the cabinet, it went to Ramsay MacDonald (1924, 1929–35), the illegitimate son of a Scottish domestic servant.[40]

Putting claims and evidence together, the following conclusions may be noted: if one takes the 1688 date, Marx and Engels have misdated the appearance of bourgeois rule by more than 200 years; if one takes 1648 as the reference point, they are off by more than 250 years. The date is one serious problem; the character of the process is another. When the shift finally occurred, early in the twentieth century, it was gradual rather than abrupt, evolutionary rather than revolutionary.[41]

Aristocracy, Bourgeoisie, and Government

William L. Langer summarizes the lessons of the British experience as follows:

The new business class appears nowhere to have been interested in securing political office. In Britain not many more businessmen were Whigs than Tories, and there were no more of them in the House of Commons after the Reform Bill of 1832 than before. Even in 1847 only about 200 members of the house in a total membership of over 800 could be classified as businessmen. The point is that these men were too engrossed in their own activities to have time for political careers. But the Reform Bill signified their victory and ensured their influence. They could and did insist on continuing reform, that is, on the modernization of the government, with due reference to the interests of the business community. The Anti–Corn Law League of the 1840's demonstrated the fact that industrialists could and would organize to impose their demands on a reluctant Parliament with its preponderantly landed membership. They did not, however, resort to revolutionary action. On the contrary, they relied on peaceful agitation and sustained pressure to attain their ends. Nowhere in Europe was this upper middle class in any sense subversive.[42]

The lessons to be drawn from this passage and from the foregoing discussion may be summarized as follows: First, throughout most of the nineteenth century, the business class, the bourgeoisie, did *not* strive to take power, that is, to occupy the top offices of government. Contrary to Marx and Engels's unequivocal judgment, that class was not revolutionary. "Accepting" or "accommodating" would be more appropriate terms to describe its outlook. The relationship of businessmen and power-holders, clearly, did not involve a dialectical confrontation. Second, one reason for this "failure" was simple: they were fully occupied with their own businesses (and, one might add, following the Taine quotation, they were generally satisfied with aristocratic management of government affairs). Third, businessmen saw their limited education as an obstacle to effective government service. Fourth, as Langer argues, they made use of pressure group activity to secure their aims, and in the major issue just mentioned, free trade, they were able to do so successfully even against aristocratic opposition.

That fourth conclusion requires further discussion. It is an easy conclusion: the league demanded and Parliament reacted. But that might involve a *post hoc, ergo propter hoc* error. The leaders of both parties, Peel and Russell, opted for free trade. That might have been a response to the Anti–Corn Law League's pressures. Another factor, one that probably carried greater weight, was the potato blight and the consequent famine. That is how Wellington saw things. "Rotten potatoes," he said, "have done it all; they have put Peel in his damned fright." The landed aristocracy was divided on the benefits of protection. It was the small and marginal farmers who most consistently opposed repeal. They, in the end, were the segments hurt by the repeal.[43]

Some additional comment on the first conclusion, the nonsubversive character of the bourgeoisie, is needed. It would have been the height of folly for businessmen to behave otherwise; playing with revolution would be as wise as the proverbial lighting of a cigar in a powder magazine. One might consider the cost-benefit analysis implicit in the Marx-Engels framework. To achieve a range of administrative reforms, ones that were being instituted in any case under the old regime, one has to imagine that the textile manufacturers and the owners of iron foundries, to hurry the pace, would conspire to overthrow kings and princes and, in the process, would arm the people. They would also have to think about the subsequent need—disarming the people after achieving their aims. In the first half of the century, they knew things were so unstable that an upset could be expected at any time. They also knew that the flimsy forces at the disposal of the government would hardly be able to contain a general uprising. Apart from consideration of those technical requirements, any businessman would know a priori that revolution, in the short run, is bad for business.[44]

The Marxian scheme, as noted, assumes that aristocracy and bourgeoisie are two separate and distinct classes. Given their different positions with respect to the "material productive forces," it follows that they have opposed interests. They are each engaged in managing, dominating, and profiting from different kinds of economic activities. The social arrangements beneficial to the one are seen as (necessarily) detrimental to the other. And for this reason, because it is a zero-sum game, the two classes oppose one another. Marx, as quoted earlier, declared the interests to be "profoundly antagonistic." In the extreme case, in France, Engels writes that the struggle "was really fought out up to the destruction of one of the combatants, the aristocracy, and the complete triumph of the other, the bourgeoisie."[45]

But what is one to make of Langer's summary review of European experience in the eighteenth and early nineteenth centuries? His paragraph reads:

It cannot be said that the European upper classes were altogether averse to business enterprise. Enlightened monarchs of the eighteenth century, notably Frederick the Great, made concerted efforts to raise the standard of living by encouraging and supporting trade and manufacture. The Hapsburgs went so far as to appoint nobles and prelates to manage mines and factories. In the nineteenth century one finds such rulers as William I of the Netherlands, who, for all his political conservatism, was a keen businessman and an active promoter. Or Louis Philippe of France, who had amassed a huge fortune before ascending the throne, and was quite at home in the company of Parisian bankers. Leopold I of Belgium was a man of the same stamp and his nephew, Prince Consort Albert, was alert to the problems as well as the possibilities of the new industrial order. It was he who provided much of the motive force behind the great exhibition of 1851.[46]

Most Marxists would know of the activities of one person in this listing, Louis Philippe having been given some attention by Marx. He is referred to as Philippe le bourgeois and as the bourgeois king. Outside of the historians' ranks, however, one still finds declarations of the ancient wisdom—that the aristocracy (and the old regime) was opposed to business, to bourgeois trade, commerce, and industry.

Pursuing the matter in the British context, Langer points to another option, that of a merger, a coming together, or a joining of interests. The aristocracy, he notes, "had been and continued to be recruited from the ranks of successful merchants and bankers." Their interests and attitudes, he reports, influenced "at least some members of the nobility." Langer points to something well known to most historians, that the aristocracy is not a fixed, unchanging hereditary class, each and every member belonging to a centuries-old family. On the contrary, all aristocracies are (must be, even) continuously renewed, wealth (or service) being a usual condition for entry. Those who argue two separate ways of life would have it that the banker-turned-nobleman would give up bourgeois profit-making for his new life of estate management. That expectation, a priori, is unrealistic and, according to Langer, empirically was not a frequent experience.

In addition to the bourgeois-turned-nobleman, we have the opposite case, the nobleman who, by accident of fate, becomes bourgeois (or perhaps has bourgeois status thrust upon him, the *bourgeois malgré lui*). "Several peers," Langer writes, "(such as the Duke of Devonshire, the Marquess of London-derry, the Earl of Durham, the Earl of Crawford, Earl Fitzwilliam) found themselves the owners of huge coal or iron deposits." Undisturbed by their noble status, they "engaged actively in the exploitation of their resources." They became involved, Langer reports, in foundries, railways, and shipping. Lord Fitzwilliam became a spokesman in Parliament "in behalf of progressive economic and social policies."[47]

A second familiar development led to the same result, that is, to the creation of bourgeois noblemen. Those whose estates happened to be located in the path of urban expansion were destined to become urban landlords and real estate operators. Concern for their aristocratic status did not deter them for a very simple reason: they stood to make a lot of money in the process. This is not to say that all noblemen were doing it. Here as everywhere some diversity is indicated. One quantitative indication of the tendency is given by Langer, who reports that in the Parliament of 1841–47, "at least a third of the aristocratic members were engaged in business, if only as directors of banks, insurance companies, railways or public utilities." Some did and some did not. John Vincent notes: "The traditional holders of power also expanded their influences as things grew fatter. Lord Lansdowne became Chairman of the Great Western, Lord Salisbury of the Great Eastern Railway."[48]

Clearly a more differentiated portrait is needed. Some aristocrats felt trade and commerce to be beneath them. But others, clearly, saw the money as more important than any traditional disdain. For some, there may have been a will but no opportunity. Some aristocrats may not have been in business because of accidents of fate—no coal had been discovered under their acres, or their fields did not stand in the way of London's expansion. Some of them may not have been on the boards of manufacturing establishments or of railways because the bourgeois directors had no high respect for their manifest talents. Custom or social taboos are not the only possibilities.[49]

It is not too surprising, perhaps, that Marx and Engels's early depictions of the bourgeois epoch should have been considerably modified in later formulations. Engels's 1847 "Principles of Communism," his draft for the *Manifesto*, contains an unambiguous declaration of the achievement; he refers to England, France, and Belgium, "where the bourgeoisie rules." The same year, in an address on the Polish question, he had announced that "the aristocracy no longer has any power in England; the bourgeoisie alone rules and has taken the aristocracy in tow."[50] But four decades later, in 1892, in his "Special Introduction" to the English edition of *Socialism: Utopian and Scientific* (1892), a strikingly different statement appears: "It seems a law of historical development that the bourgeoisie can in no European country get hold of political power—at least for any length of time—in the same exclusive way in which the feudal aristocracy kept hold of it during the Middle Ages. In England, the bourgeoisie never held undivided sway. Even the victory of 1832 left the landed aristocracy in almost exclusive possession of all the leading Government offices."

The consideration that drove the bourgeoisie to action in the early statements—the fetters on their economic activities—disappears here; the agenda of concerns shifts dramatically. One "great Liberal manufacturer," W. E. Forster, is quoted by Engels as reporting his distress when learning, as a cabinet minister, that "he had to move in society where French was, at least, as necessary as English!" The failure to take full control of the government is initially treated by Engels as a result of this deficient education: "The fact was, the English middle-class of that time were, as a rule, quite uneducated upstarts, and could not help leaving to the aristocracy those superior Government places where other qualifications were required than mere insular narrowness and insular conceit, seasoned by business sharpness." The "endless newspaper debates about middle-class education," Engels reports, "show that the English middle-class does not yet consider itself good enough for the best education, and looks to something more modest."

Engels then reintroduces his earlier claim about the continued exclusion of bourgeois leaders, this time, though, focusing on suffrage restrictions as the cause: "Thus, even after the repeal of the Corn Laws, it appeared a matter of course that the men who had carried the day, the Cobdens, Brights, Forsters, etc., should remain excluded from a share in the official government of the country, until twenty years afterwards a new Reform Act opened to them the door of the Cabinet." With no break, shifting theme in mid-paragraph, Engels moves from educational deficiencies to status problems:

> The English bourgeoisie are, up to the present day, so deeply penetrated by a sense of their social inferiority that they keep up, at their own expense and that of the nation, an ornamental caste of drones to represent the nation worthily at all State functions; and they consider themselves highly honoured whenever one of themselves is found worthy of admission into this select and privileged body, manufactured, after all, by themselves.
>
> The industrial and commercial middle-class had, therefore, not yet succeeded in driving the landed aristocracy completely from political power when another competitor, the working-class, appeared on the stage.[51]

The bold and confident bourgeoisie of the *Manifesto*—which was said to be revolutionizing all social relations, sweeping across national boundaries, and creating the world market—has become this humble and deferential class, one immobilized by a nervous concern with status. Thomas Gradgrind has been replaced by Uriah Heep. It is a remarkable transformation, one far from Marx's 1859 formulation: "The material productive forces of society come into conflict with the existing relations of production. . . . From forms of development of the productive forces these relations turn into their fetters. Then begins an era of social revolution."[52] The structural argument has yielded to an argument of social psychology. The drive to remove fetters on business activity has been blocked by poor education and feelings of inferiority.

Engels was obviously in a quandary. Events had not borne out their earlier claims about exclusive bourgeois rule. Some change, a reconciliation with undeniable fact, was clearly in order. But he is obviously extemporizing here, moving quickly from the argument of deficient education, to the need for "a new Reform Act" (a non sequitur, incidentally—the act would not alter the education of the Cobdens, Brights, Forsters, etc.), and finally to the inferiority complex claim.[53] Given the flimsiness of Engels's argument, it is perhaps not surprising that this position, shared power, has been lost in most subsequent Marxist analyses. The most striking proof of this is to be found in the related argument about Germany: this refers to the problem of German exceptionalism, that the bourgeoisie there failed to take power. An exception exists only by reference to a rule, in this case, that the bourgeoisie elsewhere—in Britain, France, Belgium, Italy, etc.—did take power.

Engels was correct in recognizing the need for historical revision. It is only in the specifics, in the handling of the subject matter, that he failed. A second attempt seems appropriate; all of the propositions offered here, it should be noted, are based on the English experience. It is useful to consider pairs of options, those provided by Marx and Engels, followed by suggested alternatives.

1. Marx-Engels: The bourgeois revolution occurred in England in the seventeenth century (in 1640, 1648, or 1688).
   Alternative: The seventeenth-century struggles were political and religious; the Glorious Revolution established parliamentary supremacy. The principal actors, the victors in that struggle, were nobles, peers of the realm, aided by their kinsmen and allies in the House of Commons.
2. Marx-Engels (initial version): The struggle between aristocracy and bourgeoisie is dialectical in character; those classes, based on opposed modes of production, have sharply opposed interests.
   Alternative: Aristocracy and bourgeoisie, initially at least, did different things. The former were landed proprietors; the latter ran manufacturing establishments, railroads, banks, and other establishments. It is a mistake, however, to see their interests as sharply opposed. Members of the bourgeoisie could and did buy land; some secured titles of nobility. An aristocrat could easily, through accidents of fate, become the proprietor of a colliery, become an urban property owner, or be the director of a bank. Over time, there was a gradual merging of interests.

3. Marx-Engels: Because of this opposition of interests, the bourgeoisie is driven to replace its predecessor; it takes power.

Alternative: Until well into the nineteenth century, the bourgeoisie was content to let the aristocracy rule the nation. The bourgeoisie was occupied with business matters and, with rare exception, had little time for politics. They did not experience aristocratic rule as a serious detriment, as fetters, to their activities. Where problems did arise, these were handled through informal contacts or, in the most famous case, the Anti–Corn Law League, through a pressure group. Even there, as noted, the causal dynamics are open to some question. Aristocratic rule was eventually succeeded by bourgeois dominance, which occurred in the first years of the twentieth century, more than two hundred years after the Glorious Revolution. The transfer of power was a slow evolutionary process.[54]

The alternatives have the advantage of being consistent with what is known about class relations in Britain in the period under discussion. The only loss is in the symmetry of the Marxian system—it is not, at least not in this episode, a history of a stochastic break between epochs. It might mean that elsewhere, too, the assumption of a sharp break between feudal and capitalist societies was unwarranted or, at minimum, in need of reconsideration. One might still maintain the rest of the system. The dialectical struggle in the next episode, however, would be between the workers and the merged forces of bourgeoisie and aristocracy. One could dispense with the search for the bourgeois revolution in the Stuart period. One could dispense with the search for failed or absent bourgeois revolutions in the nineteenth century. If the bourgeoisie was not revolutionary, if it did not seek a revolutionary overthrow of the old regime, it is hardly problematic that such revolutions did not appear. It also means one can dispense with that angry scolding found in Marxist (and some scholarly) literature.[55] The bourgeois failure (in Germany, for example) exists only by reference to the Marxian predictions. From the bourgeois perspective, it would be no failure at all, since a revolutionary overthrow of the old regime was not their aim.

Were one so disposed, a couple of options are available that might save the claim that a bourgeois revolution occurred sometime in the seventeenth century. The first possibility involves redefinition: given the manifest absence of a bourgeoisie, more precisely, of a bourgeoisie playing out the revolutionary role assigned to it, one must find that class elsewhere. An appropriate segment must be found and declared to be the bourgeoisie. Lawrence Stone points to Engels as the initiator of this approach, fitting the English Revolution into their framework "by some brisk legerdemain which changed nobles and gentry into 'bourgeois landlords', and thus made it possible to regard the Revolution as a 'bourgeois upheaval.'" This line of argument was used by Tawney, who saw "the rising gentry as progressive-minded and capitalist and . . . the Royalist supporters as old-fashioned and feudal." That equation of gentry and bourgeoisie, Stone points out, has come in for severe criticism "on both logical and factual grounds."[56] As noted above, the gentry was rather evenly divided, appearing on both sides in the civil war.

At the outset, it should be noted, this redefinition steps outside Marx's own framework. One of the most famous and most cited of Marx's works is the preface to *A Contribution to the Critique of Political Economy*. The preface opens with this statement: "I examine the system of bourgeois economy in the following order: *capital, landed property, wage-labour.* . . . The economic conditions of existence of the three great classes into which modern bourgeois society is divided are analysed under [those] three headings." The later redefinition, of gentry as bourgeois, takes a segment that is indisputably "landed property" and locates it as part of another class. Stone's use of the term "legerdemain" in this connection seems entirely appropriate. Hexter, addressing the same concern, refers to the procedure as involving "ad hoc extensions of the term 'bourgeois.'" The result, he indicates, is the "bourgeois of convenience."[57]

Another possible save focuses on the absent-documentation question, on the absence of the appropriate indications of motive. In the just-discussed preface, Marx deals with the problematical question of expressed motivations. In a brief discussion of the epochal transformations, he distinguishes between "the material transformation of the economic conditions of production" and the "ideological forms in which men become conscious of this conflict and fight it out." The former, he writes, "can be determined with the precision of natural science." But the ideological forms pose something of a problem: "Just as one does not judge an individual by what he thinks about himself, so one cannot judge such a period of transformation by its consciousness."

In another famous discussion, in the opening pages of his *Eighteenth Brumaire*, Marx offers a more extended consideration of the appearance-reality question, of what one might call the problem of murky consciousness. "The tradition of all the dead generations," he writes, "weighs like a nightmare on the brain of the living. And just when they seem engaged in revolutionising themselves and things, in creating something that has never yet existed, precisely in such periods of revolutionary crisis they anxiously conjure up the spirits of the past to their service." The leaders of the French Revolution had "the task of unchaining and setting up modern *bourgeois* society," but this, he writes, was "performed . . . in Roman costume and with Roman phrases." Bourgeois society, he declares, is "unheroic." It did, nevertheless, take "heroism, sacrifice, terror, civil war and battles of peoples to bring it into being." And it was in "the classically austere traditions of the Roman Republic [that the bourgeoisie's] gladiators found the ideals and the art forms, the self-deceptions that they needed in order to conceal from themselves the bourgeois limitations of the content of their struggles and to maintain their passion on the high plane of great historical tragedy." It was at this point that he touched on Cromwell and the English civil war and spoke of Locke later supplanting Habakkuk.[58]

The principal direction of the Marx-Engels theory asserts the powerful determining impact of material conditions which generates a coming-to-consciousness. The theory argues a developing awareness, a growth of rational understandings; it points to a wide range of factors that unveil otherwise obscure events and processes. That development of consciousness in turn leads to organization and action to achieve the real interests of an insurgent class; the class comes to act "for itself" (*für sich*). For the rising bourgeoisie, recognition of the fetters on their economic activity should, presumably, have been a clearly understood fact, something issuing out of the everyday business activities of its members. And that fact should find clear, unambiguous expression somewhere, most especially in the private writings of the bourgeois revolutionaries. In the years following the successful conquest of power, there would not, of course, be any obstacle to the open expression of such concerns.

Basically, one has two lines of argument in the Marxian texts. On the one hand, we have the argument of the rational, aware, conscious agent bringing in a new epoch; on the other, we have the argument of muddled understanding, of inappropriate dead-hand thought, of tactical needs (to add heroism to the otherwise prosaic task), or of needed self-deception. Throughout this chapter, it has been assumed that the first of these options is the "real" Marx-Engels position. Judged by the requirements of their case and by frequency of mention, the first option is, by far, the more probable logic. The successful revolution does not come about through muddled thought, inappropriate views, or self-deception. The second position seems a low probability option. It appears to be one designed to cope with a serious problem in the principal line of argument: the statements of purpose provided by the revolutionaries do not conform to the requirements of the theory.[59]

The Aristocratic Persistence

An important historical question deserves some consideration: How was it possible for the aristocracy to continue in power for so long? Why was it that bourgeois dominance appeared only in the early years of the twentieth century? The studies of W. D. Rubinstein provide some surprising answers.

First, large fortunes based on land outnumbered the equivalent urban bourgeois fortunes until late in the nineteenth century. The landed fortunes, moreover, were considerably larger than those based on bourgeois enterprise. Here is Rubinstein's summary:

> Until the 1880s more than half of Britain's wealthiest men were landowners; at earlier periods of the century the percentage was far higher. At the time of the Napoleonic Wars perhaps seven-eighths of all persons worth £100,000 or more were landowners. . . . Moreover the richest landowners were far richer than the wealthiest British businessmen until this century. The richest landowner of all during the late nineteenth century, the duke of Westminster, was reliably said to have been worth £14 million in 1895 on the basis of his London estates alone. . . . Such aristocrats as the dukes of Bedford, Northumberland, Portland, Devonshire, and Buccleuch, or Lords Derby and Lansdowne, were nearly as wealthy. In contrast, the richest British businessman of the nineteenth century left no more than £6 million."

Second, the largest nonlanded fortunes were not those of manufacturers but, rather, belonged to persons engaged in commerce and finance. Rubinstein's research "demonstrates the lead in number and wealth of commerce and finance over industry and manufacturing, and of London and provincial entrepots like Liverpool over manufacturing towns, both among the very wealthy and among the tax-paying middle class. . . . [The non-landed] wealthy of nineteenth-century Britain earned their fortunes disproportionately in commerce, finance and transport, as merchants, bankers, shipowners, merchant bankers, and stock and insurance brokers, rather than as manufacturers and industrialists."

Some sense of the proportions is useful. In the period 1858–79, the percentages of persons leaving fortunes of £500,000 or more based, respectively, on land, commerce and finance, and manufacturing were 69, 19, and 12 (N=406). If it were a simple question of money buying power, the continued dominance of the aristocracy would pose no problem at all. The landed elites had money in great quantity; the manufacturers, speaking relatively, did not. The explanation for the aristocratic persistence, in short, could easily flow out of the basic Marx-Engels arguments. But Marx and Engels, like many others, misread the frequency distribution.[60]

The demise of aristocratic power, as indicated, occurs in the early twentieth century. Arnstein links it first to the general election of 1906 and the subsequent Liberal government which, as seen, "relegated the aristocracy to a minority role in the cabinet." Lloyd George's budget of 1909 posed a serious threat to the large landed estates. The battle over the Parliament Act of 1911, Arnstein notes, fought over the issue of "the Peers" versus "the People," is frequently given as the decisive date. But the more important fact, he argues, drawing on the research of F. M. L. Thompson, was the war. On one estate, the tax on gross rents in 1914 amounted to 4 percent; in 1919, that tax was 30 percent. The budget of 1919, moreover, pushed the inheritance tax upward. On estates of £2 million or more, it went to 40 percent. "The deaths of numerous young aristocrats in the war," Arnstein adds, "meant that the same estate might change ownership twice or more during the same decade. Between 1917 and 1921 one-fourth of all the land in England may have changed hands, and the large estates were generally bought by their former tenants or by urban real estate developers."[61]

A Distant Resonance

No serious historian would accept the unrevised Marxian claim about a bourgeoisie in power in seventeenth-century England. As indicated, even Christopher Hill, the most serious defender of the position, eventually yielded or, more precisely, changed his position. Barrington Moore, the noted sociologist-historian, sums up as follows: "The critics of those who label the Civil War a bourgeois revolution are correct in their contention that the conflict did not result in the taking of political power by the bourgeoisie. The upper classes in the countryside remained in firm control of the apparatus of politics . . . not only during the eighteenth century but even after the Reform Bill of 1832." Hans Rosenberg, the eminent German historian, wrote that "England reached the great flowering of direct aristocratic rulership in the eighteenth and early nineteenth centuries." Two specialists in German history, David Blackbourn and Geoff Eley, discussing the problem of that country's failed bourgeois revolution offer a forceful summary with regard to the presumed forerunners, England and France: "The idea of Germany's failed bourgeois revolution contains one further assumption which is the most dubious of all, namely that the model of 'bourgeois revolution' attributed to Britain and France (i.e. that of a forcibly acquired liberal democracy seized by a triumphant bourgeoisie, acting politically as a class, in conscious struggle against a feudal aristocracy) actually occurred. This assumption is both basic and extremely questionable. For the thesis of the abortive bourgeois revolution [in Germany] . . . presupposes a reading of the English and French experience which is effectively discredited."[62]

Some commentators, remarkably enough, still give credence to the claim of a bourgeois revolution in seventeenth-century England. The editors of the Marx-Engels *Collected Works*, some of them eminent historians, have given full support to the claim in their many explanatory footnotes. I have not found any place where the inconsistent dates and formulations are pointed out; I have not found any indication that the basic claim lacks serious support, nor have I found reference there to any contrary evidence. Blackbourn and Eley note "that British and French historians have largely abandoned the more schematic notion of bourgeois revolution which German historians apparently still assume." Göran Therborn, a sociologist, refers to "the great bourgeois revolutions" but gives no indication to his readers that the expression might, somehow, be problematic. A review article by historian C. H. George, directed to the interested social science audience, describes an assortment of works dealing with "the English revolution" but nowhere indicates any doubts, problems, or contrary literature. Michel Foucault, without any specification or references, writes of "the process by which the bourgeoisie became in the course of the eighteenth century the politically dominant class."[63]

Some authors, clearly, refuse to give up. They are not about to be bound by evidence. Some sense of the problem may be seen in a comment reported by Jack A. Goldstone in his conclusions to a brilliant article entitled "Capitalist Origins of the English Revolution." "At a recent American Sociological Association meeting," he reports, "a prominent sociologist defended the sweep of the neo-Marxist theory by stating: 'Damn the facts. A good theory is hard to find.'" Goldstone indicated his agreement: "A good theory *is* hard to find." But, he added, "when the facts are this damning, perhaps it is time to look harder for another." Searching for "the capitalist origins of the English Revolution," he concludes, "is chasing a chimera."[64]

A Fourth Case: The Belgian Experience

At two points in this chapter, Marx and Engels are quoted with regard to a bourgeois revolution in Belgium. Consideration of the Belgian history is something of a digression here; it does, nevertheless, provide some instructive and relevant lessons. Belgium, unfortunately, has been given only limited attention in discussions of the bourgeois epoch. Relative to most other European nations of the early nineteenth century, it was economically advanced and, accordingly, was subject to all of the dynamics outlined in the Marx-Engels theory. It would constitute, therefore, another test case for assessment of the theory, evidently the point of Marx and Engels's references.

A revolutionary uprising occurred in Brussels in February 1848; it followed immediately on the arrival of news of the successful revolution in Paris on the twenty-fourth. But in this case, King Leopold, with remarkable ease, finessed the problem; he met with the insurgents, assured them of his republican sympathies, and asked only that his abdication be orderly, without bloodshed, and that he receive a pension. With calm thus restored, the reserves were mobilized, and a few days later, the insurgents were easily dispersed. Marx and Engels were both residents of the city; Engels was an eyewitness observer. This was the first of the revolutionary failures of 1848.[65]

The Belgian experience is of interest in still another respect. That nation was first created in 1830 when it broke away from the Netherlands. Marx (as quoted above, in the second paragraph of this chapter) declared it a bourgeois revolution of the same kind as had occurred twice in England and twice in France. But that seriously misrepresents the actual dynamics of the case. The Dutch king, William I, was himself very much bourgeois in orientation, a financial genius and businessman; his economic policies were exemplary for capitalist development. The problems stemmed from his social and cultural policies which aimed at national unification; these were, with considerable justification, seen as anti-Catholic and pro-Dutch. The king's extraordinarily obtuse policies outraged almost all segments of the Belgian population and generated the impossible alliance, a coalition of liberals and Catholics. His repression of a liberal journalist in 1828 led to the formation of the Union of Opposition (essentially a national liberation movement led by an assortment of intellectuals). The July Revolution in France heightened tensions. The immediate stimulus to the national uprising, however, was a cultural event—a performance of an opera by Auber, *La Muette de Portici*, described as "inspiringly patriotic."

In the face of the uprising, the king withdrew his troops from Brussels, which was quickly taken over by the insurgents. Businessmen were not a part of this movement. They were opposed to separation; at this point, their businesses were suffering. When radicals took the lead, with lower-class support, the men of wealth pleaded with the king for troops. Ultimately the aristocratic and bourgeois notables fled the city, and Frederick, the king's son, entered the city with a substantial number of troops. But, after several days, sensing that he was confronting the entire city, he withdrew, an action which decided the struggle. His judgment was based on remarkably inadequate intelligence. One rebel later reported his inability to muster even three hundred men for a decisive charge.[66]

The 1830 events in Belgium are not appropriately summarized in Marx's brief statement—that it was another instance of a bourgeoisie compelled to depose a feudal monarch. It is, in fact, another instance of a revolution that does not accord with the Marxist model. The insurgents were not those predicted; the motives were not those alleged. The struggle was cultural and national in character, not economic and not a struggle of classes. The bourgeoisie in this conflict was counterrevolutionary, favoring the status quo.

The bourgeois revolution in England, we have seen, is a nonexistent case. There was no revolution matching the Marxian description. The actual history was one long, continuous evolutionary process ultimately involving some merger of the dominant classes rather than a dialectical confrontation. In the case of Belgium, Marx has taken a real revolution and seriously misrepresented the actual dynamics. Marx's treatment of the French case, of the 1830 and 1848 revolutions, as will be seen in the next chapter, also involves serious misrepresentation of the actual dynamics.

3

MARX ON THE

1848 REVOLUTION

IN FRANCE

This chapter will review and discuss Marx's first major historical study, a work entitled *The Class Struggles in France, 1848 to 1850*. The work is not a monograph in the sense of an integrated study. It consists of three articles by Marx plus a fourth contribution by Marx and Engels. The three articles originally appeared in the *Neue Rheinische Zeitung: Politisch-ökonomische Revue*, a short-lived journal edited by Marx in 1850. In addition to the usual articles, the issues of the *Revue* also, as a special feature, provided an overview of recent events in the major European nations. Engels excerpted the sections dealing with France from the final issue and included them as a fourth chapter. Engels added an introduction and provided the title. The work was first published in this form in 1895.

The study opens with a brief history of the July Monarchy, with the reign of Louis Philippe, who was given the throne in the course of the 1830 revolution. The main effort of the work begins with the king's downfall in the revolution of February 1848. Marx reviews the actions of the provisional government and describes a series of confrontations leading up to the June Days, an important working-class uprising which was put down after several days of fighting. He then reviews events of the subsequent year to June 1849, when a democratic petty bourgeois insurgency was easily put down. The monograph, finally, carries the review of events through to August–September 1850.

Marx's account is largely descriptive, although, on occasion, some explanation is offered to indicate why things turned out as they did. It is in this effort of analysis that the work goes beyond narration of (presumed) fact to provide observations of more general importance. It is here that the monograph purports to show how the Marx-Engels analysis accounts for the principal events of the period, making sense of the complexity. It was, Engels wrote, "Marx's first attempt to explain a section of contemporary history by means of his materialist conception, on the basis of the given economic situation." Engels sets this effort in contrast to the *Communist Manifesto*, in which "the theory was applied in broad outline to the whole of modern history," and to their articles in the *Neue Rheinische Zeitung*, where the theory "was constantly used to interpret political events of the day." This work, therefore, occupies a middle ground, tracing "a development which extended over some years." The task, Engels writes, was "to trace political events back to effects of what were, in the final analysis, economic causes."[1]

Edmund Wilson, the noted literary critic, writes of Marx and Engels's "discovery of economic motivation" which enabled them "to write a new kind of history." Marx, he says, "inaugurated this work with a product of his mature genius at its most brilliant, the study called *The Class Struggles in France*." David McLellan, a leading biographer of Marx, refers to the work as "a brilliant and swift moving account of the changing political scene in France during 1848–49." The historian George Rudé commends the work for its "sustained analysis." Roger Price, author of a leading historical work on the period, describes Marx's monographs, the *Class Struggles* and the *Eighteenth Brumaire*, as "extremely influential works." Price, it should be noted, has presented evidence against many of the claims contained in those works. Validity and influence, of course, are separate and distinct issues. Evidence about the inadequacy of claims does not contradict his conclusion about influence. The political scientist Robert C. Tucker writes that the *Class Struggles* is the "most mordantly brilliant of [Marx's] revolutionary pamphlets." Another historian, Peter N. Stearns, refers to the work as "a brilliant analysis of the 1848 revolution." Maximilien Rubel, a leading Marx specialist, refers to it and several other works by Marx as "unquestionable masterpieces." Because of this importance and influence, a detailed exploration and assessment is warranted.[2]

This chapter will, first of all, following Marx's procedure, review the main points of his narrative. Second, it will discuss and comment on the various analyses as they appear in the text. And third, later in the chapter, some larger, more general issues will be addressed. Marx's account, basically, is a narrative history with interspersed analytical observations. The assessment requires a review of the claims made about the various episodes in the history, analysis and discussion of those claims, and consideration of relevant evidence on the subject. It is a complicated task, one involving many episodes of text, comment, and review of evidence. That complication, however, is necessary for a comprehensive assessment.

Historical and Theoretical Background

Marx and Engels, as we have seen, date the bourgeois epoch in England from some point in the seventeenth century. The equivalent beginning point for France comes toward the end of the eighteenth century. The date given is 1789; the French Revolution, in short, was *the* bourgeois revolution. In those revolutions, Marx wrote, "the bourgeoisie was victorious. . . . [It was] the victory of bourgeois ownership over feudal ownership." The presentation of bold claims is an easy task; the provision of evidence in support of those claims is considerably more difficult. Although the two historical claims are central cornerstone assumptions in their theory, at no point did Marx or Engels provide the necessary supporting evidence. The claims were taken as givens, as self-evident axiomatic truths. François Furet, a leading specialist in the area, writes that "although Marx considered writing a book on the French Revolution—and, indeed, commented all his life, in various contexts, on the events of late eighteenth-century France—he never did write the book."[3]

That neglect leaves many questions unanswered. The old regime was unquestionably displaced in the course of the revolution. Along with the king and queen, many aristocrats were executed, giving at least an appearance of support for the basic Marxian notion. One might see those events, especially the terror, as the effort of a victorious bourgeoisie definitively removing the previous ruling class. But the actual history is considerably more complicated. It is not at all clear that the new regime was led by or even sponsored by the rising bourgeoisie. The revolutionary period, from 1789 to 1799, moreover, contained several episodes. At first, liberal constitutional monarchists were dominant. They were displaced by the Jacobins, the authors of the terror. Then, in the course of the "Thermidor reaction," the Jacobins were overthrown by more moderate forces. It is not self-evident that any of these factions represented bourgeois interests. Then, in 1799, the entire arrangement, the First Republic, was overthrown by Napoleon Bonaparte. He ultimately established "The Empire" which, apart from the brief exile in Elba, lasted until 1815. Was Napoleon a representative of the bourgeoisie? Or did he represent himself and his own interests? The victorious allies again returned the Bourbons to the French throne after Napoleon's defeat at Waterloo, thus beginning the restoration. Did this represent the overthrow of the bourgeoisie? Had the revolution thereby been undone? Such questions are glossed over in Marx and Engels's writings.

Historian J. F. Bosher summarizes the recent evidence-based consensus as follows: "There was no rising capitalist middle class that can be identified as revolutionary, no class of rich families seeking political power by revolution, no class of frustrated or impatient professional men, no particularly revolutionary occupations, no satisfactory correlations between economic groups and revolutionary groups." Another historian, William Doyle, who provides an extensive review of evidence, declares that the "old orthodoxies," those stemming from Marx and the Marxist historian Georges Lefebvre, "are not only dead but now in urgent need of burial."[4]

The July Monarchy

In *Class Struggles in France*, Marx picks up the history with a brief review of the 1830 revolution which overthrew the Bourbons and created the July Monarchy under Louis Philippe (he being the heir to the Orleanist branch of the royal family). He reigned until early in 1848 when the February Revolution brought the monarchy to an end. The first paragraph of *The Class Struggles* gives us the basic clue to the July Monarchy. As a result of the July uprising, "the liberal banker Laffitte" led his compère, Louis Philippe, to be acclaimed at the Hôtel de Ville, the traditional setting for the declaration of revolutionary regimes. On this occasion, according to Marx, Laffitte had "let fall the words" that "*from now on the bankers will rule*." He had thereby "betrayed the secret of the revolution."

To the uninformed observer, the struggle might appear to be a dynastic conflict, merely a variant of the old regime. But, with this vignette, Marx indicates the underlying or hidden lesson, the lesson of class. A prominent bourgeois personage was obviously directing the entire operation. With this easy transformation, the basic claim of the Marxian case is established. The lesson, in brief, is that the bourgeoisie, as of 1830, was once again in command.

One might note, however, that the argument rests on a slim base, on the declaration by the author and his presentation of a single hearsay sentence.

Jacques Laffitte was a liberal banker. He was also a leading figure in the July Revolution. Opposition leaders met at his house which, after the revolution, was referred to as the Hôtel de Juillet. Laffitte was part of the cortege accompanying the new king to the Hôtel de Ville on the occasion described by Marx. Louis Philippe, however, entered the building arm in arm with the Marquis de Lafayette, a man not easily identified with either bourgeois segment. Laffitte had a long-standing close friendship with Louis Philippe. He did hold high office in the new government, first as a minister without portfolio, then, as of November 1830, as president of the council and simultaneously as minister of finance. Marx's portrait of Laffitte as power broker, however, was undone by subsequent events. By the middle of March 1831, Laffitte was out of office. He is described by one historian as a man "with little political ability or ideas, and with even less energy." Shortly after leaving office, moreover, Laffitte's bank collapsed.

Laffitte's successor in the government, Casimir Périer, was also a banker. He was, more importantly, a very capable politician. The presence of two bankers heading a government was unusual in early-nineteenth-century Europe and could easily, on the surface at least, justify the claim that France had experienced a bourgeois revolution, or, more to the point, that it was being led by a finance aristocracy. One biographer of Louis Philippe, however, argues that the naming of Laffitte was a tactical move designed to get rid of him and of a collection of left politicians. David Pinkney, moreover, possibly the leading authority on 1830 in France, writes that the revolution's leaders "included two bankers, two lawyers, one professor, two writers and journalists, and five nobles, all united for a political objective." His summary conclusion is that "political power was still firmly in the hands of the landed proprietors, the office holders, and the professional men. In this respect the July Days had effected no revolution in France."[5]

February to June 1848

The following pages review Marx's first article, which discusses events from the February 1848 revolution, the overthrow of the July Monarchy, and the creation of the Second Republic, to the suppression of the working-class uprising in Paris four months later. A welter of events occurred between those dates—a new government was formed, a constitution was written, and an election was held. With freedom of the press and freedom of assembly came an explosive growth of newspapers and clubs, all vying for influence. A series of demonstrations—*journées*—occurred; these were attempts to change the direction of government policy. Government finances were in a desperate condition. To save the situation, a new tax was decreed. A general election with broad-based suffrage was held. A job-creation program, the National Workshops, was created to deal with serious unemployment in Paris. This program, however, was viewed with increasing alarm by the leaders of the government and, more generally, by most of bourgeois Paris. The program was abruptly halted, a move that led to the working-class insurgency, the June Days.

The Finance Aristocracy

Marx's initial conclusion, about "bankers in power" as of 1830, posed an immediate problem: What was the point of the second revolution, that of 1848? An explanation is provided in Marx's second and third paragraphs. There was, he indicates, a significant division within that class, the two components being the finance aristocracy and the industrial bourgeoisie. A quotation proves useful:

> It was not the French bourgeoisie that ruled under Louis Philippe, but *one faction* of it: bankers, stock-exchange kings, railway kings, owners of coal and iron mines and forests, a part of the landed proprietors associated with them—the so-called *finance aristocracy*. It sat on the throne, it dictated laws in the Chambers, it distributed public offices, from cabinet portfolios to tobacco bureau posts.
>
> "The *industrial bourgeoisie* proper formed part of the official opposition, that is, it was represented only as a minority in the Chambers.[6]

This account differs significantly from the formulations of the *Manifesto*. The latter work focuses on the struggle between bourgeoisie and proletariat. The *Class Struggles* begins with an account of divisions *within* the bourgeoisie. That does not necessarily mean a contradiction between the two sources. The former work, as indicated, is sweeping and general (and focused on the end-phase of the struggle); the later work is detailed, concerned with an event limited in space and time, and, presumably, deals with an earlier stage of development, that is, before the clarification destined to occur in advanced capitalism. Indeed, part of the task of this work, as will be seen, is to trace the "necessary" unification of that class.

An element of carelessness appears in Marx's formulation. Marx has listed the owners of coal and iron mines as part of the finance aristocracy. One would ordinarily expect them to be classified with the industrial bourgeoisie proper. The same holds for owners of forests and those associated landed proprietors. Railways and their owner-kings pose another problem; a railroad is certainly not a financial institution. Strictly speaking, as a means of transportation, neither is it a means of production, although, given the dichotomous choice, classification with the industrial bourgeoisie seems more appropriate. The illustrative listing of finance aristocrats, in short, contains segments from the other category of that simple dichotomy plus one segment that is not easily placed. Although the names given the two factions point to a definition in terms of function, implicitly Marx appears to be defining the two bourgeois subtypes by the *use* made of those properties, that is, whether for speculative or for productive purposes.

The struggle between the two bourgeois factions involved a sharp conflict of interests, the conflict being so serious as to justify the use, by one faction, of revolutionary means. It is not the friendly rivalry of, say, two closely related clans. Marx provides some illustration here, reviewing the activities of three supposed leaders of the industrial bourgeoisie. Grandin, a Rouen manufacturer, had been "the most violent opponent of Guizot [Louis Philippe's prime minister] in the Chamber of Deputies." Léon Faucher, in the last days of Louis Philippe's reign, had "waged a war of the pen for industry against speculation and its train-bearer, the government." And Bastiat, on behalf of Bordeaux and "the whole of wine-producing France," had agitated "against the ruling system." Again there is carelessness in definition. Few readers, then or now, would expect to find the wine producers of France classified as a segment of an *industrial* bourgeoisie.

A review of relevant sources reveals that none of them assigns these men the importance Marx suggests. There are no references to these three men in two popular biographies of Louis Philippe. Pinkney's book on the last years of the regime also contains no references to them. The leading biography of Guizot contains two passing references to Bastiat, none to Grandin, and three fugitive references to Faucher. Dunham's book on French economic development from

1815 to 1848 makes no mention of Bastiat or Grandin. Fleeting references to
Faucher do not support Marx's basic claim and also indicate some important
complexities—Faucher is described as "close to the Rothschilds in their financing of French railroads." In this connection he advocated free admission of
rails or, at minimum, that duties on rails and locomotives be reduced. The
French ironmasters "quite naturally objected vehemently and succeeded in
preventing important concessions." That would make Faucher an ally of a
leading member of the finance aristocracy. It would put Rothschild, a banker
and railway king, in opposition to the owners of coal and iron mines. It would
also mean, since tariffs remained high, that the regime in this case came down
against the banker. French industry in this entire period (and afterward) benefited from high protective tariff barriers. Bastiat and Faucher were leading
advocates of free trade, following the examples of Cobden and Bright in
Britain, a position that was opposed by the protectionist industrial bourgeoisie proper. Faucher also advocated a free-trade arrangement to include
France, Belgium, Spain, and Switzerland, as a counter to the Prussian customs
union, the *Zollverein*.[7]

Before continuing with his review of government affairs under Louis Philippe, Marx inserts a brief paragraph dealing with three other segments of the
society. He mentions the petty bourgeoisie ("of all gradations") and the peasantry. Both segments, he declares, were "completely excluded from political
power." Throughout the work, Marx discusses these two segments together,
suggesting that, for most purposes, there was no need for separate analysis.
The third segment discussed at this point consists of "the *ideological* representatives and spokesmen of the above classes, their savants, lawyers, doctors, etc."
These "so-called *men of talent*" appear as no more than agents of the classes
employing them.

Marx next details the machinations of the finance aristocracy. Its members
had a "*direct interest* in the *indebtedness of the state*. The *state deficit* was really
the main object of its speculation and the chief source of its enrichment."
Profits were made through the loans required for the deficit spending,
through stock market manipulations, and use of insider information. The
majority in the chamber, we are told, had been shareholders in the railways
they caused to be built "at the cost of the state." Summing up, Marx declares
that "the July monarchy was nothing but a joint-stock company for the exploitation of France's national wealth, the dividends of which were divided among

ministers, Chambers, 240,000 voters and their adherents." Elaborating on the point, he announces: "Since the finance aristocracy made the laws, was at the head of the administration of the state, had command of all the organised public authorities, dominated public opinion through the actual state of affairs and through the press, the same prostitution, the same shameless cheating, the same mania to get rich was repeated in every sphere. . . . [The aim was] to get rich not by production, but by pocketing the already available wealth of others." The end result of this system of legalized thievery was simple: "Trade, industry, agriculture, shipping, the interests of the industrial bourgeoisie, were bound to be continually endangered and prejudiced under this system."[8]

The loose definition problem surfaces again in this sentence. The initial portrait of the bourgeois factions is asymmetric, listing key subgroups of the finance aristocracy but saying nothing about the composition of the industrial bourgeoisie proper. The "industry, agriculture, [and] shipping" of this sentence must presumably omit owners of coal and iron mines, railway kings, and some owners of forests. But which groups *are* included there? Without the railway kings, for example, which shippers remain? Was it the wagoners and teamsters and those transporting by canal? Were they the progressive (i.e., nonparasitic) bourgeoisie? Were they instigators of the February Revolution?

Marx allowed himself to be carried away by his own enthusiasm in his condemnation of this system. The number of voters given refers to the size of the electorate at that point. But the chamber, as he has already indicated, contained some opposition. Only the most generous of corrupt governments would take care of its opponents as well as its adherents. The claim of a dominated public opinion, moreover, is undone immediately in his own text. The efforts of the republican press and of a protest movement, one learns, were sufficient to overthrow the whole system. Priscilla Robertson, a leading historian of the period, gives a markedly different portrait: "The press was startlingly outspoken—a large part of its pages was given over to personal scurrility about the King and his family which would not have been allowed even in Britain with its theoretically wider tolerance."[9]

Marx's formulation is typically zero-sum in character—one side wins, the other loses. But a moment of thought suggests another possibility: both sides win. The construction of railways would serve the interests of the rising industrial bourgeoisie. The possibilities for trade would be enhanced, given the possibility of shifting from a local to a national basis. Industry, particularly the owners of coal and iron mines, would be well served by the development. The owners of forests would sell hundreds of thousands of railroad ties, with the price of all wood products aided in the process. Goods could be delivered great distances with much greater speed. The costs of transport (versus labor-intensive, slow, horse-drawn wagons) would be sharply reduced. Corruption in the construction of the railroads would mean higher costs than would be the case with a noncorrupt procedure. But those added costs would be trivial in comparison to the gains provided by the new rail network.

Marx's point, that the two bourgeois segments were sharply opposed, would be true only in the extreme case—where the parasitic finance aristocracy took resources and provided *nothing* in return, or where it provided so little as to prevent subsequent growth. Pinkney's review of French experience in the 1840s, however, convincingly demonstrates significant growth. The basis for an industrial takeoff, he argues, was established in the period. He places particular emphasis on the Railway Law of 1842, which provided for a network of some two thousand miles. Neither logic nor evidence, in short, supports Marx's claim of sharply opposed bourgeois factions. Overlooking the obvious advantages provided by the railroads, Marx provides a moralistic critique. He assesses the development against an unlikely standard, that of corruption-free enterprise. In doing so, he overlooks the real, economic, historic significance of the development.[10]

Scandal, Foreign Affairs, and Economic Crisis

Having defined the actors in the struggle and having also imputed plausible motives, Marx turns next to some of the factors that precipitated the uprising. He offers, first, a paragraph detailing the outraged attitudes of the various segments of the population in 1847: The "non-ruling factions of the French bourgeoisie cried: *Corruption!* The people cried: *Down with the big thieves! Down with the assassins!*" Paris, Marx declares, was "flooded with pamphlets" which "denounced and stigmatised" the rule of the finance aristocracy. As noted just above, this does not sound like a public opinion dominated by the agencies of the finance aristocracy. One passage here foreshadows much that was to follow (both in Marxian and in derived literatures). Marx announced that "the industrial bourgeoisie saw its interests endangered [while] the petty bourgeoisie was filled with moral indignation." Business leaders, it will be noted, have interests; they are rational and calculating. The petty bourgeoisie, in contrast, is presumably not moved by interest but rather is driven by stubbornly held moral sentiment.

Marx next considers some external events that helped to stimulate the rising. There were reverses in foreign policy. These, he says, brought "a series of mortifications to French national sentiment." Several uprisings occurred elsewhere in Europe, and these, too, apparently encouraged insurgent tendencies. The Poles arose once again, this time in Cracow in 1846. In 1847 a struggle broke out in Switzerland, the Sonderbund War, in which Catholic cantons sought independence from the predominantly Protestant state. Guizot had sided with the Catholics, which, for that era's progressives, meant siding with reaction. The victory of the Swiss liberals, however, had "raised the self-respect of the bourgeois opposition in France." And then, in January of 1848, there was an uprising in Palermo. This event, Marx declares, "worked like an electric shock on the paralysed masses of the people and awoke their great revolutionary memories and passions."

Finally, there were "*two economic world events*," the crop failures of 1845 and 1846 and a subsequent commercial and industrial crisis. The potato blight, Marx reports, led to bloody conflicts in France and across Europe. The famine created a bizarre contrast—desperate people demanding the prime necessities of life as opposed to "the shameless orgies of the finance aristocracy." The effects of the commercial crisis, he declares, were still present in February of 1848. The "electric shock" of the Palermo uprising is entirely plausible. The Neapolitan army was forced to abandon Sicily, and after three weeks of struggle, the king reluctantly granted a constitution. It is, nevertheless, remarkable how few works, then or later, refer to the event. Tocqueville, for example, offers no comment on it, nor does the comprehensive work of Roger Price.[11]

The Banquet Campaign

The factors reviewed to this point set the stage for the revolution. Marx turns now, for a paragraph, to the immediate precipitating events. The most significant development is described as follows: "Throughout the whole of France the bourgeois opposition *agitated at banquets* for an *electoral reform* which should win for it the majority of the Chambers and overthrow the Ministry of the Bourse."[12] Political meetings at that time were hampered by legal restrictions. The private subscription banquet, with accompanying toasts and speeches, was a means to circumvent the law. The first of these took place in

Paris on July 9, 1847. Some seventy banquets followed in the ensuing months, most of them in major population centers. Rather loosely organized (and open to all who could pay), several banquets fell into the hands of the left, that is, of the republican opposition. The culminating banquet, scheduled for Paris in February, was banned by the government. This was the immediate stimulus to the uprising.

The claim of bourgeois instigation, on the surface, is implausible. With the industrial bourgeoisie forming only a minuscule portion of the population at that point (and most of it already enfranchised), there is little likelihood that suffrage extension would allow it to overthrow "the Bourse." The banquet movement was the work of the *political* opposition, of a group within the Chamber of Deputies called the dynastic opposition. Unable to topple Guizot's government and having failed, in the spring of 1847, to carry a motion for suffrage extension, its leaders, Odilon Barrot and Prosper Duvergier de Hauranne, resorted to this extraparliamentary campaign. Offering no evidence on the point, Marx has simply, by declaration, transformed this political opposition into bourgeois opposition and made it an agency of the industrial bourgeoisie. As such, the claim is no more than an untested hypothesis.

Marx's claim about the role of Barrot as spokesman for bourgeois interests is implausible for another reason: the man's limited abilities and questionable loyalties. Duveau portrays him as a windbag, describing him as "a pompous, overbearing, but undeniably authoritative speaker." Later he quotes Gustave Flaubert's reference to "the righteous bellowing of M. Odilon Barrot." Baughman writes of "opportunist politicians [such] as Odilon Barrot." Tocqueville provides, at best, faint praise, describing him as a man who mixed "a touch of silliness with his weaknesses and his virtues." Stern refers to his "sonorous and empty speeches." Proudhon referred to the man as "ce grand parleur, grand imbécile." None of these authors refers to Barrot as a spokesman for business interests. Marx's comments on Barrot are unrelievedly negative—he was a "*nullité grave*," a "thoroughly shallow person," a man out for revenge, one aiming "to settle accounts with the revolutionists for thwarting his premiership." Barrot was "always fruitlessly struggling for the ministerial portfolio." And "for eighteen years [he had] hidden the rascally vacuity of his mind behind the serious demeanor of his body." A man of such doubtful talent would seem an unlikely choice as spokesman for business interests. He would seem an even less likely choice as planner and executor of their political purposes. Marx's statement itself points to a more likely alternative, that the man and his group were serving their own political purposes. They sought, at long last, to gain political power. Barrot was later chosen, in December of 1848, to be Louis Napoleon's first prime minister. That too, given Marx's later discussion, would point to opportunism and vacuity; it speaks against the argument of Barrot as an agent representing bourgeois interests.[13]

Marx inserts here a discussion of another immediate cause: the industrial crisis had forced "a multitude of manufacturers and big traders" out of foreign markets and into the home market where they "set up large establishments." That competition led to the ruin of many smaller shops. The consequence, put simply, was "innumerable bankruptcies among this section of the Paris bourgeoisie, and hence their revolutionary action in February." This claim too is, on the surface, implausible. Few big traders at any time are able to react with such dispatch. Bankruptcies did increase at this point, but that resulted from the twofold crisis, not from the entry of new competition. The bankruptcies, moreover, touched only a small part of the rank; most were hurting, to be sure, but few actually went under. Nowhere, either then or since, has it been shown that the *bankrupt* petty bourgeoisie appeared in disproportionate numbers on the barricades.[14]

Three days of confused struggle, February 22–24, 1848, brought an end, first to Guizot's ministry, then to the regime. Marx passes over these events with a few brief sentences prefaced with the phrase "It is well known." A reference to "hand-to-hand fighting between the people and the army" appears, followed by comments that "the army was disarmed" and that the "passive conduct" of the National Guard brought an end to the July Monarchy.[15] It is unlikely that those details would have been well known to Marx's German readers. The news sources of the day left much to be desired. Some two years later, the memory of even those reports would have faded. A brief review of those events proves useful.

The February Days

Sensing the revolutionary potential they had stimulated, the sponsors of the Paris banquet, scheduled for February 22, canceled the event at the last moment. Some of the more committed supporters, some students, and some curious citizens, not having heard of the cancellation, appeared as per the original plan. Most of the morning was characterized by idle milling about, the atmosphere being friendly and amiable. The appearance of some military units added a note of tension, but no confrontation followed. Tempers changed, however, with the appearance of some Municipal Guard units which proceeded to clear the streets, pushing, shoving, and charging in among those fleeing. It was this police brutality that changed the atmosphere and led to the construction of the first barricades.

Some confused, seesaw fighting followed throughout the afternoon and early evening. The same disorderly struggle continued throughout the next day, Wednesday the twenty-third. Many members of the key units, the National Guard, failed to respond to the summons; many of the units that did assemble, when confronted with crowds, dissolved and joined with the opposition. The king dismissed Guizot that afternoon and began his futile search for a new government. Given the outcome of the day's fighting and given the defeat of the offending ministry, the feeling among the insurgents that evening was one of jubilation. A crowd collected at the Foreign Ministry in the Rue des Capucines. Since it was also Guizot's residence, at this moment it was protected by a regiment of the regular army. Some shots were heard and an officer ordered his men to fire into the crowd. The reports of the resulting deaths range between sixteen and fifty-two; many more, of course, were wounded. This event generated the wrath and outrage that drove the struggle to its conclusion the following day.

Regular army units had now intervened in strength, but they were not prepared for this kind of combat. They were blocked and frustrated at many points, and here, too, fraternization undermined their effectiveness. A series of command problems aggravated an already deteriorating situation, and the troops were ordered to cease fire and withdraw. Under considerable pressure, with the situation indicated as hopeless, Louis Philippe wrote and signed a brief abdication statement. With insurgents at the doors of the palace, he walked quickly to a waiting carriage, drove off to the coast, and went into exile in England.

Marx shifts position with respect to the roles played by the classes in the February events. At one point he has it as a joint enterprise: "In common with the bourgeoisie the workers had made the February Revolution, and *alongside* the bourgeoisie they sought to assert their interests." Some ten pages later, one finds this statement: "The February republic was won by the workers with the passive support of the bourgeoisie. The proletarians rightly regarded themselves as the victors of February, and they made the arrogant claims of victors." Subsequent developments are assessed against that (presumed) fact. The working class, supposedly, felt cheated out of its victory.

The sponsors of the banquet campaign, seeking electoral reform, had intended only to replace the government. Instead, they overthrew the regime. Tocqueville reports that "all day long, [Barrot] made heroic efforts to save the Monarchy from the slope down which he himself had pushed it, and its fall seemed to have left him crushed."[16]

A Note on Causality

The lines of causality reviewed here deserve more detailed consideration. The contenders in France of February 1848 are not those indicated in the *Manifesto*. The bourgeoisie, presumably, had already taken power in France, and since this was not the proletarian revolution, it had to be an interim struggle, one with a different, unforeseen character. Marx declares it to be a struggle between two factions of the bourgeoisie. The fetters impeding bourgeois enterprise are no longer those maintained by an aristocratic regime; in this case they were imposed by one of those bourgeois factions. In Marx's first historical monograph, he had to extend the basic framework of his (and Engels's) analysis so as to accommodate experience not anticipated in the general statement. Given the special circumstances of the French case, this change, the provision of an alternative hypothesis, was entirely appropriate.

The struggle outlined in the *Manifesto* is categorical; it involves a polar confrontation of opposite classes, bourgeoisie and proletariat. The February conflict is portrayed differently: it pitted a coalition of classes and factions against a tottering regime. The revolutionary coalition linked the industrial bourgeoisie, the petty bourgeoisie, some intellectuals, and workers. No serious account of negotiations or discussions is provided, that is, of the efforts required to bring about even a modestly coordinated effort. The portrait, rather, is one of groups stimulated to revolt, essentially driven in a common direction by the force of events.

Although not a key concept in Marx and Engels's theoretical notions, the role of public opinion in this conflict is remarkable. That specific phrase does not appear, to be sure, but the concept is clearly implicit; it is central to the analysis. We are told that "the imagination of the people was offended" by the actions of the finance aristocracy. We are told that Paris was "flooded with pamphlets" which denounced and stigmatized the ruling faction. The paragraph on foreign affairs has the same character, indicating that opinion was stimulated and people moved by the news of those events.

In his final paragraph on the causes, Marx considers what might be termed pure economic factors. The first of these, the crop failures, involves a natural catastrophe, something falling outside the basic framework. It too is discussed in terms of its effects on public opinion, the contrast between human misery and "shameless orgies" moving people to insurgency. Finally, in last place among the causes considered, are the ramifying effects of the commercial crisis in Britain.

The extension of the basic Marxian framework is remarkable. The causal factors, in the order of their appearance, are the struggle between the bourgeois factions, the impacts of foreign conflicts, a natural catastrophe, and the commercial crisis. These events give rise to an outraged public opinion. Linking events and opinion, explicitly, are some media of communication—here pamphlets and, later in the text, newspapers. In this entire causal complex, only the linkage of commercial crisis, economic grievance, and insurgent sentiment may be said to be central to the basic Marx-Engels analysis. The other causal elements could easily appear in works of bourgeois (or mainstream) historians. Much of it could easily appear in any standard course on mass media and public opinion.

The New Regime

A group of notables, opposition political leaders, intellectuals, and journalists, principally those associated with *Le National*, picked up the pieces and formed the provisional government. They were quickly joined by a second group of journalist-intellectuals associated with the left republican newspaper, *La Réforme*. Under pressure from the street, some room was made for working-class representation in the positions given Louis Blanc and "the worker" Albert.

The government is best described as moderate republican with a left (or social) wing. The dominant group wished to have a republic, but one with only limited participation of the masses. While not hard-hearted, given the nation's problematical economic condition, which was immediately worsened by the success of the revolution, most of the new leaders opposed costly relief programs. Under pressure from the street and from its own left wing, however, the government announced various measures of democratization and several social measures, the most important being "universal suffrage" and the National Workshops. In subsequent months, while trying to prevent further insurgency, quiet efforts were made to take back what had been granted. Most accounts, accordingly, give considerable attention to the seesaw struggle between government restraint and mass demands. Although not a prominent focus in most accounts, economic policy was a central concern, specifically the need to get the economy moving. That policy was the key to everything: a functioning economy would mean employment and would reverse the rapidly growing welfare problem. Employed workers, of course, were not likely to be insurgent.

The provisional government, Marx wrote, "necessarily mirrored in its composition the different parties which shared in the victory. It could not be anything but a *compromise between the different classes* which together had overturned the July throne, but whose interests were mutually antagonistic." The focus, from the outset, is on the coalitional character of that government, on the diversity of groups represented, and on the incompatibility of their interests. The forthcoming struggle is again indicated as zero-sum in character; compromises or adjustment of differences are, at best, short-term solutions.[17]

Marx provides a brief review of groups and leading representatives in the provisional government. They are, first, the republican petty bourgeoisie, represented by Alexandre Auguste Ledru-Rollin and Ferdinand Flocon. This group is linked to what might be called a left-liberal newspaper, *La Réforme*. Second were the republican bourgeoisie, represented by people of the right-liberal newspaper, *Le National*. Two key figures were Armand Marrast, the editor, and Louis Antoine Garnier-Pagès. Third, the "dynastic opposition" was represented, according to Marx, by "Crémieux, Dupont de l'Eure, etc." Fourth, the working class was represented by an obscure figure usually referred to as "the worker" Albert and by Louis Blanc. The terms of analysis have shifted slightly. The republican bourgeoisie represented by the *National* is clearly the victorious industrial bourgeoisie proper. Although not stated explicitly, that faction would also, presumably, have been represented by the dynastic opposition.

Dupont de l'Eure was chosen as president of the provisional government. He is described in the *Collected Works* as a liberal politician. Born in 1767, he was, accordingly, over eighty in 1848. He had been a member of the Council of Elders in the Directorate during the Great Revolution and was active also in the 1830 revolution. A convenient figurehead, he played no significant role in the 1848 events.

The most visible member of the provisional government was the popular romantic poet Alphonse de Lamartine, who served as foreign minister. A very capable spokesman, he was, effectively, the head of the government. It was Lamartine who, under some pressure, had declared the republic. He is not easily classified, either in terms of class or interest. Marx deals with the problem as follows: "Finally, Lamartine in the Provisional Government: this [*sic*] essentially represented no real interest, no definite class; for such was the February Revolution, the general uprising with its illusions, its poetry, its imaginary content and its rhetoric. Moreover, the spokesman of the February Revolution, according to both his position and his views, belonged to the *bourgeoisie*."

Marx's conclusion is open to some question. Lamartine, a descendant of staunch royalists, was a large landowner, "one of the richest landowners in Saône-et-Loire." Given his position in the revolution, it is clear, following Marx's logic, that he must be linked to the industrial bourgeoisie proper. But Lamartine's position and views defy easy summary. Fortesque has a chapter entitled "Embracing the French Left, 1843–1848" wherein Lamartine's ideology is said to have been an idiosyncratic blend of "Christian morality and revolutionary idealism." George Sand congratulated him on joining the left wing of the parliamentary opposition in 1843. Lamartine's salon, one observer noted, included "all the left together." His friends at this point included Barrot, Garnier-Pagès, and Ledru-Rollin. A split conclusion seems appropriate: by his position, Lamartine might be counted as bourgeois; his left-liberal views, however, were not likely to have been shared by either faction of the bourgeoisie.[18]

Marx opened his account with a description of the supposedly dominant and aspiring segments of the bourgeoisie. That focus has been all but lost at this point in his text. Instead, these four poorly delineated groups have now been introduced. Two of them are said to be linked to classes: the *Réforme* group to the petty bourgeoisie and the other, two-person group to the workers. The other two were centers of political opposition: the coterie linked to the newspaper *Le National*, and the dynastic opposition, a faction in the legislature. Both of these are said to be linked to the industrial bourgeoisie.

The problem that Marx faced was, in form at least, very simple: he had invoked and wished to justify the language of class (specifically, of his nomen-clature). But the actual events were generated by several groups, which, in turn, were led by various individuals. The groups that formed and led the provisional government—those affiliated with the two key newspapers—were not easily characterized in terms of the specified classes. To make his case, Marx had to make a translation. He had to declare that a set of manifest facts (those involving individuals and coteries) "stand for" or, to use the preferred vague connective, "represent" the interests of some not immediately obvious class. Such a translation of individual and social events, if unaccompanied by evidence, is an a priori stipulation. Put in other terms, it is an untested hypothesis.

One of these ad hoc stipulations proves to be rather problematical. The first person introduced by Marx, it will be remembered, was the banker Jacques Laffitte. He, the archetypical finance aristocrat, was one of the founders of *Le National*. In the late 1820s, two young journalists, Adolphe Thiers and Armand Carrel, were the moving forces in that effort, consulting first with the aged Talleyrand. The money, however, so we are told, came from Jacques Laffitte, "the immense wealthy banker who was Louis-Philippe's financial adviser." The newspaper first appeared in January 1830. The editors and the newspaper played an important role in the creation of the July Revolution. By 1832, however, editor Carrel had changed position and now castigated the monarchy as "inglorious and corrupt."[19] The newspaper, ultimately, played an important role both in making and unmaking Louis Philippe. Where Marx portrays the banker Laffitte as the decisive figure in 1830, the role of the journalists, as will be seen below, was of even greater importance. Thiers was a central figure throughout the Orleanist period. He did not join in the banquet campaign but, in January, in the Chamber of Deputies, repeatedly attacked Guizot's policies. Like Barrot, he too was a place seeker; and also like Barrot, he wished to topple the government, not the regime.

Without any serious evidence, Marx assigns important roles to business leaders. Overlooking evidence readily available to him, he neglects or deni-grates the role of the journalists, the intellectuals, and the aspiring politicians. At best, they are treated as agents of some hidden class, never as persons acting on their own behalf.

Marx, as noted, provided no positive definition of the industrial bour-geoisie. Effectively a residual category, it contains those segments that are not part of the finance aristocracy. Moreover, apart from Grandin, the Rouen manufacturer, he has not named a single member of that segment. Had Marx named the leading figures, its notables and/or its political leaders, it would have been possible to discover their views and explore their political initiatives. Ultimately, when archival records became available, it would have been possible also to explore Marx's assertions about their ties to their alleged spokesmen. As it stands, however, throughout the work, this industrial bourgeoisie has only a shadowy existence. One is merely assured of its existence and role; it never comes on stage.

An opposite problem exists with respect to another agency, that is, the clubs. Here were groups with unquestioned importance and yet, for all practical purposes, they are missing from Marx's text. With the lifting of restrictions on the freedom of assembly, an explosion of activity followed. Peter Amann, the leading authority on the subject, reports that the number went from five at the beginning of March to more than two hundred in mid-April. These clubs had a membership estimated between fifty and seventy thousand. Led largely by middle-class figures, intellectuals, bourgeois, or white-collar employees, they had a considerable working-class following and at least claimed to speak for the masses. Several were "name" clubs, built around a dominant personality. The most important were led by various leftists, by Cabet, Blanqui, Barbès, and Raspail. The clubs organized many of the demonstrations aimed at forcing a left or revolutionary direction on the provisional government. But Marx, as indicated, neglects these voluntary associations; for him, the proletariat was acting, without the need of any intervening agency. Had he recognized the unquestionable role of these voluntary associations, he would have had yet another complication. He would have had to abandon his pure class analysis; he would also have had to make room for a range of contingent, voluntaristic factors, those generally coming under the heading of "the role of leadership."[20]

The Government: Some Policy Decisions

The February Revolution, understandably, generated considerable anxiety in business circles. Capital flight was a serious possibility. Business activity, in almost all sectors, slowed alarmingly. For the government, that meant corresponding declines in tax receipts. In the first days of the new regime, the government had eliminated several unpopular taxes (among them the salt tax, which brought in 65 million francs). While offering immediate political advantage, the moves aggravated the treasury's problems. The rapid growth of unemployment brought a need for relief payments. With treasury resources declining daily, bankruptcy was imminent.

The government undertook several measures to restore confidence. To prevent the threatened capital outflow, efforts were made to allay the anxieties of bankers and leading businessmen. One dramatic measure to secure confidence was the early payment of interest on state bonds. The move had an obvious cost in that it reduced the already modest resources of the treasury. With bankruptcy only days away, and with its options severely limited, the government instituted a 45 percent surcharge on four direct taxes. The "45-centime tax" was much resented by the peasantry. For the new regime, this expedient brought major losses, with supporters (or neutrals) becoming its dedicated opponents. Those effects did not appear immediately. News traveled slowly in provincial France; implementation of the tax, moreover, was delayed until after the legislative election a month later. Given the existence of "universal suffrage," the move ultimately proved a disaster for the new bourgeois government and its interests. The impact was clearly evident in the presidential election of December.

Almost all subsequent commentators agree that the 45-centime tax was a major policy error. Few of them review the then-available alternatives. For Marx the solution was easy—"*a declaration of state bankruptcy.*" Garnier-Pagès, the finance minister, reviewed the options (then and in a later memoir) and, along with the other members of the provisional government, concluded that the tax was the best of the options; bankruptcy, in his view, would have brought an even worse catastrophe.[21]

A second pressing domestic concern involved what is frequently called the problem of order. European nations at this point had no adequate urban police forces. A country threatened by insurrection had to call in the army, a solution that was extremely problematic, given the lack of training for urban combat and an understandable reluctance to open fire on citizens of one's own nation. The July Monarchy had the National Guard at its disposal; it was a citizen militia made up of and led by middle-class notables. But in February, those units had proven unreliable; their inactivity and, at points, their sympathy for the insurgents had been important factors contributing to the collapse of the monarchy. Under the new egalitarian arrangements, the National Guard opened its ranks to other segments of society, most importantly, to *les classes ouvrières*. Its officers were to be chosen, through direct election, by this now much-enlarged constituency. Both changes appeared to raise additional questions of reliability. To deal with the problem and to gain additional units (and, at the same time, to help alleviate unemployment), the government created a new military formation, the Mobile Guard. Young, single, unemployed workers were paid a small wage, provided with uniforms, and given military training. Marx has it that they were recruited from the *Lumpenproletariat*—thieves, criminals, vagabonds, and lazzaroni.[22]

A third pressing problem, unemployment, led to the formation of the National Workshops. Workers were taken on at a modest wage and employed in public works programs. A hasty extemporization, the demand for this employment far exceeded even the largest estimates, which meant enormous costs. With no time for effective planning, few serious projects were available, hence much of the effort was devoted to pointless make-work tasks or, worse, to no work at all. Much of this was highly visible to the gainfully employed, which stimulated considerable resentment over what was seen as a simple boondoggle. In the provinces, the link was made between the 45-centime tax and the workshops, thus adding to the disaffection. For many, the workshops were seen as a danger, as a source of revolution, and pressure grew to dissolve the entire enterprise. The moves to dissolve the workshops in turn stimulated countering efforts to defend the arrangement. The end result was the bloodletting known as the June Days.[23]

The Journées

Most histories of the first months of the republic, of events from February to June, are written in terms of a series of dates. Most of them involve demonstrations of one kind or another intended to influence the directions taken by the provisional government. Another event, possibly the most important one of the period, was the election of the Constituent Assembly.

The first of the demonstrations occurred on March 16. A few days earlier, the government had announced the abolition of the exclusive character of the National Guard. The guards, as indicated, had dissolved as serious formations in the struggles of February. Many in their ranks had opted for *réforme*, but a few weeks later, some of them discovered their enthusiasm did not extend to include equality, hence the demonstration of the sixteenth. That effort was successfully finessed by the government. But then, supposedly sensing a threat to the revolution, some 100,000 demonstrators appeared the next day to protest against the guards' elitist, counterrevolutionary demands. Marx's treatment of this event involves a significant translation. The initial demonstration, in his text, is declared to have involved "the bourgeoisie represented in the National Guard." That bourgeoisie, so one is told, "staged a hostile demonstration against the Provisional Government." His depiction, while not impossible, does seem rather implausible. Since the government supposedly was in the hands of the bourgeoisie, it would mean that the class had organized a protest against itself. There is an easy alternative—that it was, in fact, a demonstration by some of the guards seeking to maintain exclusiveness.

The proletariat, according to Marx, was put in an ambiguous position by this demonstration. They were forced, he says, to come to the defense of the government, to shout "Long Live the Provisional Government." None of the demonstrations of the period involved single or exclusive demands. In this case, for example, almost as an afterthought, the reader is told that the workers also sought to postpone the elections of the National Guard officers and, more importantly, to postpone the Constituent Assembly elections. Marx has obscured the sequence of events here. This workers' demonstration was actually organized by the clubs and had been planned some days in advance with those specific aims in view. The effort of the National Guard gave some impetus to the demonstration of the seventeenth, but the latter was not, as Marx suggests, a response to the events of the previous day. Marx's final comment on this episode stresses the increased resolve of the bourgeoisie, of its members both inside and outside the government; they now sought to "smash" the proletariat.[24]

The election of National Guard officers was rescheduled, the event being postponed a fortnight until April 16. A rumor swept Paris that day, Marx writes, that a working-class uprising aiming to overthrow the provisional government was planned. Some 100,000 men quickly assembled at the Hôtel de Ville to defend the new regime; among those present were units of the National Guard. When, somewhat later, "the workers" arrived on the scene, they learned, "to their amazement," that "bourgeois Paris" had defeated the threatened insurgency. For Marx, it was a calculated plot, one "engineered by the Provisional Government in alliance with the bourgeoisie." It was, he declared, "a very carefully calculated sham battle," its "real purpose" being to allow the recall of the army to Paris.

Most accounts give a markedly different picture of these events. A demonstration had been organized by some people on the left—no sham, in other words—to put pressure on the government. A rumor about an impending Auguste Blanqui coup did sweep Paris the previous evening; Marx is correct about that. The working-class demonstration, says Price, "only revealed the divisions and personal animosities between republicans. Lamartine, Ledru-Rollin and Barbès united in horror of Blanqui, of his person and revolutionary ideals, and the workers themselves divided." Louis Blanc also backed away from this effort. Where Marx has a sharp class-versus-class confrontation with an undivided proletariat, the actual experience was one of serious divisions within the rank, among both leaders and followers.[25]

The histories written in terms of *journées*, days on which popular uprising occurred, have a systematic bias in that they neglect popular gatherings intended to support the government or regime. The next eventful day in the history of the period was April 20. In this case, the government planned the demonstration, a celebration of the new republican regime. Called the Feast of Fraternity, it was a remarkably successful demonstration of support for the collective achievement. Most estimates put the number of participants well in excess of 100,000. This event is not mentioned by Marx. He focuses only on the failures, on the botches and fiascoes, on events that in one way or another discredited the new regime.[26]

Three days later, Easter Sunday, April 23, was the date of the election for the Constituent Assembly. It too had been postponed in response to the concern by the left for time to proselytize in the provinces. It is a date that has importance extending beyond the specific time and place, since it was the first election in modern times conducted under what was called universal suffrage. Flagrantly misnamed, it gave the franchise to adult male citizens. In contrast to previous experience, however, it was a remarkable breakthrough in the direction of citizen representation. It provided a significant experimental setting: the mute masses, for the first time in all of human history, were called upon to express themselves. The election would provide an answer to a pressing question: How serious was the threat from below?

Marx does not discuss the election immediately. His next day is May 4, the date of the assembly's first meeting. That day, like the Feast of Fraternity, was also one of celebration, a great ceremony having been planned to commemorate the event. It too was generally accounted a success. But Marx, who assigns great significance to the day, devoting three paragraphs to it, makes no reference to the celebration.

His discussion of the election itself is rather elliptic and, as a result, is seriously misleading. His principal emphasis is the failure of the reformers' expectations; the suffrage instrument had not proved the magic wand they anticipated. Instead of the fictions, he writes, the elections "brought the *real* people to the light of day, that is, representatives of the different classes into which it falls." The election, he writes, "possessed the incomparably higher merit of unchaining the class struggle." Under the monarchy, the property qualifications allowed only "certain factions" of the bourgeoisie to "compromise themselves." The others were able to "lie hidden behind the scenes." But the new suffrage arrangement threw all sections of the exploiting class to "the apex of the state" thus "tearing from them their deceptive mask."

Marx's account of the election contains only a brief reference to "the different classes." He mentions only two of them, the peasants and petty bourgeoisie. As in his previous mention, they are treated together and are again sloughed off with only a passing comment. They "had to vote under the leadership of a bourgeoisie spoiling for a fight and of big landowners frantic for restoration." Again they are declared to be groups incapable of expressing themselves and unable to organize for representation of their own interests. They are, in short, treated as pawns in the service of more powerful (or more adept) classes.[27]

Possibly the most striking fact about Marx's account of the election is an omission: he says nothing about the voting preferences of the proletariat. Duveau's summary provides some remedy for this deficiency:

A bare thirty-four representatives [from among nine hundred] came from the working class. No historian, as yet, has written a detailed account of the working-class representatives in 1848. It would be a chapter full of surprises, because the workers who did become representatives of the people revealed no strong class prejudices. They set out to please the moderates and even to win the goodwill of the more reactionary representatives. Once inside the Palais Bourbon, the very worker who had affected such a tough and uncompromising attitude in the streets . . . became a little dictator, full of assurances that the lion of the people knew of course that progress could only come about by easy stages, that the demands of the public peace must be met and so forth. All in all, it was the representatives of the workers who treated Louis Blanc with the greatest severity and allied themselves with the right wing in discrediting the actions of the Provisional government and going on to make General Cavaignac a dictator.[28]

This portrait of moderate, reformist sentiment, on first sight, seems difficult to reconcile with the events on the streets. It is entirely possible, however, that the street events dramatically misrepresent the actual lay of opinion. A large crowd, say of 100,000, even if composed entirely of workers, would still leave the majority of the class elsewhere, at home or at work. One's presence at a given demonstration might signify support for the new regime; it would not tell us anything more, such as, for example, whether the underlying sentiment was radical or reformist. The election had broader participation than even the largest demonstration; it also allowed choices across the political spectrum. It is likely, therefore, that the election result gives the more accurate portrait of public sentiment. The rate of participation, Duveau reports, was extremely high, 84 percent, a level not to be reached again either in the Second Empire or in the Third Republic. As a note of caution, one should be wary about Duveau's assumption that it was the same worker who appeared as a radical on the street and a conservative in the polling place. There is an easy alternative: one might easily be dealing with different persons. With opinion subject to many unsettling events, moreover, it would be a mistake to assume constancy of position.

Election to the assembly was from departmental lists. The Seine Department, which contained Paris, was provided with 34 seats. The result there is easily summarized: the members of the new government were the big winners. Lamartine had the highest number, receiving some 260,000 votes. He was followed closely by Dupont de l'Eure, the aged veteran of the Great Revolution, who received 245,000 votes. The working-class representatives, Albert and Louis Blanc, came in with 133,000 and 120,000, respectively. Some measure of the state of opinion is provided by the vote for General Duvivier, the commander of the newly formed Mobile Guard, who received 182,000 votes. In sharp contrast to Marx's claims about the revolutionary orientation of Paris workers, we have the following result reported by Amann: "Well-known club leaders like Cabet, Blanqui, Huber, Raspail, and Barbès had garnered between twenty thousand and sixty-four thousand votes as against the one hundred five thousand awarded the least popular of the thirty-four official winners." All five persons named were prominent leaders on the left. Those figures, Amann notes, should be taken in conjunction with the numbers present at the major *journées*, such as, for example, that of March 17.[29] It is unlikely that Marx would have been unaware of these results. The presentation appears "carefully calculated" (to borrow his phrase) so as to leave undamaged his portrait of a class-conscious revolutionary working class.

The next of the days was May 15. A crowd marched across Paris from the Place de la Bastille to the Place de la Concorde and, from there, crossed the Seine to the Palais Bourbon, where they interrupted the deliberations of the Constituent Assembly. After several hours of turmoil, they declared that body dissolved and continued the march, this time to the Hôtel de Ville. The demonstration collapsed at that point. The invasion of the assembly, understandably, was viewed as a very serious threat to the new regime. The end result, however, was the arrest and discredit of the protest leaders and of their alleged accomplices. Marx describes this episode in a single sentence: "The proletariat hastened [the coming struggle] when, on the 15th of May, it pushed its way into the National Assembly, sought in vain to recapture its revolutionary influence and only delivered its energetic leaders to the jailers of the bourgeoisie." One would not know from that statement that the demonstration was intended to support Poland's national aspirations or that the assembly that day was discussing "the Polish question."

Marx does not mention the numbers involved. Amann reports some forty thousand crossing over the Seine to the Palais Bourbon. The crowd dwindled in the course of the afternoon such that, on arrival at the Hôtel de Ville, there were, again according to Amann, less than ten thousand. Compared to the other days of the period, it was a modest venture. Omission of the numbers allows Marx to declare it another class-versus-class confrontation. The demonstration was initiated by Polish emigrés and staged by the Paris clubs. The latter had lost much of their élan as a result of their manifest defeat in the election, and some club leaders saw this as an opportunity to regain influence. Many other leaders, however, were reluctant participants and tried to contain what they saw as a problematic undertaking. Possibly the most "energetic" of those leaders delivered to jail was Auguste Blanqui, who had addressed the assembly and was expected to call for a new insurgency. But according to most accounts, he was not at all energetic but instead attempted to calm the demonstrators.[30]

The events of the next weeks are linked, in one way or another, to the National Workshops. These had been formed in response to working-class demands (and in an effort to fend off development of the left). The organization of these units had been entrusted to Emile Thomas, a young, capable, charismatic, nonrevolutionary leader. He formed the workers into quasi-military units and maintained close, continuous contact with them. He also moved the units about—in some cases to demonstrations in support of the government, in others, away from demonstrations when the government appeared to be threatened. In the language of the later social sciences, he had successfully co-opted those workers. It was, on the whole, a brilliant organizational achievement.[31]

But the reality of his achievement was not appreciated by bourgeois Paris, and many reacted to the somewhat distorted appearances. There was the reality of the monumental cost. And there was the equally obvious reality of either make-work or, as some saw it, no work. Some saw the entire project as socialist and, as such, a threat to society. The idea of publicly supported workshops was identified, erroneously, as having originated with Louis Blanc, a man seen by many as a dangerous radical and one who, at this point, was a member of the government. Few saw or appreciated that the venture was never in the hands of the radicals or that, as a threat, it had been completely tamed. It was on the basis of the misperception that the triggering decisions were made.

On May 26, Thomas was dismissed. More precisely, quietly, in the dark of night, without prior notice, and without even permission to communicate, he was sent off to Bordeaux. Not too surprisingly, there was an instant shift in the attitudes of workshop members. The radicalization of these workers, it will be noted, dates from late May. It was not the case, as Marx would have it, that the workers were radical in outlook from February onward. One proof of this appeared in the results of June 4 by-elections when, in Paris, support for the left improved considerably over the dismal level of April.[32]

On June 21, the government's plan for dissolution of the National Workshops was published along with decrees announcing its immediate implementation. For single eighteen- to twenty-five-year-olds, the choice was between enlistment in the army, for six-year terms, or being struck from the workshop rolls. For others, a second option was available: rural work projects in the provinces. The first "volunteers" were transported that day. Others demonstrated that evening in a massive parade, chanting "We Won't Go!" and "Bread or Lead!" For members of the ateliers, dissolution had a more ominous meaning. Without that modest subsidy, tens of thousands would be completely destitute.[33]

The June Days

On Thursday morning, the twenty-second, some 1,500 workers demonstrated at the Place de la Bastille. Events escalated throughout the day, so that by nine in the evening 100,000 persons were assembled, the activity then having shifted to the Hôtel de Ville. On the following day, barricades went up, and after some delay by the government forces, the conflict began. Marx declares: "The workers were left no choice; they had to starve or take action. They answered on June 22 with the tremendous insurrection in which the first great battle was fought between the two classes that split modern society. It was a fight for the preservation or annihilation of the *bourgeois* order. The veil that shrouded the republic was torn asunder."[34]

Given Marx's claim about the total character of the struggle—workers versus bourgeoisie fighting for power—it is important to have estimates of the numbers involved. The maximum estimate given for all insurgent forces is 50,000 with only about 10–15,000 directly involved in the fighting (the rest providing backup support). If one were to accept that high overall figure and were to assume that all of those insurgents were workshop members, that still would not involve even half of the June enrollees (some 120,000). Judging from arrest records, however, many of the insurgents were not enrolled. Any relaxation of the two extreme assumptions, therefore, would mean a smaller minority of workshops enrollees among the insurgent forces. Some workshop members, moreover, were present within the reformed National Guard units fighting against the insurgency; their numbers have been estimated as close to that of their fellow workers among the insurgents.

If one takes all Paris workers as the base for discussion, it means of course a still smaller working-class involvement in the uprising. Alfred Cobban offers the following judgment: "The number involved in the actual fighting must not be exaggerated; they were probably not more than 20,000, one in ten or less of the workers of Paris." If one went by the previous maximum estimate, that would put another 30,000 in backup or support roles. That would mean, at minimum, three of four Paris workers did *not* join in support of the June rising. Some workers participated as counterinsurgents, either in the Mobile Guard or in the National Guard. The remainder, in all likelihood, stayed home.[35]

General Cavaignac, the commander of the government forces, held back during the initial hours of the insurgency, which gave the insurgents time to construct an extensive network of barricades. Cavaignac's aim was to move only with large massed formations. Having learned the lesson of February, he wished to prevent any softening of the ranks, any possibility of fraternization and dissolution. His forces included units of the regular army, of the National Guard (now anxious to make up for its behavior in February), and of the new Mobile Guard. Most of the actual fighting occurred on Saturday and Sunday. By Monday, the twenty-sixth, all resistance had ended.

The struggle was characterized by much bitterness and, at its conclusion, by vindictiveness. Marx reports that it is "well known how the bourgeoisie compensated itself for the mortal anguish it suffered by unheard-of brutality, massacring over 3,000 prisoners." Marx does not mention arrests and deportations in *The Class Struggles*. In *The Eighteenth Brumaire*, he twice declares that "15,000 were deported without trial."

Duveau estimates that 4–500 rebels were killed in the fighting but adds, repeating Marx, that "more than three thousand were massacred by the soldiers of the *garde mobile* and the regular army after the fighting was over." Nearly 12,000 arrests followed. "A few of these were executed and some were sentenced to forced labor, but by far the most common penalty," Duveau reports, "was deportation" as "unwilling colonists" to Algeria. Those statements, however, are not accurate.

A review of these matters by the historian Frederick A. de Luna reads:

There is no doubt that the victorious forces shot some captive insurgents. Yet the view that such *fusillades* killed thousands is probably a gross exaggeration. One extreme estimate was that of Louis Ménard, an insurgent who published a book in which he claimed that only four or five hundred of his comrades had been killed on the barricades, but that about 3,000 were executed afterwards. However, the contemporary who was the most impartial and most scrupulously accurate of those who wrote about the revolution, Madame d'Agoult, concluded that only about 150 prisoners were shot. . . . Those atrocities that did occur were the work of Mobile and National Guardsmen; the regular army displayed no vindictiveness, and many officers sought to protect prisoners.

Madame d'Agoult (Daniel Stern) gives, without comment, a figure from the official police report declaring a total of 1,460 deaths in the June fighting, two-thirds of them suffered by the army and National Guard.

Duveau's report of the treatment of the arrestees is also misleading. Actually some 15,000 were arrested, more than 3,000 of whom were released "within days," yielding the 12,000 figure. In December, when Cavaignac left office, only about 2,700 remained in custody. Some 2,200 of these, according to de Luna, were freed during 1849. Early in 1850, 459 insurgents were sent to Algeria. The "most common penalty" thus appears to have been six months to a year of incarceration in France.[36]

The Question of Motives

Marx's declaration, as indicated, held that the struggle was "for the preservation or annihilation of the *bourgeois* order." Backing up that claim, he provides two of the slogans. The workers, he says, had proclaimed *"Overthrow of the bourgeoisie! Dictatorship of the working class!"* It is remarkable the extent to which Marx's portrait has "veiled" our understanding of the June Days. The insurgents' own slogans indicate more limited aspirations—the word "bread" is prominent in their statements. And the National Workshops, at that critical point, were the principal means for achieving even that limited goal. That agency may be described quite simply as a government-sponsored job-creation program. It was, put differently, an early primitive step in the direction of the modern welfare state. Borrowing from another vocabulary, the innovation would be termed a reformist measure by any orthodox Marxist. The insurgent workers, in their desperate circumstances, were making use of exceptional means, armed insurrection, to maintain a reformist institution. Passing over the specifics, over the concrete aims of the insurgents, however, Marx declared the effort to be maximalist, an attempt to overthrow and replace the bourgeois regime.

That reading of the June Days was of considerable importance for Marx. For him, it was "the first great battle" between the classes in the capitalist era. It was, as such, a decisive proof of his claims, the cornerstone of his historical enterprise. His reading of the event, his definition of the entire class as radical and as mobilized for pursuit of the maximal aim, postponed the discussion of reformism versus radicalism, of "possibilism" versus "maximalism," of "economism" versus the larger political purpose, for some decades. If one accepted that reading of the June 1848 events, it would be necessary, in subsequent treatments, to provide some explanation for the deradicalization of the workers in the following decades (or at least until the Paris Commune in 1871). There is, however, another possibility, namely, that the insurgent workers had reformist goals.

In support of this alternative, we have a striking fact: none of the other sources referred to here reports use of the maximalist slogans Marx attributed to the workers. Engels's account in the *Neue Rheinische Zeitung* makes no mention of the maximalist slogans cited by Marx. Engels cites two inscriptions: "Bread or Death!" and "Work or Death!" Amann points to "The social and democratic Republic!" as an important war cry. But that focuses on programmatic content, what the republic should be doing; it says nothing about overthrow or class dictatorship. De Luna cites the slogan "la République démocratique et sociale" as expressing the most common demand. Before the fighting began, at one of the barricades, François Arago, a member of the government, a respected scientist, and a proven republican, remonstrated with insurgents. One of them responded: "Monsieur Arago, we are full of respect for you, but you have no right to reproach us. You have never been hungry, you don't know what poverty is." Other slogans expressed hostility to the regime that had betrayed them—for example, "Down with Lamartine!" "Down with Marie!" "Down with Thiers!" and "Down with the traitors!" One slogan focused on the forced move to the provinces—"We won't go!" Other slogans focused on the immediate pressing need: "Bread or bullets!" and "Work! Work! Bread! Bread!"[37]

Marx gives little attention to workers' perceptions, outlooks, or motives. His arguments or assumptions, for the most part, are implicit and, again for the most part, depend on a single, exclusive logic: the workers, now wide-awake and fully conscious, had fought on the barricades in February. Then, denied the fruits of *their* victory, they demonstrated for at least a share of the benefits. Finally, when provoked by the bourgeoisie, they took to the streets in this attempt to overthrow the government. If that were the insurgents' goal, it should have appeared in their "bold slogan," which should have read, as Marx declares, "Annihilation of the bourgeois order!" Instead, the leading slogan appears to have been "Pain ou Plomb!"—"Bread or Lead!"

Marx's single, exclusive logic seems a rather unlikely reading of the participants' motives. The wide-awake (or fully conscious) workers would have to see a "dictatorship of the working class" as a solution to their problems. But to take over a nearly bankrupt state would hardly mean improvement. The situation of the treasury would not be improved. The capital outflow that would follow any such takeover would bring a substantial increase in the already high level of unemployment. A maximalist struggle, in short, could only make things worse. The more limited struggles occurring since February had dampened business activity, making clear the implications. That recognition might well explain the choice of many workers during the June Days—that is, to stay out of it.

Marx divides Paris into two exclusive segments—it was "a *revolution of the proletariat against the bourgeoisie.*" All interests are identified with one or the other of those segments. But the real world rarely divides with such categoric simplicity. Some participants were forced into revolutionary service. This statement was the most frequently given, by those arrested, in the course of subsequent interrogations. Many of those declarations were doubtlessly self-serving, the most plausible of the available excuses. Some of them, not many to be sure, were probably genuine. Tocqueville reports that one of his colleagues, while out on official business, was forced to help in the construction of a barricade. Some people might have favored the insurgency but, to save their skins, avoided direct involvement. For individuals, the "free rider" option is always the most rational economic choice. The motivational and interpersonal dynamics operating, in summary, were more complex than is suggested by that image of a sharp confrontation with clear understanding and commitment on both sides.[38]

The nonparticipants, those who sat out the struggle, could easily recognize other interests—survival, health, and welfare—of themselves, and of their families, friends, and associates. They could easily conclude that their interests were not well served by either side, by neither the bourgeois government nor the insurgents. At the same time, being fully aware, having true consciousness of the situation, they would also recognize their own powerlessness. They could not stop (or otherwise influence) the actions of the government or those of the insurgents. Their situation was similar to that of various groups at the time of the English civil war; as discussed in the last chapter, many sought to avoid any involvement.

This discussion of what we might call the third option, it will be noted, is largely speculative. We have no information at all on the motives of those who opted out. Revolutions are not written from the perspective of nonparticipants. Most analyses assume a complete mobilization of the people and therefore sense no need for consideration of nonparticipation.

Some simple facts of life might easily account for the neutralist tendency. Most accounts of revolution overlook the simple fact of family. The overwhelming majority of the barricade fighters were male. Wives and daughters remained at home; at best a tiny minority appeared in support roles. Many wives, it seems likely, would do everything they could to prevent participation by their husbands. And it seems equally likely that mothers and nonparticipant fathers would do all they could to prevent the involvement of sons. In short, the normal family dynamics—love, affection, and economic need—would serve as powerful deterrents to participation. This again, however, is speculation, part of the never-recorded history.[39]

Something must also be said about another key segment of the proletariat. Marx has it that those recruited into the Mobile Guard were from an easily corrupted underclass, the *Lumpenproletariat*. Mark Traugott's recent research, however, has demonstrated that members of the Mobile Guard and the National Workshops were virtually identical in terms of occupational background. Both groups were recruited across the board from the working-class ranks. The major differences between them were in terms of age and marital status, both of these stemming from the initial criteria for recruitment. The guard recruited young, single persons; the workshops recruited single and married persons. Many of the latter, of course, had children, and they also, of course, would have had a somewhat higher average age. There was an obvious logic involved: the former organization was looking for fighters; the latter aimed to alleviate economic suffering. Given the selection procedures and given the basic finding, the identity of backgrounds, it follows that the struggle was not one of workers versus lumpenproletarians. It would have been quite possible for the conflict to have pitted brothers against brothers. The Mobile Guard, however, was generally used outside its home arrondissement, thus avoiding that source of strain. Basically, two separate organizations had been recruited from the same class milieu.[40]

Some comment is also in order with respect to bourgeois outlooks and orientations. Marx has written the history as if, for the workers, it was a foreordained tragedy. The movement of those events, however, was not due to some blind fate. It is presumed that the bourgeoisie consciously, systematically, and with plan and foresight directed events toward that confrontation with the workers. Central to this plan was the perception of the National Workshops as a threat, as a challenge to their rule. But, as indicated, under the management of Emile Thomas, the workshops were just the opposite of a threat. The workshops had contained any radical potential, had removed workers from threatening demonstrations, and, in some instances at least, had brought them to demonstrations in support of the regime.

The workshops, however, posed a serious economic problem. The costs of the arrangement proved to be immense, going beyond any foreseen limit. Worse still, those costs continued to increase as, unexpectedly, the membership continued to grow. With the economy foundering, in great measure because of the revolution, the workshops were seen as an obstacle to a revival, adding an important element of uncertainty and, to some extent at least, taking workers from employment in the private sector. Given the haste and lack of planning in this job creation effort, critics could point to obvious boondoggles. Combined with these economic problems was a political concern—the perception, largely mistaken, that the workshops formed the basis for an army of insurrection. It is not surprising, given the cluster of concerns, that the government, with strong backing in bourgeois circles, concluded that it was necessary to end the arrangement—*il faut en finir*.

The decision by the government to dissolve the workshops was easy enough; the economic realities provided ample justification. But, given the dependence of workers on this primitive welfare arrangement, it was a difficult resolution to carry through, and, as seen, the decision and its execution ultimately provoked the uprising. But Marx's account missed these dynamics; his portrait has a vicious bourgeoisie pressing for a showdown with the workers. In his discussions of the workers and the bourgeoisie, Marx has missed these alternative readings of the motivational dynamics. By doing so, he has allowed himself support—spurious support—for his determinist reading of the history.[41]

Most accounts of the 1848 revolution, understandably, are very much Paris-centered. Marx's history, too, shares that emphasis. His account also, as just indicated, is essentially bipolar in character: it describes a struggle between the Paris bourgeoisie and proletariat, with the rest of France looking on as spectators. For most of the account, one segment of the Paris population, the petty bourgeoisie, disappears from view. Another category, one forming the vast majority of the French nation, also disappears: the peasantry. In one of the last paragraphs of this article, Marx allows these two classes another appearance, one that again is best described as fugitive. The statement reads: "With the proletariat removed for the time being from the stage and bourgeois dictatorship recognised officially, the middle strata of bourgeois society, the petty bourgeoisie and the peasant class, had to adhere more and more closely to the proletariat as their position became more unbearable and their antagonism to the bourgeoisie more acute." It is a remarkable claim: the petty bourgeoisie, having just fought this life-and-death battle against the workers, now feels it must adhere to them. And the same is supposed to be true of the majority, the peasantry. This statement, not surprisingly, comes without a shred of supporting evidence.

This supposed 180-degree shift of direction is all the more remarkable given the strength of Marx's formulations elsewhere. On the opening page of the subsequent article, for example, he states that the petty bourgeois "democratic republicans" (Ledru-Rollin, the *Montagne*, the *Réforme*) had "conspired on April 16 against the proletariat, [and] together [with the republican faction of the bourgeoisie] they had warred against [the proletariat] in the June Days." A worker-peasant linkup seems even more unlikely given Marx's conclusion, on the same page, about "the unleashed property fanaticism of the peasants." An even stronger statement about the petty bourgeoisie, indicating the strength of the sentiments involved, appears a few pages later: "No one had fought more fanatically in the June days for the salvation of property and the restoration of credit than the Parisian petty bourgeois—keepers of cafés and restaurants, *marchands de vins*, small traders, shopkeepers, handicraftsmen, etc."[42]

The final paragraphs of the first article turn to what one might call foreign affairs, that is, to the international implications of these domestic events. The victory over the proletariat raised the self-assurance of the bourgeoisie everywhere. It also caused the bourgeoisie, everywhere, to "league" openly with "the feudal monarchy" against the people. This brief comment, one may note, signals an unexpected, non-Marxist option, a coalition of rising bourgeoisie and old regime, as opposed to the bourgeoisie demanding and taking power in its own right.

The June struggle contained a lesson also for "the despotic powers of Europe." It indicated that France "must maintain peace abroad at any price in order to be able to wage civil war at home." The struggles for "national independence" going on at this time were thus left to their fate; Russia, Austria, and Prussia now had a free hand to undertake their suppression. The fate of those national revolutions, the Hungarian, Polish, and Italian, thus depended on the fate of the proletarian revolution. The practical implication is stated by Marx as follows: "Finally, with the victories of the Holy Alliance, Europe has taken on a form in which every fresh proletarian upheaval in France directly involves a *world war*. The new French revolution is forced to leave its national soil forthwith and *conquer the European terrain*, on which alone the social revolution of the nineteenth century can be accomplished."[43] For some, this call by Marx for a world war may come as something of a surprise. It is a call to follow the course taken in the Great Revolution. In 1792, to secure and extend their advances, the leaders of the revolution had declared war on the reactionary powers of Europe. That strategy was seen as appropriate by Marx, his sense of things being derived from the history of interventions by the reactionary powers observed from then through to 1848–49.

June 1848 to June 1849

The heart of the revolutionary drama of 1848 is contained in Marx's first article, which deals with events from February to June. In his second article, Marx reviews (and rewrites) some of the politics of that period; he then discusses events up to June 13, 1849 (that date is the title of the piece). Rather anticlimactic, this article focuses on events in the government, specifically the conflict between the executive and legislative branches. This article too is organized in terms of a series of days, but these, with one exception, mark struggles in the assembly. The most significant development in this article is a change in the dramatis personae, the actors and agencies in this drama, for the most part, being different from those of the first act.

Since the action is rather complicated, a brief overview of the developments may prove helpful. The most significant event of the period was the election of

Louis Napoleon Bonaparte as president of the republic in December 1848. He brought in a wide array of July Monarchy notables to form a new cabinet. Among them was the previous leader of the opposition, Odilon Barrot. That government came into immediate conflict with the Constituent Assembly, the result being a series of no-confidence moves by both sides. Upon completion of its task, the writing of a constitution, that assembly, with some reluctance, dissolved itself. A legislative body, the National Assembly, was elected in May 1849. Given the history of botch and blunder by the previous assembly, the original republican faction virtually disappeared. The new assembly had a decidedly antirepublican majority made up of Legitimists, Orleanists, and a small group of Bonapartists. It also had an unexpectedly large, left-liberal republican opposition party which called itself *la Montagne*.

The second most important figure in this phase of the history was Alexandre Auguste Ledru-Rollin, a left-liberal and the leading figure of the *Réforme* group. In the legislature, he was the leader of *la Montagne* (which for Marx was a pale, ridiculous replica of the revolutionary original of 1793). The date of the title refers to Ledru-Rollin's attempt to check the reactionary tendency. When that failed, he went to the street, attempting to generate a rising in support of the revolution. But that too collapsed when there was no response from the workers. Following the route of Louis Philippe, of Karl Marx, and of Louis Blanc, he too went into exile in Britain.

The Contending Forces

Marx begins with a review of the republic's two leading political factions (or coteries). There was the petty bourgeois faction, referred to as the democratic republicans. In the first months of the republic, Marx writes: "The republicans in the sense of the *petty bourgeoisie* [were] represented in the Executive Commission [cabinet] by Ledru-Rollin, in the Constituent National Assembly by the party of the *Montagne* and in the press by the *Réforme*." This group, Marx notes, had "conspired" with the bourgeois republicans against the proletariat but, with the latter defeated, "they were dismissed." No longer the useful subordinates of the bourgeois republican group, they could wring no concessions from them, and yet whenever the republic appeared to be in jeopardy, they had to follow. Without the backing of the proletariat, their efforts counted for nothing.[44]

The second group, actually the principal agency in the original governing coalition, was the bourgeois republican faction. It was *the* victor in both the February Revolution and the June Days. It had undone the old regime, defeated the workers, and subordinated the petty bourgeois faction. That victory, it will be remembered, was said to have been the victory of the industrial bourgeoisie over the finance aristocracy. That sharp, dialectical confrontation of the two bourgeois factions does not appear here in Marx's initial discussion. The victorious faction of February, the industrial bourgeoisie proper, has been redefined in the second article:

> Since 1830, the *bourgeois republican* faction, in the person of its writers, its spokesmen, its men of talent and ambition, its deputies, generals, bankers and lawyers, had grouped itself round a Parisian journal, the *National*. In the provinces this journal had its branch newspapers. The coterie of the *National* was the *dynasty of the tricolour republic*. It immediately took possession of all state dignities, of the ministries, the prefecture of police, the post-office directorship, the positions of prefect, the higher army officers' posts now become vacant. At the head of the executive power stood its general, *Cavaignac*; its editor-in-chief, Marrast, became permanent President of the Constituent National Assembly.[45]

The class faction has now, appropriately, become a coterie grouped around a newspaper. The faction was originally moved by pressing economic concerns, ending the predatory regime of the finance aristocracy. Here the members are defined politically; they are the supporters of the "tricolour republic." In contrast to the earlier statement, some unnamed bankers appear as part of the winning coalition.

Marx is passing over many inconvenient facts here. The *National* coterie had taken the lion's share of the ministries in February. Lamartine, however, easily the leading figure in the provisional government, was not part of that group. A compromise had to be arranged with the *Réforme* coterie, the result being that Ledru-Rollin, viewed by many as a dangerous leftist, was made minister of the interior and thus the man charged with organizing the election for the Constituent Assembly. Popular pressures in the first days of the new regime forced a second compromise, making some place for the left, for Louis Blanc and Albert.

After the election, a new government, now designated the Executive Commission, was chosen by the Constituent Assembly. Many persons in the *National* coterie wished to exclude Ledru-Rollin, but due to the strenuous efforts of Lamartine, the man continued to hold office, although no longer as minister of the interior. Lamartine, who had been supported by, among others, a wide spectrum of conservatives, lost much of his following as a result. Those conservatives, who had voted for him as their protection against Ledru-Rollin, saw it as a betrayal. In the midst of the June conflict, the Constituent Assembly conferred executive power on Cavaignac, and the Executive Commission resigned. Cavaignac named a new cabinet, one made up of moderate republicans (and with the left completely excluded). The *National* coterie was still well represented. That government ruled until December, when the new president, Louis Napoleon, chose its successor.[46]

Marx's reference to Cavaignac as the *National*'s general and chief executive is without justification. Marrast did become president of the Constituent Assembly—which does not mean, as Marx implies, that he controlled it. Here Marx has taken a history of persons, of a coterie, transformed it into a history of a class faction, and declared its political dominance. That domination, presumably, was nowhere more clearly exemplified than in the Constituent Assembly. Some others, even revolutionary French writers, Marx notes, had mistakenly thought the assembly to be controlled by royalists. Marx, however, declares it to be "the *exclusive representative* of bourgeois *republicanism*." Subsequent scholarship has established that the assembly was in fact dominated by royalists.[47]

Within the assembly, according to Marx, the bourgeois republicans undertook *their* political business. They formed a commission of inquiry to study the events of May 15 and of June. Their inquiry focused, Marx declared, on Louis Blanc, Caussidière, and Ledru-Rollin, that is, on the leaders of the working-class and petty bourgeois factions. The former two were recommended to the courts (all three ultimately found refuge in Britain). A series of repressive laws were enacted by this assembly in this period of reaction. At the same time, most of the progressive measures decreed in the first days of the revolution were eliminated. Cavaignac, on July 3, decreed the termination of the National Workshops.

Marx devotes several paragraphs to the petty bourgeoisie (as distinct from its agency, the *Réforme* coterie). The members of that class—all of them, presumably—were heavily indebted and faced imminent bankruptcy. They, accordingly, sought debt relief, "an extension of the term of payment . . . and the compulsory liquidation of creditors' claims in consideration of a moderate percentage payment." The adjustments were called friendly agreements— *concordats à l'amiable*. After some discussion, the assembly rejected the adjustments in "most essential points." Having alienated the peasantry, the workers, and now the urban petty bourgeoisie, the bourgeois republicans had made an opponent of every significant segment of the society. The emerging problem was signaled in by-elections on September 19. Louis Bonaparte was elected to the assembly along with "the Communist Raspail." The bourgeoisie, Marx declares, elected "the Jewish money-changer and Orleanist Fould." All of these signs pointed to an open declaration of war against the Constituent Assembly and bourgeois republicanism.[48]

The principal task of the Constituent Assembly, of course, was the writing of the constitution. This effort was overseen by Armand Marrast, formerly the editor of *Le National* but now, as noted, president of the assembly. The task was soon accomplished, their document providing for a single legislative body and for a presidency, both to be elected by universal suffrage. The "right to work," the problematical phrase that had given rise to the National Workshops, was replaced by another, by a "right to assistance." There was some other tidying up, such as a ban on progressive taxation and a measure on the irremovability of judges. Banning progressive taxation, according to Marx, was one further denial of petty bourgeois hopes. The writers of the constitution thereby rejected "the only means of binding the middle strata of bourgeois society" to the republic. The bourgeois republican regime, in short, wrote a constitution that, in all respects but one, was ideal for the interests of the bourgeoisie. That single exception, the "fundamental contradiction of this constitution," Marx calls it, was the suffrage provision. It allowed the now disaffected segments of the population to vote out the entire ruling coterie. As opposed to a history governed by insistent economic facts, this history, it will be noted, is written in terms of human political errors, of blunders that were in no way foreordained.[49]

A paragraph appearing at this point introduces a significant emendation of Marx's basic portrait of the bourgeoisie. "But what class," he asks, "then remained as the mainstay of their republic?" He replies: "The big bourgeoisie. And its mass was anti-republican." The *republican* bourgeoisie, the instigator of the revolution, is here declared to be a minority in its own rank, something not hitherto disclosed or in any way suggested. The lesson, clearly, is that the industrial bourgeoisie, the segment fettered by the rule of the finance aristocracy, was about to lose out. Marx makes no comment on this problematical development.[50]

Louis Napoleon and the Peasantry

The presidential election, on December 10, 1848, is described by Marx as "the day of the *peasant insurrection*." They had their February in December. The successful candidate, by a vast margin, was Louis Napoleon. He received 5,434,226 votes, nearly three-quarters of those cast. Cavaignac, with 1,448,107, was a very distant second. Louis Napoleon is a problematical presence for Marx's larger theory; he is an individual not easily fitted into any of the class categories or clearly identified with any of those class interests. Marx again makes no comment, deferring consideration for a later point.

A long paragraph is devoted to the peasants. It is the most extensive discussion in the entire work of this segment, which formed the majority of the French population. Marx draws a parallel between Louis Napoleon, here referred to as a symbol, and his peasant supporters: "The symbol that expressed [the peasantry's] entry into the revolutionary movement, clumsily cunning, knavishly naive, doltishly sublime, a calculated superstition, a pathetic burlesque, a cleverly stupid anachronism, a world-historic piece of buffoonery and an undecipherable hieroglyphic for the understanding of the civilised—this symbol bore the unmistakable physiognomy of the class that represents barbarism within civilisation." In lieu of thought, analysis, or explanation, Marx offers vituperation. For the peasantry, the merely unflattering description contained in the *Manifesto*—the "idiocy of rural life"—here becomes one of intense hostility. It is one of the many (as will be seen) instances of unremitting denigration of the farm population in the writings of Marx and Engels. There was a simple logic in the choices made by the farmers, one indicated immediately by Marx himself. The republic, after all, had "announced itself to this class with the *tax-collector*." The peasants, accordingly, had marched to the polls, Marx declares, with shouts of: "No more taxes, down with the rich, down with the republic, long live the Emperor!" Hidden behind that choice, he states, was "the peasant war." The republic they had voted down was "*the republic of the rich*."[51]

Bonaparte had gained more than peasant support. The proletariat had also voted for him, presumably as a vote against Cavaignac. The petty bourgeoisie had voted for him in order to create, so they thought, the "rule of the debtor over the creditor." Marx also claims that the majority of the *haute* bourgeoisie supported him; they were voting against the momentarily dominant industrial bourgeoisie whose rule had become intolerable to them. Marx, it will be noted, is interpreting election results and, like many commentators, is imputing motives to each of these segments. The advantage of Bonaparte's candidacy, he argues, was that he was unknown but, at the same time, the bearer of a great name and tradition. "Just because he was nothing," Marx writes, "he could signify everything save himself . . . [however] different as the meaning of the name Napoleon might be in the mouths of the different classes, with this name each class wrote on its ballot: Down with the party of the *National*, down with Cavaignac, down with the Constituent Assembly, down with the bourgeois republic." His candidacy, in short, provided an ideal opportunity for the expression of protest.

Marx considers also the significance of two minority candidates, Ledru-Rollin and Raspail. They were the candidates, respectively, of the petty bourgeoisie and of the revolutionary proletariat, at least of the "more advanced sections" of those classes. Marx invests Raspail's votes with special significance. They were cast against any presidency, against the constitution, and against Ledru-Rollin. The latter claim is announced as "the first act by which the proletariat, as an independent political party, declared its separation from the democratic party." This was a proof of one element of the Marx-Engels system. One problem, however, is glossed over. Although the proletariat has been portrayed, since June, as highly conscious, Marx gives no clear explanation for its overwhelming support of Louis Napoleon; a vote for Raspail, after all, would be a much more effective protest against all developments since February. Nor does Marx reveal that Raspail's support from all of France amounted to only 37,000 votes.[52]

Cavaignac resigned office and Louis Napoleon was sworn in as president of the republic, promising to uphold the constitution. To head the government, he chose Odilon Barrot, the leader of the dynastic opposition during the July Monarchy. Marx makes much of this appointment, noting that the last minister of Louis Philippe thus became the first minister of Louis Napoleon. His point, elaborated for several paragraphs, is that the new government was a coalition of prerevolutionary leaders who were now back in power. There is another easy hypothesis. Louis Napoleon, as Marx recognizes, came out of nowhere and, initially at least, had no party and no serious following. There was, in short, no shadow cabinet ready when the occasion arose.

After the failure of his Strasbourg coup attempt in 1836, Louis Napoleon had called on Barrot to lead his defense. When Louis Napoleon was sent into exile without trial, Barrot had his brother Ferdinand undertake the defense of the man's accomplices. After Louis Napoleon's second coup attempt, during his imprisonment in the 1840s, some opposition deputies in the chamber took up his cause and visited Louis Philippe to seek his release. Bonaparte's principal friend in this group was Odilon Barrot. In March 1848, when considering whether to run for the Constituent Assembly, he sought the advice of Barrot. Louis Napoleon's subsequent naming of Barrot therefore is not as surprising as it might first appear. The lack of an experienced organization would also explain his choice of Orleanists for other positions; they were the only group having experience in government. This embarrassing problem is one that faces any individual or group coming to power either for the first time or after a long time in opposition. They must either make do with less than optimally experienced personnel or draw on those with some previous training.

Marx is mistaken in his claim about the old leaders now back in power. The three persons named by him were all in opposition to the July Monarchy. In addition to Barrot, "the Orleanist," there was "the legitimist and Jesuit Falloux." Léon Faucher is there as minister of the interior. Marx identifies him at this point as "the Malthusian," neglecting his earlier description of him as an opponent of the finance aristocracy. For the rest, one found "a combination of Legitimists and Orleanists." The same pattern of appointment is reported in other positions. A Legitimist officer was given command of the armed forces in the Seine Department; an Orleanist officer was given command of the Alpine army. Posts high and low were "filled with old creatures of the monarchy," the result, clearly, being a "restoration of the old royalist administration." This transformation meant that "the party of the *National*," the leaders and administrators of the February Revolution, was "relieved of all the higher posts, where it had entrenched itself."[53]

The Constituent Assembly continued in office for several months, serving, according to Marx, as "the last asylum of the bourgeois republicans." A struggle for power followed with the leaders of the assembly attempting to topple and replace the Barrot ministry. Government finances were a persisting problem, and Barrot proposed to retain the salt tax which had been abolished by the outgoing government. With evident enthusiasm, looking toward favor from the peasantry, the assembly rejected the proposal. A series of confrontations between Louis Napoleon's government and the Constituent Assembly followed. The government wanted the assembly to dissolve, since its task, writing the constitution, was now complete. The assembly, however, according to Marx, sought to exert power. Several no-confidence motions were introduced, but all were defeated. Another contradiction appears here. Earlier Marx had declared that the bourgeois republicans had the upper hand in the Constituent Assembly. And later, as seen above, he had declared the assembly to be the exclusive representative of bourgeois republicanism. It is curious that a group with the upper hand could not carry its own no-confidence votes. Although Marx spends many pages on this seesaw struggle, he offers no explanation for the paradox. Nothing is served by reviewing that narration; largely descriptive (and embellished with heavy derogatory comment), it contains nothing of lasting importance. The struggle between legislative and executive branches ended in mid-May when the assembly dissolved.

The National Assembly

The campaign for the election of a legislative body, the National Assembly, had already begun in March. In this connection Marx provides a long paragraph reporting the appearance of two new parties, indicating also their relationships to the underlying classes. These were the Party of Order and the Social Democratic (or Red) Party.

The Party of Order, Marx declared, combined all but one of the segments of the dominant classes. The single exception was the *National* coterie, which put forward its own party. The secret of the Party of Order was its coalition of Legitimists and Orleanists. This is to say that it brought together the supporters of the main Bourbon line (those ruling from 1815 to 1830) and those of Louis Philippe (who ruled from July 1830 to February 1848). Since those are divisions within the royal family—not divisions of class—that too requires explanation, something that is forthwith provided. The monarchy restored in 1815, according to Marx, represented the big landed proprietors. The July Monarchy, which Marx initially declared to be the agency of the finance aristocracy, now is said to have been the agency of *both* bourgeois segments. This reformulation reads: "The bourgeois class fell apart into two big factions, which had alternately maintained a monopoly of power—the *big landed proprietors* under the *restored monarchy*, and the *finance aristocracy* and the *industrial bourgeoisie* under the *July monarchy*."

This claim stands in direct contradiction to the central explanation for the February Revolution offered in the first article. This does not appear to be a careless error, since the point is reiterated with even greater emphasis: "*Bourbon* was the royal name for the predominant influence of the interests of the one faction, *Orleans* the royal name for the predominant influence of the interests of the other faction." It is, clearly, a major change. The work began with a delineation of the February Revolution as a struggle between two rival bourgeois factions, finance and industrial; one article later, both of those factions are merged (and their struggle submerged), and their joint interests are now set in opposition to those of "bourgeois" landed proprietors. Their separate interests are hidden under cover of the royal houses. With a few strokes of the pen, it will be noted, Marx has relocated those Legitimist landowners. In most accounts they are portrayed as aristocrats and as adherents of the old regime. Here, without any comment on the transmogrification, the entire aristocracy has become a bourgeois faction. It is another case of the "bourgeois of convenience."[54]

Restoration would normally be the prime concern for a royalist faction. But this now posed a problem, since the Party of Order was "the *coalition* of *Orleanists* and *Legitimists* into *one party*," which meant they had to forgo restoration. As Marx puts it, "the *nameless realm of the republic* was the only one in which both factions could maintain with equal power the common class interest without giving up their mutual rivalry." Both royal factions, for the sake of their material interests, became what one might call practical republicans. This argument—the republic as practical ideal—is repeated several times in later articles. It is a bold argument. Royal houses become bourgeois factions; antirepublican factions discover the merits of the republican form. These transformations left the *National* group "confused in its own mind" and, initially at least, the royalists themselves were no less "deceived."[55]

Earlier, the *National* was linked to the industrial bourgeoisie. Now, in passing, it is said that the group "did not represent any large faction of their class resting on economic foundations." The group's sole importance was to have recognized (and "idealised and embellished") the republican form as the ap-

propriate arrangement for transcending the interests or egoism of each bourgeois faction. That point required elaboration. The *National* coterie had done
more than merely recognize the ideal form. They had made it reality. It was
perhaps understandable that the combined ruling segments should dismiss
the coterie and form their own party, since at this point the bourgeois republicans were thoroughly discredited. It is surprising, however, that the bourgeoisie should be so ungrateful for the remarkable services that had been provided.[56] Marrast, the editor of the *National*, was to die in poverty within a
few years. There is, of course, another possibility: the coterie was self-directed,
not an agency of the bourgeoisie or of any of its segments. This alternative,
the possibility of an autonomous intelligentsia, will be discussed below in
Chapter 5.

A second long paragraph reviews the program and resources of the Party of
Order. The program, in brief, championed property, family, religion, and
order. It had "enormous money resources," had organized branches everywhere, had "all the ideologists of the old society in its pay," had the government power at its disposal, and had "an army of unpaid vassals in the whole
mass of petty bourgeois and peasants [who] found in the high dignitaries of
property the natural representatives of their petty property and its petty prejudices." Marx once again displays a remarkable indifference to what he had
written earlier. In the previous paragraph, as just indicated, he wrote that the
National group, "confused in its own mind," had gone its way and formed its
own party. Hence, not all of the ideologists of the old society were in the
pay of the Party of Order. And then too, he announced that the petty bourgeoisie, after the June Days, "had to adhere more and more closely to the
proletariat." Then, in December, they had had their revolution and voted in
Louis Napoleon. Finally, they are declared to be "vassals" in the bourgeois
coalition.[57]

Petty bourgeoisie and peasantry, it will be noted, are once again declared to
be hopeless political incompetents. They have no independent views, no independent organization, and no stability of position. The petty bourgeoisie and
peasantry, Marx writes, could still maintain the illusion that Bonaparte had
been prevented from "manifesting his wonder-working powers" by the machinations of the Constituent Assembly. Of Louis Napoleon and his following,
Marx provides this brief comment: "We have not mentioned the Bonapartists
in connection with the party of Order. They were not a serious faction of the

bourgeois class, but a collection of old, superstitious wounded veterans and of young, unbelieving soldiers of fortune."

The election, as indicated, yielded a victory for the bourgeois coalition. Heavily dependent on the votes of its vassals, the Party of Order sent a large majority to the assembly. For Marx, therefore, the now-consolidated bourgeoisie had secured power in the legislative branch.[58]

Marx next considers the opposition, that is, the Social Democratic or Red Party. That may sound like a party of the proletariat; it is, however, the party of the petty bourgeoisie. The *Montagne* was the floundering agency led by Ledru-Rollin. This party had the support of "the sections of the petty bourgeoisie and peasant class already revolutionised," those who "naturally" had to ally themselves with "the revolutionary proletariat." This seems an improbable choice. One is supposed to believe that sections of those two classes, both of undisclosed but presumably nonminuscule size, had turned to the revolutionary proletariat. The industrial proletariat in France at that time was itself a minuscule segment; the revolutionary portion of that class must have been infinitesimal. One has to assume, moreover, that the larger segment, peasants located throughout France, would look to workers in Paris, Lyons, Lille, or Strasbourg for political direction. Despite the manifest implausibility of the claim, Marx nevertheless recapitulates the theme at the end of his long description: "A considerable part of the peasants and of the provinces was revolutionised. Not only were they disappointed in Napoleon, but the Red party offered them, instead of the name, the content, instead of illusory freedom from taxation, repayment of the milliard paid to the Legitimists, the adjustment of mortgages and the abolition of usury."[59] It is a point of more than passing interest: this "red" party was making appeals to the peasantry, basically offering them tax and debt relief. It constitutes an early foreshadowing of what, in later discussions within Social Democratic circles, came to be called the *Agrarfrage*, the agrarian question. This subject will be discussed at greater length in Chapters 4 and 5.

Marx again discusses the petty bourgeoisie at this point. They are, he declares, "a mass hovering between the bourgeoisie and the proletariat, a mass whose material interests demanded democratic institutions." That demand, presumably, stems from their concern with debt relief, such measures not being likely under restricted suffrage and the rule of creditors. That mass, we are told, had voted overwhelmingly for Louis Napoleon in December 1848;

they had, rather gullibly, seen this "nonentity" as representing or standing for their interests. Five months later, we are told, the same mass was serving as an army of vassals for the Party of Order. No explanation is given for this majority choice; it is especially problematical, since the Party of Order was not enthusiastic about democratic institutions.

As noted, some segments of the petty bourgeoisie, both urban and rural components, had aligned with the revolutionary movement. But no indication was given as to the size of these minorities. Moreover, no clue was given as to the source of the division. The two segments shared common class locations, yet some went one way, some went another. Marx here provided a statement of fact but, despite an obvious need, offered no explanation or analysis.[60]

This second article ends with a brief, elliptical reference to the events of June 13. On June 11, Ledru-Rollin brought in a bill of impeachment against Napoleon. On June 12, the assembly rejected his motion. Then, Marx declares, "the proletariat . . . drove the *Montagne* onto the streets, not to a street battle . . . but only to a street procession. It is enough to say that the *Montagne* was at the head of this movement to know that the movement was defeated, and that June 1849 was a caricature, as ridiculous as it was repulsive, of June 1848." In the subsequent article, Marx declared that thirty thousand demonstrators were present. Price puts the number at between six thousand and eight thousand. Marx concluded the second article with the statement that "the party of Order had won, it was all-powerful." The statement overlooks the presence of an important power-holder, Louis Napoleon, the president of the republic.[61]

June 1849 to March 1850

The third of Marx's articles begins with a half-dozen pages on the *Montagne* fiasco. Various acts of repression are reviewed, including military actions, dissolution of unreliable National Guard units, and limitations on press freedom and the right of association. The indications of changed public sentiment are reviewed, such as many notables distancing themselves from the revolution and the republic. A couple of paragraphs review the efforts of Barrot's ministry in the National Assembly. Several pages are given to the maneuvering of Legitimists and Orleanists, each aiming for their restoration.

The third period in the life of the constitutional republic, Marx declared, dates from November 1, 1849, when Louis Napoleon dismissed Barrot and named a new government. The "ministry of the royalist coalition" was now out of power, and Napoleon thus became an independent agent. The new d'Hautpoul ministry, Marx announced, "was the ministry of Bonaparte, the organ of the President as against the Legislative Assembly." The Party of Order, the party of the coalesced bourgeoisie, it will be noted, was declared all-powerful in June; in November, it proved powerless.

A three-way struggle for dominance, between Legitimists, Orleanists, and Bonapartists, had been under way within that party's ranks. Marx again puts forth his formula: the republic is the form in which the special claims of the factions "remain neutralised and reserved," hence the ideal form for the bourgeoisie. The factions, however, were striving for "usurpation and revolt." In this thin reed of analysis, Marx bypasses all of the key problems: Why did the bourgeois factions not recognize this ideal arrangement as the one best serving their interests? Why did they continue to scramble for dominance, thus threatening the arrangement? Given the existence of that scramble, of what value is his declaration of this abstract ideal?[62]

Louis Napoleon's Government

Neglecting those analytical problems, Marx proceeds with his exposition. Louis Napoleon named Achille Fould, a "stock-exchange wolf," as his finance minister. It was a move, Marx claims, that Louis Philippe would never have dared. The "bourgeois republic" had thus "pushed into the forefront what the different monarchies, Legitimist as well as Orleanist, kept concealed in the background." In what seems a clear contradiction, Marx now declares that the republic, "from the first day of its existence, did not overthrow but consolidated the finance aristocracy. . . . With Fould, the initiative in the government returned to the finance aristocracy."

Marx asks how the remaining bourgeois factions could "bear and suffer the rule of finance" which had excluded and subordinated them in Louis Philippe's reign. The answer, he declares, "is simple." The leading figures in the new republic, he reports, are the Orleanists, the "leading lights . . . old confederates and accomplices of the finance aristocracy . . . the golden phalanx of Orleanism." As for the Legitimists, they too "had participated in practice already under Louis Philippe in all the orgies of the Bourse, mine and railway speculations. In general, the combination of large landed property with high finance is a *normal fact*. Proof: *England*; proof: even *Austria*."[63]

This conclusion is remarkable in three respects.

First, it entirely ignores the initial argument of the *Class Struggles*, the claim of a confrontation between two bourgeois segments, financial and industrial, a struggle from which the latter emerged victorious.

Second, and more importantly, it introduces a new line of analysis, one with major implications for the entire Marxian framework. Where that framework is based on the notion of a dialectical opposition of old and new ruling classes, here we find, for the second time, a new possibility or, more precisely, the declaration of a new reality—a merger, a coalescence of those classes. It is even said to be the normal condition. From the perspective of readily available evidence, it seems an entirely plausible option. But if it is entirely normal, why is the opposite claim, that of epochal struggles, even asserted? Why, in the more frequent formulations, is the normal condition said to be one of dialectical confrontation, of life-and-death struggle between those classes? The problem is not addressed here. It is, obviously, not even indicated as a problem.

To this point, the "industrial bourgeoisie proper" has not yet appeared in this new analysis. Recognizing the problem, Marx provides several paragraphs of explanation. "In a country like France," he argues, with its enormous national debt, government bonds form "the most important object of speculation." People "from all bourgeois or semi-bourgeois classes," accordingly, "must have an interest in the state debt." And, for Marx, it follows that these "interested subalterns" find their "natural mainstay and commanders" in the finance aristocracy. To guard their interests (and those of the subalterns), this faction needs to control, if not the state, at least the Ministry of Finance. The finance aristocracy in power may then profit from the trade in state indebtedness and, a necessary corollary, shift the mounting tax burden to others.

It was only one faction of the Party of Order—the manufacturers—who sought the overthrow of the finance aristocracy. They wished to reduce the costs of production, one of these being the heavy taxes required to pay the interest on the state debt. But, unlike England, where industry dominates, in France, agriculture is the predominant economic activity. And that means "French industrialists . . . do not dominate the French bourgeoisie." Unlike the equivalent English, they cannot "take the lead of the movement and simultaneously push their class interests to the fore." Their initial effort is explained as follows: "In February they had misunderstood their position; February sharpened their wits. And who is more directly threatened by the workers than the employer, the industrial capitalist? The manufacturer, therefore, of necessity became in France the most fanatical member of the party of Order. The reduction of his *profit* by finance, *what is that compared with the abolition of profit by the proletariat?*"[64]

The February Revolution, in short, was a mistake. The industrial bourgeoisie misunderstood their own position and their own interests. One would have to assume an unusually obtuse bourgeoisie for this claim to be valid. How was it that they did not see the implications of, to borrow an Engels phrase, "playing with revolution"? It is possible, of course, that the "reigning princes of the manufacturing interests" were so thoroughly out of touch, so confused by some "false consciousness," that they unwittingly triggered the February events. It should be noted, however, that Marx never established his initial proposition, that the February Revolution, in some way, was the work of the industrial bourgeoisie.

Those manufacturers may have misunderstood; they may have misconceived their real interests. Marx also clearly misunderstood. In the opening pages of *The Class Struggles*, with evident approval, he portrayed the industrial bourgeoisie as seeking to oust the finance aristocracy, no indication being given there that the effort was in any way mistaken. Only later, some seventy pages into the text, did Marx make the discovery.[65]

A third problem appears in Marx's discussion of the new ministry. It was, Marx said, "the ministry of Bonaparte." It was the president *against* the Party of Order and the assembly. But, only a few paragraphs after this unambiguous declaration of presidential independence (or autonomy), "the bourgeoisie," the again-dominant financial segment, is declared to be in power, this time in the cabinet. That conclusion remains to the end of the monograph. For Marx, the bourgeoisie, whether in whole or in part, is never far from the centers of power. And no upstart, no usurper such as Louis Napoleon, is allowed to be an independent or autonomous actor. The possibility of autonomy, of Bonapartism, was thereby postponed. It became the central theme of Marx's second major historical monograph, *The Eighteenth Brumaire*.

The Emerging Opposition

Marx proceeds to a discussion of Fould, the Finance Ministry, taxes (specifically to the retention of the wine tax), and the circumstances of the peasantry. The latter is considered at some length, yielding a conclusion that the exploitation of the peasantry differs only in form from the exploitation of the industrial proletariat. It is also concluded that "only the fall of capital can raise the peasant; only an anti-capitalist, a proletarian government can break his economic misery, his social degradation." Everything depends on "the votes that the peasant casts into the ballot box. He himself has to decide his fate." The Party of Order did what it could to deflect recognition of this simple fact. But a review of by-elections, Marx indicates, showed a "gradual revolutionising of the peasants."[66]

Two processes were occurring simultaneously in early 1850: strains were showing with increasing frequency within the Party of Order, and there was a manifest increase in the strength in the opposition party. The latter development is described as follows:

Little by little we have seen peasants, petty bourgeois, the middle classes in general, stepping alongside the proletariat, driven into open antagonism to the official republic and treated by it as antagonists. *Revolt against bourgeois dictatorship, need of a change of society, adherence to democratic-republican institutions as organs of their movement, grouping round the proletariat as the decisive revolutionary power*—these are the common characteristics of the *so-called party of social-democracy, the party of the Red republic*. This *party of Anarchy*, as its opponents christened it, is no less a coalition of different interests than *the party of Order*. From the smallest reform of the old social disorder to the overthrow of the old social order, from bourgeois liberalism to revolutionary terrorism—as far apart as this lie the extremes that form the starting point and the finishing point of the party of 'Anarchy'.[67]

An obvious conclusion—imminent revolution—is suggested here. Marx provides some further review of issues and arguments and again offers a conclusion emphasizing tendencies leading to a polar confrontation: "Just as in the party of *Order* the *finance aristocracy* necessarily took the lead, so in the party of '*Anarchy*' the *proletariat*. . . . [The] different classes, united in a revolutionary league, grouped themselves round the proletariat." It is a remarkable fancy—the overwhelming majority of the society, one with rather diverse interests and concerns, accepts the leadership of a class that, at the moment, was minuscule in size, badly defeated, and showed no signs of taking any leadership role.[68]

This article, as indicated, treats developments in the third period of the revolution, an episode beginning in June 1849 and ending on March 10, 1850. The latter was the date of the most recent by-elections, a day which, according to Marx, brought *"the revocation of June 1848 . . .* [and] *the revocation of June 13, 1849."* Conservative candidates were rejected, and three representatives of the opposition coalition were the victors. According to Marx, "March 10 was a revolution." It represented a new phase for the constitutional republic, *"the phase of its dissolution."* Marx dilates on the theme at some length: "The moral influence of capital is broken; this means that the bourgeois assembly now represents only the bourgeoisie; this means that big property is lost, because its vassal, small property, seeks its salvation in the camp of the propertyless." It is a weighty conclusion resting on a modest base of evidence—the results of three by-elections.[69]

The threat facing the Party of Order forced the quarreling factions of the bourgeoisie to unite again "among themselves and with Bonaparte." Louis Napoleon, Marx declared, was again "their *neutral man.*" The article ends with the prediction that the bourgeoisie must now repress the looming insurgency; specifically, it must abolish universal suffrage. The bourgeois coalition was now obliged to "retreat from the *constitutional republic*—the only possible form of their *united* power, and the most powerful and most complete form of their *class rule*—to the subordinate, incomplete and weaker form of the *monarchy.*" Whether republic or monarchy, however, for the bourgeoisie, the situation was hopeless. Marx's closing comment in this third article is that March 10, 1850, "bears the inscription: Après moi le déluge!"[70]

After the Deluge

The final article, as indicated earlier, is a joint Marx-Engels product, drawn from their review of European events to the autumn of 1850. One topic covered was the effort to abolish universal suffrage; hence, it complements and follows up the argument of the third article, which, as just shown, ended with a prediction of imminent revolution. In an introductory paragraph written for the 1895 edition, Engels provided an unexpected transition. In this review, he announced, "it was shown how the prosperity of trade and industry that again set in during the course of 1848 and increased still further in 1849 paralysed the revolutionary upsurge."[71] The famous quotation attributed to Louis XV, it should be noted, appears on the immediately preceding page of the monograph.

In the first paragraph of their joint text Marx and Engels review at length this previously overlooked return of prosperity. "The Parisian industries are abundantly employed. . . . The cotton factories of Rouen and Mulhouse are also doing pretty well." There is discussion of the "development of prosperity in France," of the increased export of French commodities, and of the "growth of capital." The desperate condition of the petty bourgeoisie and workers has changed, since now "a swarm of companies has sprung up, the low denomination of whose shares and whose socialist-coloured prospectuses [*sic*] appeal directly to the purses of the petty bourgeois and the workers." But this, one is assured, is all "sheer swindling" such as "is characteristic of the French and Chinese alone."[72]

The peasantry are excepted from this portrait of well-being; some 25 million of them "suffer from a great depression." They continue "in debt, sucked dry by usury and crushed by taxes." But, in marked contrast to the preceding accounts, which had them as participants in the developing insurgency, here it is declared that "the history of the last three years has . . . provided sufficient proof that this class of the population is absolutely incapable of any revolutionary initiative."[73]

A paragraph follows, stating the general Marx-Engels position with respect to the conditions under which revolutions appear. Because of the importance of this idea, quotation is useful: "With this general prosperity, in which the productive forces of bourgeois society develop as luxuriantly as is at all possible within bourgeois relationships, there can be no talk of a real revolution. Such a revolution is only possible in the periods when *both these factors*, the *modern* productive *forces* and the *bourgeois forms of production*, come *in collision* with each other. . . . *A new revolution is possible only in consequence of a new crisis. It is, however, just as certain as this crisis.*"[74] This linkage of crises and revolution is one of the clearest, least ambiguous predictions in the entire Marx-Engels repertory. It is, simultaneously, one of the least adequately supported of all their claims. The 1848 events, it will be noted, are only tenuously linked to the collision they describe, the economic collapse across Europe being in great measure due to a natural catastrophe, the crop failures. Economic crises came and went with regularity over the remainder of the nineteenth and much of the twentieth century. Possibly the most serious of these in Marx and Engels's lifetimes was the depression of the 1870s. There was much suffering, to be sure, but no revolution resulted. The world wide depression of the 1930s, possibly the most serious economic crisis of the entire modern era, did not trigger the kind of revolution they anticipated.[75]

Having tabled the revolutionary question for the moment, Marx and Engels proceed to a review of political events in France. The third article ended with three-plus pages of exuberant comment on the significance of the March 10 by-elections. That "victory of the people," it was now reported, in a remarkable about-face, was "annulled" in the later by-elections of April 28. The exuberance is replaced with the tepid comment that "the victory of March 10 ceased to be a decisive one." The confident prediction, in short, had a validity of only seven weeks. Marx and Engels pass over this difficulty quickly, providing no indication that they had erred in their previous analysis. Instead, in mid-paragraph, they turn to ridicule of the candidates and parties. The novelist Eugène Sue, for example, was one of the candidates; he is described as a "sentimental petty-bourgeois social-fantasist, which the proletariat could at best accept as a joke to amuse the grisettes."[76]

Four paragraphs are given to the passage of a new election law which "abolished universal suffrage." Marx and Engels do not indicate specifically what was involved. The law changed the residency requirement in the commune from six months to three years, a move that disfranchised about 3 million of the 10 million electors. Most of those disfranchised would have been workers, especially the migratory laborers. A new press law provided another range of restrictions.

All these developments led to the same result: forestalling a new revolution by the proletariat. Those events are listed in a summary paragraph: a large army in Paris, an "appeasing attitude" in the now-tame press, the "pusillanimity of the *Montagne* and of the newly-elected representatives," the "majestic calm" of the petty bourgeois, and, "above all, the commercial and industrial prosperity."[77]

For the Party of Order, one problem remained. Their coalition of forces included—presumably—the president of the republic, Louis Napoleon. But that fact posed a serious problem: the constitution restricted him to a single term, and therefore he had to retire in May 1852. The bourgeoisie, Marx and Engels report, saw "the only possible solution" in the "prolongation of the power of the President," that is, in the extension of his term. After some further discussion, they conclude that the National Assembly, which was to reconvene on November 11, 1850, would have to address the question at that time. The Party of Order, they declared, will "be compelled to prolong the power of the President [and] . . . Bonaparte . . . will, despite all preliminary protestations, accept this prolongation of power from the hands of the National Assembly as simply delegated to him." But events did not unfold as they predicted. The assembly did not begin discussion of the constitutional revision until late May 1851. And then, in mid-July, the proposal was rejected. On December 2, 1851, Louis Napoleon conducted the coup d'état that ended the Second Republic. It is, of course, still another instance of failed prediction. Those events would be the subject matter for Marx's second historical monograph, *The Eighteenth Brumaire of Louis Bonaparte.*[78]

Conclusions

First, Marx's much-acclaimed work, *The Class Struggles in France*, is a remarkably inadequate accomplishment. A spectacular lack of consistency appears with respect to some major elements of the basic framework; this inconsistency is most striking in the treatment of the bourgeoisie.

The revolution, presumably, was somehow precipitated by an industrial bourgeoisie, a group that had been thwarted by the machinations of its class peers, the finance aristocracy. Marx's carelessness, we have seen, begins on the very first page, where one finds owners of coal and iron mines and some landed proprietors classified as part of the finance aristocracy. But then, within a few pages, that distinction drops from sight to reappear only peripherally in subsequent discussion. Later in the text, the competing royal houses, the Legitimists and the Orleanists, are said to be the decisive ruling factions; these, it seems, are merely the disguised segments of the bourgeoisie. The competing segments then merge to form the Party of Order, which is successful in capturing the National Assembly. Louis Napoleon is elected president of the republic, and Marx declares him to be the neutral spokesman for the united bourgeoisie. The Bonapartists, as a party, are said to be insignificant, counting for nothing. The united bourgeois coalition, which dominates both the legislative and executive branches, is clearly in control.

Marx then offers his republic-as-ideal claim: for the competing royal houses (and bourgeois segments), the republican form allows collective advantage. Although put in a clear indicative form, the optative form would have been more appropriate—the bourgeoisie *should* recognize the advantage—since the next episode in his narration recounts a tripartite struggle for dominance between Legitimist, Orleanist, and now, suddenly sprung to life, Bonapartist factions. In a brief interlude, the industrial-versus-finance dichotomy again appears. Given the way things are in France, it follows "of necessity" that things must be run by the finance aristocracy. It is logical that, under Louis Napoleon, they are once again in leading positions. The initial event in the history, the revolution instigated by the industrial bourgeoisie, one learns, was a mistake. Alarmed over the results of a handful of by-elections, revolution appearing to be imminent, the bourgeois factions cease their squabbling and again coalesce. But then, as revealed in the next article, subsequent by-election results showed there was no real cause for alarm. But by then, the government had in many ways alienated most segments of the population and, given "universal suffrage," now faced the imminent loss of power. The analysis ends with the "obvious" claim—that the coalesced bourgeoisie would be forced to extend Louis Napoleon's term of office.

A different analytical problem arises with respect to Marx's depiction of the petty bourgeoisie; no plausible explanation is provided for their behavior. At the outset, they—the small shopkeepers and producers of Paris—are being crushed by the competition of the big bourgeoisie. Nevertheless, in the June Days, they align with the big bourgeoisie against the proletariat. Then, with the defeat of the workers, they find themselves helpless vis-à-vis the bourgeoisie and now turn toward and follow the lead of the workers. The farm proprietors too, the majority of the population, are in desperate circumstances. They too, one is told, are being radicalized and turn more and more to the proletariat. Neither the urban nor the rural segments of the petty bourgeoisie, however, undertake any serious political initiatives of their own. They vote for parties and candidates and are instantly betrayed, basically with respect to the tax burden, and yet, showing remarkable gullibility, they continue to ally with their oppressors.

The *Manifesto*, it will be remembered, put forth two basic claims with regard to the petty bourgeoisie. The principal option was that this class would be reactionary; it would "fight against the bourgeoisie" to save its position. The second possibility was that some of its members, by chance, would adopt the standpoint of the proletariat. In *The Class Struggles*, Marx has all but abandoned the principal option. Instead, he has given considerable emphasis to the second position, arguing that after the June Days it was the general response. A third option, vacillation, has a prominent place in this monograph. Marx provides no explanation for the bizarre choices made by this class. In lieu of analysis, he offers only vituperation and denunciation.

The proletariat, at all times, is reported to be revolutionary; it is either actively engaged in revolutionary struggle or, between episodes, waiting for the next opportunity. The formulations are comprehensive and all-embracing; when discussing the proletariat, Marx generally avoided the use of partitive expressions. While in the early months of the history their consciousness possibly was not "fully developed," by June of 1848 the workers, unlike the befuddled and confused petty bourgeoisie, were moved by logic and understanding.

A second conclusion involves a comparison with the claims appearing in the basic programmatic statement, *The Communist Manifesto*. Two principal shifts occur in Marx's 1850 analysis of France, as compared with the framework put forth two years earlier. The portrait contained in the earlier work was one of advanced or fully developed capitalism. The social transformations were there, already achieved, and continuing at a rapid rate. That accomplishment was a "present fact" in Britain and France, it will be remembered, with the Communists then turning to Germany, a latecomer that was rapidly catching up. In actuality, however, that claim of advanced capitalist development could not be sustained for France at mid-century. Marx was, therefore, forced back to the more realistic portrait of France as a nation still at an early stage in its economic development. That, of course, meant the French bourgeoisie and proletariat were also in the early stages of their development. It meant that both would be small, even minuscule classes, not the dominant actors in that final, titanic struggle.

Where the *Manifesto* has the final struggle as a polar confrontation of two classes, each acting in its own interest, that imagery is not possible for the French case, certainly not in 1848. Hence the need for the second principal shift in his analysis, a shift to a focus on coalitions. The leading actors, because of their small size and importance, must move in conjunction with other classes or segments of classes. Much of Marx's account here focuses on the (presumed) fact of alliances, describing their formation, dissolution, and re-constitution. The shift is certainly legitimate and, under the circumstances, entirely appropriate.

This pluralist development, however, opens up some rather indeterminate possibilities. To save his basic theory, Marx places his favored actors at the head of each coalition. The bourgeoisie (in various combinations) heads the forces of order. The proletariat, after the June Days, is placed at the center of the insurgent coalition; the urban and rural petty bourgeois segments are said to approach and follow the workers. It is, of course, a most implausible argument, one which, in another context, might easily be termed a utopian fantasy. The obvious hypothesis at this point in France's economic development would be that the peasantry, which, as Marx noted, constituted two-thirds of the nation, formed the opposite pole in any direct confrontation. That majority class would be the central actor in any forthcoming struggle. The argument of coalition, with workers stipulated as leaders, is the only way Marx can make the struggle one of bourgeoisie and proletariat.[79]

A third major conclusion involves problems of evidence. The evidence required for support of his arguments is either remarkably inadequate or missing entirely. This problem appears at virtually all points in Marx's account. He makes claims, for example, about the major classes present in France. He reports the state of consciousness within each class (and within all major segments thereof). He knows, somehow, that each segment has a distinctive position. Other possibilities are excluded a priori; these include shared reactions, wide dispersion of responses, options based on other lines of cleavage (e.g., religion, generation or cohort experience, or regime loyalties), and, most obvious of all, indeterminacy—not knowing what to think or do. Overlooking all rudimentary epistemological problems, Marx provides definitive reports on the actions of all the segments he has delineated. Such conclusions are difficult under any circumstances, let alone during the rapid movement of revolutionary events and in the flux of subsequent reconstitution. But, with no evident qualm, Marx declares what "they," the various classes and segments, thought and did. The problem is perhaps best illustrated by his comment on one relatively small group, the nine hundred members of the newly elected Constituent Assembly. Many observers, including several members of the assembly, grappled with this problem, trying to decipher the character of that body, many of whose members had surfaced for the first time. It stood to reason that many of them were at best only republicans of convenience, persons hiding their basic loyalties and adapting to the times. Many people, he admits, suspected a strong royalist presence. But Marx—somehow—knew that body to be "the exclusive representative of bourgeois republicanism."

The Class Struggles, in short, shows serious empirical problems at almost all points. This is evident in matters that Marx should have known or could have easily researched, such as that of Laffitte's role in the 1830 revolution and in the subsequent government. Many simple factual questions, especially those involving individuals, could have been checked and verified through his own investigation. But in matters involving classes, their consciousness and actions, any comment would, at best, be tentative or hypothetical. Marx deals with this problem by focusing on individuals, coteries, and the putative classes. He then makes allegations about the links between them; a given individual or coterie is said to stand for or represent the class whose involvement is not immediately evident.

The striking fact about Marx's use of this method is his failure to document, or in any other way, establish the alleged links. Odilon Barrot, for example, described as "the incarnation of liberalism," is presumably, somehow or other, a representative of or spokesman for the bourgeoisie. As noted, Marx sees some unusual significance in Barrot's being chosen, finally, by Louis Philippe and then by Louis Napoleon. But those facts are hardly compelling evidence of the alleged links. There are, moreover, implausibilities in the logic of the case. Louis Napoleon chose this supposed representative of the industrial bourgeoisie at a point where that segment was said to be losing out to the finance aristocracy. Why did Napoleon choose a man tied to the "wrong" faction? And, a more serious problem, Marx has told his readers that Barrot is a windbag; he is a *nullité grave*. Why should any segment of the (presumably) conscious and aware bourgeoisie choose or recommend a shallow nullity for this ultimately important task, managing the affairs of their government? There was, as was noted, another easy possibility, limited options and a personal choice. Having no party of his own, without a ready and competent following, Louis Napoleon chose the one person he knew who, with any semblance of plausibility, could undertake the task.

Marx showed a remarkable indifference to questions of number, of quantity. When one fills in the blanks, when those numbers are present in consciousness, many of his theoretical claims become instantly implausible. Some basics:

The 1851 census of France gives the population of the nation as 35,783,000. The population of Paris is given as 1,053,000 persons. Figuring generously, Paris contained 3 percent of the French population. The next largest cities were (figures in 1,000s) Marseilles, 195; Lyons, 177; Bordeaux, 131; Rouen, 101; Nantes, 96; Toulouse, 93; and, both with 76, Lille and Strasbourg. Taken together with Paris this "large city" population still does not form even one-tenth of the population. Industrial Lille is at best only a large town at this point. Other industrial cities of later decades, Roubaix, Mulhouse, and St. Etienne, for example, do not even appear in this list of large cities. Taking a much lower cutting point, populations living in communities of 2,000 or more, only one in four were located in urban places. Roughly four-fifths of that urban population, moreover, was living in larger villages, in market towns, and in provincial capitals rather than in Paris or the other large cities.

Those figures are, of course, cross-sectional, freezing the movement at one point in time. But Marxism is a theory about movement, specifically, in the modern era, about rapid change. But here too the numbers show a different pattern, one of slow change. In the first half of the nineteenth century the percentage of the population living in communities of 10,000 or more went from 9.5 percent to 14.4 percent. The rate of change, in short, amounted to an increase of one percentage point per decade. The major lesson of this review is that the overwhelming majority of the French population was rural. At that rate, even well into the twentieth century, the majority of the French population would still be living in towns, villages, and rural areas. That reality stands in stark contrast to Marx and Engels's exuberant declarations in the *Manifesto*: "The bourgeoisie . . . has created enormous cities, has greatly increased the urban population as compared with the rural. . . . It has agglomerated population."[80]

What can one say about the Parisian working class? The 1847 industrial census by the Paris Chamber of Commerce gives the number of workers as 343,000, roughly a third of those enumerated. But that census counted only those in industrial occupations, thus omitting service workers, domestics, and transport workers. It also omitted the unemployed. Daumard has provided estimates based on that source and on general census results, those of 1831, 1841, and 1846. She has more than half, 56 percent, classified as *milieux populaires*. That segment would form 62 percent of the civilian labor force. Roughly three-fifths of the Parisian population, then, might be counted as workers (or as members of working-class families).

Is that Paris majority, then, the industrial proletariat, the central actor in the unfolding drama? If by that term one means wage workers in large (and growing) manufacturing enterprises, the answer to the question, on the whole, must be negative. Amann reports that the average "industrialist" in Paris "employed no more than six or seven workers." Price summarizes one 1847 study as follows: "Only 318 workshops [of 64,816] in the department of the Seine used mechanical power or employed more than twenty workers. Only about 30,000 workers [of the 343,000] were employed in these [larger shops], with countless more employed in smaller and more technically primitive workshops. . . . The scale of production was small and its form is best described as artisanal."[81]

One characteristic of all European cities of the period deserves more than passing attention. They all had extremely high population densities, probably the highest in all of modern European experience. The problem was particularly acute in working-class districts. And that meant it was virtually impossible to locate large manufacturing establishments there. The new manufacturing establishments had to be located elsewhere, outside the city walls, in the suburbs, or in smaller cities. The industries of the large cities, accordingly, in Paris and elsewhere, were typically small-scale, handicraft enterprises. In the *Manifesto* one is told: "Modern industry has converted the little workshop of the patriarchal master into the great factory of the industrial capitalist. Masses of labourers, crowded into the factory, are organized like soldiers." Marx does not amend that portrait in *The Class Struggles*. He does not tell his readers that the average "industrialist" in Paris "employed no more than six or seven workers." Large manufacturing establishments were present in France in 1848, but they were located elsewhere. Price, drawing on 1847 figures, reports that twenty-one departments of northeast France, the area of greatest industrialization, had an average of fifty-five persons per establishment. The concentration was greatest, he reports, in towns of the north and east, Lille and Mulhouse, rather than in Lyons, France's third largest city. Lyons, the center of silk manufacture, like Paris, showed the combination of small shops and working-class insurgency. The centers of modern industry, on the whole, were not centers of insurgency in 1848; they were remarkably quiescent. Marx and

Engels regularly predicted a close association between modern industry and revolution. In France of 1848, the relationship was directly opposite to the one they predicted.[82]

Marx had to submerge both number and quality in order to achieve this necessary transmogrification, to make the workers into a large and important class, one about to take the lead in historical events. The same kind of transformation was necessary with respect to the bourgeoisie. The *Manifesto* unambiguously focuses on Modern Industry. The opening section spells out the central features of the capitalist era: "Steam and machinery revolutionised industrial production. The place of manufacture was taken by the giant, Modern Industry, the place of the industrial middle class, by industrial millionaires, the leaders of whole industrial armies, the modern bourgeois."[83] Given the bold announcement of the basic position, it is rather surprising, to say the least, that in *The Class Struggles* large landowners come to have such a central place within that class. Again a transformation was required; the number of industrialists was small, so much so as to make implausible any claim about their importance. To save the argument, large landholders—nobles and commoners alike—had to be added to the category in order to make the bourgeoisie the dominant class.

It is *The Class Struggles* that presents the accurate portrait, not the *Manifesto*. The two largest fortunes in France, far ahead of all other contenders in 1848, were those of Louis Philippe (a major landholder) and James Rothschild (the leading banker). André-Jean Tudesq's comprehensive study of France's *notables* makes it eminently clear just how central landowning was in the nation's economic affairs. The bourgeoisie, in Marx's original meaning, as the leaders of Modern Industry, was a minuscule class, both in terms of size and influence in 1848. Roger Price summarizes one aspect to Tudesq's research as follows: "Of the 512 richest men in France . . . 377 were exclusively landed proprietors, only 45 were bankers or merchants and 26 industrialists." Of the 512, he adds, "238 were aristocrats and 78 had pretensions to nobility. A large proportion of them, Price suggests, were likely to be Legitimists. The bourgeoisie was also, as Marx eventually indicated in *The Class Struggles*, a subordinate class operating within a framework set by others, by political and financial leaders. But Marx and Engels still wished to have the bourgeoisie at the center of things, and this could only be achieved by quiet redefinition of the term—by extension of the boundaries so as to include landed proprietors.[84]

The economic reality of France in 1848 entirely contradicts the claims of the *Manifesto*. That account argues a struggle of modern forces, of a developed class of industrial workers and a dominant industrial bourgeoisie. But the reality was one of persistent artisanal production and a nowhere-near-dominant industrial bourgeoisie. Marx modernizes this backward reality by obscuring the character of the working class and by merging landowners with the mini-segment, the modern industrialists. The dynamics, both of economic development and of the class struggle, are changed as a result. This is especially the case with Marx's belated recognition of the mistake made by the insurgent industrialists. That leaves France's entire development problematical, or, borrowing a term from a later strand of the theory, France, like the United States and Germany, is "exceptional." As the analysis trails off, the industrial bourgeoisie remains in the same situation described in the opening pages—fettered by the machinations of the resurgent finance aristocracy.[85]

Another problem present in Marx's analysis of France's class structure is that of an absent (or hidden) class. The nation is portrayed as one without a class of government officials. The problem is especially acute in this account with its focus on the nation's capital: Paris is a city without civil servants. The latter are not easily fitted into any of Marx's categories: they are not bourgeois, petty bourgeois, or workers (in his use of that term). This class is simply bypassed. But they were present, of course, observing events and in one way or another participating in the history he describes. The omission, of course, means an incomplete analysis. It also means that the discussion of "the bureaucracy," an important segment of the "new middle class," was not faced at that time but, rather, was postponed for some other occasion.[86]

A fourth major problem with Marx's analysis involves an important omission. The events of the February Revolution, it was noted, are passed over with no comment or analysis. What actually happened in those three days of February? What precipitated those events? And what factors determined the outcome? Put differently, what were the dynamics of those events that, according to Marx, were so well known as to not require his (or the reader's) attention? Those events, as was seen, provide a range of data that allow further testing of the Marx-Engels framework. By avoiding the topic, Marx avoided that test.

Those three days were filled with contingent events. A provocative banquet was planned; at the last moment, the event was called off. Many people did not get the word and thus arrived for the festivities. Some needlessly harsh reactions by the Municipal Guard changed the public mood. A confrontation between army and demonstrators in the Rue des Capucines brought the deaths and generated the resentments that carried the struggle to its conclusion. The National Guard, a bourgeois citizens' militia, had been neglected for some years and now, when needed, proved unreliable, not fighting at all or protecting the insurgents or joining them. Muddled decisions were made all along the chain of command. One of those decisions determined the outcome: the decision to withdraw the troops. Those contingencies are not easily reconciled with Marx's broad portrait of a determinate history.

Some consideration of the movers in the February events is in order. The visible movers, the protagonists, those who set the events in motion, were politicians, the leaders of the dynastic opposition, and intellectuals (journalists), the leaders of the opposition press. The first group, through the banquet campaign, sought a modest increase in the size of the electorate in order to gain power hitherto denied them. Whether a segment of the bourgeoisie stood behind the scenes, directing the operations of Barrot and the others, as Marx alleges, is at best an unsupported hypothesis. Pending the appearance of that confirming evidence, the best conclusion is that the event generating the revolution was the work of political and intellectual leaders (factions thereof), not of a bourgeois faction. The conclusion, in short, is that what *appears* to be the case, political and intellectual leadership, *was in fact the case*. That standard element in the Marxian dramaturgy, the notion of a hidden reality behind the given appearance, depends on the presentation of evidence establishing the unseen linkage. Until the appearance of that evidence, the February Revolution, judged in terms of its leadership, is best described as the product of two loosely aligned groups. It was, first, the unintended result of the banquet campaign, the effort undertaken by the political opposition, by Odilon Barrot and company. And, aiding, abetting, and benefiting from that campaign, it was, in part at least, a "revolution of intellectuals."[87]

With events set in motion, it was easy for other actors to join in and to make their contribution. While the banquet campaign had relatively high-status leadership and support, a new, largely working-class constituency was soon present and involved in a series of street actions, barricade construction, and open conflict. Their agenda, not too surprisingly, was very different from that of the political and intellectual protagonists; they wished to see full (male) suffrage and a social republic. With the release of political prisoners and the sudden formation of clubs (with related newspapers), new and highly vocal agencies were present on the scene, reinforcing those leftist demands and generally, so they said, speaking for the workers. Clubs and newspapers cost money. The new government made meeting rooms available and provided some subsidies, but these were withdrawn as tensions rose. Given the deterioration of the economic condition and, already in May, with declines in club membership and attendance, it is likely that the constituency became more predominantly middle class. It would have been a leftist segment of the class, one which probably was not as well-off as the segment supporting the banquet campaign.

While Marx offers his behind-the-scenes direction hypothesis, suggesting calculation, planning, and control by the bourgeoisie, other possibilities easily come to mind. There might easily be other actors operating in their own right, *für sich*, independently of other's plans, control, or influence. Against the direction and control hypothesis, in short, there is an independence or autonomy hypothesis. Individuals and groups, in other words, are capable of charting and following their own courses.

There are obvious difficulties also with the assumptions of planning and control. One easy possibility is the mistaken plan, as with the (supposed) stimulation of the revolution by the industrial bourgeoisie. There is, moreover, the possibility of failure in the execution of plans, as with the instigation of the banquet campaign by Barrot and others, with the effort to call off the Paris banquet, and with the efforts of the authorities to control the public disturbances. The clubs planned many things but achieved little of what was intended. Their most important achievements were not intended—undermining their initial strength and undercutting the legitimacy of the new regime.

Marx senses a logic and clear lines of control existing somewhere behind the scenes. An alternative, a "dissociative hypothesis," seems more likely, at least a priori. This assumes more actors or agencies than Marx allows and a wider range of outcomes, including failures and the unexpected. There is no reason for such discussion to remain on a purely speculative level. If there had been plan, logic, direction, and control, it should be possible to provide some documentation.[88]

The situation of another key mover has also been left offstage in Marx's account. On the morning of February 24, the third day of the uprising, Louis Philippe's situation turned from poor to desperate. The offstage fact in this case was the availability of a substantial and intact army which was, of course, directly under his command. Some advisers pressed him to make use of those forces. Instead, the troops then facing the barricades were withdrawn. Another option considered was a tactical retreat to St. Cloud and a return the next day with sixty thousand troops. That option too was refused. The withdrawal determined the immediate outcome; the regime came to an end within the hour. It was clear that Louis Philippe would have to make a hasty retreat. Unlike the retreat of his predecessor, this flight was likely to be a dangerous venture, a life or death undertaking. For him too, either the richest or second richest man in France, it would probably mean the loss of his fortune. It would mean, at least so it seemed at the time, losses for the entire Orleanist contingent. And yet, in contrast to the easy anticipation of a struggle to the death, the man simply gave up: he abandoned power. With the fact hidden, it is no surprise that explanations are virtually nonexistent.

There appear to be two lines of explanation: First, the king was completely demoralized; the events of the previous forty-eight hours had broken his will to continue. Second, Louis Philippe recognized that use of those troops would mean a vast shedding of blood, far beyond what had already occurred. And he did not wish to be the cause of that additional catastrophe. The lesson, in short, is an unexpected one; it is a lesson of human decency. A rich and powerful man gave up both riches and power in order to save thousands of lives. It is curious: why should one hide evidence of human decency?[89]

A fifth major problem appears in the treatment of the economic factor. Marx and Engels provide a general formula which describes the conditions under which revolution occurs. This revolution, they write, "is only possible in periods when . . . the *modern* productive *forces* and the *bourgeois forms of production*, come *in collision* with each other."[90] The collision referred to is an economic crisis stemming from the deficiencies of the capitalist economy. But in France, the modern productive forces were only just beginning to appear. The 1846–47 crisis of the French economy was due largely to a natural catastrophe, to crop failures, not to that fundamental collision of forces and forms. The efforts of Odilon Barrot and his fellow banqueters do not appear to have been linked to "the bourgeois forms of production." And finally, the working-class involvements in the revolutionary events proved to be linked to premodern productive forces. The events of the February Revolution, in short, do not support the general formula.

For Marx, as noted, economic crisis is *the* fundamental source of working-class insurgency. That crisis, in his analysis, stems from irremediable flaws of the capitalist economic system. The problem stems from the lack of plan or direction of such economies; a simple slogan, the anarchy of capitalist production, points to the basic difficulty. But in this case, in 1848, the crisis was said to have had two sources: the commercial collapse in Britain and the natural catastrophe—the failure of two major crops, grain and potatoes. Those events had different origins and different consequences. A commercial crisis is deflationary; a natural crisis is sharply inflationary with respect to food prices and deflationary for almost all others. Revolution might, conceivably, be seen as a way to improve the organization of production, to deal with commercial crises and anarchic production; it is not easily seen as a means for overcoming a natural catastrophe.[91]

The timing of those economic events, of the key causal factors, is only very sketchily indicated in Marx's text. He points to the crop failures of 1845 and 1846 and then refers to the "dearth of 1847." The last phrase is at best a half-truth, one hiding the good harvest that came later in the year. Marx does not mention, following that good harvest, that in February 1848 there were signs that the nation was emerging from the depression. Nor does he indicate that the revolution halted the recovery and, worse, caused a rapid deterioration. The revolution itself, in short, created the spring crisis that did so much to generate the June Days. It is a causal link that hardly requires documentation. That revolutions cause unemployment is not a hidden fact (or one that operates only behind the scenes). It is, however, a connection that has been hidden by many commentators writing on those events in the subsequent sevenscore years. It is unlikely that workers (and their families) would have missed the connection. Many of them, accordingly, would have opposed revolutionary initiatives as detrimental to their interests. For that reason, then, quite apart from the grounds reviewed earlier, it is not at all surprising that the majority of workers in Paris were not on the barricades in June.[92]

Another element of the economic history is missing from Marx's account of France in 1848 and 1849. It is certainly appropriate, for any history of the period, that considerable attention be given to the economic catastrophe present from March to June 1848. But it is, to say the least, rather mysterious that the crisis should disappear with Cavaignac's subjugation of the workers. A simple question: what happened then? Cavaignac had decreed an end to the workshops, thus ending the financial support for 120,000 members. What were the employment levels in July, August, and September? And the levels of desperation and misery? What of the business recovery? Marx's narrative (and those of many later commentators) proves to be curiously truncated. From January to June, one is provided with economic and social history. But after June, the account is almost exclusively political. The omission is strikingly obvious. His account of working-class misery in June of 1848 is followed by many pages discussing "other things." Then, suddenly, without any previous hint, in the final article, written in the fall of 1850, the reader is informed of the economic upswing. It must have had earlier origins.[93]

Some comment on the sources available to Marx is appropriate. The MECW editors report that Marx "used French newspaper reports, reports published in the *Neue Rheinische Zeitung*, and accounts given by witnesses—French and German revolutionary refugees, among them Ferdinand Wolff, the *Neue Rheinische Zeitung* Paris correspondent, and another Communist League member, Sebastian Seiler, who was a stenographer to the French National Assembly in 1848 and 1849 and wrote a pamphlet on the events of June 13, 1849, which he presented to Marx. Marx was also probably familiar with Ledru-Rollin's pamphlet on the same subject."[94] Ultimately a remarkable number of memoirs became available, since almost all key figures wrote about what they had done, seen, or heard. But most of them appeared later, after Marx had written this account in 1850. Paris had many newspapers already in February 1848; several have been mentioned in the text. Between February and June, moreover, some two hundred new ones appeared on the scene. One would not realize from Marx's text or from the editors' footnotes (either those of the MECW or MEW) that Marx's closest ties were with the democratic "petty bourgeois" journal *La Réforme*, his most likely 1848 source. The MECW's list of possibilities overlooks another option—direct observation of at least some of the events. Marx was in Paris from March 5 to April 6 of 1848, which means he was there at the time of the March 16 and 17 demonstrations. He was in Paris again from June 3 to August 24, 1849, at the time of Ledru-Rollin's June 13 demonstration. The Marx biographies cited earlier say nothing about his activities during those *journées*. Two scholarly commentators have suggested that he was present in the June 1849 demonstration.

The links to *La Réforme* antedate the events of February. Engels wrote articles for the newspaper in 1847. He used that paper as a prime source for his contributions to *The Northern Star*. In several of the latter, he extolled the virtues of *La Réforme* and praised its attacks on *Le National*. In late February, while still in Brussels, Marx received a letter from Ferdinand Flocon, an editor of *La Réforme*, a barricade fighter, and, at this point, a member of the provisional government, announcing the lifting of Guizot's expulsion order. Arriving in Paris on March 5, Marx, the very next day, wrote an open letter for the newspaper, reporting on his treatment by the Belgian authorities. On March 10, he wrote a second piece for them, this time on the treatment of foreign radicals by the Belgian police. Engels also wrote an article for *La Réforme* on the same topic.

Much of Marx's time in Paris was spent on Communist League activities and in working against the "adventurist" German Legion effort. Marx visited Flocon at the office of *La Réforme* on the fourteenth of March, several days before the first of the major *journées*. On the sixteenth, the day of the National Guard protest, Marx was busy with Communist League affairs, seeking to expel Bornstedt for his support of the German Legion. The leading chronology has no entries for the day of the demonstration, March 17. Most of the rest of his time in Paris was occupied with league affairs and, more importantly, with the plans for his return to Germany and for publication of the *Neue Rheinische Zeitung*. Marx had another meeting with Flocon, who offered money to support their paper, but this was declined.

As for Marx's 1849 stay in Paris, particularly for his whereabouts from June 11 to 13, the chronology provides no information. The accounts of Marx's activity during this visit appear to be very limited. He published a letter on July 30 in *La Presse* correcting its account of his recent movements. Seiler was with him much of this time. It is striking that no record is available to establish Marx's presence at Ledru-Rollin's futile demonstration. If Marx had been present at either the March 1848 or the June 1849 demonstrations, he would surely at some point in his later years have mentioned it. Engels's direct involvement in the last futile struggles of the German revolution have been recounted on many occasions. But, so it would appear, Marx passed up two opportunities for such participation, for a demonstration of "the unity of theory and practice."[95]

The Class Struggles in France, as we have seen, is basically a narrative with interspersed analysis. It is the analysis which goes beyond simple description ("mere journalism") and thus could have some more general significance. But as was also seen, most of that analysis is of dubious merit. The explanations appear to be ad hoc, spur of the moment exercises, basically extemporizations designed to account for the immediate problem posed in the narrative. Subsequent extemporizations give little or no recognition of what has come before; thus the work is filled with sharp breaks in logic. It is, in short, filled with inconsistencies. There are serious misrepresentations—beginning with his treatment of Laffitte on the first page. There are many obvious gaps, instances where the logic of the argument is not pursued. Persons alleged to be leading the events disappear with hardly a mention in subsequent pages. Actors presumed to be rational and knowledgeable, members of the bourgeoisie, embark on what, for them, would have to be considered foolhardy, dangerous ventures. Then later, as with the February Revolution itself, they recognize it as all a mistake. Those arguments, or rather allegations, come without benefit of any serious supporting evidence.

This chapter and these conclusions have focused on the factual and analytical elements of Marx's work. That overlooks a considerable part of the text which is not adequately described with the words "narrative," "fact," or "analysis." Much of his text is given to ridicule, mockery, or denigration. Entire paragraphs are devoted to drawing historical analogies, not for any analytic purpose, but rather for the purpose of an unflattering or, more appropriately, damning comparison. Much of the text, in short, is given over to personal attack, to ad hominem argument. It is certainly "mordant," as one commentator has described it. But a corrosive comment is not necessarily an accurate one.

What is one to make of those testimonials cited earlier? Three of them, those of McLellan, Tucker, and Stearns, use the word "brilliant" in connection with this work. John Merriman tells his readers that "Marx proved himself a generally astute contemporary observer" of the French scene. Jerrold Seigel, historian and Marx biographer, reports that Marx "followed the French events of 1848 with close attention." Referring to *The Class Struggles* and *The Eighteenth Brumaire*, Gordon Wright declares: "Although [they] fused propaganda with history, they contained such a remarkable combination of shrewd insight and plausibility that [Marx's] analysis continues to be widely accepted in our day. In muted form, it reappears in many non-Marxian works." Roger Price, as seen throughout this chapter, has provided a substantial data-based critique of many central claims in *The Class Struggles*. His judgment of it is unambiguously negative. What is one to make of Charles Tilly's conclusion? Roger Price, he declares, "offers many a cavil and not a few nuances, but ends up in basic agreement. The broad lines of Marx's analysis have survived more than a hundred years of historical criticism."[96]

Testimonials are one thing; investigation and assessment is something else. Declaring a work to be "brilliant," by itself, says nothing about the validity of its claims. Such testimonials vouch for the work without directly commenting on its validity. The unsuspecting reader might easily draw a mistaken conclusion—that *The Class Struggles in France* is a credible history.

Those attesting to the merit of the work are claiming that it offers some distinctive contribution to human knowledge. If that were so, the proof would be easy. All that is necessary is to provide a list of propositions, a series of statements, indicating those worthwhile contributions. Some guidelines may be noted. The use of class analysis is no unique contribution as Marx himself indicated.[97] His analysis of the classes in France at mid-century, as seen here, is a rather dubious achievement. Many of the other observations contained in the work, while clearly valid, are not unique or distinctive contributions. Many of them represent no distinctive contribution flowing out of a Marxist framework. Many commentators, for example, recognized that the provisional government, the executive commission, and Cavaignac's government, sought to undo many of the achievements gained in February. A recognition of the obvious hardly qualifies for the list of brilliant achievements.

The proof of the pudding, it is said, is to be found in the eating. A testimonial attesting to its merit—that Jeremiah Finchley, a leading expert in such matters, for example, found the pudding to be a brilliant achievement—is no substitute for the more direct approach. The proof of a meritorious intellectual achievement is to be found in a statement of (or a listing of) its distinctive virtues. None of the authors of the just-cited testimonials provides such a statement.[98]

4

ENGELS ON

GERMANY'S CLASSES

This chapter will compare four analyses by Engels of developments in Germany, along with the more familiar account of *The Communist Manifesto*. As will be seen, several positions appear in these less-known historical writings. Put differently, several divergent "Marxisms" are contained in the original work. To be considered are, first, an Engels essay written in 1847 (but not published until 1929), "The Status Quo in Germany"; second, Engels's *Germany: Revolution and Counter-Revolution*, a series of articles written in 1851 and 1852; third, Engels's preface to the second edition of his book *The Peasant War in Germany* (1870); and fourth, an addendum to that preface, written for the third edition of *The Peasant War* (1874).

The principal tasks here will be those of exposition and analysis. A comprehensive empirical assessment of the historical claims contained in these works would require an extensive review of monographic studies. For the most part, therefore, the questions raised will focus on the logic and plausibility of the analyses. One can indicate logical inconsistencies and one can also make rule-of-thumb estimates of the possibilities, that is, of the likely "realism" of the claims. One can, moreover, indicate those points where the bold assertion lacks support, where the claim is nothing more than an unsubstantiated hypothesis in need of empirical assessment. On several key points, however, on questions of special importance where historical evidence is readily available, direct assessment of claims will be made. This first engagement, as indicated, will focus on German history from roughly 1840 to 1875. A brief review of that history is clearly in order.[1]

Historical Background

Three decades of peace and relative stability in continental Europe followed the defeat of Napoleon in 1815. The terms of the peace, the international arrangements, were worked out at the Congress of Vienna. With the Karlsbad Decrees of 1819, Prince Metternich, the Austrian chancellor, imposed a repressive domestic policy designed to reverse and suppress the liberal movement of the period. The leaders of the continental powers, basically, agreed on a mutual security arrangement designed to stabilize boundaries and to ensure their conception of the appropriate "domestic tranquility." The period up to 1848, apart from some eruptions in 1830, was one of general stability or, perhaps better, of quiescence.

No Germany existed at that time—at least no state with that name. Instead, there was a German federation, a loose assemblage of thirty-eight states operating within the territory of the old Holy Roman Empire. The largest states in that federation, Austria and Prussia, at first shared the management of German affairs, the smaller states either following their lead or quietly attempting to pursue an independent course. Engels declared 1840 to be the turning point in this episode of the history. That date has a rather unexpected un-Marxian significance. It is the year in which Frederick William IV ascended the throne of Prussia. Some events were then set in motion, Engels alleges, that eventually culminated in the revolutions later in the decade. The first spark, undoubtedly the most important and the most dramatic of the series, came in Paris in February 1848. Uprisings followed in other European cities, in Munich, Milan, Vienna, Berlin, Budapest, and in many smaller centers.

That might be taken as proof for the Marxian case, as instances of the rising bourgeoisie attempting to displace a previous ruling class. But it is best not to prejudge the issue. At mid-century, the German states were still very backward economically. Britain's leading industrial center at that point was the city of Manchester. It was also Engels's home in the fifties and sixties. The city was a giant, rapidly growing manufacturing center with over 400,000 inhabitants. The nearest equivalent in the German states, the leading textile center for the time, was the city of Barmen, where Engels was born and raised. At mid-century it had not yet passed the 40,000 mark; it continued at that level, showing only modest growth, until the 1870s. The German economic takeoff, for all practical purposes, came only in the seventies; thus the image of powerful bourgeois contenders in the forties and fifties is, to say the least, somewhat premature. Marx and Engels read their interpretation into the events of 1848. But, given the laggard German development, it follows that the actual history must have had a strikingly different character.

In the end, all of the 1848 revolutions were defeated. In France, as noted, Louis Napoleon was elected president and then overthrew the Second Republic. In Austria, the military defeated the national uprising in northern Italy and, aided by Russian troops, defeated the national rising in Hungary. "Order" was then ultimately restored in Vienna. In Prussia, the undefeated army reentered Berlin and restored the authority of the monarch without having to fire a shot. The old order was restored also in the smaller states of Germany, in many instances with the assistance of Prussian troops. In Prussia, the newly secured regime promulgated a constitution. It was, at best, a modest advance over the pre-1848 arrangements.

A new period of quiescence followed. Marx and Engels made regular predictions about the forthcoming revolution. They saw it coming with the next downswing of the economy. But the next revolution was many decades away. When it did come, it was in markedly different circumstances; it was in November of 1918, as the final episode of the world war.

Two socialist parties had been founded in the 1860s. One, Prussia-based, was led by Ferdinand Lassalle; the second, based largely outside of Prussia, was led by Wilhelm Liebknecht and August Bebel, both of whom had close ties to Marx and Engels. The major events of that decade, however, were not generated by the working class. They were not the product of social history but, in great measure, stemmed from the maneuvers of Otto von Bismarck, minister president of Prussia. With remarkable cunning, he stimulated three quick wars in the course of six years. In 1864, in alliance with Austria, he moved against Denmark and captured the disputed territories, Schleswig and Holstein. Then, precipitating a struggle over the spoils, he moved against and defeated his former ally. The defeat of Austria at Königgrätz in July 1866 made Prussia the dominant power in the German-speaking world. Finally, in another effort of manipulation, Bismarck encouraged the gullible French emperor to attack. This allowed Bismarck to bring an array of smaller German states into a "defensive" alliance. This episode ended with the defeat of Louis Napoleon at the battle of Sedan in September 1870.

The culmination of this series of foreign-policy moves was a major achievement of domestic policy, Bismarck's unification of Germany. In January 1871, most of the German states joined together to form the new *Reich* (empire). Austria, rather ostentatiously, was left out of the new German unity. The King of Prussia, William I, was elevated to the rank of *Kaiser* (emperor).

That easy summary phrase—the unification of Germany—hides a wide range of contention and detail. There had been years of discussion over the boundaries (whether *Grossdeutsch* or *Kleindeutsch*, that is, big or small; with or without Austria; or, the same issue, whether with Catholic or Protestant dominance). Serious struggles also took place over the internal constitution of that unity. Marx and Engels favored the *Grossdeutsch* solution. For them the nationality and religious questions were of no significance and should have been discounted. Marx and Engels also favored a unitary centralized state. That would facilitate the development of a large, unified working class. But in both respects, despite their initial enthusiasm, Bismarck had failed them. He had created "small Germany" and, even worse, had created a federal state, one leaving many powers with the component states. The kings, dukes, and lesser rulers continued in their offices until 1918. Only foreign affairs (including tariffs) and the conduct of war were centralized, that is, were to be handled by national offices located in Berlin.

The two socialist parties experienced occasional reverses but, on the whole, showed considerable growth. A merger was achieved in 1875, at the Gotha conference, to create what soon became the world's leading socialist party, the Social Democratic Party of Germany (called, for short, the SPD). Marx and Engels paid considerable attention to these developments, guiding the party and attempting to direct its course. Although the most significant quantitative growth came outside the period under immediate review, one key episode, the struggle over the *Agrarfrage*, the farm question, did fall here, and Marx and Engels both intervened to affect the outcome. The resolution of that question was to have long-ranging implications for the political development of Germany.

For this discussion, one must follow the writings of Engels, who, in their informal division of labor, was the German specialist of the pair.

"The Status Quo in Germany"

The first Engels contribution to be considered here, a brief account entitled "Der Status Quo in Deutschland," was written in the spring of 1847, less than a year before the *Manifesto*. Not published until 1929, in the Soviet Union, it does, nevertheless, provide us with a first view of the German topic. It is also, as will be seen, an unusually detailed and comprehensive account. One West German specialist, Iring Fetscher, declared "The Status Quo in Germany" to be "one of the most brilliant criticisms of the (German) bureaucracy and political backwardness to be written by a revolutionary intellectual in the nineteenth century."[2]

The work begins with a discussion of the German bourgeoisie, contrasting it with the equivalent classes in England and France. The account, on the whole, is very much in keeping with standard Marxian views: it portrays a rising class aspiring to take power. The treatment is clear and unambiguous: "In Germany the bourgeoisie is not only not in power, it is even the most dangerous enemy of the existing governments." He speaks in this connection of the "aspiring" (*andrängende*) bourgeoisie. The point is repeated in subsequent discussion, with Germany being contrasted with the two leading forerunners: "While in France and England the bourgeoisie has become powerful enough to overthrow the nobility and to raise itself to be the ruling class in the state, the German bourgeoisie has not yet had such power."[3]

If not the bourgeoisie, who, then, does rule? One might think it was simply the aristocracy, but that was not Engels's position, at least not in the discussion that follows. "While in France and England the *towns* dominate the *countryside*, in Germany the countryside dominates the towns, agriculture dominates trade and industry." He then turns, appropriately, to consider the nobility, "the class of big landed proprietors." Their complete domination of society appears in the feudal system. But that system, he reports, has "everywhere declined" due to the rise of a competing "industrial class" (*gewerbetreibende Klasse*). That new class, one learns, is not the *haute* bourgeoisie, as one might anticipate, but rather the petty bourgeoisie (*Kleinbürger*). The outcome of this development, rather unexpectedly, is a compromise between the nobility and the petty bourgeoisie which "amounts to resigning power into the hands of a third class: the bureaucracy." Since the nobility is the more powerful of the two (actually, "represents the more important branch of production"), members of that group hold the highest posts in the civil service, while the petty bourgeoisie must settle for the lower ones. "The petty bourgeoisie," Engels declares, "can never overthrow the nobility, nor make itself equal to it; it can do no more than weaken it. To overthrow the nobility, another class is required, with wider interests, greater property and more determined courage: *the bourgeoisie*."[4]

This formulation is distinctive in four respects: First, the discussion by-passes the monarchy entirely, treating it as of no importance. It is, to say the least, an unusual portrait of the Hohenzollerns, Habsburgs, Wittelsbachs, and the lesser royal families. Second, it assigns a power and a role to the petty bourgeoisie that is seldom seen elsewhere in the Marxian literature. Third, the portrait of rule is coalitional in character; that unexpected pluralist argument, seen in the previous chapter, appears again in this brief analysis. And fourth, there is an ad hoc delineation of a new class, the bureaucracy, a group not appearing in most accounts of the basic nomenclature; this class is treated as a dependent force, apparently, in some way, executing the will of the coalition partners. The latter claim, it should be noted, again bypasses consideration of the monarchy; the civil service serves this coalition of classes, not the king.

Engels next provides an extended discussion of the petty bourgeoisie, con-trasting them with the bourgeoisie. It is one of the most detailed accounts to be found anywhere in the Marx-Engels work. The bourgeoisie grew out of the petty bourgeoisie in those countries sharing in world trade and large-scale industry, in those with free competition and concentration of property. The bourgeoisie engage in worldwide trade; the petty bourgeoisie, by contrast, deal locally or, at best, in a regional market. (Curiously, Engels makes no mention of the obvious intermediate option, of a national market.) Corre-spondingly, there appears a difference in the breadth of their outlooks: the petty bourgeoisie have only local concerns, but the bourgeoisie have *general* interests. The petty bourgeoisie settle for and are happy with small gains, indirect influence in national legislation being adequate for their purposes; participation in local administration is all that is required. The bourgeoisie, in contrast, cannot secure their interests without direct, continuous control over the central administration, foreign policy, and national legislation. This point has considerable importance for later discussion in this chapter: it says direct and continuous control is required over, effectively, *all* government operations. Engels here denies the representational possibility, that some other group or class could serve as its agent; the bourgeoisie itself must undertake the task. One final statement in this comparison touches on the differing politics of the two classes: "The petty bourgeois is conservative as soon as the ruling class makes a few concessions to him; the bourgeois is revolutionary until he him-self rules."[5]

Germany's bourgeoisie has a rather unexpected historical origin. Engels declares that "the creator of the German bourgeoisie was Napoleon." It is a statement worthy of a Carlyle—or of a Treitschke (who argued that "men make history"). It was Napoleon's continental system and the resulting pressure for freedom of trade that gave Germany its modern industry and extended the development of mining. Then, already in 1818, the Prussian government felt compelled, much against its will, to create a protective tariff, this being its first official recognition of the new class. The Prussian Customs Union followed, and then the bourgeoisie "developed rather quickly." Although lagging behind England and France, "it has nevertheless established most branches of modern industry, in a few districts supplanted peasant or petty-bourgeois patriarchalism, concentrated capital to some extent, produced something of a proletariat, and built fairly long stretches of railroad."[6]

The 1818 arrangement, as W. O. Henderson has summarized it, "swept away some sixty internal duties, abolished prohibitions, admitted raw materials free of duty and levied import and consumption duties of only 10 percent on manufactured goods and 20–30 per cent on colonial goods [foodstuffs] and wines." Eliminating internal trade barriers and increasing the size of the trade territory are both key elements of the liberal program. A pure liberal might have wished no tariffs at all, but the Prussian program could easily be counted as "steps in the right direction," especially since most import duties were "levied at much lower rates than those of other countries on the Continent." Free trade, the abolition of the Corn Laws, it will be remembered, did not come to Britain until 1846.

An empirical question: Did the Prussian government only reluctantly institute the tariff? Historical research on the subject indicates just the opposite—the government ("the bureaucracy") pursued the task with enthusiasm. It was relatively easy for that government to eliminate trade barriers within Prussia and to establish the 1818 tariff. Then, through sustained diplomatic efforts, the ministers succeeded in extending the arrangement to include other German states, yielding the Customs Union (*Zollverein*) of 1834. It was, Henderson declares, "the most liberal tariff in Europe." The explanation for the zeal—of Prussia and of the other participating states—is very simple: following basic liberal principles, the move would mean substantial increases in trade and equally dramatic increases in state revenues. The Prussian civil servants responsible for *Zollverein* affairs, we are told, "had been educated at universities at which doctrines of the classical economists were taught." It was the civil servants, moreover, who had taken the initiative; business leaders, generally supportive of the innovations, complained only that they had not been consulted.[7]

The actual history, in short, does not square with Engels's account of the bureaucracy. He has the top ranks filled with members of the aristocracy (an accurate portrait) and, presumably, serving the interests of that class. But the actual history shows them serving the interests of "the state." Arguing liberal principles, they claimed their policy served also the general welfare. The actual history points to an independence or autonomy of the state (or the government, or the civil service). The policy was not something derived from (or "a reflection of") the will or interests of a dominant (or rising) class. Engels's account misses this actual history; his treatment is such as to lend plausibility to the basic Marxian notion of the centrality of the classes.

Apart from the actual historical evidence, it should be noted, the logic of the argument is implausible. In 1818, it is argued, the Prussian government felt compelled (*genötigt*) to institute the tariff. But at that time the bourgeoisie must have had minuscule influence. It is only after the *Zollverein* (Engels omits the date, 1834) that he can speak of the "rather rapid development" of the class, it still, even in the twenties, thirties, and forties, lagging far behind its British and French equivalents. He has assigned an influence to that class which, at that early date, is most unlikely. There is also a motivational problem: why would the higher civil servants—aristocrats with interests opposed to the bourgeoisie—foster a policy that, presumably, would damage *their* class interests? It is clear from logic alone that something else must have been operating.

The rise of the bourgeoisie, Engels declares, meant a loss for the previously dominant classes. The German nobles, he claims, ever since Napoleonic times, had become more impoverished and burdened by debt. The ending of feudal labor services increased their costs; Russian, American, and Australian competition squeezed them. They failed, moreover, to use the newest developments in farm technology. The decline of the nobility, it should be noted, is not simply a function of economic facts. An important role is assigned to outlooks or attitudes, to laziness on the one hand and to profligacy on the other. The German nobles, Engels reports, like their English and French forerunners a century earlier, were squandering their fortunes. Engels writes: "Between the nobility and the bourgeoisie began that competition in social and intellectual education, in wealth and display, which everywhere precedes the political dominance of the bourgeoisie and ends, like every other form of competition, with the victory of the richer side. The provincial nobility turned into a Court nobility, only thereby to be ruined all the more quickly and surely. The three per cent revenues of the nobility went down before the fifteen per cent profit of the bourgeoisie."[8]

The introduction of the attitudinal factor, of the element of will, changes the character of the analysis; it is no longer, strictly speaking, economic determinist. It thereby becomes contingent history; the nobility, if so disposed, could have made use of the newest advances in agriculture, could have given serious attention to the management of their estates, and could have refrained from ostentation and frivolous display.

The bourgeoisie, as noted repeatedly, is generally treated as an urban class, the word itself in its etymology signifying an urban base. But Engels here points to the appearance of bourgeois farmowners, to a new class of industrial landowners. The differences between them and the nobility are again, unexpectedly, matters of will or character rather than legal or purely economic ones. "This class carries on agriculture," Engels declares, "without feudal illusions and without the nobleman's nonchalance, as a business, an industry, with the bourgeois appliances of capital, expert knowledge and work." This agricultural segment of the bourgeoisie is essentially at one in outlook with its urban peers. Some of the nobility, those "wise enough not to ruin themselves," joined with this industrial landowner class. Engels's conclusion here is that "the nobility has therefore become so impotent, that a part of it has already gone over to the bourgeoisie."[9]

Engels returns again to discussion of the petty bourgeoisie. This class is weak in comparison with the nobility and, even more, in relation to the bourgeoisie. Indeed, after the peasants, it is "the most pathetic class that has ever meddled with history." Its heyday was in the late middle ages, but even then its concern with petty local interests brought it only to local organizations, local struggles, and local advances. It led a tolerated existence alongside the nobility; nowhere, however, did it achieve a general political domination. With the coming of the bourgeoisie, the petty bourgeoisie loses "even the *appearance* of historical initiative." At this point, the petty bourgeoisie, Engels writes, is caught in between, overwhelmed by the political power of the nobility and pressed by the economic power of the bourgeoisie. Given this position of conflict, Engels announces, the class divides into two factions; the richer, urban petty bourgeoisie, "more or less" timidly, joined the revolutionary bourgeoisie; the poorer faction, especially from the rural communities, joined with the nobles to protect the existing arrangement.

That all seems clear enough. However, in the same long paragraph one is provided with another scenario. Under current circumstances, in the prevailing status quo, the ruin of the petty bourgeoisie is certain, something clearly recognized by the poorer faction. Seeing their only chance in the possibility of mobility into the bourgeoisie, they follow the leadership of that class. The "more certain its ruin," Engels declares, "the more it ranges itself under the banner of the bourgeoisie."

When the bourgeoisie attains power, the petty bourgeoisie divides once again. At that point its members must either ally with the proletariat, an option mentioned only in passing, or surrender unconditionally to the bourgeoisie. This process had already occurred in England, most clearly in periods of economic downswing, and was currently to be seen in France. The same development is just beginning in Germany. It was only now in the phase of abandoning the nobility. The petty bourgeoisie, Engels concludes, "places itself every day more and more under the command of the bourgeoisie."

To summarize, the petty bourgeoisie is backing away from the declining nobility. But, at the same time, it finds no clear positive option. Seen first in alliance with the nobility (those two classes staffing the bureaucracy), it then divides, one part maintaining the link, the other joining with the bourgeoisie. Then, in a third development, virtually the entire class submits to the bourgeoisie. A minor option, forming ties with the proletariat, as indicated, receives only a brief mention. For the moment, the German petty bourgeoisie has allied with—has entrusted its fate to—the bourgeoisie.[10]

The next class considered by Engels is the farmers (*die Bauern*), including here the smallholders and tenants. This account notes some similarity between farmers and the urban petty bourgeoisie. Unlike the *Manifesto* and *The Class Struggles in France*, it also recognizes a point of difference. Like the urban segment, this group is a "helpless class," one incapable of any historical initiative. The two differ, however, in character. The farmers, it is said, show "greater courage" than the petty bourgeoisie. Where the absence of a nobility or bourgeoisie allows them to rule (Norway and the Alpine cantons of Switzerland are mentioned), they are given to "pre-feudal barbarianisms, local narrow-mindedness, and dull, fanatical bigotry." On the positive side, Engels notes, they show "loyalty and rectitude."

Where the farm class persists, as in Germany, the farmers find themselves squeezed, just like the petty bourgeoisie. Accordingly, one finds division in their ranks, the condition of the holding being the decisive factor. Some, those with larger farms—those in the east—tend to ally with the nobility. Elsewhere the tendency is to ally with the bourgeoisie. As with his discussion of the petty bourgeoisie, Engels makes no attempt at quantification. He does say, in a final passage, that they, "for the greatest part," have put themselves at the disposal of the bourgeoisie. One might wonder, in the absence of any serious evidence on farmers' outlooks or behavior, how Engels knows about these mass reactions. At this point he gives us a clue as to his research procedures. "That this is actually the case," Engels writes, "is proved by the Prussian provincial diets [legislatures]."[11] That rather imprecise proof assumes a direct, unbiased system of representation, broad suffrage, and free elections. But the comments of such spokesmen, at all times and places, must be recognized as providing, at best, only very oblique reflections of underlying mass opinion. Any such conclusions, therefore, must be viewed as extremely tenuous.[12]

Finally, Engels discusses the working class. His main task is to indicate the fragmentation present: the class contains farm laborers, day laborers, journeymen in the crafts, factory workers, and *Lumpenproletariat*. These groups are spread thinly over a wide territory with only a few weak points of concentration. As a result, it is difficult for them to develop an understanding of their common interests and to form themselves into a single class. They, as a consequence, focus on their respective immediate interests and see these linked to the conditions of their employers. Each segment, accordingly, forms an auxiliary army in the service of its employers. The farm laborers and day workers support the interests of the nobility or the farmer, and so on. The "Lump" fights for whoever pays a few Taler. The workers, clearly, are not at all prepared to take over the direction of public affairs.

Engels summarizes as follows: "The nobility is too much in decline, the petty bourgeoisie and peasants are, by their whole position in life, too weak, the workers are still far from sufficiently mature to be able to come forward as the ruling class in Germany. There remains only the bourgeoisie."[13]

A more detailed discussion of the condition of the bourgeoisie follows. Its situation in Germany is compared with the experience of other nations, principally with England and France. The immediate conclusion, not at all unexpected in this case, is that Germany's bourgeoisie is destined to overturn the status quo. This follows both from the general historical experience and from the particular constellation of forces in Germany. Although only a small and relatively undeveloped class (especially as compared with those of England and France), its strength comes through its leadership of a broad combination of forces. Engels concludes that the bourgeoisie is "the only class in Germany which at least gives a great part of the industrial landowners, petty bourgeoisie, peasants, workers and even a minority among the nobles a share in its interests, and has united these under its banner."[14]

Engels also reports on the state of bourgeois consciousness. It is the only class in Germany that has definite plans, that knows what to put in place of the status quo. He reports at some length on the aims of the bourgeoisie, on its plans and organization. It is a portrait of knowledge, understanding, and of actions designed to attain their ends. The portrait, in short, is one of a class having a high state of awareness and a will to action. In the familiar Marxian terms, it possesses a fully developed class consciousness; it is a class for itself.

Some additional questions are considered in the remaining pages of the incomplete manuscript. The principal concern is with the "why" question: Why does the bourgeoisie seek to overturn the status quo? These pages provide a rather detailed account of the fetters argument, of the obstacles placed in the way of bourgeois trade and industry by the old regime. It explains that class's needs, taking up matters on an issue-by-issue basis. In this respect it is a rare performance; most later discussions simply refer to the fetters, assuming the obviousness of the argument and neglecting the details. Exploration of those details here would require a major digression. One may focus, however, on the conclusion: Engels argues that the bourgeoisie must become the ruling class. Its interests must take priority in legislation, in administration, in the judiciary, in matters of taxes, and in the conduct of foreign policy. The logic of that "must" is neither clear nor all that compelling. The argument, moreover, has an all-or-nothing character—the bourgeoisie "must develop itself to the full . . . *in order not to be ruined*." But there might be other possibilities: sharing power, muddling through, compromise arrangements (especially to be recommended for coalitions), representational alternatives, and so on. If the bureaucratic-monarchical regime could serve the nobility and the petty bourgeoisie, might it also be of service to the developing bourgeoisie?[15]

The Communist Manifesto

"The Status Quo in Germany" and the *Manifesto* show important differences in the character of the analyses. The first and perhaps the most striking difference, is the shift from complexity to simplicity. In the article, six classes receive at least a paragraph-long treatment. In the *Manifesto*, including the single paragraph on the *Lumpenproletariat*, there are four classes. The change, in part, stems from a difference in focus. The article deals with prerevolutionary Germany; hence the classes of two epochs are present and contending. The *Manifesto* is focused on the bourgeois era; the first and principal analytic section considers the dynamics of the presumably already-existing bourgeois epoch. Hence, for that reason, the nobility receives only a few casual mentions. The farm populations are there treated as part of the bourgeois economy and are classified with the petty bourgeoisie. The bureaucracy exists as a separate entity in "The Status Quo"; it is not present in the *Manifesto*.

Simplification occurs in still another way. "The Status Quo" recognizes the possibility of internal differentiation; some diversity of outlooks within classes is clearly indicated. The *Manifesto*, in contrast, provides strong categorical formulations—the bourgeoisie does this, the proletariat does that. The former work sees contending coalitions of forces; it is the alliance of the bourgeoisie with other groups that challenges the status quo. By itself, the bourgeoisie would be too weak to achieve the task. The *Manifesto*, in contrast, says nothing of such alliances. The bourgeoisie is a bold, competent, and capable class; it goes its way, charts its own course. The linkage with the *Lumpenproletariat* involves the purchase of services, something quite different from a conventional alliance. Differentiation within the bourgeoisie is recognized, but the minority factions defect; they "go over to" the workers rather than allying with them. It is the class-versus-class formulation of the *Manifesto* that has dominated subsequent thought, both in Marxist and non-Marxist analyses, rather than the coalition-versus-coalition portrayal.[16]

The coalitional focus, it will be noted, has a counterpart in contemporary thought, that is, in the pluralist framework. That line of theorizing, reaching back to Montesquieu and Tocqueville, assumes multiple centers of power and processes of negotiation between them to achieve satisfactory compromise results. Engels's "Status Quo" account clearly has a strong pluralist character. There is a recognition of the multiple power centers and, although not a strong emphasis, there is a recognition of the negotiated or compromise out-comes. But where the pluralists normally give consideration to the negotia-tions, discussing the terms of the compromise, Engels neglects that subject, treating the alliances as the natural or automatic outcomes of the larger social developments. The introduction of negotiations into the discussion would have problematical implications in that the determinist history would again become contingent. A role for the individual, for the shrewd, adept negotia-tor, would appear; moreover, one would also have to allow some place for the accident, for the fluke in such negotiation efforts.

There is also a problem of inconsistent predictions. The most important of these appears with respect to the petty bourgeoisie. In "The Status Quo," that class is allied with the aristocracy and then, so it is claimed, will join with the bourgeoisie, that being the most forcefully stated option. Any links with the proletariat are mentioned only in passing. In the *Manifesto*, as was seen in Chapter 1, the petty bourgeoisie either acts for itself, wishing to "roll back the wheel of history," or, a part of it at least, joins with the workers. In the *Manifesto*, all segments of the class "fight against the bourgeoisie." There is no suggestion of a "surrender" into the hands of the bourgeoisie. This indicates a remarkable flexibility of position within the span of only a few months.[17]

Germany: Revolution and Counter-Revolution

The next account to be considered here is Engels's *Germany: Revolution and Counter-Revolution*. This work is a collection of articles that were written under Marx's name for the *New York Daily Tribune* in 1851 and 1852. Leonard Krieger, who edited the version to be used here, declares that "the work has been recognized as a classic by historians of all persuasions." As a historical study, he adds, "its repute and its utility remain eminent." He refers also to "the prece-dence which it has recently enjoyed over all the contemporary and even many of the subsequent histories of the 1848 revolution in Germany."[18]

This history opens with a delineation of five classes (plus some "subordinate gradations"). Two classes mentioned briefly in "The Status Quo," the indus-trial landowners and the *Lumpenproletariat*, do not appear here. The signifi-cance of those missing classes will be considered at a later point.

The first class discussed is the nobility. Again comparison is made with England and France, where feudalism was "entirely destroyed" or, in England, reduced to a "few insignificant forms" due to the efforts of a "powerful and wealthy middle class." But in Germany "the feudal nobility" retained "a great portion of their ancient privileges," including "jurisdiction over their tenants." In addition to this "supremacy over the peasantry in their demesnes," they were also exempt from taxes. The feudal arrangement was stronger in some localities than in others. Regional variation within Germany is a central theme found throughout Engels's discussion; there were, after all, thirty-eight separate states within the loosely organized German federation. The nobility, officially, was the first "Order" of the land. It "furnished the higher Government officials" and, almost exclusively, "officered the army." One point deserves special emphasis: The nobility was not a ruling class. Engels is very clear on this point, referring to them as "deprived of their political privileges, of the right to control the princes."[19]

The nobility in this 1851 portrait bears little resemblance to that of Engels's 1847 account. There is nothing on their backwardness, on their failure to use modern technique; there is nothing on their outlooks, on either laziness or profligacy; there is nothing on their competition with the bourgeoisie for status, nothing on their "three per cent incomes"; and there is nothing on their role as "flunkies" at court. In 1847, Engels places great emphasis on their relative impoverishment. In 1851, that also disappears, the only comment now being that some of them are "very wealthy."

The bourgeoisie, in this account, is portrayed as relatively weak and backward, but growing in strength. It is certainly not the bourgeoisie of England or France. The most serious problem is that of division, there being no large centers of trade or manufacturing. Much of the trade passes through foreign ports, Dutch and Belgian principally, thus creating the bourgeoisie of other nations. There is, moreover, the problem of division into some three dozen states. The basic problem was a want of numbers and particularly of concentrated numbers; this prevented them from taking power, as was done in the leading capitalist nations.

The governments of Germany were "compelled to bow," reluctantly, he says, to the immediate material interests of the bourgeoisie. Engels again mentions the Prussian tariff of 1818 and the *Zollverein* as prime examples. It was, however, a seesaw struggle, the governments, in subsequent periods of reaction, recapturing ground previously lost. The argument of fetters on trade and industry appears again, this time without any detailed specification. Bourgeois activity

is "checked" by the political constitution of the nation, by the "random division" of territory "among thirty-six princes with conflicting tendencies and
caprices," by "the feudal fetters upon agriculture and the trade connected with
it," and by the "prying superintendence" of an "ignorant and presumptuous
bureaucracy." Despite these obstacles, trade continued to grow, bourgeois
links and consciousness to develop. The commercial classes of the various
states were brought closer together, their interests equalized, and their
strength centralized. The "natural consequence," Engels reports, is that the
"whole mass" of them passed into the camp of the Liberal Opposition. He
gives this move a precise date, 1840, described as "the moment when the
bourgeoisie of Prussia assumed the lead of the middle-class movement of
Germany."[20]

The next class discussed is the petty bourgeoisie. That expression, however,
is not used; here it is referred to as the "small trading and shopkeeping class."
Because of the limited development of the bourgeoisie, this class has special
importance in Germany. "In the larger towns," Engels writes, "it forms almost
the majority of the inhabitants; in the smaller ones it entirely predominates
[due to] the absence of wealthier competitors or influence." Engels assigns this
class a considerable role in the revolutionary events of 1848. "During the recent
struggles," he says, "it generally played the decisive part."

Once again we have a discussion of the distinctive intermediate position of
this class. Its members are, he says, "eternally tossed about" between "the hope
of entering the ranks of the wealthier class, and the fear of being reduced to the
state of proletarians or even paupers." Unlike the bourgeoisie, which knows its
position, and unlike the proletariat which soon will know where it stands, the
petty bourgeoisie is "extremely vacillating" in its views. The class is "humble
and crouchingly submissive" under feudal or monarchical governments; it
turns "to the side of Liberalism" under the ascendant middle class and is even
"seized with violent democratic fits" when the middle class "has secured its
own supremacy." But then, when the proletariat attempts its own independent
movement, the class "falls back into the abject despondency of fear." All these
positions, he says, are evidenced in the events of the German revolution.[21]

This portrait of the petty bourgeoisie, the third of the Marx-Engels portraits
reviewed thus far in this chapter, differs markedly in the specific assertions
made about the class. The *Manifesto* had it that they would either be reactionary or, those recognizing their fate, would join with the workers. The former

option is not mentioned specifically here, although the "abject despondency of fear" statement might be an oblique reference to that possibility. The second option, joining with the workers, is not mentioned at all. The development described in "The Status Quo," the alliance of petty bourgeoisie and nobility sharing power through the bureaucracy, also is not mentioned in *Revolution and Counter-Revolution*. The minor option mentioned in "The Status Quo," alliance with the proletariat, has disappeared. The major alternative mentioned there, "unconditional surrender" to the bourgeoisie or serving "under the command of the bourgeoisie," may be implicit in at least two phases of the present sequence, although here the relationship appears freely chosen as opposed to the helpless "act of submission" of the earlier work. And finally, where that earlier work left the class under the command of the bourgeoisie, the last act in the 1851 scenario has them leaving that command, evidently to support the monarchy.

Engels again is showing unusual flexibility in his statement of the petty bourgeoisie's role. The recurrent evidence problem surfaces once again: How could Engels have known about the reactions of hundreds of thousands of persons scattered across "three dozen" central European states? It is clear that no adequate epistemological method—way of knowing—was available at that time and that he, to put it simply, was freely extemporizing.

The German working class, like that nation's bourgeoisie, has a laggard development. This is the only place where Engels's discussion is clearly dialectical in character. The working class develops in opposition to the bourgeoisie. "Like master, like man," he writes. But the "mass" of German workers are employed "by small tradesmen, whose entire manufacturing system is a mere relic of the Middle ages." The consequence is a lack of development, an absence of modern ideas. Just as there is "an enormous difference between the great cotton lord and the petty cobbler or master tailor, so there is a corresponding distance from the wide-awake factory operative of modern manufacturing Babylons to the bashful journeyman tailor or cabinet-maker of a small country town, who lives in circumstances and works after a plan very little different from those of the like sort of men some five hundred years ago."

Given the condition, it was not surprising, as Engels reports, that "at the outbreak of the Revolution, a large part of the working classes should cry out for the immediate re-establishment of guilds and Mediaeval privileged trades corporations." That reactionary tendency has been well documented in later scholarship. That single sentence is the only statement in the entire account that recognizes the backward-looking character of the working-class movement of 1848. Beginning with the next sentence, Engels turns to the opposite movement, to consideration of the emerging radical tendencies. In the manufacturing districts where the "modern system of production" predominated, where greater movement and communication was possible, a different "mental development" was possible. There, a "strong nucleus" formed "whose ideas about the emancipation of their class were far clearer and more in accordance with existing facts and historical necessities; but they were a minority." Those qualified formulations disappear in his later pages. There, even before the March revolution, "the working classes of the larger towns looked for their emancipation to the Socialist and Communist doctrines." And a page later, he reports that "the proletarians were preparing to hurl down the bourgeoisie."[22]

The fifth and last category considered in this account is "the great class of small farmers, the peasantry." Together with the farm laborers, it constitutes "a considerable majority of the entire nation." This class, Engels reports, is divided into four subcategories or factions. These are the more wealthy farmers (who have allied with the "antifeudal middle class of the towns"); the small freeholders, a group that is, on the whole, impoverished, burdened by mortgages, and so forth; feudal tenants—those not easily turned off the land, persons obliged to pay "perpetual" rents or labor services; and the agricultural laborers. The last three groups "never troubled their heads much about politics" before the revolution. Although they see new opportunities for themselves in that development, Engels does not portray them as actors in those events. It is evident, he says, something "borne out by the history of all modern countries," that the farm population, being dispersed and unable to develop their ideas and to coordinate action, "never can attempt a successful independent movement; they require the initiatory impulse of the more concentrated, more enlightened, more easily moved people of the towns."

Wealthy farmers, the *Gross* and *Mittel-Bauern*, it will be noted, are explicitly declared to be a faction of "the great class of the small farmers, the peasantry," although that does not seem appropriate. The "class of industrial landowners" of "The Status Quo" has disappeared as a separate category. The second and third factions, freeholders and tenants, classified with the farm class in "The Status Quo" and with the petty bourgeoisie in the *Manifesto*, are again part of the farm class. No clear role is attributed to them in this work: they had an opportunity, saw it, and did nothing with it. Farm laborers, explicitly excluded from the farm class in "The Status Quo," presumably to be counted as proletarians, now are counted along with the *Gross*, *Mittel*, and *Klein* farm proprietors. The inconsistent placement had no great significance because, according to Engels, none of the factions played a serious role in the revolutionary events he is describing.

That portrait of do-nothing farm populations, however, is not accurate. Violence was widespread in the German countryside in the year prior to the revolution, with burning of manor houses a frequent event. The farm populations showed considerable "initiating impulse." Engels's treatment of the historical record here involves serious distortion. He makes much of minor working-class skirmishes (for example, the "insurrections" of Silesian and Bohemian weavers) but gives no attention to the much more serious farm insurgency. For those not knowing anything of the history, that selection would confirm Engels's claims—that the future would be decided by the proletariat and that farm populations generally would count for nothing in the unfolding drama.[23]

The German case, in contrast to Britain and France, is complicated by the diversity problem, that is, by the presence of many states (or statelets). The contending classes have a different mix in "every district, in every province." Moreover, there is no great center, no London or Paris, where a decisive battle could occur. There is, accordingly, a necessity for "fighting out the same quarrel over and over again in every single locality." Given such "incoherence," it is not at all surprising that Marx and Engels were ardent supporters of German unification; it would simplify all of that complexity and allow a rapid acceleration of the historical development.

The previous paragraphs summarize Engels's first *Daily Tribune* article, which briefly describes the five classes of his nomenclature and gives some indication of their dispositions in the 1848 struggles. It is not at all clear from this particular account which sides were contending. Given the trained expectation of a class struggle, one might anticipate a conflict of bourgeoisie against aristocracy. But that is not the case. The antagonists, the defenders in the struggle, are the monarchies headed by the princes. The protagonists, the revolutionary forces, are arrayed against political regimes, not against ruling classes. Engels's portrayal of these regimes, initially at least, is rather nebulous, providing no clear link to the just-described classes. At the opening of the second article, for example, they are described as "half-feudal, half-bureaucratic Monarchism." Those regimes, it will be noted, are autonomous political agencies. Engels has indicated earlier that the aristocracy had been deprived of political power; power now was in the hands of monarchs and their agencies, principally, bureaucracy and army. Those regimes stand outside the classes and interests he has delineated. No sooner is the Marxian class analysis under way than the strict lines of that framework are abandoned.

Most knowledgeable persons would expect a structural analysis to follow, one proceeding independently of persons and individual motives; in fact, in the opening pages, Engels promises just that kind of analysis. His actual analysis, however, centers on individuals, their whims and fancies. In his discussion of Prussia, the subject of the second article, he focuses on the king, Frederick William IV, who came to the throne in 1840. That date is given repeatedly as the beginning point of the new ferment. The king's political preferences and his foibles, speeches, and behavior are reviewed at length, the net result, it is said, being "to estrange from him the sympathies of the middle class."[24]

An extended discussion of the troubled relationship of king and bourgeoisie follows. The conflict resulted in a high level of consciousness on the part of the middle classes. They knew they were "on the eve of a revolution and prepared themselves for it." For this purpose they "sought to obtain by every possible means the support of the working class of the towns, and of the peasantry in the agricultural districts." Curiously, Engels omits the petty bourgeoisie, the class that he said played the decisive part in the towns. It is a puzzling observation: Why would the bourgeoisie neglect its most obvious ally in this struggle? Why would bourgeois leaders instead attempt to mobilize two rather distant classes, ones that would be disposed to dangerous positions on questions of suffrage, indebtedness, and property?

The final paragraph of this discussion depicts two contending coalitions—not a polar confrontation of opposed classes. Engels's summary reads:

> While the higher nobility and the older civil and military officers were the only safe supports of the existing system; while the lower nobility, the trading middle classes, the universities, the schoolmasters of every degree, and even part of the lower ranks of the bureaucracy and military officers were all leagued against the Government; while behind these there stood

the dissatisfied masses of the peasantry, and of the proletarians of the large towns, supporting, for the time being, the Liberal Opposition, but already muttering strange words about taking things into their own hands; while the bourgeoisie was ready to hurl down the Government, and the proletarians were preparing to hurl down the bourgeoisie in its turn; this Government went on obstinately in a course which must bring about a collision.

A similar portrait appears at the end of the following article, one focused on the smaller states of Germany. Again it is an account of "a heterogeneous mass of opposition," this "more or less led by" the bourgeoisie.[25]

The basic portrait offered in *Revolution and Counter-Revolution* differs considerably from that provided in the *Manifesto*. The former account, like the "Status Quo" article, depicts a struggle of coalitions, one weak and fumbling, the other large, angry, and confident. The account does not show, as in the *Manifesto*, a sharp class-versus-class confrontation; it does not show a *class* struggle. This divergence, however (as noted in the discussion of "The Status Quo"), does not represent a contradiction but stems rather from a difference in focus. The *Manifesto* gives only a truncated portrait of the historical process and thus provides a misleading clue to the larger framework.[26] It begins with a bourgeoisie already in power and concentrates on the end-phase of the capitalist epoch. The final struggle, so it is announced, will find "two great classes directly facing each other." In that struggle, the proletariat, a powerful, self-conscious majority, will have no particular need for allies. The options available to the bourgeoisie, as compared with earlier points in the epoch, will be limited and without promise, since only the dwindling petty bourgeoisie and the *Lumpenproletariat* remain. Given the unreliable character of both segments and given the odds against them, negotiations by the bourgeoisie could not significantly alter the situation. The pluralist analysis, in short, would no longer be applicable in the end-phase of the epoch.

But in those previous struggles, in those assumed (and bypassed) in the *Manifesto*, the conflict would have had a different character, one for which a pluralist analysis would be most appropriate. In fact, only with difficulty could it be avoided. With aristocracy and bourgeoisie together not making up even 10 percent of the population, any social conflict would, almost of necessity, involve coalitions of forces. There would, in other words, be considerable incentive for the principal contenders to seek aid from among "the other 90 percent." Accounts of those earlier struggles would have to consider discussions of the terms; they would have to consider quid pro quo arrangements—what rewards for what support? Analyses of the defeats, where appropriate, would also have to consider the unraveling of those agreements. What led participants to withdraw from a coalition? What led some to change sides?

Engels provides only a brief sketch of the revolutionary coalition. He assumes the bourgeoisie to be revolutionary in orientation. He declares the movement to be "more or less" under bourgeois direction. Other groups seeking redress of their grievances have been drawn into this effort. But no serious evidence is provided to back up any of these claims. No evidence is offered to show the revolutionary orientations of the bourgeoisie. We have nothing on the bourgeois leadership, and no detail is provided on the negotiations necessary to form the coalition. Some important considerations, in short, are missing from Engels's analysis.

Something must also be said about the other contender in the revolutionary struggle, the "half-feudal, half-bureaucratic" monarchical regimes. They evidently are in power. It is also evident that these regimes are not reducible to (that is, are not the agencies of) any of the five classes described in the opening article. Individual rulers now appear, and their outlooks and orientations make a difference. In the Prussian case, Frederick William's peculiarities play a "decisive part" in stimulating the formation of the opposition. These rulers, moreover, do not stand alone; they operate through a bureaucracy, a civil service. And just as decisively—a key aspect of the arrangement—they operate with the aid of armies. The entire cluster—monarch, bureaucracy, army—stands outside Engels's basic analytic framework. Since he cannot very well ignore these ruling agencies, they enter through the back door, in ad hoc discussions. This means there is no serious analysis of the key agencies in the struggle, of the so-called absolute monarchies. Those agencies, therefore, have a phantom existence in his account.

One should, in addition to these purely analytical objections, consider the empirical implications of Engels's analysis. If the bourgeoisie was "more or less" organizing the effort, that should be reflected in the surviving documentary record. A simple question arises: Where is that leadership role empirically established? If the bourgeoisie were as unified and conscious as Engels claims, that too should be indicated in the documentary record. Again some simple questions: Is that the case? Do the letters, diaries, memoirs, pamphlets, etc., written by the bourgeoisie (especially by the leaders of that class) show such awareness? Were they seething with resentment over the fetters imposed by the monarchical regimes? Did they actively seek to replace those regimes? Did they make contacts and negotiate with that range of allies in order to implement their aims? One would have to demonstrate all these things in order to establish Engels's case. Such a demonstration would probably be beyond Engels's reach, especially given his day-to-day obligations and commitments in Manchester and given the lack there of prime source material. But for the historical researcher in the intervening 130 years, for the diligent and concerned social historian, provision of that documentation should be a relatively easy task—if the claims were accurate. And if they were not accurate, if the bourgeoisie was thinking or doing something else entirely, that too should long since have been established.

Diefendorf provides an answer with respect to businessmen in the Prussian Rhineland. He notes the relatively close contact that existed between business and government, first achieved under the French occupation, then carried over by the new Prussian administration after 1815. The relationship deteriorated somewhat after 1830, after the passing of the reform generation of Prussian bureaucrats. This did not, however, "lead to any sort of revolutionary opposition." Businessmen remained "politically loyal [to] the Prussian state." Although opposed to specific policies and wishing to see reforms, they "did so as a loyal opposition, seeking improvements in a system that they basically approved of." The Rhenish liberal businessmen "wanted a fair share in directing the state, not complete control or sovereignty, over it. They wanted to join the crown and bureaucracy as leaders, not to replace them." A reaction did occur in the 1840s; this was stimulated, as Engels rightly observes, by Frederick William's arbitrariness and by his appointment of conservatives in the bureaucracy. But this led businessmen to join the movement for constitutional reform—not one for revolutionary change.[27]

On the eighteenth of March 1848, Engels reports, "the people of Berlin rose in arms and, after an obstinate struggle of eighteen hours, had the satisfaction of seeing the king surrender himself into their hands." That portrayal is, to say the least, somewhat misleading. In a muddled decision-making process, the king and his advisers and generals agreed that the troops should be withdrawn from Berlin and that a siege was to follow. But the execution of the plan was flawed in that the army exited before the royal family was evacuated, and thus, as a result of a blunder, the king was obliged to "surrender himself." The army, it should be noted, was not defeated in that obstinate struggle. Engels's treatment of the revolutionary events in Germany, it should be noted, parallels Marx's account of the February revolution in Paris in two respects. It is brief: he gives only one sentence to the revolution in Berlin. Marx also, it will be remembered, failed to mention a crucial fact—the withdrawal of undefeated troops.

No attempt was made to abolish the monarchy, to declare a republic. Despite widespread dissatisfaction with the incumbent, Frederick William was not deposed. No Revolutionary Council intervened to take over (or even to circumscribe) his right to rule. These facts provide telling evidence about the aims of the revolutionaries. They clearly had no intention of overthrowing the regime.[28]

The remainder of the revolutionary history may be easily summarized. The Prussian king named a new cabinet led by two eminent bourgeois notables: Ludolf Camphausen was appointed minister president of the reform government; David Hansemann was named finance minister. A Prussian assembly began work on a new constitution. Within a few months, however, the Prussian king and his circle, a group of tough reactionaries referred to as the camarilla, took heart. In November, the king ordered his still-intact, undefeated troops to reenter Berlin, and, without firing a shot, he reestablished control. The revolutionary insurgents of March had disappeared, had changed position, or had lost the will to fight. In early December, the king dissolved the constituent convention and, by royal decree, promulgated the constitution that remained in force until 1918.

A more important body, the National Assembly, was elected by "independent citizens," with delegates chosen in all German states. It met and discussed in Frankfurt, in the Paulskirche. The Frankfurt Assembly, in March 1849, offered the king an emperor's crown, inviting him to reign over the new, democratic united Germany. But he refused it; he would not accept such a gift "from the gutter." Eventually, with Prussian troops, the revolution was defeated in all the states of northern and western Germany. In Austria a more complicated history had been played out because of the ethnic and national complexities, specifically because of the Italian uprising and the Hungarian insurgency against Vienna's rule. But there too, the result was the same: the

Austrian military, aided by Russian troops in Hungary, defeated the revolution at all points. The decisive agency in both contexts was the army, not a class or coalition of classes. This led Engels, belatedly, to a recognition of its importance and of its autonomy. "The army," he declared, "again was the decisive power in the State, and the army belonged not to the middle classes but to themselves." We have here a new agency and a new hypothesis—that the military, under some circumstances at least, can be an agency acting on its own behalf, that is, *für sich*.[29]

How does Engels deal with the counterrevolution? Basically, his "analysis" consists of a heavy ad hominem attack on the bourgeois ministers in Prussia and on the representatives in the National Assembly. Camphausen and Hansemann, the two key cabinet appointees in Prussia, are attacked for their faintheartedness, for their fears (of revolutionary workers), and for their inactivity. Described as "poor deluded wretches," they are faulted for their zeal to restore "order" and for their failure to carry through any serious changes. "Not a single bureaucrat or military officer was dismissed," he writes, "not the slightest change was made in the old bureaucratic system of administration." It is curious: in place of analysis or some argument stemming from the initial theoretical statement, we find personal attack, the imputation of fault, and blame. In the first paragraphs of the first article, Engels had announced that the causes of the defeat "are not to be sought for in the accidental efforts, talents, faults, errors, or treacheries of some of the leaders." But here, in one key episode, he focused exclusively on the faults and errors of two leaders.[30]

Engels's angry condemnation of the bourgeoisie comes in lieu of the appropriate step—provision of a straightforward conclusion. It might read as follows: Our prediction, that the bourgeoisie would at least attempt to take power, has not been confirmed; in this case, at least, the claim has proven mistaken. That conclusion, in turn, should have stimulated a review and reconsideration of the original argument. Engels's procedure, however, is akin to that of a physicist berating cowardly particles for their untoward behavior or that of a botanist railing against plants for failing to confirm his prediction about the inheritance of recessive traits. Condemnation of the key actors in the historical drama is a theory-saving device; it deflects attention from the key fact, that the claim was not supported. This procedure continues to assume, despite the immediate failure, that the prediction is justified, that it is correct.

That faultfinding, moreover, departs from the basic commitment to scientific history; it no longer is delineating and explaining fact but, rather, is invoking normative judgments. It is Engels's standard, moreover, that provides the basis for judgment, or, more broadly, it is that of the Marx-Engels position; it is their conception of what the bourgeoisie should be doing. But that avoids a basic empirical question: How did they, Camphausen and Hansemann, see things? What did they want? What were their priorities? Did they see the institution of a bourgeois regime as a first priority or even at this moment as important? That reading of bourgeois motivations, basically, is dependent on Marx and Engels's assumptions. But if Camphausen and Hansemann did not adopt the Marx-Engels program as their own, they can hardly be faulted for neglecting it.

An alternative possibility is that Camphausen and Hansemann's reading of events was accurate, that they did what was the right, wise, or appropriate thing to defend the interests of the bourgeoisie. Put differently, it is possible that Marx and Engels were mistaken about the bourgeoisie's appropriate response. Diefendorf describes bourgeois reactions to the outcome of the revolution in Prussia as follows: "A Prussian national legislature was created, the members to be elected by a three-class electorate, the voting weighted in favor of the propertied classes, and the rule of law and the independence of the judiciary was established. Remaining feudal privileges were abolished, and censorship was ended. Many of these reforms resemble the proposals made by Hansemann in 1830; in fact, he served on the commission that modeled the new national franchise on the Rhenish three-class franchise of 1845. Certainly the Rhenish business leaders were basically satisfied with the results of the revolution in Prussia." All of the businessmen active during the revolution, Diefendorf declares, "strongly endorsed" the new Prussian constitution decreed by the king. Gustav Mevissen, one of the business leaders, said it offered more "than pre-March Rhenish liberalism had hoped for."[31]

It was the immobility of the new bourgeois government that, presumably, led the other parties of the revolutionary coalition—petty bourgeoisie, workers, and farmers—to defect, to drop their support for the enterprise. Again Engels's treatment is very sparse, providing little discussion of the terms of the trade—what, for example, did the workers want? And what could the new bourgeois government give? Discussion of the pluralist bargaining, of the negotiation, is missing. This allows him to avoid an important conclusion—the new government was not able to pay off its presumed allies. They were certainly not able to pay off the workers with money, with increased wages; as good liberals concerned with eliminating fetters, they were not about to restore guild privileges. Where Engels is arguing that they had positive options, that they could have saved the situation, his vague calls for decisive action hide the actual options facing them. The only area in which they could have taken decisive action was the political sphere, by taking control of the military and of the police. Engels, it appears, wished the bourgeoisie had used force; the *imposition* of their plans was the appropriate course of action. But that, of course, again assumes they wanted to take power. It assumes they would have seen their interests enhanced by such a bold move.

The failure of 1848, in Engels's view, was a function of the weakness of the bourgeoisie, too small in numbers and too timid in execution of its task; the revolutionary coalition, as a consequence, fell apart and dissolved. The situation is summarized as follows:

> It was, in fact, evident, even from the beginning of the revolutionary drama, that the Liberal bourgeoisie could not hold its ground against the vanquished, but not destroyed, feudal and bureaucratic parties except by relying upon the assistance of the popular and more advanced parties; and that it equally required, against the torrent of these more advanced masses, the assistance of the feudal nobility and of the bureaucracy. Thus, it was clear enough that the bourgeoisie in Austria and Prussia did not possess sufficient strength to maintain their power, and to adapt the institutions of the country to their own wants and ideas. The Liberal bourgeois ministry was only a halting-place from which, according to the turn circumstances might take, the country would either have to go on to the more advanced stage of Unitarian Republicanism, or to relapse into the old clerico-feudal and bureaucratic regime.

What eventuated, obviously, was a relapse. But the 1848 events, Engels assures his readers, was but the first act of the revolutionary drama. Given the same causes, the same tendencies, the next act would find a larger, more aware, and more confident bourgeoisie—and a weaker feudal-clerical-bureaucratic monarchical regime. The work ends with the assurance that soon, after "probably [a] very short interval of rest," we shall see the "beginning of the second act of the movement."[32]

Preface to
The Peasant War in Germany

That second act was obviously delayed, and thus, some years later, an explanation was needed. One such account appears in a brief preface to the second edition of Engels's *The Peasant War in Germany*. In his original preface, written in 1850, he had spoken of Germany's "modern big bourgeoisie" and had claimed this class was "quickly subjugating" the princes of Germany by means of the state debt. By 1870, when Engels wrote the second preface, it was clear that such was not the case, and he therefore reversed his position, indicating now that "too much honour was given to the German bourgeoisie." It could have quickly subjugated the monarchy "by means of the State debt" but failed to use the opportunity.[33]

Describing first the recent Austrian events, he says that nation "fell as a boon into the lap of the bourgeoisie after the war of 1866." But then, he adds, "the bourgeoisie does not understand how to govern. It is powerless and incapable in everything." Turning to Prussia, he discusses the constitutional struggle there in which Bismarck had recently subjugated the Prussian legislature. Again the bourgeoisie, although possessing a majority in the chamber, did not move to take control. Engels does not wish to blame the "National Liberals" for this collapse; they, after all, had been forsaken by their clientele, by "the mass of the bourgeoisie." That mass, it seems, "does not wish to govern. 1848 is still in its bones."[34]

Although some advances of bourgeois interests were made in the intervening period, this was all "within limits befitting bureaucracy." This "system of bureaucratic concessions," incidentally, is described as "the main evil." The source of the problem, once again, is not the previously dominant class, the aristocracy; it is, rather, "the government." One of the principal tasks of the new preface is to explain and to account for cowardice: "How, then, is it possible that the bourgeoisie has not conquered political power, that it behaves in so cowardly a manner toward the government?"[35]

The explanation, he declares, is that the German bourgeoisie is a latecomer on the scene. Its "period of ascendency" coincides with the "downward path" of the bourgeoisie in "other western European" countries, that is, England and France. In England, one is told (as was noted earlier, in Chapter 2), that "the bourgeoisie could place its real representative, Bright, into the government only by extending the franchise which in the long run is bound to put an end to its very domination." In France, he reports, "the bourgeoisie, which for two years only, 1849–50, had held power as a class under the republican regime, was able to continue its social existence only by transferring its power to Louis Bonaparte and the army."[36] The basic problem is that the growth of the bourgeoisie entails the growth of the proletariat. It is fear of the proletariat, first clearly recognized in 1848 in the June Days in Paris, that causes the hesitation, that leads the bourgeoisie to reject its historic mission.

Sensing the threat, recognizing the presence of the proletariat, of this "second self" that has outgrown it, the bourgeoisie "loses the power for exclusive political dominance." At this point, Engels announces, the bourgeoisie "looks for allies *with whom to share its authority, or to whom to cede all power, as circumstances may demand*" (emphasis added). The point is summed up as follows:

> In Germany, this turning point came for the bourgeoisie as early as 1848. The bourgeoisie became frightened, not so much by the German, as by the French proletariat. The battle of June, 1848, in Paris, showed the bourgeoisie what could be expected. The German proletariat was restless enough to prove to the bourgeoisie that the seed of revolution had been sown also in German soil. From that day, the edge of bourgeois political action was broken. The bourgeoisie looked around for allies. It sold itself to them regardless of price, and there it remains.
>
> These allies are all of a reactionary turn. It is the king's power, with his army and his bureaucracy; it is the big feudal nobility; it is the smaller Junker; it is even the clergy. The bourgeoisie has made so many compacts and unions with all of them to save its dear skin, that now it has nothing more to barter. And the more the proletariat developed, the more it began to feel as a class and to act as one, the feebler became the bourgeoisie.[37]

Once again we see a remarkable revisionist portrait, even more of a deviation than the previous ones reviewed. Again we see the need for a coalition of forces, for negotiation and concession. Once again, in other words, we find this other, this pluralist Marxism. But this time, going a significant step farther down the revisionist road, we have a bourgeoisie that has given up the demand for power, that now, because of an assortment of deals, is no longer capable of taking power. Power must now be shared with a collection of allies.

Engels next considers the German proletariat. He reviews various indicators to show the growth of proletarian consciousness. The working class of Germany, Engels notes, is more advanced than its counterparts elsewhere. "It is to the credit of the German workers," he writes, "that *they alone* have managed to send workers and workers' representatives into the Parliament—a feat which neither the French nor the English had hitherto accomplished." But this class forms only a minority of the German people, and, as a consequence, it too is "compelled to seek allies." The only possible allies are the petty bourgeoisie, the *Lumpenproletariat* of the cities, the small peasants, and the wage workers of the land. The remainder of the preface is devoted to discussion of each of these possibilities.

The petty bourgeoisie, master artisans, and merchants remain unchanged, Engels writes. "They hope to climb up to the big bourgeoisie, and they are fearful lest they be pushed down into the ranks of the proletariat. Between fear and hope, they will in times of struggle seek to save their precious skin and to join the victors when the struggle is over. Such is their nature." The basic point is repeated later: The class is "entirely unreliable except when a victory has been won. Then its noise in the beer saloons is without limit." Engels's only positive statement about this class is that "there are good elements among it, who, of their own accord, follow the workers." Of the several options delineated earlier, the vacillation thesis is now given the principal emphasis.[38]

The *Lumpenproletariat* once again comes in for unrelieved condemnation: "This scum of the decaying elements of all classes, which establishes headquarters in all the big cities, is the worst of all possible allies. It is an absolutely venal, an absolute brazen crew." Any working-class leader making use of these "gutter-proletarians," he declares, "proves himself by this action alone a traitor to the movement."

Turning to the farm populations, Engels here makes two changes in his portrayal. In *Revolution and Counter-Revolution*, it will be remembered, the more wealthy farmers, the *Gross* and *Mittel-Bauern*, were treated as a faction of "the great class of small farmers, the peasantry." That segment was allied with the "antifeudal middle class of the towns." In the preface, they are reclassified. The "bigger peasants," Engels notes, in a brief parenthetical statement, "belong to the bourgeoisie." He later refers to "middle and large land ownership" and, along with "the large peasants," to the "still larger feudal masters" but does not explicitly classify them. Following the logic of the parenthetical statement, however, they too must "belong to the bourgeoisie." The second change comes in Engels's delineation of four subgroups of "small peasants"— those "in serfdom," persons "bound to their lords and masters"; feudal tenants; smallholders; and farm laborers. The category of serfs has been added to the three outlined nearly two decades earlier.

Little was said about the farm segments in that earlier account, it will be remembered, except that they can never proceed independently. They require the "initiatory impulse" of the "more enlightened" people of the towns. Here, with complete consistency, he details and recommends just such an impulse: it is the workers' major task. The paragraphs are remarkable in that they give such extended attention to the *Agrarfrage* (the farm question). The choices of those populations are treated here as key to the subsequent historical development.

Since the bourgeoisie has "failed to do its duty" by the "serfs," that is, to free them from serfdom, it should not be difficult to convince them that "salvation" can come "only from the working class." As for the feudal tenants, their situation, he reports, is "almost equal to that of the Irish." With high rents and uncertain yields, they are left entirely at the mercy of the landlords; the bourgeoisie provides relief only under compulsion. Where, he asks, "should the tenants look for relief outside of the workers?" The third group of farmers, the smallholders, are also in desperate circumstances. Heavily indebted, they face the bourgeoisie directly; it is the "capitalist usurers" who "squeeze the lifeblood out of them." "It will be necessary to make clear to these people," Engels writes, "that only when a government of the people will have transformed all mortgages into a debt to the State, and thereby lowered the rent, will they be able to free themselves from the usurer. This, however, can be accomplished only by the working class."[39] The promise or tradeoff in this case, rather unexpectedly, is that the working class will undertake, somehow, to rescue this segment of the petty bourgeoisie.

The "wage-workers of the land," the agricultural proletariat, appear "wherever middle and large land ownership prevails." In those areas, they "form the most numerous class." It is here, Engels claims, that the urban workers "find their most numerous and natural allies." Engels sees this group as pivotal for the subsequent historical development. His final sentences read:

The agricultural proletariat, the wage-workers of the land, is the class from which the bulk of the armies of the princes is being recruited. It is the class which, thanks to universal suffrage, sends into Parliament the great mass of feudal masters and Junkers. However, it is also the class nearest to the industrial workers of the city. It shares their conditions of living, and it is still deeper steeped in misery than the city workers. This class, powerless because split and scattered, but possessing a hidden power which is so well known to the government and nobility that they purposely allow the schools to deteriorate in order that the rural population should remain unenlightened, must be called to life and drawn into the movement. *This is the most urgent task of the German labour movement.* From the day when the mass of the workers of land have learned to understand their own interests, a reactionary, feudal, bureaucratic or bourgeois government in Germany becomes an impossibility.[40]

This last recommendation is almost Tocquevillian in its call to educate likely allies to remove them from the opposing coalition and to bring them into the ranks of the progressive forces. An important breakthrough has occurred in this discussion: farm segments have been treated as significant political actors worthy of attention.

The formulation in this preface has serious implications for the larger Marxian theory. History, according to that theory, unfolds dialectically. The proletariat, it will be remembered, is formed in opposition to the bourgeoisie; its consciousness is formed in the process of struggle with the dominant class. Although, as noted, modern history opens with a complicated heritage of classes and institutions (all of that obscured by outmoded or misleading ideologies), a vast simplification results when the bourgeoisie comes to power and creates its "historically necessary" institutional arrangements. That simplification, in turn, facilitates the development of working-class consciousness as the implications of bourgeois rule become ever-more transparent, open, and obvious. That is the meaning of the frequently used term "unveiling."

But what is one to make of this new argument? If things develop as Engels now claims, that entire line of argument would have to be either abandoned or seriously reworked. With power dispersed among a wide range of allies, the polar confrontation of opposites would not occur. The enemy could not be defined simply as the bourgeoisie, since all groups in the conservative coalition would be part of the problem. Given that sharing of power, one should expect compromise policies among those various segments; Engels says just that in his statement about sharing authority with allies as circumstances demand. One result would be disadvantage for bourgeois interests; it would mean the possibility, the likelihood even, of retained, reinstituted, or new fetters hampering the development of capitalist production and accumulation. And if the bourgeoisie does not develop as predicted, if it does not do the things anticipated, would the proletariat experience its predicted dialectical development?

With government policies reflecting a plurality of interests, the targets for working-class resentments would accordingly also become rather diverse. The social processes, in short, would be such as to complicate things, or to reverse the cliché, they would re-veil those events. One alternative for the workers, possibly, if suitably guided, would be to target the entire system. If no longer facing a clearly defined bourgeois opponent, the workers might focus on the entire reactionary-feudal-bureaucratic-monarchical-bourgeois government. But another problem arises with this revisionism. If the bourgeoisie can make deals with such a wide range of groups, if it no longer requires total control, what would stop it from making deals with the proletariat, in whole or in part? Why would it not, for example, provide various welfare programs, thus rewarding workers and generating thereby a sense of gratitude or loyalty? Engels's formulations here, his raising of the pluralist option, makes clear that choice is involved. He has thereby erased the supposed necessity of the Marx-Engels argument; a new voluntarism and, hence, a new element of contingency has made its appearance.

Engels's final point is also of considerable importance, although it is largely neglected in comment and assessment of the German case: he has introduced and emphasized the importance of the *Agrarfrage*. It is a question of extraordinary importance, the proletariat of any nation being formed, for the most part, of ex-farmers or children of farmers. How one addresses farmers, before their "fall" into the working class, might well determine their later responses. The simplest alternatives are that one could make friends of them or one could turn them into enemies. Engels, at this point, recognized the importance of the issue, but there was to be little subsequent follow-through. The German Social Democrats took up the issue and discussed it again in 1895. But the handling of the question was disastrous; the issue, in effect, was tabled. The next serious discussion of the *Agrarfrage* came in 1927, when it was too late to gain the favor of Germany's farmers.

The Addendum to the Preface

Apparently sensing some problem with his 1870 statement, Engels wrote a brief addendum in 1874 for the third edition of *The Peasant War*. Here one finds still another portrait of German class relations and the dynamics of their development. The Prussian victories of 1870 and the unification of 1871, by adding millions of non-Prussian Germans, have transformed things, displacing "the entire foundation of the Prussian State edifice." The "Junker dominance," one learns, had become ever-more intolerable, even for the government itself. This is the first time, it will be noted, that the Junkers are said to be dominant in the Prussian government. In *Revolution and Counter-Revolution* he states explicitly that they had been deprived of power. Now one learns that the monarchy was maintaining an equilibrium in the struggle between nobility and bourgeoisie. The monarchy, he declares, was "protecting the nobility against the onslaught of the bourgeoisie." But then, sensing the more serious threat of proletarian revolution and the threat to all forms of property, the monarchy has taken the task of "protecting all propertied classes against the onslaught of the working-class." The most convenient arrangement for this purpose was a "Bonapartist monarchy." The Junker, he reports, is gradually losing his "feudal privileges." Slowly, belatedly, he "is forcibly being transformed into something akin to the English squire," essentially a bourgeois, market-oriented farmer, a businessman just like any other.

The character of the arrangement, the tacit agreement, is simple: The government "reforms the laws at a snail pace tempo in the interests of the bourgeoisie; it removes the impediments to industry"; and, on the other hand, the bourgeoisie "leaves in the hands of the government all actual political power. . . . The bourgeoisie buys its gradual social emancipation for the price of immediate renunciation of its own political power." The bourgeoisie, in short, abandons its historical political mission. It is, as indicated, a major deviation from the main line of the Marx-Engels framework. Although the bourgeoisie proves "miserable" in the political realm, it does, nevertheless, perform its task in the economic realm. "As far as industry and commerce are concerned," Engels declares, the bourgeoisie "fulfils its historic duty." The class itself has developed, so that "at last we have world trade, a really big industry, and a really modern bourgeoisie." And that means, simultaneously, "a truly mighty proletariat." The remaining paragraphs of this brief article are focused on the workers, providing an encomium, a brief comparative study, and some words on the immediate practical tasks.[41]

German workers, it seems, came through the Franco-Prussian War with flying colors: "Not a trace of national chauvinism made itself manifest among them. . . . In no country have the workers stood such a difficult test with such splendid results." The working-class parties came under considerable attack and, in the years immediately following, arrests, imprisonment, and general harassment were regular occurrences. Despite the onslaught, however, in the elections of January 1874, the party came through with a victory "unique in the history of the modern labor movement."[42]

Two principal reasons are given for this success, the first of these being that German workers "belong to the most theoretical people of Europe." We are told they retain "that sense of theory which the so-called 'educated' people of Germany have totally lost. Without German philosophy, particularly that of Hegel, German scientific Socialism (the only scientific Socialism extant) would never have come into existence. Without a sense for theory, scientific Socialism would have never become blood and tissue of the workers. What an enormous advantage this is, may be seen on the one hand from the indifference of the English labour movement towards all theory, which is one of the reasons why it moves so slowly."[43] Workers in France and Belgium, by contrast, suffer from the "mischief and confusion" created by Proudhonism. Worse still, the Spanish and Italian workers suffer from Proudhonism in its "caricature form" presented by Bakunin.

This argument, one might note, appears burdened with more than a trace of national chauvinism. At the same time, it points to the role of those bourgeois intellectuals who break away from their own class and provide enlightenment for the otherwise untutored workers. That focus on "the most theoretical people of Europe," that emphasis on a cultural factor, deviates from the strict materialist theory of history. It might be that there is some economic explanation for the theoretical character of the Germans, for the atheoretical character of the English, and for the mistaken-theoretical character of those Latin peoples. The argument, however, if there is one, is not spelled out. As it stands, it is purely cultural; the differences depend on the national tutors, whether Bakunin and Proudhon or Hegel, Marx, and Engels.

A second reason for the preeminent position of the German working class is the factor of sequence. This group arrives after the earlier English and French developments; it has developed "on the shoulders of" the English and French movements. Utilizing that prior experience, the German movement has been able to avoid others' mistakes. The end result is that the German workers now "form the vanguard of the proletarian struggle." That 1874 conclusion, it will be noted, was foreseen earlier in the *Manifesto* passage cited in the opening chapter.

A discussion of the tasks facing the workers follows. The "specific duty of the leaders," Engels states, is to "gain an ever clearer understanding of the theoretical problems, to free themselves more and more from the influence of traditional phrases inherited from the old conception of the world, and constantly to keep in mind that Socialism, having become a science, demands the same treatment as every other science—it must be studied." A further task for those leaders is "to bring [that] understanding . . . to the working masses." This part of the directive, borrowing a term from later discussion, is Leninist in character. Another task assigned those leaders is not at all Leninist: it is to undertake electoral activity. The task, Engels declares, is "to wrest from the enemy's hands one city, one electoral district after the other." The farm question, so heavily emphasized in the 1870 introduction, here, curiously, receives only a single sentence: "Encouraging as may be the successes of the propaganda among the rural population, more remains to be done in this field."[44]

The explanation for the sudden, though temporary, interest in the *Agrarfrage* in 1870 may be found in the topical issues then under discussion in the European left. The International Workingmen's Association met in Basel in September 1869. Then under Marx's direction, the delegates had passed a resolution affirming the "right and duty" of society to collectivize privately owned farm properties. This posed a problem for the Social Democratic Workers' Party (SDAP) of Liebknecht and Bebel. If the resolution was accepted, it would mean a break with their left liberal, middle-class allies in the German People's Party. It would also, Liebknecht recognized, make it difficult for them to campaign among the small farmers. He at first opposed acceptance, but then, sensing the tide of opinion within the party, came out in favor of acceptance, even writing a pamphlet to justify the move. Expropriation of major landowners presented no problem; that was clearly in order. Liebknecht recognized the need for a positive approach to the small farmers. He argued that education should be used to persuade them "to renounce their property." At the SDAP congress in June 1870, the resolution carried easily. The event was decisive for both party and nations. Liberals and the left, from then on, went separate paths. That the *Agrarfrage* was central for Engels in 1870 ("the most urgent task of the German labour movement") but worth only a passing mention in 1874, suggests that the concern reflected immediate tactical needs rather than the more lasting requirements of a scientific theory.[45]

Conclusions

Two sets of conclusions follow: the first deals with the classes, the second with larger issues, of method and theory.

The bourgeoisie, not too surprisingly, occupies a central position in all five analyses reviewed here. This class, meaning here the *haute* (or *grande*) bourgeoisie—big business, the owner of the major capitalist enterprises— receives serious discussion in all five accounts and is assigned some major role in all of them. A decisive shift of position appears with respect to the major aim or task of this class; that is the first of our conclusions. In the first three accounts, written at mid-century, the bourgeoisie aspires to take power; that is its major historic mission. The accounts of the 1870s, however, give another portrait, in which the German bourgeoisie abandons its task. It is then willing, anxious even, to share power with other groups through a series of trades or deals designed to save its skin. By 1874, it is portrayed as happy to leave power with the monarchy, that agency providing the vehicle for balancing the demands of the major property-holding classes of Germany.

This new portrait constitutes a significant deviation from what might be termed the main line of Marxist thought, which, as stated in the *Manifesto*, holds that the "executive of the modern State is but a committee for managing the common affairs of the whole bourgeoisie." In this new version, it becomes a committee for managing the common affairs of several classes. This might well be termed the first of the many subsequent revisionism efforts. The key elements of this new direction are the abandonment of the historical mission and the substitution of what might be called the pluralist settlement. These accounts, actually little more than brief preliminary sketches, provide two different portraits: in one, the bourgeoisie itself negotiates the plural settlement or the power sharing; in the other, the monarchy works out the arrangements. Marx, it should be noted, was alive and well at this point. Engels was living in London at this time, and the two met regularly for extended discussion of their many common concerns. We have no indication that Marx objected to these new formulations.

Although these works are intended to support the scientific socialist perspective, one key aspect of the bourgeoisie's behavior, its abandonment of the historical mission, is explained in terms of a character failing: it is due to cowardice. But if bravery-versus-cowardice is to be the decisive factor, history will lose its determinant character; it no longer follows a "necessary" pattern. The German bourgeoisie, so it is claimed, saw the implications of the workers' rising in Paris in June 1848 and accordingly decided to arrange its affairs differently, in effect, leaving government to someone else. That character failing, that cowardly behavior, however, appears as such only from the perspective—from the *logic*—of the Marx-Engels position. Members of the bourgeoisie, who were very much occupied with the management of their growing enterprises, appear to have been satisfied to leave government to others, as was the case in Britain. From *their* perspective, acceptance of the current arrangement may have been the logical, the best, or the most appropriate conclusion.

The second conclusion involves the proletariat, the most consistently portrayed of all the classes; it received serious attention in all five accounts. It is consistently said to be developing in numbers and in consciousness. Its aim is invariably given as revolutionary; its goal is to take power. No suggestion appears anywhere in these accounts of a reformist tendency within the working class; the argument of the later revisionism associated with Eduard Bernstein does not appear here. The portrait of the workers is clear, consistent, and unambiguous. This is the case even though its dialectical opposite, the bourgeoisie, does not perform as expected. The bourgeoisie's exercise of political power in its own interests would precipitate clashes with the workers and would unveil the entire process. Although a key cause is absent, Engels nevertheless affirms the consequence, the growth of working-class consciousness. A key task—reconsideration of the causal dynamics—has been avoided.

The *Lumpenproletariat* is the subject of the third conclusion: it receives very little attention, a trace in "The Status Quo," a paragraph in the *Manifesto*, and one in the preface. It is ignored in the remaining two accounts. Where mentioned, the accounts are entirely consistent—this is a dangerous class. The reason for the spare treatment is easily established: the *Lumpenproletariat* plays no role whatsoever in Engels's discussion of the German developments. Its only role is, so to speak, offstage, in Paris during the June Days. That event provides merely a cautionary reminder, something for German workers and their leaders to keep in mind. The repeated mention of a class that plays no role is rather puzzling. The references to the *Lumpenproletariat* have an almost ritualistic character; it is part of the standard litany.

The petty bourgeoisie, the subject of the fourth conclusion, receives serious attention in four of the five accounts (it is missing entirely from the brief addendum). Within the context of modern society, the class is consistently portrayed as having "lost its place." It has no proper function, no task that it performs well that could provide the basis for a satisfactory existence or for political power. With respect to predictions of effects, of consequences, however, the petty bourgeoisie is the most inconsistently portrayed of all the classes; an extraordinary range of options is announced. It is in alliance with the nobility and is in process of backing away from that alliance. It is portrayed as a class for itself, as one pursing distinctive reactionary goals. It is said to support whichever class provides rewards. It is said to fight against the bourgeoisie; it is said to submit itself to the bourgeoisie. It is said to be vacillating, to be opportunistic, identifying first with one side, then with another, depending on which seems to be the winner. Some factions are said to identify with workers in the developing struggle. The petty bourgeoisie is a wild card in Engels's deck. No serious evidence is offered to support any of these diverse claims; they are merely declared. Table 2 attempts to summarize this diversity.

Two possibilities, it will be noted, do not appear in this list. The easiest prediction of all, especially in the age of liberalism, would be that of individual responses. A myriad of rational, calculating individuals could develop scores of options yielding a diversity that would defy easy categorization. While easily conceived (and easily defended), this possibility does not appear in the Marx-Engels repertory. Their predictions involve sweeping categorical judgments; the class as a whole, or at best, a couple of "fractions" of the class, will react as collectivities. Given the categorical preference, it is remarkable that one such

Table 2. Predictions Made about the Petty Bourgeoisie

Work	Predictions
"Status Quo"	1. Stage One: The richer urban segment joins with the revolutionary bourgeoisie; the poorer rural segment joins with the nobles. 2. Stage Two: The poorer segment joins with the bourgeoisie. 3. Stage Three: Unconditional surrender; puts itself under command of the bourgeoisie; a few concessions and it is conservative.
Manifesto	4. All fractions fight against the bourgeoisie to save their middle-class existence; they are reactionary (i.e., a class for itself). 5. Some, by chance, adopt the standpoint of the proletariat.
Revolution and Counter-Revolution	6. Extreme vacillation; shifting alliances, none of them clear parallels to foregoing claims.
Preface	7. Extreme vacillation; allies itself with winners. 8. Some good elements follow workers. (One line—same as no. 5 above.)
Addendum	No mention

response is also among the neglected possibilities: some "fractions" might conceivably retain traditional ties or loyalties. One possibility, especially important in the German context, would be the religious factor. But religion, where mentioned, is viewed as a derived phenomenon and as one destined to lose significance. In the final analysis, it is treated as having no importance.

In one respect, these portraits of the petty bourgeoisie display a remarkable consistency: in all of them the petty bourgeoisie is shown in extremely negative, unflattering, derogatory terms. The class is consistently denigrated or, to use the language of our age, it is consistently put down. The petty bourgeoisie, in this extension of the basic litany, is capable of no good; worthwhile, elevated, idealistic, or decent actions are not to be expected from this segment of society.

The fifth conclusion involves the farmers. This collection of "fractions" is described as a class in three of the five analyses. In one account, in the *Manifesto*, "the peasant" is included in a list of petty bourgeois occupations. The portrayals, in general, closely parallel those of the petty bourgeoisie. The farm populations are not quite so insistently denigrated as the petty bourgeoisie, although the principal tendency is clearly negative as, for example, in the *Manifesto* remark about the "idiocy of rural life." The consistent emphasis here is on their incapacity. Because of their territorial dispersal, they cannot initiate or carry through any serious historical movement. This claim is puzzling because, as was noted, it is clearly contrary to fact for the German states in 1848. The claim can be supported only by withholding evidence of widespread rural insurgency. The comments about the farm populations generally focus on the passivity of the farmers; they also point to the long-term historical tendency, to their impending "fall" into the proletariat. Only in the 1870 preface is there discussion of the needs of farmers and the kinds of appeals that socialists should make in order to gain their support. At that point, a strong "voluntarist" emphasis appears, stimulated, presumably, by the issues then under discussion in left circles. When no longer a current theme, the farmers were again treated with characteristic indifference.

Only one of the five texts reveals a simple fact—that the farm population was the largest single segment of German society. Those persons employed in farming and forestry made up more than half, actually 55 percent, of the employed population of Germany in 1852.[46] In 1871, when Engels was writing his later contributions, those groups had declined somewhat, to 49 percent of the total. The absolute number of persons so employed increased in that period. The numbers continued to increase up to World War I, although, to be sure, the relative decline continued.

We have no precise comparable measure of the size of the urban proletariat. Those employed in industry and handwork taken together with those in mining formed 25 percent in 1852 and only 29 percent in 1872. That category, however, includes artisans (part of the petty bourgeoisie) as well as managers, professionals, and clerical workers in industry. Some workers, to be sure, would be found elsewhere (e.g., in transport, in banks, in insurance firms, and linked to the military). It seems unlikely, were one able to reassemble the categories, that the proletariat would have formed as much as one-third of the labor force even in the early seventies.

A sixth conclusion involves what might be termed the missing agency. The reference is to the regimes, to the monarchs heading the states, and to the bureaucracy, the civil service, and the military—the principal instrumentalities of those regimes. The writings of Marx and Engels display a general reluctance to focus on governments and their personnel. One might hazard the guess that "the bureaucracy" in those decades would be as important quantitatively as either the nobility or the bourgeoisie. In terms of political importance—the ability to make things happen (or to prevent their happening)—monarchs and their bureaucracies would be more important than those minuscule classes. The importance of the regimes is indicated by Engels himself, who describes both nobility and bourgeoisie as not in power. Although the regimes are not part of his central framework, Engels does find it necessary, in later discussion, to fill in, to provide his readers with an ad hoc sketch. The regimes, therefore, as indicated, have a phantom existence in these works. The ad hoc treatment is all the more remarkable since the regime (along with an assortment of allies) is *the* antagonist in the struggles being described. The alliance of "rising" and disaffected classes (or factions thereof) is after all contending with a government—not with a ruling *class* such as, for example, the aristocracy.

A regime, especially a monarchical one, does not fit into the basic analysis, with the claim of *class* struggle as the constant in all hitherto existing societies. Kings and other monarchs, dukes, electors, barons, and so on, are not classes. To focus on them means, unavoidably, to focus on the role of individuals—on their whims, fancies, and idiosyncrasies. One cannot avoid that reality. To do so, it would be necessary, for example, to assert that it made no difference to Prussia whether the monarch was Frederick II (called the Great) or Frederick William II (his successor, the king during the first years of the French Revolution). It would, in short, be necessary to reduce the significance of these individuals to zero. In practice, however, Engels does not do that. He brings in discussion of individuals when needed, of Frederick William IV, for example, and provides long descriptive passages about their importance. Engels is obviously having it both ways. He announces his "new" historiographic rules in the first paragraphs of *Revolution and Counter-Revolution*: The "causes . . . are not to be sought for in the accidental efforts, talents, faults, errors, or treacheries of some of the leaders." But later, as if he were a student of Leopold von Ranke, he portrays the king's foibles at length and attributes to them a decisive role in generating the subsequent events.[47]

The treatment of the bureaucracy is equivocal. In "The Status Quo," it is referred to as a class. But it does not easily fit with the basic Marxian portraiture of exploiting and exploited classes. This segment is "something else," not easily placed in terms of its "relationship to the means of production." The few comments or observations made about this class are again ad hoc in character. The basic procedure is to suggest its derivation from other classes, as if the policy preferences found in the bureaucracy would reflect those origins elsewhere. But then, here and there, one finds an important alternative, that the bureaucracy might have a direction or an interest of its own.[48] It could also, on occasion, move against the interests of those other classes. The bureaucracy, in several contexts, is portrayed as moving against the interests of the aristocracy, even though it is staffed, especially in the leading positions, by persons of aristocratic origin. There is ample historical justification for this claim and, one might add, a good explanation for it. The requirements of one's current position might easily override the training and influences associated with a person's origin. One might well develop new loyalties, especially where all major rewards (e.g., money, prestige, advancement) depend on performance in the bureaucracy.[49] The choice of liberal over aristocratic values was aided by some of the lessons of Adam Smith and the classical economists taught in the universities. The universities, it should be noted, were (and still are) part of the larger category, that is, of the bureaucracy.

Like the previously discussed division of the bourgeoisie into two subcategories, big and little, most discussions of the bureaucracy prove to be remarkably crude. Governments in continental Europe in the nineteenth century typically contained a foreign ministry, a finance ministry, a police agency, a justice ministry, a cultural ministry (attending to religion and education), and, last but not least, a war ministry. Many complexities were involved, such as differences in background, in subsequent training, and in loyalties and interest, complexities not in any way captured by a simple reference to the bureaucracy. Any serious intellectual contribution must recognize that underlying complexity and must, at minimum, consider some detailed hypotheses. The minimum requirement, as in the present case, is to signal doubt as to the adequacy of the crude, all-encompassing formula. With no serious analysis of the monarchy or of the bureaucracy, it follows that the relationship between the two will also be neglected.

We have a simple possibility: strong monarchs dominate their bureaucracies, making them instruments of their policies; weak, indifferent, ineffectual, or lackadaisical monarchs show little interest in ruling and hence allow their bureaucracies considerable autonomy. Frederick the Great, as long as his health allowed, dominated his bureaucracy. His successors, three indifferent Frederick Williams, in one way or another allowed their bureaucracies considerable latitude. It would be a mistake to read the result as bureaucratic determinism. The key consideration was the orientation or zeal of the monarch. At a later point, when William II, the last kaiser, chose to conduct his own foreign policy, he did so, regularly overriding his foreign ministry in the process.[50]

The seventh conclusion addresses the question of Marx and Engels's method. The five works in question show an extraordinary flexibility in their treatment of the classes. Borrowing a musical image, these works, produced over a quarter of a century, appear to be extemporizations, creations of the moment designed to explain events as they had unfolded to that point. It would be a mistake, remaining with the musical image, to see them as free inventions; they are obviously constrained, bound by some rules that limited their development. It would be more appropriate, therefore, to see them as variations on a theme. The basic theme, of course, is that of class. The classes under discussion show a relative constancy over the period from 1847 to 1874 (see Table 3). A wider range of variation appears, as indicated in the previous conclusions, in the specific treatments, that is, in the claims made about the consciousness, the quantitative and qualitative development, the outlooks, and the internal cohesion of the various classes.

One might argue that this flexibility represents growth or development, in which case the diversity might be seen as the normal or expected occurrence in a scientific enterprise. But that is not the case. Growth refers to something added, something stemming from a previous state or condition. The new shoot grows out of the branch which, in turn, grows out of the trunk of the tree. But the new variations in this case do not have that kind of organic connection to the previous exposition; they constitute new starts not suggested or in any way foreshadowed in the previous work. No new insight is provided into the logic of the previous argument such as would mandate a change of position. Nor is new evidence presented (for example, on the motivations or outlooks of the lower middle class) such as would force modification of a previous claim. The appropriate terms then are consistency and

Table 3. Class/Agency Discussed

| | Marx-Engels's Work | | | | |
| | "Status Quo" | *Manifesto* | *Revolution* | Preface | Addendum |
Class/agency	(1847)	(1848)	(1851)	(1870)	(1874)
Nobility	X[1]	T	X	X	X
Industrial landowners	T				
Farmers	X	T[2]	X	X	
Monarchy and/or bureaucracy	X		X	X	X
Bourgeoisie	X	X	X	X	X
Petty bourgeoisie	X	X	X	X	
Proletariat	X	X	X	X	X
Lumpenproletariat	T	X		X	
Number of discussions	6	4	6	7	4

[1] An "X" signifies an important discussion, in most instances one of at least paragraph length. A "T" (for Trace) signifies a passing reference, usually a sentence or two. The total given in the bottom line is for Xs only. This table, it should be noted, does not include the radical intellectuals or the military.

[2] The farmers here are counted with the petty bourgeoisie.

inconsistency, not growth and development. The procedure is declamation, not discovery. No attempt at reconciliation of the different versions is made. There is no recognition of the error of the previous claims nor, of course, are reasons given for the shifts of position. In short, positions are abandoned, and new ones are simply declared.

The conclusion may be stated analytically, that is, without the metaphor, as follows. The *Manifesto*, supposedly, states the general Marx-Engels position. It provides the basic outline of the larger framework. That outline cannot deal with the multiplicity of events occurring within a given nation in any episode of its current development. To account for such episodes, some additional study and analysis are required. If the general framework is adequate, appropriate, or correct, it should provide the guidelines for those detailed analyses. The proof of the integrity of the intellectual system would appear in the links made between the general position and the specific historical analyses. If one is in fact dealing with a consistent framework, then the principal conclusions of the general scheme should appear, clearly supported, in the specific studies. The latter will unquestionably contain many supplemental lines of analysis and additional conclusions, but fundamental to the claim of unity would be the clear, unambiguous, integral role of the key general propositions.

Another proof of the integrity of the system would appear in the links between the specific analyses. The conclusions drawn at $Time_2$ should have a logical connection with those drawn at a previous $Time_1$. The subsequent conclusions should, ideally, indicate confirmation of the previous findings (showing either the identical pattern or a continuation of previously established trends). If, however, the conclusions shifted dramatically from one point to the next, those results would not demonstrate the logic, the power, or the usefulness of a consistent theoretical system. Error, to be sure, is always a possibility. A correction, an explanation of the earlier mistakes (for example, a mistaken derivation from the general scheme or an inadequate understanding of relevant fact), would attest to the usefulness of the original system. But the pattern found here, the succession of declarations and abandonments, points to an opposite direction. What one has is a nonsystematic procedure, a series of ad hoc extemporizations.

Another approach to the same problem involves the short-run versus the long-run distinction. The *Manifesto*, it is said, focuses on the entire capitalist epoch, that is, on the long-run development. The specific historical analyses deal with the short-run occurrences. The discussions of the short run will (of course) cover different terrain and have different specific contents. But this distinction does not avoid the objection contained in the above paragraph. The key propositions of the general analysis should still, somehow or other, be visible within the framework of the short-term analyses. The long term, after all, is the sum of a collection of short terms. If the long-term predictions are accurate, their reality (their coming-into-being) should be manifest in the short-term accounts. But in these instances, where Engels has contingency, personal interventions, royal willfulness, mentality factors, diverse options, and unforeseen coalitions, it is difficult to see how indeterminant short-run episodes will add up to a determinant long run. The opposite conclusion is more clearly appropriate: the short-run analyses undermine the claims of the long-term analysis.[51]

An eighth conclusion also involves method: the works make persistent use of attitudinal arguments. People in the same objective circumstances behave differently, the diversity being explained, again in an offhand way, with declarations of different outlooks or orientations. The nobility and the industrial landowners, for example, do the same thing—they have the same relationships to some means of production—but with sharply different outcomes. The difference is due to an attitude or outlook. On one dimension it is a matter of easygoing versus hard-driving work habits; on another it involves the choice of traditional versus modern farm technology. The result is a difference in rates of return—3 percent versus 15 percent—and, accordingly, changes in the relative positions of the two classes over the long term. The explanation is cultural (and, perhaps, social psychological) as opposed to the purely economic.

While from one perspective commendable (it demonstrates an openness to alternative lines of explanation), reference to such cultural arguments should appear as more than casual asides. The explanation should be stated explicitly and the implications explored. One should explore the sources of those cultural orientations (as Max Weber tried to do in his famous work on the Protestant ethic). One should also consider possible consequences. Economic structures, generally speaking, are givens; they are unalterable facts. Culture does not have that same fixed character. It is one of those things that can be changed. At its simplest, the wide-awake aristocrat could see his opportunity and could respond accordingly. He too could make use of the most advanced farm technology; he could also, of course, change his work habits. Bourgeois practice unveils possibilities for him also. Recognizing the substantial differences in rates of return, moreover, he would have considerable economic incentive to make those changes. The implication, of course, is that claims about outlooks make for much greater complexity; they allow for greater diversity in the range of possible historical development. History is no longer so narrowly determined as in the basic version of Marx and Engels's theory. New options for development—and for alliance—make their appearance, and again one is traveling on the road to conditional, contingent explanation.

Rather than follow their road consistently, in this respect, Marx and Engels operate on two levels, as with their treatment of the phantom agency. There is the basic theory, and then there is the ancillary theory, the latter appearing only in casual, offhand references. Although treated as not entirely presentable, the ancillary theory is a necessary adjunct to the basic position. It contains the range of additional or supplementary explanations that make the basic theory viable. That being the case, there is no excuse for not bringing the ancillary arguments up front, and incorporating them into the basic package. But were one to do that, the basic line of argument would itself be transformed. It would lose its distinctive character, no longer standing in sharp opposition to conventional or bourgeois analysis. It would no longer provide the unique, distinctive weapon for assault on the status quo. The world would once again become complicated, difficult to comprehend, and, more seriously, difficult to predict. None of the predictions, moreover, once encumbered by the contingencies of attitudinal outlooks, would have the same initial or surface plausibility they had in the basic version of the theory.

The ninth conclusion involves another of the submerged components of the Marx-Engels position. The invocation of attitudes, as noted, indicates a voluntarist component in the theory. That voluntarism, the role of will, of choice, of personal options, appears frequently in these works. The previous conclusion focused on presumed *existent* outlooks or preferences. But in other contexts Engels focuses on might have beens, on choices that, for one reason or another, were neglected. The most important of these appears in his discussion of the bourgeoisie, where its political task, taking power, was abandoned. The reason given, it will be remembered, was failure of nerve or, more precisely, cowardice.

That focus on character failure avoids the question of what Engels thinks they should have done. The negative judgment is clear—they did the wrong thing; the positive option is not spelled out clearly. Engels argues that the bourgeoisie could not have gone it alone in 1848; they needed allies. But there is no discussion of what they should have done to secure the support of those allies; he is, therewith, again withholding something. Either the argument is cryptopluralist or it is crypto—something else.

If one assumes the former, it is necessary to consider the options: What could be negotiated? But here it is clear that the bourgeoisie had little choice. At that point, inspired by laissez-faire doctrines, they were not about to create even a primitive welfare state so as to relieve working-class grievances. They were not about to offer debt forgiveness so as to gain the support of small farmers. Devoted to the inviolability of private property, they would not favor expropriation of large landholders so as to allow redistribution. They were not likely to respond to artisan demands by, say, reinstituting guild privileges, since they wanted to see free entry to all trades. It is not clear what they could have offered the rest of the petty bourgeoisie to protect them from the competition they themselves, the *haute* bourgeoisie, provided. The bourgeoisie, in brief, had virtually no negotiating options, at least none that they would have seen as acceptable. The pluralist option, tradeoffs for support, was not open to them.

That leaves the crypto—something else. What was it that Engels had in mind when he called for decisive action from the bourgeois leaders? The answer, no mystery surely, is that they should have taken over the instruments of the state, specifically the bureaucracy and the army. The lesson, put simply, was this: If they could not achieve their goals by negotiation, they should have imposed them by force. It is, in short, an early, though rather indirect, lesson in Leninism.[52]

Many find the logic of Marx and Engels's system compelling. They emphasize the consistency and durability of the framework. They claim brilliance, profundity, and penetrating insight on the part of the authors. In contrast, this review has found casual, easygoing procedure to be typical; there is infirm logic, many less-than-profound declarations, and a remarkable array of inconsistencies.

5

THE LESSONS

OF HISTORY

One of the most important lessons of history found in the Marxist analysis is the claim that modern capitalist nations have a tripartite class structure consisting of bourgeoisie, petty bourgeoisie, and workers (or proletariat). From the beginning, however, that formulation proved inadequate for both description and analysis of the complex events found in those nations.

Marx and Engels's analyses of capitalist societies centered on urban populations. Modern Industry was located in the large cities; it was there, accordingly, that the crucial class dynamics would occur. In an early formulation, Engels stated the point as follows:

> If the centralisation of population [in the great cities] stimulates and develops the owning classes, it drives forward even more rapidly the development of the workers. The workers begin to feel themselves as a class, as a whole. . . . The separation from the bourgeoisie [allows] the development of outlooks and ideas peculiar to the workers, corresponding to their position in life. The consciousness of oppression awakens and the workers attain social and political importance. The great cities are the birthplace of the working-class movement. In them, the workers first began to think about their condition, and to fight against it. In them, the opposition between proletariat and bourgeoisie first made itself manifest.[1]

Marx and Engels regularly exaggerated both the extent of the changes that had occurred in the capitalist societies and the pace of current developments.

Marx's analysis of the 1848 revolution in France, as we have seen, did not report the small shop, handicraft character of industry in the capital. Nor did Marx report that Paris, the principal setting for his history, contained only 3 percent of the nation's population. Only in passing, usually in isolated sentences, did those authors acknowledge that the farm populations still formed the majority in most of the countries they analyzed. Somehow or other, these populations had to be placed in the basic nomenclature. Basically, their continued presence was viewed as a passing event: the farm proprietors, most of them small farmers, were destined to lose out in competition with the large property holders and would fall into the proletariat. Farm laborers, of course, were already part of the proletariat. Both segments, in the end, would be forced into the cities and to jobs in Modern Industry. Their understanding (or consciousness) would then be transformed by the more transparent conditions and by contact with the advanced working-class majority. In the meantime, the farm populations were an inert factor; they had no decisive role to play in the unfolding historical struggle.

Marx and Engels recognized also that the bourgeoisie was not satisfactorily treated with that easy division into two components, *grande* and *petite*. Their analyses, accordingly, were regularly supplemented with discussions of divisions within those classes and of coalitions across class boundaries. Most of those analyses, as we have seen, depended on ad hoc declarations, actually guesses or hypotheses, about the behavior of the classes and of the various "fractions." When a given claim was no longer feasible, another was announced and put in its place. The presence of salaried white-collar workers also posed something of a problem. Although present from the beginning of modern times, most notably in governments, in the civil service they were largely neglected until the revisionist controversy of the 1890s.

One group within the population, the intellectuals, was given only peripheral attention. Two subgroups were delineated. The first consisted of spokesmen for various classes; they were treated as agents, conscious or unconscious, for some group or segment that was hidden behind the scenes. That subgroup, therefore, was easily assimilated to the basic analysis of the class structure. The second subgroup, however, the advanced or vanguard intellectuals, were portrayed as having a floating or baseless existence. In later literature, they were sometimes said to be free floating (*freischwebend*), an expression used by both Marxist and non-Marxist commentators. It is an unusual assumption for the social sciences which normally see the world as highly determined; one group is singled out and said to be above any such determination. When so baldly stated, the view is easily recognized as unacceptable. Few commentators, however, have pointed out the curiosity—that the productions of some intellectuals were being treated as an "uncaused cause." Few have critiqued the claim and declared it to be patently ridiculous. Just the opposite has been the case: the *freischwebend* image has been accepted by many intellectuals themselves as both a valid and a flattering portrait. They alone rise above the conditions affecting others in the society; they alone discover and reveal the higher truth.[2]

Another striking feature of the portraits of intellectuals is that their efforts are treated as epiphenomenal—they do not cause historical events to happen. At most, they retard the development (as with the ideological agents of conservative classes) or accelerate events (as with the vanguard). But in both instances, their contributions are viewed as secondary; they are not independent causal agents. The historical process, so it is said, is immanent, something moved by the material conditions of human existence. Intellectuals may comment on those basic conditions, but they do not create them; they are not the prime movers of history.[3]

There is, of course, another possibility, that intellectuals or groups of them might well cause events, that is, independently of any underlying economic structures. Recognition of that possibility, however, would mean one must leave the terrain of economically determined history and thus lose the (largely presumed) predictive power of the theory. This alternative, that intellectuals might play an independent causal role in historical events, would presumably be greatest where they acted (or campaigned) en bloc in support of a given program or direction.

The importance of this possibility was signaled by Engels at two points in his analysis of Germany in 1848. His discussion of the smaller states opens with a description of "a race of Liberal lawyers," these being the "professional oppositionists" found in the small assemblies (legislative bodies). These "talkative attorneys" (also described as traders "in politics and opposition") helped form the public opinion required for the subsequent uprising. The second causal factor indicated by Engels was "German literature" which, he says, "preached . . . a crude Constitutionalism, or a still cruder Republicanism." In a striking formulation, he declares that "poetry, novels, reviews, the drama, every literary production teemed with what was called 'tendency,' that is with more or less timed exhibitions of an anti-governmental spirit." At a later point, Engels argued a similar, although weaker, cultural influence in the Austrian context. All of this, incidentally, occurred in the face of repressive regimes with (presumably) heavy censorship.

That a collection of free and undetermined minds showed the same tendency, that they happened to float in the same direction, to opposition, is, to use a cliché, no accident. It means, of course, that they were not free floating but instead were subject to some undiscussed (and hence unexplored) determination. One might consider an analogy: If a coin came up heads in one hundred consecutive tosses, how many commentators would see that as an undetermined result, as the result of a free-float? There is, clearly, a suggestion of conformity (or groupthink) in the pattern reported by Engels. He saw "the habit" particularly among "the inferior sorts of literati," among those making up for "the want of cleverness in their productions."[4]

The critical examination of Marx and Engels's discussions of the classes has revealed many serious deficiencies. The classes and their roles are simply declared rather than established. Causal processes are also declared with both links and weights (importance) stipulated rather than researched. When subsequent events showed an analysis to be faulty, a new one was extemporized. Classes always occupy a central place in the analyses; in the a priori weighting, intellectuals always had a secondary or ancillary role. That was in keeping with their fundamental hypothesis, the primacy of material conditions as the determinant of history.

A more detailed review of the lessons about those classes or segments is appropriate, that review being the principal task of this chapter. The following categories will be considered: bourgeoisie (the *grande* or *haute* segment), petty bourgeoisie, workers, farmers, and intellectuals. The review will focus on substantive and methodological issues: it will consider both what has been said (what claims were made) and the procedures used to generate and support those claims. Later in the chapter, the questions considered in this work will be treated more generally. In the famous Weydemeyer letter, Marx summarized his specific contribution, the formulations there rising above any particular (or concrete) historical analysis. Those lessons too will be reviewed and assessed.

The Classes

The Bourgeoisie

The Marxist analysis of capitalist society begins with the bourgeoisie, the ruling class of the epoch. Marx's first historical monograph, *The Class Struggles in France*, opens with a discussion of that class in connection with the events of 1848. That analysis contains some instructive lessons. Marx began, it will be remembered, with a modification of his basic argument, delineating a cleavage within the rank and arguing that one segment, the industrial bourgeoisie, was now overthrowing the other, the finance aristocracy. This free and easy declaration foreshadows the style of analysis found throughout the work. The first and foremost task, research, some kind of documentation of the claim, is missing entirely. To validate the claim, an obvious first step would be definition: one must, in some way or other, indicate the boundaries of the bourgeois segments, industrial and financial. That done, it should be necessary to draw up a list—even if only illustrative or rule of thumb—of the key figures in each segment. This step, it may be noted, would be a simple elaboration of the direction signaled by Marx himself with his listing of Faucher, Grandin, and Bastiat as spokesmen for the insurgent faction. The third step would be to establish their views and to show what part they played in the events of February 1848. But even those tasks were neglected.

For that research, Marx would have had to rely largely on newspapers or on the reports of observers close to the events. Later commentators would have published memoirs as well as the documentation contained in archival sources. In Marx's account, the task of definition, as we have seen, was undertaken so carelessly as to involve patent errors and implausibilities that clearly required further explanation. The most obvious example, of course, was the inclusion of various industrial segments in his description of the finance aristocracy. The listing of actors—members of the respective segments—was also casual in the extreme. Apart from the problematical listing of the three spokesmen, no leaders of the insurgent industrial bourgeoisie are named. Marx mentions one leading figure in the finance aristocracy—the banker James Rothschild. Two simple questions arise: What was his attitude toward the events of 1848? And what role did he play? Marx provides no answers to those questions, although, as will be seen, they were easily available.

A recent biography of James Rothschild, written by a descendant, Anke Muhlstein, provides some basic information. Rothschild, head of the family's Paris operations, was intimately involved with the Louis Philippe regime, providing financial services both for the state and the monarch. The February Revolution took Rothschild completely by surprise, and the immediate collapse of business activity caused him and his firm considerable problems. One might think that this key figure in the finance aristocracy would be in hiding and planning to escape the country. But the reality did not correspond to that expectation. Toward noon on the twenty-fourth of February, as the monarchy was collapsing, a member of the National Guard saw two men walking calmly toward the Tuileries and recognized one of them as James Rothschild. Pointing out the obvious dangers, he advised the banker to return home. Rothschild, however, continued on his way—to the Ministry of Finance— declaring it his duty to see if they might not need his experience and counsel.[5]

The members of the provisional government recognized the imminence of economic catastrophe; the clues were unambiguous. An instant consensus arose on the need to generate confidence, to prevent the outflow of capital (and capitalists), and to stimulate investment. Central to this effort was the choice of the finance minister. Rothschild was present and a participant in the discussions that led to the appointment of Michel Goudchaux, a fact, Muhlstein reports, that was "noted by various newspapers." Goudchaux combined two traits that were useful to the negotiators: he was a radical and a banker. Recognizing the overwhelming problems, Goudchaux was reluctant, feeling that he was not up to the task. Lamartine and Arago, however, begged him to take the position, at least for the time being. One argument they offered was that "M. de Rothschild and the principal members of the banking community were preparing to leave Paris." For the sake of "the prompt establishment of commercial interests, it was vital that he accept the Ministry of Finance." After accepting, he was visited by Rothschild, who announced his reassurance and declared his intention to remain in Paris.

Goudchaux resigned on March 5 and was replaced by Louis-Antoine Garnier-Pagès. He had been a deputy since 1842, a member of the opposition in the Orleanist period, and an active participant in the banquet campaign. By one account, he was a "courtier de commerce" (commercial broker) since 1825. In his own history of 1848, Garnier-Pagès is more specific. He reports having been, for twenty years, a member of "Les Courtiers de commerce près la Bourse de Paris." He was a stockbroker.

A second appointment of relevance in this connection was that of Adolphe Crémieux as minister of justice. His presence in the government is curious in that he was linked neither to the *National*, the *Réforme*, nor to the streets. He was a lawyer of considerable ability and a member of the dynastic opposition—a defense attorney who defended persons and newspapers prosecuted by Louis Philippe's government. A leading member of the Jewish community, he had also defended Jews in Syria against charges of ritual murder back in 1840. In that capacity he had made the acquaintance of Rothschild. The appointment of Goudchaux and Crémieux, of these two "old friends," Muhlstein states, allayed the banker's concerns. He recognized that Crémieux "would provide him with a source of reliable information." To dramatize his approval of the new government, Rothschild gave fifty thousand francs to a fund for the benefit of those wounded in the recent fighting.[6]

Some rumors circulated to the effect that the government had Rothschild's banking house under surveillance. Louis Blanc "wasted no time" in denying the rumors. The new government, Muhlstein reports, "relied heavily on James' support." His services were appreciated not only by the moderates but also by two prominent figures on the left, Louis Blanc and Marc Caussidière. Those links between Rothschild and members of the provisional government show how far removed Marx's portrait was from the actual development.[7]

After the June Days, Rothschild continued his efforts to establish connections, a process made relatively easy by the quiet reappearance of former political leaders. Muhlstein quotes a letter from one of the Rothschilds which reports: "We were yesterday at Cavaignac's. Same people as usual." Pointing to the absence of experienced leaders, the biographer asks: "How could it have been otherwise?" Rothschild had quickly severed all ties with Louis Philippe. He later, not too surprisingly, had close contacts with the Party of Order. He also established contact with "an old acquaintance," with Louis Napoleon. Quite early he had recognized the likelihood of his success in the presidential election and, "sensing the inevitable," had loaned him money. Rothschild was not personally close to Louis Napoleon, but like Thiers and Marx, he thought Napoleon could be easily led. That did not turn out to be the case. On the morning of the coup, a group of bankers met at Rothschild's mansion and accepted the event as "more or less inevitable."

Marx, it will be remembered, saw a return of the defeated finance aristocracy in November 1849, signaled by Louis Napoleon's naming of Achille Fould (a "stock-exchange wolf") as finance minister. "With the nomination of Fould," he wrote, "the finance aristocracy announced its restoration in the *Moniteur*." This means Marx had missed the significance of the Goudchaux, Crémieux, and Garnier-Pagès appointments, which signaled a continuation of the ties between the government and the finance aristocracy. Marx missed something else by treating the faction as a cohesive body, as one with a common will and interest. For some time Fould wanted to replace Rothschild as the state's leading banker. Now, thanks to Louis Napoleon, he achieved his aim. Marx could conceivably have missed this detail in 1849 and 1850. He might have picked it up had he been open to an alternative hypothesis—to the possibility that bankers (and businessmen generally) compete with one another.[8]

The striking fact about Rothschild's history is that he had established contact and done business with all governments in France from that of Louis XVIII at the restoration through the provisional government in 1848 and the Cavaignac government of that year. The character of James's relationship with those governments deserves some attention. Rothschild and his brothers sought out the power-holders and offered their services. These services, on the whole, were enthusiastically welcomed. Muhlstein describes the process as follows: "James stepped over the wreckage of each fallen regime. His relationship with the various administrations was always characterized by a transparent simplicity: the give-and-take of mutual accommodation and advantage. Those currently in power protected him and allowed his business affairs to proceed. In return, he offered the benefits of his advice and support. . . . He felt bound by no traditional commitments to party or person, thereby evincing an absence of political principle that was inevitable, given the total, unquestioned primacy he accorded his fortune and the glory of his family."[9]

Rothschild did not initiate the political events of the period from 1815 to 1848. He reacted, adjusted, and sought advantage in those developments, in most instances, after the fact. He and his brothers had an impressive intelligence system that allowed them early warning of many coming events. They offered guidance, counsel, and information to power-holders in an effort to achieve their own goals. But other people, monarchs and politicians in most instances, led the way. They held power and made the political decisions. In the face of revolutions, however, that decision making left much to be desired, with the result that power slipped away from them, often with remarkable ease. On those occasions, Rothschild stood ready to do business with their successors. One final observation: None of the Rothschild biographies mention an opposition group that could be termed the "industrial bourgeoisie proper."

Two conclusions flow from this case study, one methodological, one substantive. The first conclusion is that one should research, document, back up, or somehow support claims made, especially those central to one's position. The second conclusion involves the role of the capitalists. In opposition to the claim of leadership, of direction and control, this example shows France's leading capitalist reacting to events created by others, by politicians and intellectuals. As such, it provides a clear challenge to a central claim in the Marxian repertory, namely, that the bourgeoisie had taken over the state and now used it for their purposes.

One might easily—and justifiably—object that the French experience reviewed here is limited and maybe atypical. A similar conclusion has been put forth with regard to the 1789 experience, the point at which, according to Marx and Engels, the revolutionary bourgeoisie was taking power, overthrowing the old regime. Speaking of the orientations of businessmen at that time, a leading historian, Robert R. Palmer, reports as follows: "Seldom did business men take any initiative in bringing on revolution. Very commonly they accepted it, benefited from it, and supported it once it was an accomplished fact." The business-as-reactive claim, as sketched out here, might reasonably be counted as a weakly supported hypothesis. But weak support, in the ordinary run of things, is better than no support; it is better than the hypothesis accepted on faith alone.[10]

The Petty Bourgeoisie

The next class in the Marx-Engels hierarchy is the petty bourgeoisie. As indicated in Chapter 1, the *Manifesto* provides two hypotheses about the behavior of this class. The principal option is that of reaction; it aims to "roll back the wheel of history." A second possibility was that some part of the class, by chance, would join with the proletariat. In the *Class Struggles*, a third option— vacillation—makes its appearance; the class moves from one side to the other with little serious (or plausible) explanation provided for those shifts. Engels's treatments of the class within the German context, as seen, were remarkably diverse, essentially following the needs of his current argument.

Claims are one thing; evidence is something else. The epistomological problem here, the problem of how one knows, is much more complex than in the case of the bourgeoisie. The leading coterie of the bourgeoisie in any country, the power elite, might be no larger than a medium-sized committee. They normally have considerable prominence both in their own time and in the subsequent historical record. In the case of the petty bourgeoisie, however, the problems of knowing outlooks and behavior, especially in the nineteenth century, are virtually insurmountable. The class itself is sizable, depending on the country, running to the hundreds of thousands or millions. Because of its size and necessary dispersion, it would not ordinarily have a core of leaders equivalent to that found within the bourgeoisie. One could, as Marx does, name some individuals (Ledru-Rollin, for example) as the leaders of the class. But such stipulations provide no assurance that they did in fact lead or that they in any serious way represented the underlying constituency. Even if one were dealing with the leaders of a voluntary association, with some trade association or pressure group, the assurances of linkage and representation are not justified, because, first, any such organization, especially in the nineteenth century, would include only a trivial percentage of the total and, second, lacking the possibility of direct inquiry, one cannot establish, support, or justify the claim of representation, that the leaders do in fact speak for the membership. One should be skeptical about such claims at any time.[11]

Even that crude procedure, however, is only imperfectly followed in Marx's account. As indicated in Chapter 3, Marx reported that "we have seen peasants, petty bourgeois, the middle classes in general, stepping alongside the proletariat" early in 1850. This tendency he had discovered in "the so-called party of social-democracy." Within this party, referred to as a "revolutionary league," he had recognized, "necessarily," that the different classes had "grouped themselves round the proletariat." But none of those claims is in any way established. He does not indicate where the Social-Democratic votes came from. He does not indicate the class backgrounds of those elected. He does not indicate the issue orientations of the party. And he does not provide any evidence to support his claim of a petty bourgeoisie grouping round the proletariat.

The election of the National Assembly, in May 1849, was the first in modern times in which mass participation and mass parties were present (these, to be sure, being rather primitive formations). The Party of Order won a majority of the votes. But the left opposition did surprisingly well, gaining approximately one-third of the total. The "démocrates-socialistes" were a loose coalition of rather diverse forces ranging from moderates to the *montagnardes*. Marx points to that diversity indicating a range of concerns extending from "the smallest reform of the old social disorder to the overthrow of the old social order, from bourgeois liberalism to revolutionary terrorism." Such diversity would ordinarily pose difficulties for understanding and interpretation. But for Marx there were no difficulties, those extremes representing, respectively, "the starting point and the finishing point" of the party.

Marx describes the party in terms of its class basis. But that involves a serious misrepresentation, since region was the most obvious factor underlying the election results. The party's one-third share of the overall vote was very unevenly distributed. Sixteen departments (of the then eighty-six) gave the party more than 50 percent, and fourteen gave less than 20 (the extreme percentages were 67.6 and 5.3). Some rural communes, in other words, voted for the "party of Anarchy," some (most of them) voted for the "party of Order." Marx neglected the obvious and, accordingly, provided no explanation for this key result. The party did well in urban working-class areas, but given their small overall size, that contribution to the party's strength was not large. More than three-quarters of those elected came from twelve rural departments. If Marx had detailed the party's geographic basis, some major claims would have lost surface plausibility. Paris workers are at the center of his analysis; the party's support, however, was centered in such places as Nièvre, Haute-Loire, Cher, Dordogne, Allier, Haute-Vienne, and Corrèze.

Information on the occupational backgrounds of those elected was doubtlessly not as accessible as the voting results. The broad outline, nevertheless, should have been clear, especially for the analyst seeking to discover and predict the emerging tendencies. A study undertaken more than a century later found "the large majority of the elected democrats and socialists were from the petty or middling bourgeoisie." Of the 211 persons for whom information was available, 127 were listed as "Capacités intellectuelles"—76 lawyers, 25 doctors, 13 journalists, and 13 teachers or writers. Nineteen had farm occupations (no "paysans," only "quelques propriétaires"), and the same number were from commerce and industry. Twenty-seven were employed in various public service positions. And finally, 11 were listed as workers.[12]

Occupation (or class) per se tells nothing about issue orientation, that is, whether favoring "the smallest reform" or the overthrow of the old order. If Marx had revealed the broad outline of that party's composition, his claims would again have lost even surface plausibility. Would the hundred plus intellectuals have grouped around the eleven workers? What did those workers stand for? Where were they on the political spectrum? Did those workers represent the party's finishing point?

The election results available to Marx allowed plausible judgments about the voting preferences of two segments: farm populations and urban workers. A minority of the former, a limited regional grouping, supported the "party of social-democracy." Urban workers across the board appear to have provided strong support. Beyond that, little can be said with certainty. A vote is ordinarily an obscure indicator of underlying sentiment: a voter indicates a preference for a given party or candidate but says nothing about the reasons for the choice. One point deserves special attention: the voting preferences of the urban petty bourgeoisie are nowhere indicated in those results, neither in the aggregate nor in the regional breakdowns. Unlike farmers and workers, they are not normally concentrated in such a way as to allow any serious conclusion. That knowledge would only become available many years later, with the development of multivariate statistical techniques and/or through the use of polls and surveys. Until those new tools were developed and used, judgments about the attitudes and behavior of the middle class in general were unsupported hypotheses, at best based on limited odd-lot impressions.

Many accounts written subsequent to Marx and Engels's work did not make use even of the indirect indicators of underlying sentiment; they simply declared the petty bourgeois tendency to be reactionary, that conclusion resting on the common consent of like-minded authors. Conclusions drawn about the thought and behavior of a large and diverse class have been accepted at face value for over a century, even though, as a moment's reflection would indicate, the claims involve experience that was almost unknowable. Worse still, beginning in the 1940s and 1950s, when the developing social science technology first made it possible to gain reliable information on this crucial class, the opportunities for empirical testing of the received wisdom, with rare exceptions, have been declined.

The focus on class as a key concept, it will be noted, assumes both differences (vis-à-vis other classes) and commonality (a strong central tendency, that is, shared attitudes and behavior within a given class). Without investigation, neither of those assumptions can be taken as anything more than unsupported hypotheses. It might well be that the differences—say, in attitude toward the established government—are so small as scarcely to deserve mention. The internal homogeneity hypothesis has no more justification, a priori, than a contrary internal heterogeneity hypothesis. The exponents of class analyses, from the time of Marx and Engels, have found it necessary, almost immediately, to invoke an opposite claim, an assertion of deviant segments or factions (called fractions) of the class. But even that involves unsupported hypothesis: without investigation, one cannot be sure that the class is in fact divided along the alleged line of cleavage. One cannot know the size of any faction, and without that knowledge it is impossible to say whether it is typical, the majority or modal case, or deviant.

The few actual studies available report a pattern of small class differences and considerable internal diversity. Possibly the most important source of diversity, religion and/or religiosity, rarely receives attention in popular or scholarly accounts. One could easily add political socialization (family tradition), family background (whether of middle-class, working-class, or farm origins), city size, and neighborhood characteristics as additional factors dividing the petty bourgeoisie. Here too a simple question arises: How much explanatory power does class itself have, that is, apart from the influence of these other factors? If the explanatory power of those other factors proves greater, why are they not at the center of the going styles of analysis?[13]

The Workers

The Marx-Engels discussions of the working class show many of the same difficulties found with respect to the lower middle class—difficulties posed by any large and faceless category. In one respect, however, the compelling conclusion is easier than with the petty bourgeoisie. In the case of an uprising based in neighborhoods with working-class majorities, it is easy to identify the base, easy to establish that workers were in revolt. But beyond that simple statement, the problems begin.

The first of the problems in Marx's analysis involves his portrayal of the workers as industrial, as factory workers in modern capitalist enterprises. The major finding from recent studies of social history has been the "discovery" that in 1848 the working class was based, largely, in premodern craft industries; it was made up of artisans as opposed to factory workers. And those insurgent artisans were looking backward, aiming to fend off the development of Modern Industry. They were, as Craig Calhoun has called them, reactionary radicals. Given the primitive development of Modern Industry, especially in France and Germany at that time, the working class could hardly have been anything else. To support the claim of a unique historical role for the industrial proletariat, some quantification was clearly in order. What part of the class was industrial? What part artisanal? What were the aims and interests of the two segments? Were they shared or opposed goals? And, finally, did both segments participate in the February events in France or in the March events in Austria and Prussia?[14]

It might be objected that Marx and Engels could not have known of these subsequent developments in historical scholarship, since the artisanal character of the working class was first revealed only late in the twentieth century. But that would be inaccurate. The "discovery" was there for any interested observer in 1848. That small shop, artisanal dominance would have been visible to anyone walking the streets of Paris or Berlin. The subsequent accounts, Hamerow's 1958 publication, for example, involved a recovery of information. Petitions drawn up by workers in 1848 were once again brought to light more than a century later. Engels knew of those petitions; he signaled his recognition of the workers' reactionary aims in one isolated sentence.[15]

For Marx and Engels, the question of motivations and outlooks posed no serious problem. Workers were, actually or latently, revolutionary in orientation. If at a given moment the workers were of another persuasion, that was merely some temporary false consciousness, an outlook destined to be replaced as the inevitable flow of events moved them. That exclusiveness, however, indicates a poverty of invention with regard to the immanent possibilities. The question that dominated Social Democracy at the turn of the century—that is, whether the workers were revolutionary or reformist—is entirely absent from their mid-century accounts.

An equally important question, one bypassed entirely, involves that of action, of participation. In their accounts of the revolutionary struggles, Marx and Engels assume full participation—the workers rose in arms. But, judging from the June 1848 experience in Paris, most of the workers opted out; they stayed home. Since Marx and Engels have focused exclusively on the reasons or grounds for participation, they have provided nothing—no theory, no analysis, no explanation at all—for the behavior of the majority of workers. Even for that participant minority, serious questions must be raised about their aims or goals. Marx claims they sought a revolutionary overthrow of the new bourgeois government. But the only statement of revolutionary slogans appears in Marx's account; the other accounts, with remarkable consistency, point to reformist aims, the most important obviously being the preservation of the workshops, the sole source of livelihood for many workers at that point.

As indicated, a much wider range of motivational hypotheses could easily and plausibly be invoked to account for working-class responses. Working-class wives and daughters were not present in the actual fighting. It seems likely that many of them would have pressured husbands, sons, and brothers not to participate, for reasons of hard, unambiguous economic interest. One curiosity about much of the thinking in the contemporary social sciences is that hard factors are regularly preferred over soft. Put differently, economic interest, often declared to be "hard," is thought to be more plausible than personal sentiment. But one such sentiment, love and affection, might well have had considerable importance; would-be combatants might have been deterred by the pleas of (and concerns for) loved ones.

There is, of course, the possibility of a rational choice. Marx and Engels spell out a rationale or logic underlying the workers' behavior. But that is simply one reading of the event and, lacking confirming evidence on the motives, it is an untested hypothesis. Many workers, as indicated, could easily (and with justification) have read the evidence differently. They would have known from their own experience that economic conditions were better than 1846 and early 1847, some recovery having occurred prior to the February Revolution in Paris. They would have known, again through their own immediate experience, that conditions deteriorated rapidly in the days and weeks that followed. It would be easy for them, therefore, to see the revolution as the cause of their economic difficulties. Rather than identifying with the revolution and defending it as their own, many workers, conceivably (an alternative untested hypothesis) would have rejected it. Since the February Revolution was triggered by the banquet campaign, an effort led by opposition politicians easily identified with the middle class, and since the new government was largely in the hands of coteries linked to the *National* and *Réforme*, it would have been easy to see the revolution as someone else's venture.

It would also have been easy for any worker to recognize that revolution was bad for business and, as a consequence, bad for workers. One would not need statistics or neoclassical logic to recognize that fact. Any tailor, construction worker, home builder or repairer, or cabinetmaker would know that new orders had all but disappeared. Given the small size of the typical shop, that knowledge would be available to all persons present—to the masters, of course, but also to the apprentices and journeymen. Given the small shop size, the maximalist option would seem most implausible. Would the three or four workers in a tailoring shop see their employer as a member of the hated bourgeoisie? Would they see him as their enemy, as the immediate source of their problems? Would socialization of the means of production provide new orders for the cabinetmakers? That reading of workers' motives, the maximalist imputation, requires an extraordinary leap of logic.

At this late date, adjudication between these two competing rationales is difficult. Since few participants have left a record of their motives or outlooks, one appropriate conclusion would be "don't know" or "cannot definitively say." One could, of course, indicate the range of explanatory possibilities. The stipulation of an exclusive option—a fully mobilized working class in pursuit of maximalist goals—is an imposed solution. It is also one that is challenged by two facts: by the minority participation and by the insurgent workers' own slogans.

Marx and Engels offered some predictions about subsequent working-class behavior. The defeat in June was temporary. The next economic crisis would again educate the workers; they would engage at that point with greater understanding and commitment and would be victorious in that next struggle. Revolution, in their view, was regularly linked to downswings in the business cycle, to rising unemployment and the accompanying deprivation experienced by workers. But that prediction did not prove valid. The next rising of Paris workers came in 1871 with the famous commune, more than two decades after the defeat of June 1848. And that rising followed a military collapse, the defeat of France by Prussia, rather than an economic crisis. The defeat of the commune was followed, over many decades, by further economic crises, but no proletarian revolution occurred. Looking elsewhere, there was no proletarian rising in Britain at any time, that is, no equivalent either to February or June of 1848. Although the Communists, so Marx and Engels wrote in 1848, "turn their attention chiefly to Germany," that country produced no successful revolution, bourgeois or proletarian, until November 1918. Again, the antecedent fact was defeat in a war, not a downswing in the business cycle. In the three key cases chosen by Marx and Engels, within the time span they had indicated, the predictions proved unambiguously mistaken.

The normal expectation in scientific study is that a failed hypothesis will be rejected and, possibly, that its original justification will be reexamined. In the Marxist science, in all but one of the variants (the original revisionism), that has not been the case. Instead, the practice has been a series of post hoc revisions designed to explain the failure of the original claim. It is the various welfare measures that, momentarily, moderate worker attitudes. Or it is a transfer of the class struggle to the colonial world, again a temporary phenomenon. Or it is some sophisticated strategy of legitimation that deludes the workers. Or it is some cunning use of the mass media that deludes them. It will be noted that all the various saving strategies involve procedures adopted by the capitalist system to fend off the inevitable. None of those options questions the inevitability hypothesis.

It is useful, once again, to speculate about worker motivations and outlooks. A simple question: How did the participants themselves see and react to the revolutionary events in Paris of 1848?

Some lessons may be gained by a consideration of the experience of the single worker present in the provisional government. This man, the first worker in modern times to be a member of a government, is generally referred to simply as Albert. He is introduced, for example, in the early pages of Karl Marx's *The Class Struggles in France* in this enigmatic sentence: "The working class had only two representatives, Louis Blanc and Albert." Louis Blanc, the well-known author and political leader, required no introduction. But Albert, except possibly in club circles, was unknown. This working-class representative received only three mentions in Marx's work. All three have the exact same two-word format—"and Albert." He is treated as an appendage to Louis Blanc.[16]

Most subsequent accounts are also brief and cryptic in their treatment of the man and his role. Frederick de Luna's work, an exception to that rule, provides some basic information. Albert, he reports, was added to the provisional government in response to the demands of the crowd at the Hôtel de Ville on the twenty-fourth of February. De Luna introduces him as "a worker named Alexandre Martin and called Albert" who had been "a member of a vaguely republican secret society." The new government consisted of seven moderates and a radical wing of four which included Albert (and Louis Blanc). Albert was one of the seventeen workers elected to the Constituent Assembly (out of a total of nine hundred). He came in twenty-first in the Seine among the thirty-four elected, a remarkable achievement, since well-known radicals Barbès, Raspail, Considérant, and Cabet all lost. Even Louis Blanc did not fare as well, coming in only twenty-seventh. On May 15, Albert was present at the National Assembly when the crowd broke it. After the "dissolution," Albert continued with the crowd to the Hôtel de Ville, where he and Barbès proclaimed a new provisional government and where both were arrested. The assembly later voted to prosecute its members who were said to have been involved. The original accusation included also Louis Blanc, Ledru-Rollin, and Caussidière. But Ledru-Rollin was dropped from the list and Blanc and Caussidière were allowed to escape, both reaching England "without difficulty." All this time, Albert "languished in the dungeon at Vincennes."[17]

Donald McKay's 1933 study of the National Workshops provides some further information on the man and his fate. A footnote reads: "Albert . . . , 'ouvrier mécanicien,' had taken a prominent part in secret societies under the July Monarchy. He was also one of the founders and anonymous editors of the *Atelier*. The precise reasons for his selection as member of the government, as opposed to some other worker, are obscure. . . . He was condemned to deportation, 1849, for his part in the events of May 15, 1848, amnestied in 1859, and refused thenceforth to play a political role, although he was subsequently made a member of the *commission des barricades* by the Government of National Defence in 1870."[18]

Maybe something is to be learned from McKay's footnote comment, from the statement that Albert "refused thenceforth to play a political role." Having paid a heavy price for his involvement, he simply withdrew from politics. One possibility worth consideration is that of leadership loss. Marx and Engels assumed that the class struggles, even failed engagements, would yield net gains in leadership numbers and skills. But there is an easy alternative, that of net losses. Some leaders died in the struggles, some were jailed, and others went into exile. Most of the estimated fifty thousand insurgents of June 1848, however, not having suffered any of those penalties, probably remained in Paris. Most of them must have returned to their normal everyday routines in the months and years following. Judging from the quiescence of the subsequent two decades, most of the June 1848 participants, like Albert, appear to have refused further revolutionary involvements.

For the workers of June 1848, for both the combatants and the majority who did not participate, it would have been easy to recognize a simple fact, one stated sixscore years afterward by the eminent historian William L. Langer: "Not a single radical leader participated." All of the left notables and club leaders who were still free after the May fiasco were located elsewhere, sheltered somewhere behind the government's forces, during the June Days. Historian Bernard Moss stated the same point some thirteen decades after the fact: "Not a single radical leader or major club—not even the Rights of Man—joined the uprising. Student radicals and intellectuals, who normally led the charge were conspicuously absent. Few of the politically conscious workers from the Luxembourg or elite crafts were implicated." The vocal bourgeois radicals from the other side of Paris escaped from the debacle, in one way or another, leaving the workers to pay the price.[19]

Maybe Albert, along with thousands of other workers, concluded that revolution was a dangerous, ultimately lethal game. It was one that bourgeois intellectuals played at. They stimulated events, nurtured them, and pushed them along. But then, at the crucial moment, those suppliers of "enlightenment and progress" disappeared and remained safely (and quietly) in the protection of government troops. Maybe it became part of the folk wisdom of the working class, part of working-class culture, something passed on by fathers and mothers to their children, that one should stay clear of those people and their ventures. The experience, in short, may well have educated the workers; it may have provided them with a lesson: radical intellectuals may be hazardous to health and welfare. Given the workers' experience and given the absence of the intellectual vanguard, that conclusion would constitute a hard and unambiguous element of true consciousness.

Eventually, once the smoke cleared, the progressive intellectuals again began to ply their trade. They wrote accounts of the 1848 events. They explained the origins of the revolution in terms of the economic crisis, neglecting the faint signs of recovery early in 1848 and overlooking the source of the spring crisis. They told of the June Days, of the desperation of the workers. And they told of the rapacity and ruthlessness of the government forces. The working-class uprising, they wrote, was put down by force, by the spilling of workers' blood. In most accounts, they neglected the dubious role played by the bourgeois intelligentsia. So for them, and for those who read their books, the eternally puzzling problem came to be that of the subsequent quiescence of the workers. Why did they have such *false* consciousness? Why did they accept things as they were? Why did they not rebel? It never occurred to most of these critics, helpless prisoners of their own conceptions, that there might be an easy, entirely understandable explanation for that behavior.

In recent years phenomenology has been very much in vogue within some intellectual circles. In rough translation, that term appears to mean seeing things from the perspective of the actors. In this case it would mean, somehow or other, trying to gain a sense of how workers in Paris would have seen things, say in the last half of 1848. But little effort is expended to gain that perspective. It is something that should be on the research agenda for radical sociologists or for the enthusiastic supporters of the new social history. How did the workers react in the aftermath of other revolutionary ventures? How, for example, did the workers of Munich react in mid-May of 1919, after the revolution and after the counterrevolution, in which some six hundred of their members had been killed? Our accounts are peculiarly one-sided. They describe (or dramatize) the rising of the workers but neglect the subsequent phase of the cycle. It is as if economists focused only on the upswings of business cycles. Such study ought to be more wide-ranging in its invocation of explanatory hypotheses. In addition to the "dynamics of capitalism" and the use of force (bourgeois brutality), one might give consideration to the three possibilities suggested here: revolution and the resulting unemployment as a source of working-class quietism, net losses of leadership, and the behavior of radical intellectuals.[20]

The Farmers

The farm populations figure only as distant offstage segments in the Marx-Engels accounts. It is a peculiar and problematical portrait: the workers are front and center in the staging, declared at times to be the majority, and at all times said to be the protagonist in the forthcoming drama. But in most European countries throughout most of the nineteenth century, rural populations formed either the majority or the largest minority. In France, the second capitalist nation in Marx and Engels's view, three-quarters of the population in mid-century was rural, a proportion that fell only gradually in subsequent decades (to 69 percent in 1872). Some of those employed in rural settings were in nonfarm occupations, but even taking those directly engaged in the primary sector (agriculture, forestry, and fishing), the picture is little different. That sector contained 51.4 percent of the active population in 1856. Two decades later, that level had declined only marginally, to 49.3 percent. Somewhat larger declines came later, to 45.3 percent in 1896 and 43.2 percent in 1906, but even then the primary sector remained a major part of the total.

Even late in the century, the farm populations persisted, a declining force to be sure, but still more than a trivial presence on the scene. England, the most advanced capitalist nation, was clearly exceptional: in 1891, only one-seventh of the men in the labor force were in farming. In France, as just seen, more than two-fifths of the men in the labor force were employed in the farm sector, the majority of them being farm proprietors. France at that time had more workers in agriculture than in manufacturing. Thirty-six percent of Germany's male labor force in 1895 was in agriculture, that sector still being slightly larger than manufacturing (31 percent). Four and five decades earlier, when Marx and Engels first expounded their position, the farm sector would have been much larger and the working class correspondingly smaller, especially that part of it involved in Modern Industry.

At all times in the nineteenth century, moreover, in all countries, large percentages of the workers were born and raised on farms. For most of them, migration meant a move to a nearby town or city, which in turn meant that many of those first-generation workers were able to maintain ties with those family members and friends who remained on the farm. The exclusive categorical reading, that people are either on the farm or in the city, subject to one or the other influence, is a view with only limited applicability.[21]

Marx and Engels, as we have seen, often treated the owners of small farms as another petty bourgeois segment (although usually considered separately from their urban counterparts). The farm populations were not treated as a class *für sich*, as one capable of acting in its own interest. Instead, they were regularly denigrated, portrayed as stupid and incapable. They were said to lack the wit and wisdom necessary to organize for the pursuit of their goals.

The farmers faced the same problems as their urban counterparts in that the competition from the more efficient large farms would lead to their ruin. Like the shopkeepers and small producers of the cities, they too would lose their independent status and would fall into the proletariat. Given this inevitable fate, there was no point in developing meliorative programs designed to stem the flow of events. Any such programs would, at best, involve stopgap measures. They could, possibly, slow down the pace of events; the eventual outcome, however, would not be altered. The party of workers, in any event, would not see its task as providing aid for another class, particularly to one whose activity was seen as problematical for the welfare and improvement of the workers' condition.

For Marx and Engels (and for the later Marxist parties) this analysis led to a peculiar treatment of the segment. Farm populations were told, in one way or another, that their situation was hopeless (and that they were lacking in intelligence). The programmatic statements, basically, offered them nothing; there were no immediate appeals that would move them to support Social Democracy. Basically, farmers were offered the long-term prediction: You are destined to fall into the proletariat. At that point, the party will, for the first time, represent your interests.[22]

There is a hidden corollary to this argument: those persons falling into the proletariat would then adopt the values and outlooks of the workers. It is another indication of the (untested) assumption of the power of class. Class position, supposedly, is so powerful that it would overwhelm any prior training and experience. The extreme options, basically, are that persons falling into the proletariat would bring their traditional values with them into their new position (in effect, transferring false consciousness to a new location) or they would convert, abandoning their previous thought patterns and adopting the new, appropriate framework (true consciousness). The Marxian argument, both in the original and in the subsequent literature, assumed the dominance of conversion.

The question of transplantation versus conversion is largely unexplored. Despite the many bold predictions about the consequences of downward mobility, few studies have actually investigated subsequent attitudes and outlooks. As mentioned earlier, the assumption of easy conversion stands in sharp opposition to the logic put forth in other contexts. The petty bourgeoisie, it is said, fiercely defends its middle-class status, doing everything possible to prevent that downward movement. In the extreme case, as was argued in a later literature, they would embrace the ruthless solutions provided by fascist movements, so as to prevent their loss of position. But then it is suggested that, having fallen, they would abandon the fetishistic attachment to their old status and, with no evident strain, would make common cause with the workers. The logic of the argument is implausible; it assumes a remarkable indifference to one's previous background and experience.

There is an easy alternative hypothesis: If a segment of the electorate is regularly denigrated by the leading spokesmen of a party, who offer no solution to the problems faced by that segment, one possibility is that even after the fall, those persons would not view the mocking antagonist with any favor. They would, even as members of the proletariat, continue to support non-socialist parties. The cynical indifference of the socialist leaders, in other words, might conceivably have helped to block the historical movement. Those leaders might, to borrow a phrase, have helped generate an opposite to their own movement. A similar development appeared within the liberal parties, although without this element of denigration; given their laissez-faire stance, they too had no plausible solutions for the problems facing small farmers. Until the relatively late development of farm support programs, both socialists and liberals, in short, helped set the stage for subsequent demagogic appeals to the farmers.[23]

Neither of these hypotheses, transplantation versus conversion, captures the complexities involved in the *Agrarfrage*. Both farmers and workers are embedded in social networks that provide influences guiding and directing social and political consciousness. The competing hypotheses discussed here overlook the impacts of such networks. A bankrupt farmer does not leave one milieu, a supportive farm setting, and move to the city, locating in an opposite, working-class setting. In general, where choice is possible, people move into what one might call like-minded settings. They move to settings that in significant ways match their former experience. The simplest example involves the familiar process of chain migration, people following after another family member who moved earlier. The literature of internal and international migration is filled with evidence showing community-to-community and region-to-region moves. For many persons, then, the uprooting move involves a change from the community of origin to another setting having a similar character, one in which re-rooting is relatively easy. And that, in turn, would mean the new community would, on the whole, support and reinforce the values held prior to the move.

The commentators schooled in the mass society tradition (elements of which are present in Marxism) automatically assume the existence of insistent corrosive processes associated with urbanization. But if there were also significant corrosive effects associated with Marxism, if its themes and presentations alienated rather than attracted, then those new urban communities containing large numbers of farm-to-city migrants might, on balance, hold up rather well against the effects of the city. The religious tie, conceivably, is of special importance in this connection. With remarkable insistence, socialist parties have attacked religion. They were, in the process, attacking beliefs that, for many, were strongly held. They were also attacking an institution that could and did fight back. The anticlerical efforts might well have firmed up the ranks of the faithful. With equally remarkable insistence, it might be noted, subsequent commentators have overlooked the role of the religious factor and the consequences of this distinctive conflict.[24]

The discussions of farm-to-city movement focus on uprooting, on people leaving a small community and moving to the large, impersonal city. The enormous size of that movement is frequently documented by presentation of census figures showing the growth of cities over many decades in the modern era. But part of that change, the smaller part to be sure, involves no uprooting at all. It involves what might be called city-to-farm movement—moving the city boundaries outward to embrace surrounding countryside. That process changes administrative jurisdictions (and relocates people for statistical purposes), but those changes have little or no impact on established social networks. Scores of villages many kilometers from Berlin became, on one night, part of the metropolis.[25]

From the first exposition of the claim that the move from independent farm proprietorship into the proletariat represented a fall, most commentators have accepted it uncritically. That assumes the previous condition, independence, was an unambiguous good and the dependent proletarian condition an unambiguous bad. While that assumption is perhaps an undoubted truth when viewed from the perspective of advanced philosophy, the participants themselves might see things differently. The circumstances of the petty bourgeoisie, it will be remembered, are routinely portrayed as depressed (miserable might be the better term). The life of the small farmer involves hard work, uncertainties (linked to weather and markets), and powerlessness, combined with, at best, modest financial returns. For many of those farmers (or for many of their children), blue-collar work in nearby towns might well be viewed as a step up in the world. It might be seen accurately as yielding a net improvement in the quality of life. That would mean the farm-to-city movement, in many instances, did not result from a push (a loss of position) but was due rather to a pull, from the sense of, or recognition of, that net gain. Germany's National Socialists were ardent ideological agrarians who sought to turn back the clock and return people to the land. Much to their surprise, they discovered that many of the people they were trying to help actually preferred the city.[26]

This discussion of the farmers has been largely speculative. It brings together the findings of migration studies with the largely untested assumptions of easy conversion implicit in the Marxist theory. No long-term studies are available that establish the extent of the political conversion (or transplantation) associated with farm-to-city moves. Few studies are available showing the locational choices made within the cities. Studies of the political influences present within their new interpersonal networks are rare. Perhaps of even greater importance, we have no serious studies of the reactions to Social Democratic (and later Communist) programmatic themes. Commentators aligned with those parties generally assume the validity of their basic logic and, accordingly, view those program elements as having positive effects. But the consequences of that sophisticated deprecation of the farm population may well have been negative. That possibility, however, is rarely considered.[27]

All in all, the treatment of the farm sector is the most curious of all elements in the Marxist theoretical repertory. There has been a systematic refusal to face up to the majority status of this sector in most nations for most of the nineteenth century. One might refer to this as the problem of the misplaced majority. The tendency in the theory and practice of Marxist parties, moreover, has been to denigrate and ridicule that majority rather than analyze, understand, and appeal to them. The praxis appears to have been one that would alienate, offend, or insult those falling into the proletariat, rather than attracting them. That practice is likely to have put obstacles in the way of the movement's advance. If so, we would have a remarkable example of a compelling theory aiding and abetting the conduct of foolish policy. Foolishness is frequently seen as behavior having no remarkable consequences. In this case, however, the foolishness may well have had "world historical" consequences—by "setting the stage for" the later National Socialist electoral victories.

A Note on Mobility

Classes are not fixed, immovable social formations; they are in movement in all societies, even if the pace is at best glacial. Moreover, again in all societies, there is movement of individuals and families up and down in the class hierarchy. Two basic questions arise: the directions and quantity of movement—

basically, How much movement occurs in each direction?—and the effects—What are the consequences of those moves?

For Marx and Engels, mobility presented no problem. For them, the principal flow was downward, into the proletariat. This yielded the increase in the size of the working class that, ultimately, would make it the majority. Implicit in their argument, as already noted, is the assumption of conversion; persons falling into the proletariat would convert and adopt the appropriate revolutionary politics of their new class.

The basic questions require more detailed consideration. First, there is the matter of flows, the question of the amount and direction of movement. Looking at the nonfarm segments, the best current evidence decisively rejects the hypothesis of a net downward flow. The analyses of intergenerational movement, those comparing fathers' and sons' occupations, show a net upward movement. The proportion of working-class sons arriving in nonmanual occupations amounts to roughly one-third of the total; the proportion of middle-class sons employed in manual occupations amounts to roughly one-quarter of that segment. The quantity of upward movement is even greater than these fractions suggest, since the absolute number of manual fathers is larger than the equivalent nonmanual figure. The conclusion, it should be noted, is data-based.[28]

That conclusion, incidentally, flows logically from one of the major structural developments of the modern era, that is, from the growth of bureaucracy. That long-term development means the addition of many layers of hierarchy to what were once small, two- or three-layer firms. If the firm of Ermen and Engels, for example, went from three to eight levels of hierarchy over its first half-century, that would mean five entirely new layers of hierarchy. All of those elevated into those new ranks would experience upward mobility. Most of the expansion of government in the twentieth century had the same effect. There too, the additional layers of hierarchy required upward moves.

The second question, the political correlates of mobility, is considerably more difficult. Apart from the rule-of-thumb judgment, it is something that is best answered with survey evidence, with studies asking appropriate questions and containing sufficient numbers of mobile persons. Much popular or journalistic speculation in subsequent decades recognized the dominance of the upward movement. But it too, as with Marx and Engels, assumed conversion. The consensus on this point, however, was that the workers who arrived in the middle class would shed their former views and adopt the values and political dispositions of their conservative (or moderate) neighbors. Much of that speculation flourished in the United States in the 1950s when the class shift hypothesis, the coming of the middle-class majority, was first elaborated. The combination of the upward mobility and the moves to suburbia made it easy to believe that conversion was the only possible outcome. The election of Eisenhower and a Republican congress in 1952 provided plausible evidence in support of this logic. Some subsequent research, however, showed evidence for the alternative hypothesis, that is, for transplantation. Many people carried their original values with them into those new settings.[29]

That continuity of outlook suggests a weighting of the two factors. It suggests that political socialization (and possibly subsequent reinforcement) outweighs the impact of current class position. While little more than a weakly supported hypothesis at this point, the presence of considerable mobility does provide the occasion for repeated testing of the competing claims. If class is a significant factor (or a powerful predictor), that should become manifest subsequent to the move into a new (and politically different) class. The appropriate investigation ought to answer the following questions: How much weight should be assigned to socialization and social influences? How much to class?

The Intellectuals

Marx and Engels's discussions of the farm sector might, at many points, be treated under the heading of "the missing majority." In like manner, the intellectuals might be treated as a missing coterie. And because it is missing, it is also, like the farmers, an unanalyzed segment. Marx and Engels regularly put the bourgeoisie at the center of events in France. When it came to the major revolutions of 1789, 1830, and 1848, it is the bourgeoisie (or factions thereof) which—from behind the scenes—were said to direct events. But that argument, as has been seen repeatedly, comes largely without benefit of evidence.

The Great Revolution went through several phases in its ten-year existence before being overthrown by Napoleon Bonaparte. Marx and Engels manifested special affection for the Jacobin period, which was characterized by dictatorial control, the use of terror against opponents, and aggressive military action vis-à-vis the European powers. Although the revolution was called "bourgeois" Marx and Engels did not indicate what that term meant in 1792–94, nor did they establish that the Jacobin leaders were themselves bourgeois (or, at minimum, the agents of bourgeois leaders). In the Jacobin period France was ruled by twelve men, the members of the Committee of Public Safety. Robert R. Palmer, the author of the leading work on the group, describes them simply as follows: "All twelve were intellectuals." Moreover, in more than a dozen passages in his book, Palmer indicates strong antibourgeois sentiments and antibourgeois actions on the part of the twelve.[30]

The 1830 revolution, according to Marx, was somehow directed by "the banker Laffitte." But that brief and cryptic claim, as already noted, omits much of the history. A key agency in the July uprising was a newspaper, the *National*, then led by three rising young men who combined intellectual, journalistic, and political interests. These were Adolphe Thiers, his lifelong friend François Mignet, and Armand Carrel. They did have close ties to Laffitte, although, as will be seen, the significance of that link is open to some question. Thiers was the author of a ten-volume work *Histoire de la Révolution*, that had appeared between 1823 and 1827. It was "one of the first narrative accounts" dealing with a subject "in which most educated Frenchmen were passionately interested." Mignet had written two volumes, *Histoire de la Révolution française*. And Carrel had published *Histoire de la contre-révolution en Angleterre*, which, as one historian put it, drew "a long and menacing parallel between the Stuart and Bourbon restorations." The coterie proceeded, following their British model, to transform the French government. They were most explicit about this, seeing Louis Philippe as their William III.[31]

The repressive decrees that set in motion the events leading to the overthrow of the restored Bourbon line were directed against the press, not against the bourgeoisie. Thiers and his associates took the lead in February 1830. They organized the initial response by the city's liberal journalists, all this being planned in the offices of the *National*. The initiative then passed to the opposition politicians, with Thiers serving as liaison. Laffitte was out of the city at the onset of the difficulties and returned only on the twenty-ninth, at which point his house became the headquarters of the insurgency. It was Thiers who then argued for the Duc d'Orléans, with Laffitte being described merely as "a willing listener." The revolution, in short, was moved by the intellectual coterie. Marx's brief prefatory comment hides that fact and, as indicated, makes Laffitte the central actor. Marx thus omitted important elements of the history—elements that could hardly have escaped his attention. Lenore O'Boyle writes that "the part played by the press in the overthrow of Charles X and the profit the journalists drew from that event were obvious to all observers." Marx's account of the moving forces of history, at this point, is sustained by restaging the drama, by neglecting those leaders who were on stage at the time.[32]

Laffitte soon disappeared from the scene. His brief government was a failure; his bank collapsed and, therewith, his influence came to an end. The intellectual coterie also had no long-term success in relation to the regime it had created. Carrel was soon disenchanted and, within two years, had become a strong opponent. Thiers led the government a decade later but, checked by the king on a key foreign-policy issue, also found himself in the opposition until called to office once again, on February 23, 1848, when it was too late to do anything. Again in 1848, in this unintended revolution, the driving forces were coteries of intellectuals centered around the *National* and the *Réforme*. Together with the circle of opposition politicians, they had set events in motion. With the dynastic opposition momentarily eclipsed, it was the intellectuals alone who managed the transition to the republic.

The central position of intellectuals in these three revolutions should be indicated in subsequent historical and theoretical accounts. But Marx, as we have seen, pushed them aside, assigning them only subordinate roles. Where an appearance is unavoidable, he treated them as agents standing in for some unnamed bourgeois leaders said to be operating behind the scenes. Curiously, many non-Marxist historians, although not accepting the materialist conception of history, have followed this outline, and they too have submerged or played down the role of the intellectuals while accepting nebulous claims about direction of events by the bourgeoisie.

This easy acceptance of the consensus position—treating the intellectuals as peripheral—is all the more remarkable given their presence in almost every setting. Louis Philippe's reactionary prime minister, François Guizot, was also an intellectual and a politician, having written, among other things, *Histoire de la civilisation en Europe* and *Essais sur l'histoire de la France*. He also wrote *Histoire de la révolution d'Angleterre*, which deals with Charles I. The de facto leader of the provisional government, Alphonse de Lamartine, was the most obvious, the most visible intellectual in the new regime. While known as a romantic poet, the most eminent in all of France, he was also the author of an important political work, the eight-volume *Histoire des Girondins*, which was published in 1847. Some contemporary accounts claimed it to have been a major contributing cause of the revolution. It certainly received much publicity, including a banquet (this in the period of the banquet campaign). Louis Blanc was the author of an influential critical account of the first decade of Louis Philippe's regime, *L'Histoire de dix ans* and then, on the eve of 1848, his *La Révolution française* appeared. In some listings of the causes, mention is made of Jules Michelet, the eminent historian of the 1789 revolution who, early in January 1848, was fired from his post. Except for the stubborn prejudice, any serious commentator would have to focus on the central role of intellectuals in the 1848 events.[33]

Some obvious conclusions flow from this discussion. Intellectuals can have a major causal role in the unfolding of historical events. They can, moreover, play independent causal roles, that is, independent of bourgeois leadership. The business of intellectuals, after all, is a low-cost enterprise; the capital requirements, particularly in the mid-nineteenth century, were so modest that any talented person could compete. If the work sold well, that person could gain considerable influence. That influence could be multiplied if the intellectuals had a common outlook, direction, or tendency.

The writers, artists, musicians, and intellectuals of the era did share a common tendency; with only occasional exception, they were critics of the established regimes. Most writers were advocates of a general liberal viewpoint. Their works illustrated and commented on aspects of that outlook; this was accompanied by steady criticism of handed-down conservative practice. These didactic offerings, clearly, were oppositional in character, that is, challenging the dominant or ruling authorities of the age. Although writers frequently complained of oppression, of close and insistent controls, their productions, on the whole, managed to overcome those obstacles. The dominant movement of the age, it will be remembered, was romanticism, the literary or artistic counterpart to liberalism (the political program). Victor Hugo, the "recognized leader of French Romanticism," summarized the point as follows: "Romanticism is . . . nothing more than liberalism in literature." The intellectuals, in short, with few exceptions, were selling a program designed to undermine "the established social order." Charles-Augustin Sainte-Beuve described the generation as one which had "fought with virtual unanimity under the Restoration against the political and religious *ancien régime*." They clearly played a decisive role by undercutting the claims to legitimacy of both the Bourbon and Orleanist regimes.[34]

It is important to note the character of the intellectuals' audience. It would, necessarily, be a part of the literate population of the society which, of course, would be a relatively well-off group, possibly among the most affluent fifth of the society. Those "counterculturals," the Byron and Shelley enthusiasts, the readers of George Sand, Lamartine, and Heine, would be found largely within the upper and upper middle classes. We are regularly misled about this fact by "critical" intellectuals who, with remarkable insistence, portray themselves as a beleaguered minority fighting against the forces of philistinism. The upper and upper middle classes are portrayed as an unbroken rank of reactionaries, in matters of both politics and culture. But that imagery cannot be accurate. If the upper classes were solid and unbroken, how could one explain the ever-threatening presence of liberalism within the legislative bodies of the period? The restrictive suffrage arrangement means the people who voted for them were highly placed in the social structure. And given various combinations of rotten boroughs and corruption, it means they are not represented in proportion to their numbers. Given the basic facts of literacy, the audience for those critical cultural productions must also have been located in the higher circles.

It is difficult to estimate the numbers. Judging, however, from the popularity of the various literary productions, a fair-sized segment of the upper and upper middle classes in the first half of the nineteenth century must have been free spirits with open, innovative, antitraditional, and antiauthority attitudes. Among other things, this means the upper and upper middle classes were not solidly conservative; they were not uniformly in support of established arrangements. Thanks to the intellectuals, a significant faction was willing to consider and support other options, some of which were clearly and unambiguously revolutionary in character. Their revolution, however, had few points of convergence with any revolution that might issue out of the masses. The sources of the revolutionary sentiment, in short, were widely divergent. The problem for these upper- and upper-middle-class players was that their revolution could very easily stimulate that other, more dangerous variety, the mass uprising. The intellectuals' revolution was based on the west side of Paris. But the center of gravity of the social movement, as we have seen, could easily shift to the east side of the city.[35]

The upper classes, as indicated, were seriously divided. An important line of cleavage ran through their ranks, separating the conservatives (the practical or pragmatic tendency) from the liberals (the critical, oppositional, counter-cultural tendency). If one fails to recognize (or to reckon with) that cleavage, another difficulty follows: the relationship between the intellectuals and their upper- and upper-middle-class audience will remain unexplored. We have some easy hypotheses about that relationship. There is the familiar romantic portrait of the rejected artist: an indifferent or hostile public (the bourgeois philistines) leaves the artist to starve, typically in a garret. Another option has it that the bourgeoisie can and does buy off the dissident—the familiar "he who pays the piper" line is invoked. Those with money can easily control or dominate the less powerful segment. As is generally the case, however, the reality is considerably more complicated. A brief review proves instructive.

Corti's account of the Rothschild banking house contains, here and there, some suggestive lessons. At one point, Moritz Gottlieb Saphir, the "much-dreaded wit, critic, and journalist," is introduced. The man "wrote with extraordinary facility, and his output was considerable." He was also, we are told, "insanely vain, and violently persecuted anyone who showed him ill-will. When he had money he spent it recklessly in giving most magnificent parties." Solomon Rothschild, the leader of the Austrian branch of the family, "often footed the bill" for these entertainments, "for the very good reason that it paid better to have him as a 'dear' friend than as a cheap enemy." Eventually, however, this proved "irksome," and the banker worked out another arrangement. The next time "the revolutionary satirist" appeared seeking funds, Rothschild proposed that he should, in exchange for "a substantial income," write "in Metternich's interest." Saphir requested some time for consideration. The next day, he accepted the proposal and "entered the service" of the Austrian government. It was a simple case of venality, a support-for-money transaction.

The Rothschild family was coming up in the world in the 1830s and 1840s and undertook considerable effort to break into society. They were, on the whole, successful in this effort. Nathan's family in London had prominent members of the nobility, including Wellington, as house guests. Present also were leading artists such as Grisi and Rossini. Even more striking was the success of James Rothschild in Paris. The two leading composers of the age, Rossini and Meyerbeer, were regular guests. In the mid-thirties, a famous German exile, Heinrich Heine, was also a frequent visitor. He was there, for example, at the first ball in the new mansion, following the premiere performance of Meyerbeer's *Les Huguenots*. Balzac too was a regular visitor. Even more remarkable, perhaps, he was a friend of the banker's.[36]

Heine at this point was the leading poet writing in the German language. Most of his writing was bitter, caustic, and sardonic; he was a dedicated opponent of the established regimes of Europe, although that opposition was more cultural or aesthetic than economic; and he was more concerned with the position of the poet than with that of the proletariat. It was Rothschild's wife, Betty (Solomon Rothschild's daughter, incidentally), who maintained connections with the artists and intellectuals. She was charming and accomplished and, initially at least, a supporter of Heine (who in turn dedicated several poems to her). There was still another link. Heine's father "had known the Rothschilds well," Corti reports, "having been constantly associated with the House in financial matters." James also had connections with the poet's uncle, Salomon Heine, an extremely wealthy Hamburg banker. Both bankers supported the poet financially, Rothschild with several gifts, the uncle, ultimately, with a regular annual pension.[37]

It is easy to think of the artist in this relationship as a dependent suppliant. But that does not appear to have been the case. Heine taunted the banker, both in private and in print. At one dinner the hosts were entertaining, among others, Heine, Rossini, and the Austrian poet and playwright Franz Grillparzer. The latter found Heine's mean-spirited remarks offensive; if he disliked his hosts, he should not have come. Grillparzer wrote that James and Betty "were afraid of Heine."[38]

Following the 1848 revolution, French government files were opened. A file in the Foreign Ministry bore the heading "Service extraordinaire" and listed the recipients of secret subsidies. Heine was indicated as the recipient of 4,800 francs annually. He had been supported, it seems, from the mid-thirties until the revolution, which means he had been aided by both the liberal Thiers and the conservative Guizot governments. Heine declared it to have been a simple act of generosity by the French government; it was help for "exiles seeking freedom." He asked that the pension be continued but Lamartine had it stopped. If some fee for service was intended, it is not at all clear what that service was.[39]

The relationship of poet to bourgeois, or of poet to regime, it is clear, is not entirely one-sided. The portrayal of the poet as victim, as martyr, is a useful tactic. One could describe it as a self-serving myth or, putting the point more directly, as simple dishonesty.

This sketch of the role of intellectuals does not constitute an argument for intellectual determinism. It does not put intellectuals in the exclusive position occupied by the bourgeoisie in the Marxist framework. The intellectuals, rather, prove to be one factor among many. In 1830, for example, the intellectuals of the *National* were moving in tandem with some important business leaders, the most important of whom was Jacques Laffitte. The intellectuals in Paris of 1848 were moving together with a group of opposition political leaders led by Odilon Barrot and company. Their audience in that period would, at best, amount to a tiny segment of the adult population. Even a best-selling writer, such as George Sand, would probably not reach even as much as 5 percent of the nation (approximately 70 percent were illiterate; many others would have been only marginally literate and hence were beyond the reach of "sophisticated" literature).[40] The vast majority of the population, in short, would not have been touched by those intellectual influences. The roots of the majority's behavior would have to be found in some other factors.

The focus on entire populations is mistaken. In the initial stages of the revolutions of 1830 and 1848, less than 5 percent of the adult population of France would have been involved. The influence of intellectuals in the initial events would be much greater than in any later episodes, which had considerably greater popular involvement. When universal suffrage engaged the entire adult male population, the influence of intellectuals in determining outcomes was altered and, in all likelihood, substantially reduced.

The intellectual self-conception, the self-portrait, also deserves attention. Intellectuals portray themselves as, for example, in the case of Marx and Engels, commentators or reporters of events, frequently offering the claim that they bring a unique truth. They simultaneously reject the notion that they themselves cause those events to occur. In fact, in much of that self-portraiture, intellectuals are said to be powerless or, in another frequent version, to be alienated. The recurring image of Prometheus presumably describes their circumstances. If the power of intellectuals were to be admitted, some significant modification of the basic Marxian framework would be necessary. It would no longer be determinate; the moving forces would no longer be exclusively those immanent in the structure of the economy. It would be necessary to pay attention to the determinants of intellectual outlooks, to explain and account for their typical directions. Given the independence of the intellectual directions, one would also have to deal with the possibility of divergence, that the forces of history as represented in working-class movements might take entirely different paths from those chosen by the intellectuals of a given age. It is possible, since intellectuals have, on occasion, been swayed by momentary trends or fashions, that their plans or programs were not based on some unique truth. They might easily have been based on some unique, self-generated error or misunderstanding. Were that the case, then, unlike Prometheus, their contribution might not be a benefit to all mankind.

Marxism:
The Distinctive Contribution

Shortly after publication of *The Class Struggles in France*, his first historical study, Marx wrote his friend Joseph Weydemeyer and, in a justly famous letter (dated March 5, 1852), summarized his intellectual achievement. He began with a disclaimer: "I do not claim to have discovered either the existence of classes in modern society or the struggle between them. Long before me, bourgeois historians had described the historical development of this struggle between the classes, as had bourgeois economists their economic anatomy." In this regard, of course, Marx is entirely accurate. "My own contribution," Marx continues, "was 1) to show [or establish, to prove] that the *existence of classes* is merely bound up with *certain historical phases in the development of production*."[41]

Has Marx done that in *The Class Struggles*? The answer, clearly, is that he has not. A general proposition is not proved with a single case study. In this case study, moreover, as we have seen, the demonstration is seriously flawed. At the outset, Marx stated that an industrial bourgeoisie had emerged and taken power, its historical phase evidently having arrived. But, because so patently erroneous, Marx abandoned that argument (distancing himself from it even) in the third installment of his text. It was nowhere established that the finance aristocracy was bound up with a "certain historical phase." Speculators, after all, have been present (some of them linked to power-holders) throughout recorded history. And finally, Marx missed entirely the specific character of the working class in France, failing to recognize the continuing dominance of artisanal production. His portrait of mid-century France, of its "certain historical phase" and the resulting classes, in short, is mistaken.

Another step in the argument deserves attention. The development of production gives rise to a specific formation of classes and leads to the subsequent conflict between them. That second link in the causal chain is also inappropriate as applied to the French experience. The French Revolution of 1789 was not bound up with the development of production. It had its origins in an economic crisis, to be sure, but it was not the kind of crisis indicated by Marx and Engels. It began with a *fiscal* crisis: government expenditure (interest charges on the debt) had outstripped current revenues. The heavy indebtedness, moreover, resulted from earlier foreign-policy ventures, from France's involvements in the Seven Year War and in the American War of Independence. The crisis was accentuated by an extremely bad harvest in 1788, a disaster which had effects lasting well into 1789. The problem, in short, was not caused by the development of production but rather by failures of the existing arrangements. The crisis, ultimately, led to the calling of the Estates General which in turn set other events in motion.

The next revolution, of 1830, as we have seen, found politicians and intellectuals moving to block repressive legislation; together they set in motion the events that brought down the reestablished Bourbon monarchy. In 1848, the insurgency was again stimulated by opposition groups, by politicians and intellectuals who sought to enhance their power and advantage. A natural catastrophe, a failure of agricultural production, was again a major contributing factor.

Looking elsewhere in Europe in 1848, it is the range of causes that proves of interest, none of them fitting the case developed by Marx and Engels. The original rising in Palermo in January resulted from demands for national liberation. The same was true of the uprising in Milan, where the demand was for an end to Austrian rule. The later struggle in Hungary, much praised by Marx and Engels, was also national, also aiming for liberation from Austria. The revolution in Bavaria focused on the king and his relationship with Lola Montez, a virtual comic opera, rather than something bound up with productive phases. The most intriguing of all those struggles occurred in Prussia. There too, in a remarkable parallel to France of 1789, one causal chain involved a fiscal crisis. To secure needed revenues, the king was forced to call the United

Landtag (legislature). The fiscal crisis in Prussia had its origins in the crop failures of the mid-forties.

The Belgian experience of 1830 and 1848, as was seen earlier, also does not follow any course predicted by Marx and Engels. England, as we have seen, had no bourgeois revolution in the seventeenth century and no such revolution in later centuries (although a late evolution early in the twentieth century was indicated). Britain had no proletarian revolution, either in 1848 or in any later decade. The experience in the most developed capitalist nation is perhaps the most telling failure of this basic prediction. This is the nation, it will be remembered, whose experience would show to the less developed "the image of its own future."[42]

The diversity of causes in these various struggles is remarkable. The two revolutions that most clearly had economic origins were not of the variety specified by Marx in the Weydemeyer letter. A natural catastrophe and the resulting famine is a markedly different event from the cause he predicted. Not a single case among those revolutions fits within the framework of his specific predictions.

Marx's letter to Weydemeyer lists two other contributions. The second of his distinctive achievements was his proof "that the class struggle necessarily leads to the *dictatorship of the proletariat*." This claim involves a prediction about a future state or condition. As such, it is not something that can be proved through past or present experience, nor, obviously, can it be proved "of necessity." The third conclusion holds that "this dictatorship itself constitutes no more than a transition to the *abolition of all classes* and to a *classless society*." It also involves a prediction about future circumstances and, as such, cannot be proved through the analysis of past or contemporary developments. In both instances, Marx violates a fundamental principle of his system; the portrayal of future conditions—*Zukunftsbilder*—crosses the line separating scientific from utopian analysis.[43]

Most of the claims contained in the *Manifesto*, it will be noted, are scientific in character. Capitalists are forced to create great cities; national boundaries and local provincialism will disappear; work will lose its charm; and so forth. Those are hypotheses capable of some testing within the range of capitalist experience. That the class struggle leads to the dictatorship of the proletariat is not capable of such test, at least not in Marx's time, since there had been no experience that would allow the needed investigation. The same point, of course, holds for the assumption of a classless society. Those two exercises in "futurology," moreover, contain a hidden assumption—life in that next epoch would be good. The human condition then would be positive, desirable, beneficial, and qualitatively superior to present-day conditions, to those conditions described and analyzed in their empirical studies. But the assumption of beneficence is nowhere justified or defended; it is merely assumed.

The claims are clearly separable. The first conclusion, a class struggle driving events in a specified direction toward a revolutionary overthrow of capitalism, could be entirely accurate. But that would say nothing about the validity of the second or third, those assuming subsequent beneficence. In the absence of evidence, one could easily entertain the opposite conclusion, that conditions after the revolution would be worse. It is, after all, unlikely that the proletariat as a whole would rule. Some kind of delegation, some representation would be necessary. One could easily imagine tough, ruthless, and manipulative leaders emerging from the revolutionary struggle. They would exercise power, but no necessity would compel them to represent the working-class masses. Rather than abolish all classes, this new class of leaders would continue exploitation of the overwhelming majority, only the "specific form" being changed. The dictatorship of the coterie, in short, is an easy hypothesis. If Marx's first claim, the scientific one, were valid, it could mean that historical events were moving capitalist society toward a catastrophe. If that historical process were determined, it might mean workers (and all other groups) were, of necessity, moving toward the abyss.

The Marxian system, of course, is not strictly determinist: "conditions" provide the framework or structures within which people act. But those people, individually and collectively, have some impact on events, attempting to accelerate the movement, attempting to slow down those processes, or doing nothing. If workers recognized the negative character of the utopia promised them, they might easily, if fully conscious, join the ranks of the counterrevolutionaries. Or they might choose an intermediate option, supporting the revisionist position first outlined by Eduard Bernstein, one that would continue the economic improvement they had experienced and the gradual process of democratization.

The Marx-Engels utopianism differs in one significant aspect from those provided by their leading competitors. Their competitors provided detailed accounts of how things would be in that future state, thus inviting assessments of likelihood or plausibility. Marx and Engels also offered an argument of comparative advantage, but, except for one key stipulation, they did not detail the alternative case. All that is revealed of their utopia is the single predicate: it will be good. No specifications are indicated because on good scientific ground, they had no basis for such prediction. They could only describe, analyze, and predict on the basis of past and present causes. What determinants would be operative in that future state was anyone's guess. The argument is impeccable, entirely in keeping with routine assumptions of scientific analysis. It is, however, flagrantly violated by that assumption of beneficence. How could one know the quality of life in that future condition when, prior to the appearance of the successful revolution, all evidence was lacking?

This unacknowledged utopianism carried with it some remarkable advantages. It is easy for the Marxist critic to compare any ongoing capitalist society and the elements sketched out in the utopian plan (say in those of Owen, Cabet, or Fourier).[44] Moreover, since many of those plans were actually attempted, a direct test of the realism of those proposals was soon at hand. The Marx-Engels utopian sketch avoided the problem of such testing. It possessed the singular advantage of comparisons between the experience of any capitalist society, past or present, and an untrammeled vision. As a general rule, any comparison of existent practice and a formal ideal allows an easy judgment in favor of the latter. It is a rule that follows (almost) of necessity. Every ongoing society will have hierarchy, corruption, incompetence, ignorance, exploitation, deprivation, and suffering. Against that experience, the unexamined ideal always wins.[45]

It is this device, conceivably, that has given "scientific socialism" such power over the minds of so many followers. Lest that contrast, by itself, be not sufficiently compelling, Marx and Engels portrayed existing capitalism in the most unfavorable terms possible. This was seen, for example, in Chapter 3 in Marx's portrayal of the bourgeoisie as murderous, killing workers after the June fighting had ended and punishing thousands of others.

Following in the tradition of Descartes, Marx once declared his motto to be *de omnibus dubitandum*—doubt everything.[46] In the case of the first principles stated in the Weydemeyer letter, however, there was to be no doubt.

History and Its Lessons

It is remarkable how often George Santayana's most famous line appears in intellectual discussions. Some blunder is recounted, reference is then made to the lessons of history, and, for a final touch, one is reminded of the philosopher's apothegm: "Those who cannot remember the past are condemned to repeat it."[47]

But like so much of the handed-down scholar wisdom (our equivalent of folk wisdom), what sounds eminently sensible dissolves in an instant with a modicum of thought. The "lessons of history" claim, of course, is both pretentious and absurd. We, the bearers of the humanity's collected and distilled wisdom, have a package of lessons—rules for the guidance of conduct. If properly applied, they will solve most, if not all, of the world's problems. That child described by Hans Christian Andersen might well ask: "What are the lessons? Are they written down somewhere? Where will I find them?" But, of course, they do not exist. It is merely a manner of speaking. The phrase, in short, does not reflect any obvious reality.

One not-so-obvious reality, however, is implicit in this oft-repeated ritual. The Promethean myth is there once again. Those who so readily agree to the Santayana claim are portraying themselves as the bearers of truth, as the bringers of light. And once again, the awesome claim is made—*J'ai seul la clef.* But then, still drawing on the romantic imagery, even with the key revealed, other people—the powerful, those occupied with their own affairs, or the indifferent—show no interest in the truth which is offered. That is the tragedy (or perversity) of the human condition.[48]

The romantic image begs an important question. The Bearer of Truth, in the many manifestations of the myth, declares the truth, and a willing audience accepts the claim. The Promethean hero, so it is assumed, provides a true and accurate guide in those lessons about the human experience. Only the "crude philistine" (or Andersen's child) would raise questions about validity.

But what if Prometheus, for some reason, was giving us a distorted or false account? Maybe the "truth" reported was something he had heard in a casual conversation. Or maybe he read about it somewhere. Or perhaps it was something he had learned in a course taken many years earlier. Or maybe he had a political aim and had chosen to reveal only part of what he knew. Or perhaps he was a member of a political group and, for tactical reasons, had agreed to suppress some damaging information.

If the self-announced critical thinkers were genuinely committed to the Cartesian principle, if they were really set to doubt everything, why should they make an exception in the case of Prometheus? Or, for that matter, why should one except any prophet, poet, or visionary? Why should any claim rest on the authority of some favorite? Why should conclusions—especially those of critical thinkers—depend on a declaration of faith such as in those familiar prefatory phrases, "As Marx said" or "As Santayana said"?

Santayana did indeed write the statement. But is it true, accurate, valid? Or is there, perhaps, more to be said on the question? Santayana wrote of those who cannot remember the past. But did he formulate the problem accurately? Is the problem one of remembering? Or is it one of never having known? For many, especially in recent decades, the past was not learned because it was dropped as a requirement in high school and university programs. And who, one might ask, changed those requirements? Was it not the responsibility of educators? Was it not, in part at least, the work of critical intellectuals, of those now quoting Santayana?[49]

We do not have a certified list of the lessons from the past. All such offerings are selective. The various narrations or theories are simplified summaries of extremely complicated events. That simplification is one of the tasks of the scholar, commentator, or social theorist—deciding what is important and what is not. But that conclusion—of selectivity—does not lead into one of relativity, as if one selection were as good as the next. Learning the lessons depends on assessment of the available accounts; some judgment of adequacy is appropriate. Such assessment involves consideration of an account's coverage of important events (i.e., that there be no serious omissions) and its accuracy (that the major claims be valid or, at minimum, not patently invalid). The citizen denied even that rudimentary knowledge of history is denied the most basic tools needed for any such assessment.

The problem is compounded by another consideration. The student-citizen who does not know the past, is regularly told by various authorities that this, the Marxian account, provides a valuable portrait of human experience, one deserving serious consideration. Even if, here and there, found wanting on a specific point, the larger framework stands; it is well worth one's attention. In the circumstance, the student-citizen is doubly vulnerable. The failure of the educators to require history leaves the student without any tools for direct assessment. Instead of some dimly remembered fact and a flimsy knowledge of sequence, now there is only a blank. If in that circumstance some expert gatekeeper then declares a given framework to be worthy, the poorly educated citizen is faced with a simple choice: to accept the judgment of the authority or, blindly, to reject the judgment. The latter option is often difficult because of an insistent and, in part, understandable question—Who am I to challenge the judgment of that authority?

The self-declared critical thinker enjoins his (or her) audience to question authority. It seems a reasonable proposition. But one should do so consistently; the effort should not be selective or one-sided. Following the ancient adage, that sauce for the goose is sauce for the gander, one ought to question the authority who asks us to question authority. Why would an intellectual authority, for example, vouch for patently inadequate historical accounts? Why would a "critical" authority be indifferent to the need for research, for documentation of claims? Why would an authority declare a viewpoint to be consistent when inconsistency is its most obvious characteristic?

Santayana's statement applies only obliquely to those influenced by such authorities. For them, the problem is not one of remembering the past, but, rather, is one of a false or distorted record. It is not at all clear that those so influenced would be condemned to a repetition of past mistakes. They might be condemned to new and different mistakes. It is clear, however, that an inadequate record of human experience, a misleading map of the terrain, provides poor guidance for those seeking direction, for those preferring to know where they are going.

NOTES

In the following pages, when referring to Marx and Engels's writings that appeared originally in German, I have cited the collected works published by the Institut für Marxismus-Leninismus in the German Democratic Republic: Karl Marx and Friedrich Engels, *Werke*. Some sense of the extent of those works is given by the number of volumes involved, the last of these, published in 1983, being volume 42. There are also two index volumes and two later supplementary volumes. The *Werke* will be abbreviated as *MEW* followed by the volume and page numbers. A new complete edition, the new *Gesamtausgabe*, is being produced, this by the same Institut, beginning in 1975. When complete, it is expected to have over 130 volumes.

I have also, wherever possible, provided references to English versions of those texts, in most instances to those contained in Karl Marx and Frederick Engels, *Collected Works*. This 50-volume collection, which is not yet complete, is not a translation of the *Werke* but, rather, is an independent effort undertaken by editorial commissions in Great Britain, the United States, and the Soviet Union. The *Collected Works* will be abbreviated here as *MECW* followed by the appropriate volume and page numbers. Deviations from this procedure will be indicated as they appear.

Unless otherwise indicated, italics within quotations appear in the original.

Chapter 1

1. Most English translations of German originals given here are taken from the *MECW*. When possible, I have compared the passages cited with the German versions, with those appearing in the *MEW* and, where appropriate, have made corrections. In a few instances I have supplied my own translations of German originals. Where a work originally appeared in English, the text, again when possible, has been checked against the original (as, for example, in the case of the *New York Daily Tribune* articles).

2. The quotations are from Marx's preface to the first German edition of *Capital*, 1:8–9. This work has not yet appeared in the *MECW* edition. For the German, see *MEW*, 23:12.

On occasion, Marx and Engels's writings on a given country have been collected and published separately. The volume *On Britain*, with 584 pages of text, allows an easy overview. Engels's *Condition of the Working-Class in England* occupies almost three-fifths of those pages. An assortment of journalistic articles, twenty-nine of them, make up another third of the volume. The remaining pages contain letters (or parts thereof). The attention paid to France and Germany, as will be seen immediately, is enormous by comparison.

One could, justifiably, also add some chapters from *Capital* to the list of works on Britain (for example, the famous chapter "The Working-Day"). Despite its importance, I have not included that work in this assessment. The work is, of course, focused on economics, on the economic dynamics of capitalist economies. Much of that analysis is general in character, the conclusions applying to all capitalist nations. The work, it will be remembered, opens with more than a hundred pages on "Commodities and Money," these introducing the distinction between use-value and exchange-value. A key chapter, entitled "The General Law of Capitalist Accumulation," contains a section of some seventy pages with illustrations from the British experience. Limitations of time and space do not allow review and assessment of those discussions.

Assessments of Marx's economic theories may be found elsewhere. For a useful review of claims and evidence, see Gottheil, *Economic Predictions*. One of the earliest critiques was that of Böhm-Bawerk, *Karl Marx*. See also Lindsay, *Marx's Capital*. For a recent appreciation, see Heilbroner, *Marxism*, especially chap. 4.

3. Louis Napoleon's coup d'état of December 2, 1851, posed an obvious challenge for Marx's general theory. To deal with that problem he wrote a second monograph, *The Eighteenth Brumaire of Louis Bonaparte*. Later, after the Paris Commune of 1871, he produced a third monograph, *The Civil War in France*. An earlier work, *The Poverty of Philosophy* (1847), challenged the position of France's leading socialist, Pierre-Joseph Proudhon. This achievement, three historical studies and one theoretical treatise, contrasts sharply with the attention paid to Britain. In addition, there were a wide range of journalistic contributions. Two of Marx's daughters had French husbands and lived in France. Laura's husband, Paul Lafargue, was a leading figure in French socialist circles. The correspondence, accordingly, is extensive. See the three volumes of Engels and Lafargue, *Correspondence*.

4. Marx and Engels, "Manifesto of the Communist Party," *MECW*, 6:519, and for the German, *MEW*, 4:493.

The *Manifesto* was based on an Engels draft entitled "Principles of Communism," *MECW*, 6:341–57 (for the German version, see *MEW*, 4:363–80). Marx then reworked the draft into the final version. That Germanocentric view does not appear in the draft, nor is Germany said to be "on the eve of" the bourgeois revolution. In Germany, so reads the draft, "the decisive struggle between the bourgeoisie and the absolute monarchy is still to come." Engels's original also differs in its claim about sequence and about the facilitating conditions. The revolution, he writes, "will develop more quickly or more slowly according to whether the country has a more developed industry, more wealth, and a more considerable mass of productive forces. It will therefore be slowest and most difficult to carry out in Germany, quickest and easiest in England" (*MECW*,

6:356, 352). This example illustrates the ease with which fundamental empirical judgments were altered. Other examples appear in the following chapters. Engels's draft also appears in Henderson, *Friedrich Engels*, 1:332–79.

5. Engels wrote three monographs dealing with aspects of German history. There was *The Peasant War in Germany*, on the peasants' uprising of 1525–26 (1850). Also in 1850 he produced *Die deutsche Reichsverfassungskampagne* (*The Campaign for the German Imperial Constitution*). The best-known of the three is his *Germany: Revolution and Counter-Revolution* (1851–52). There are many lesser contributions, such as the topical articles in the *New York Daily Tribune*. Marx and Engels both commented on aspects of the Franco-Prussian War and on the subsequent unification of Germany. Marx also wrote a scathing commentary on the Gotha Program (1875). The extent of their writing on Germany may be seen in a large, two-volume collection put out by the Institut für Marxismus-Leninismus, *Zur deutschen Geschichte*. Some of the articles contained there, however, are by Lenin, some by Stalin. Several large collections of letters also attest to the extent of the concern, those exchanged between Marx and Engels and various German-based correspondents—Bebel, Bernstein, Bracke, Kautsky, Kugelmann, Lassalle, and Liebknecht.

A review and assessment of the entire corpus of Marx and Engels's writings on Germany would require several volumes. As indicated, the present work can deal with only a small part of that total. Only a portion of Engels's *Germany: Revolution and Counter-Revolution* will be discussed here. A full assessment would require a monograph-length study.

6. *MECW*, 6:482–85, *MEW*, 4:462–63. Some reference is made to other classes, but these are at best fleeting. The feudal nobility is mentioned on several occasions, but only as a class that has been displaced by the bourgeoisie. The latter, for example, was once "under the sway of the feudal nobility." When the bourgeoisie has gained the upper hand, it will "put an end to all feudal, patriarchal, idyllic relations" (*MECW*, 6:486; *MEW*, 4:464).

7. *MECW*, 6:486, 489, *MEW*, 4:464, 467. These paragraphs represent exposition of a viewpoint, not agreement with the claims offered.

8. *MECW*, 6:493–94, *MEW*, 4:471–72.

9. *MECW*, 6:491–92, *MEW*, 4:469. The German version refers to "Rentiers" rather than "retired tradesmen generally."

10. *MECW*, 6:494, *MEW*, 4:472.

11. I have been making use of the official (and revised) version of the *Manifesto* attested to by Engels. For the record, it should be noted that the first of the quotations given above, in the German original, reads, "*Die bisherigen kleinen Mittelstände, die kleinen Industriellen,*" etc. The second reads, "*Die Mittelstände, der kleine Industrielle, der kleine Kaufmann,*" etc. (*MEW*, 4:469, 472). Some might translate *Mittelstände* as "middle ranks." Engels, however, was obviously satisfied with the expression "lower middle class."

12. The quotation is from *Germany*, p. 128. All references to this work will be to the

readily available Krieger edition (rather than to the *MECW*). An assistant, Yuhui Li, has checked that text against the *New York Daily Tribune* original. The Krieger volume also contains Engels's *The Peasant War in Germany*.

13. *MECW*, 6:494, *MEW*, 4:472. In German, the paragraph begins with the words *Das Lumpenproletariat*. "Dangerous class" is not an accurate translation of that original.

Again, it may be noted, we have the transformation of quantitative differences, those of degree, into differences of kind. Again, as with the lower middle class, there is some unexpected (and unexplained) indeterminacy—the *Lumpenproletariat* "may, here and there," etc.

14. This work deals with Marx and Engels's formulations, not those of subsequent followers. It might be that every fault indicated here has been adjusted and corrected in later work. That might be the case, but then again it might not. In any event, that is a topic for another monograph. For a brilliant analysis and critique of some recent major efforts in the Marxist tradition, see Van den Berg, *Immanent Utopia*.

15. Gouldner, *Two Marxisms*, p. 34. For the *German Ideology* quotation, see *MECW*, 5:35, *MEW*, 3:25.

16. For Marx's references to their division of labor, see his letter to Engels of July 31, 1865, *MEW*, 31:131, *MECW*, 42:172. The Marx quotation in the text is from *Herr Vogt*, *MEW*, 14:472, *MECW*, 17:114. Engels's letter to Bernstein (February 22–25, 1882) is in *MEW*, 35:284.

17. For recent presentations of the anti-Engels case, see Levine, *Tragic Deception*; Bender, *Betrayal*; and Carver, *Marx and Engels*.

18. The Marx quotation, about following in Engels's footsteps, is from his letter, July 4, 1864, *MEW*, 30:418, *MECW*, 41:546. For descriptions of Engels's lectures, see Gustav Mayer, *Friedrich Engels*, 1:209–19, and Henderson, *Friedrich Engels*, 1:45–47. For the text, see *MEW*, 2:536–57, *MECW*, 4:243–64.

Frederic L. Bender, as editor of a "critical edition" of the *Manifesto*, makes Marx the sole author of that work. Engels's role was peripheral—he "presumably . . . was consulted throughout." See Bender, *Communist Manifesto*, p. 14. Marx declared, unambiguously, that the work was "jointly written by Engels and myself." See his preface to *The Critique of Political Economy*, *MEW*, 13:10, *MECW*, 29:264. For other evidence on the joint character of the effort, see Henderson, *Friedrich Engels*, 1:119.

19. Carver agrees with my point about the basic agreements "before 1859," indicating the similarities of their historical works and declaring that they "used a common analytic method—class analysis" (*Marx and Engels*, p. 142). For more recent contributions on the subject, see Levine, "Engelsian Inversion" and "Lenin's Utopianism," and Carver, "Marx, Engels, and Dialectics" and "Marx, Engels, and Scholarship." The latter is a response to challenges to his position by Welty, "Marx, Engels, and 'Anti-Dühring,'" and by Stanley and Zimmermann, "Alleged Differences."

For further discussion, including extensive criticism of the anti-Engels argument, see Kolakowski, *Main Currents*, 1:399–408; Gouldner, *Two Marxisms*, chap. 9; Horowitz and Hayes, "For Marx/Against Engels"; and Kline, "The Myth." For a useful brief counterstatement, see Randall Collins, *Three Sociological Traditions*, pp. 56–62. Also of some relevance is Hammen, "Alienation."

Many of the arguments about Marx-Engels differences first appeared in earlier writings, the names of Lukács, Korsch, and Gramsci being most frequently cited. For middle-period reviews of the problem, see Lichtheim, *Marxism*, pp. 58–61, 234–58, and Avineri, *Social and Political Thought*, pp. 65–73. See Henderson, *Friedrich Engels*, for further details: for the collaboration on *The German Ideology*, see 1:79–93; for *The Communist Manifesto*, 1:106–33; and for the *Revolution and Counter-Revolution* articles, 1:206.

The citations presented here, incidentally, are by no means exhaustive. I am especially indebted to Axel van den Berg and to Helmut Smith for their assistance on this question.

20. Anderson's comments are from *Lineages*, p. 237n.

Chapter 2

1. From an article in the *Neue Rheinische Zeitung* dated January 22, 1849, *MECW*, 8:263, *MEW*, 6:192.

The Stuarts, during most of the seventeenth century, reigned in two separate nations, England and Scotland. It was only in 1707, with the Act of Union, that a single nation, Great Britain, was formed. The struggles to be discussed here occurred in England; it was the English (not the British) civil war. The same point would hold, of course, for a bourgeois revolution.

Marx, as noted, assumes a unity, an identity of interest between king and aristocracy. His summary statement quoted in the text (that "state power in the hands of a king" is "state power in the hands of the old society . . . in the hands of the feudal social estates") does not adequately describe medieval England. Its history contained the Magna Carta, the rise of the House of Lords, and the Confirmation of Charters. Between 1327 and 1485, five kings were deposed. See Dunham and Wood, "Right to Rule."

2. *MECW*, 6:486, *MEW*, 4:464. The observations made here are all commonplace for anyone with passing knowledge of the Marxist theory. They would hardly need mention but for the flexible tendency found among some of the theory's defenders, the propensity for post hoc adjustment when faced with contrary evidence followed by a conclusion declaring the basic position to be completely vindicated.

3. Christopher Hill, the Marxist historian, noted that Marx and Engels never wrote "a consecutive history" of the English seventeenth-century revolution. In an early article, Hill "tried to illustrate their ideas" on the subject but, touching on the difficulty, indicated he had "not [tried] to synthesize them." See his "English Civil War," p. 133.

A minor point: a unified nation bearing the name Germany (*Deutschland*) did not appear until 1871. Prior to that time there was a scatter of German-speaking nations,

Austria, Prussia, Bavaria, Baden, Hanover, and so on, all officially linked in a rather powerless federation, the German Bund.

4. *MECW*, 6:485, *MEW*, 4:463.

5. The first quotation is from Marx's letter to P. V. Annenkov, December 28, 1846, *MECW*, 38:97, *MEW*, 27:453. The other two Marx quotations are from *Neue Rheinische Zeitung* articles, those of December 15, 1848, *MECW*, 8:161, *MEW*, 6:107–8, and January 26, 1849, *MECW*, 8:293, *MEW*, 6:201. The Engels quotation is from *Germany*, p. 126.

In a remarkable series of articles written early in 1844 (and published later that year), Engels laid out all of the basics of the Marxian historical theory. He declared "that Germany, France and England are the three foremost countries at the present moment in history," a fact, he added, that "I can doubtless take for granted." He refers to "the English revolution of the seventeenth century," which "provides the exact model for the French one of 1789." He sees a parallel between the "three stages" of the Long Parliament and the evolution of France's revolutionary government. Cromwell, he asserts, "is Robespierre and Napoleon rolled into one." Later, however, his focus is on the "revolution of 1688." He writes of the "foundation of 1688." From "The Condition of England," *MECW*, 3:471, 472–73, 490–91.

6. Chodorow et al., *Mainstream*, p. 537. A correction: absolute monarchy, such as appeared on the continent, was never successfully established in England. Charles had no standing army, no paid bureaucracy, and no independent revenue to support either agency. What Parliament destroyed in the years 1640–41 was prerogative government. For more detailed reviews, see Ashton, *English Civil War*, chap. 6, and Roots, *Great Rebellion*, pp. 38–42.

It would be a mistake to see the collapse of the monarchy as the result of a couple of policy errors. For an important review, one that covers the long-term development, see Goldstone, "State Breakdown," and "East and West."

7. Ashton, *English Civil War*, pt. 2; Roots, *Great Rebellion*, pp. 69–134. For Cromwell's coup d'état and the Protectorate, see Roots, *Great Rebellion*, pp. 163–80.

A successful revolution has two aspects or phases, one military, one political. There is the conflict phase, one requiring broad-based involvement. On the occasion of success, on gaining power, the political leadership then creates new institutions, bringing about the revolutionary changes. The conclusion of the first phase in this instance may easily be dated as 1649. But that marks only the beginning of the new institutional experimentation.

For a brilliant comprehensive overview, see Stone, *Causes*. See also his long essay, "Results," chap. 1. For a sweeping review of the historiography over three centuries, see Richardson, *Debate*. The leading Marxist accounts are those of Hill. For his earliest statement, see *English Revolution*. For a brief review of Hill's extensive work in the area, see Richardson, *Debate*, pp. 110–27.

See also Aylmer, *Rebellion or Revolution?*, and Morrill, *Reactions*. For accounts of the most prominent actor, see Paul, *Lord Protector*; Hill, *God's Englishman*; and Fraser, *Cromwell*.

8. *MECW*, 11:105, *MEW*, 8:116. Hill makes a flat-out declaration of the point: Puritanism was "the ideology in which the bourgeoisie expressed their revolutionary aspirations" ("English Civil War," p. 132). The problem touched on here will be discussed at greater length later in this chapter.

9. From Engels's "Special Introduction," p. 96; *MEW*, 22:301. A note on that *MEW* page indicates some differences between the German and English versions of the text. The "three great bourgeois risings," incidentally, are "the Protestant Reformation in Germany" (which also includes Calvinism), the English civil war, and the French Revolution.

Engels's 1892 formulation, it should be noted, makes no mention of the gentry as a factor in the conflict. The claims about the gentry as the decisive insurgent segment were not to appear for another half-century. This subject will also be discussed in more detail below.

10. For an overview, see the essays in J. R. Jones, *Restored Monarchy*.

11. The editors of the *MECW* (39:600 n. 36) offer the following one-sentence account: "The 'glorious revolution' of 1688 in England established a constitutional monarchy based on a compromise between the landed aristocracy and the financial bourgeoisie." The *MECW* editors provide no supporting evidence on this latter point, nor do they refer to any scholarly sources. The editors, it should also be noted, do not mention the birth nor, obviously, its implications for the religious settlement. Also omitted is any indication of Mary's identity, that she was the eldest daughter of James II and, until birth of the son, heir to the throne. She and her sister Anne (also destined to be a queen of England) were children from James's first marriage, and, the salient factor in the history, both were Protestant. In the *MEW* account, the editors (22:610 n. 260) do not even mention Mary. The revolution, it is said, "overthrew the Stuart dynasty" and transferred the royal power to William of Orange. Mary and Anne, of course, were both Stuarts.

For an older classic, an enthusiastic Whig history, see Trevelyan, *English Revolution*, and, for an account sympathetic to the king, see Haswell, *James II*. For overviews, see J. R. Jones, *Revolution*, and Speck, *Reluctant Revolutionaries*. The definitive biography of the king is Miller's *James II*. For a discussion of the resolution of one central issue, the king's purse, see Roberts, "Constitutional Significance."

12. Engels, "Special Introduction," p. 97; *MEW*, 22:301.

13. See Stone, "Results," pp. 64–65.

14. The strongest arguments for the seventeenth-century bourgeois revolution appeared, as indicated, in the work of Christopher Hill. But even Hill, in his later work, abandoned the bourgeois-instigation position and instead put forth an argument of consequences—the 1688 settlement yielded legislation that favored the rise of the bourgeoisie. For this new argument, see his essay, "A Bourgeois Revolution?" The argument of favorable consequences appears there on pp. 111 and 115. Even in the aftermath of the civil war, Hill writes, "there was no direct takeover of power by 'the bourgeoisie'" (p. 131). Some additional aspects of this changed position are considered below in n. 59.

15. Stone, *Causes*, pp. 30, 34.

16. Ibid., p. 49; for more on the same theme, p. 51. See also Stone's 1980 conclusions, as cited above in n. 13.

17. Stone, "Results," pp. 40, 46. Goldstone provides a similar conclusion with regard to the character of the conflict: "Wherever one looks in mid-17th century England, one almost never finds conflict between classes; instead one finds conflicts within classes and shifting coalitions—among the Crown, lords, gentry, merchants, and popular groups— that cross and obscure class lines" ("State Breakdown," p. 259).

18. Stone, *Causes*, pp. 55 (emphasis added), 71–72, and for other statements of the point, pp. 127–28 and 144. For research on the orientations of a key segment, see Pearl, *London*; Brenner, "Civil War Politics"; Howell, "Urban Politics" and Howell, "Neutralism."

Some commentators have made much of the fact that London was on the side of Parliament throughout the conflict. Given the presence of the merchant elite, it is easy to conclude that they opposed the king and his policies. But, as Stone indicates, that conclusion depends on an ecological fallacy. The city's ruling elite, he argues, citing sources, "were predominantly royalist in their sympathies, and had to be ejected from power by a revolution from below before the political allegiance of the city could be shifted to Parliament. The same appears to be true of Newcastle and York, while the citizens and patriciates of Bristol and other cities were mostly neutral, anxious above all to save their homes and shops from the horrors of military occupation by disorderly troops, siege and sack." See his "Bourgeois Revolution," p. 280.

19. Stone, *Causes*, pp. 55–56. For reviews of the gentry controversy, see Stone, *Causes*, pp. 26–29; Hexter, *Reappraisals*, chap. 6; Richardson, *Debate*, 103–6, 136–40; and Ashton, *English Civil War*, chap. 4. Hexter's conclusion reads as follows: "Economically gentry and peerage were of the *same* class—the class that ordinarily drew the larger part of its income from exploitation of proprietary rights in land" (p. 128). His comments on pp. 140–41 are also relevant.

In a 1985 publication, Stone provided some evidence, more than a shred, on the point. This evidence, he writes, "not only does not support, but tends directly to contradict the theory that bourgeois attitudes towards land management led to support of Parliament" ("Bourgeois Revolution," pp. 284–87). For a review of other works dealing with the composition of the contending forces, see Richardson, *Debate*, pp. 155–66.

20. Stone, *Causes*, pp. 56–57 (emphasis added).

21. Engels, "Special Introduction," p. 97; *MEW*, 22:301.

22. One would have to show, for example, that the Immortal Seven, the signators of the invitation to William of Orange, were themselves bourgeois or were representatives of that class; see Speck, *Reluctant Revolutionaries*, pp. 219–25. On December 11, 1688, abandoning the throne, the king fled London, aiming for refuge in France. Before leaving, James "deliberately set out to create a governmental vacuum." Immediately after his departure, a group of notables met to deal with the alarming situation. The group, called together by the earl of Rochester and the bishop of Ely, was composed of

peers and bishops. No indication is made of bourgeois representation, for example, of merchants, bankers, or financiers. See J. R. Jones, *Revolution*, pp. 305, 308–9, and Speck, *Reluctant Revolutionaries*, pp. 88–89.

Also of considerable interest, reviewing both the Restoration and 1688, is McInnes, "When Was the English Revolution?"

23. Marx to Engels, January 24, 1852. This is my translation based on the *MEW* text, 28:12–13. The *MECW* version (39:21) differs in some minor but inessential details.

24. *MECW*, 6:526, *MEW*, 4:499–500.

25. Marx's article "In Retrospect," dated December 29, 1854, appeared in the *Neue Oder-Zeitung*, *MECW*, 13:554–56, *MEW*, 10:588–90.

26. Engels, *Germany*, p. 7. The passage is from Engels's 1870 "Preface to the Second Edition" and *MEW*, 16:396–97. On the Palmerston-Bright relationship, see Ridley, *Palmerston*, pp. 565 and 491. Bright's position, as bourgeois representative in the government, will be considered in more detail just below in the text.

On the 1867 suffrage extension, see Magnus, *Gladstone*, pp. 177–82; Blake, *Disraeli*, chap. 21; and Bradford, *Disraeli*, chap. 17. Gladstone and the Liberals first introduced the reform bill, only to have it denounced and defeated by Disraeli and his supporters. Disraeli then introduced a similar measure and, making a complete turnabout, defended it and saw it enacted. Many workers, for the first time, were allowed to vote. The results, however, were a disappointment to Engels, who wrote as follows to Marx: "What do you say about the elections in the factory districts? The proletariat has once again made an awful fool of itself. Manchester and Salford return 3 Tories against 2 Liberals. . . . In Ashton it looks as if Milner Gibson has gone to the wall. Ernest Jones nowhere, despite the cheering. . . . If any party has gained strength from the new voters, it is the Tories. . . . The increase in working-class votes had brought the Tories more than their simple percentage, and has improved their relative position. . . . It remains an appalling display of weakness [*Armutszeugnis* 'certificate of poverty'] by the English proletariat" (November 18, 1868, *MECW*, 43:163–64, *MEW*, 32:207–8).

It may be noted, in passing, that a series of failed hypotheses appear in these passages. Engels, in 1847, predicted an imminent move by the bourgeoisie to "complete the victory." Marx, in 1854, saw "war with Russia" as the ultimate threat to aristocratic rule. Workers, they thought, would vote for working-class leaders (e.g., Ernest Jones) or the more progressive wing of the Liberals, not for Conservatives.

27. Gash, *Aristocracy*, p. 347.

28. Entitled *Notes sur l'Angleterre, 1860–1870*, it first appeared in 1872. I have quoted from Taine, *Notes on England*, p. 155. The key passage also appears in Shannon, *Crisis of Imperialism*, pp. 22–23. The first chapter of Shannon's book argues a history of aristocratic persistence down to at least 1865, the date of Palmerston's death; the 1867 electoral reform is reviewed in his chap. 3.

29. Vincent, *Formation*, pp. xxvi–xxviii.

30. Ibid., pp. 18, 164–68. W. E. Forster, a manufacturer, entered Parliament as a Liberal in 1861. Two years later, he wrote that the party needed a leader, someone to take

over after Palmerson: "The want of the liberal party of a new man is great, and felt to be great; the old whig leaders are worn out; there are no new whigs; Cobden and Bright are impracticable and un-English, and there are hardly any hopeful radicals." From Woodward, *Age of Reform*, p. 176.

31. Hinde, *Richard Cobden*, p. 269. For an account of Cobden and Bright's most famous effort, see McCord, *Anti–Corn Law League*. For comment on Bright's lesser role, see pp. 171–72. In the period of league agitation (it dissolved in 1846), the leaders did not want cabinet offices and advised members against the opportunity (p. 214). For more detail, especially on their diminished role after 1846, see McCord, "Cobden and Bright."

32. Guttsman, *Political Elite*, pp. 77–78.

33. On Salisbury, see Kennedy, *Salisbury*. Salisbury's third son, Lord Robert Cecil, was a prominent British statesman, a principal author of the League of Nations Covenant and, in 1937, winner of the Nobel Peace Prize. The British ambassador to the United States from 1961 to 1965 was David Ormsby Gore, Lord Harlech. He was a great-grandson of Salisbury (from the *New York Times* obituary notice, January 27, 1985).

It would be easy to read in some notion of an upper-class plot, of a small group of wealthy noble families holding onto power over centuries. But the experience of Peel, Disraeli, and Gladstone, among others, would require some revision of that view. Moreover, as one knowledgeable commentator observed: "Only by the rarest of chances did a great house like Hatfield [i.e., the Cecils] revive its primitive glories." See Percy, *Some Memories*, p. 12.

34. Guttsman, *Political Elite*, pp. 78–79. For this purpose, he has defined aristocracy as "all those who were descended from a holder of a hereditary title in the grandparent generation, thus excluding the sons of the newly ennobled or those who have received hereditary titles themselves" (p. 77). Winston Churchill, thus, by this definition, is counted appropriately, given his background, as an aristocrat. The term "middle class" as used by Guttsman, it should be noted, is not the same as "bourgeois" (in Marx and Engels's usage). The category is much wider, including sons of professionals, administrators, etc.

Kennedy also argues an end-of-the-century transition, quoting Winston Churchill on the point. Kennedy writes: "The Prime Ministers of two centuries of British history had been drawn from the same class and much the same environment. Lord Mersey, in his *Prime Ministers of Britain*, shows statistically that the typical Prime Minister between 1700 and 1900 was born in the peerage, brought up in the country, educated at Eton and Oxford (except when he emerged from Harrow and Cambridge)" (*Salisbury*, p. 5). Winston Churchill, it will be remembered, was prime minister long after the turn of the century, first during World War II, and again in 1951. His ancestor John Churchill (later the Duke of Marlborough) played a decisive role in 1688 by denying military support to King James.

35. Guttsman, *Political Elite*, pp. 77–78.

36. The markedly aristocratic character of Palmerston's last cabinet was reported

above. Guttsman offers the same basic conclusion: "It contained three dukes, two Earls and six other aristocrats out of a total of fifteen members." This cabinet brought together two factions of the Liberal Party. In the previous negotiations, Bright (according to Engels, the bourgeoisie's real representative) had asked that in forming the government "some attention . . . be paid to members below the gangway." As a result, Guttsman reports, "Milner Gibson was appointed President of the Poor Law Board (with a seat in the Cabinet). Bright was angered at this cavalier treatment of the radicals" (ibid., p. 77).

37. See Arnstein's brilliant comprehensive overview, "Survival of the Victorian Aristocracy." The number of English peers—the dukes, marquesses, earls, viscounts, and barons—those entitled to sit in the House of Lords, was remarkably small: 304 in 1830, 502 in 1896. Scottish and Irish peers sat in the Commons. There was a larger group of lesser nobles, the baronets, to add further complication. Arnstein's table (p. 210) separates cabinet members into three categories: peers, lesser aristocrats, and commoners. The second category includes "Irish peers, baronets, and sons or sons-in-law of peers. Untitled country gentlemen and cabinet members related to the peerage in other ways are defined as 'commoners.'" For Guttsman's procedure, see n. 34 above. Arnstein's discussion of Salisbury's 1895 cabinet appears on pp. 207–9. Tuchman, his source for much of the Salisbury discussion, is quoted on p. 207. See chap. 1 of Tuchman's *Proud Tower*. Entitled "The Patricians, England: 1895–1902," it gives a rich account of this last episode of aristocratic rule. Another useful source, one providing a wide range of detail on political leaders, cabinet composition, and policies, is Ensor, *England*.

38. Arnstein, "Survival," pp. 211, 209. On the hostility of established Tory and Whig leaders toward Disraeli and Gladstone, see Bradford, *Disraeli*: for Disraeli's relationships with the Tory squires, see pp. 223–24, 253; for Gladstone's with the equivalent Whigs, see pp. 255–60. In the late sixties, Bradford writes, "the future belonged to two men who were outsiders in terms of the traditional political establishment, who had risen by ability alone and who were regarded by their respective parties with distrust and even loathing" (p. 259).

39. Thompson, *English Landed Society*, p. 295. Political leaders are often categorized in either/or terms, being tagged as having either landed or bourgeois (or manufacturing, or business) backgrounds. The case of Gladstone makes clear that one could easily have both, his father being a cotton manufacturer with substantial estates. Without extensive research, it would not be possible to say, in any given case, which of those backgrounds was most important, either in the family's finances or in its preferences or loyalties. Gladstone himself did not see things in either/or terms; he saw merit in both kinds of economic activity and in both life-styles.

40. Arnstein, "Survival," p. 254.

41. The aristocratic persistence, it should be noted, was recognized by a wide range of contemporary observers. Alexis de Tocqueville, in his 1833 visit to England, saw that class as still dominant: "The English aristocracy has a hand in everything." He quotes Bulwer Lytton to the same effect: "The aristocracy still has considerable strength with

us." At that point, however, Tocqueville thought the aristocracy would soon, with the coming of democracy, be overwhelmed by "the people." In 1857, on the occasion of his last visit, he revised that judgment, recognizing that it was "the same old England." Matthew Arnold, in 1861, wrote that "the aristocracy [still] . . . administers public affairs; and it is a great error to suppose, as many persons in England suppose, that it administers but does not govern." See Tocqueville, *Journeys*, pp. 67, 55, and 59–61; Arnstein, "Survival," p. 217; and, for the Arnold quotation, Guttsman, *Political Elite*, p. 34.

42. Langer, *Political and Social Upheaval*, p. 51. For further discussion of this point see below, Chapter 5, n. 10.

43. The Corn Law repeal is reviewed in Arnstein, "Survival," pp. 217–19. For some decades, Arnstein notes, commentators pointed to the famous acts, those of 1832, 1846, 1867, and 1884, as "neat signposts" attesting to the achievement of middle-class rule. He reviews all of these, indicating the complexities involved (pp. 214–21). Given what has been reported thus far in the text, it is clear that they did not bring about middle-class rule. All of the acts, Arnstein points out, received significant support from aristocrats and their supporters in Lords and Commons (otherwise they could not have been carried). In some respects, he indicates, the reforms strengthened the aristocracy. The 1832 reforms, for example, ended the embarrassing and indefensible "rotten boroughs." A tariff on imported grain (easily tagged a "bread tax") is an embarrassment at all times. It was extremely problematic in the midst of a serious famine.

Arnstein raises an intriguing question: "Why have so many general historians, British and American alike, been so insistent on seeing a middle-class triumph in 1832?" He suggests two answers (actually, hypotheses): First, "a feeling, conscious or unconscious, that a Marxist analysis demanded a British equivalent to the French Revolution of 1789. If 1640 did not fit the bill because it required an explanation for the aristocratic revival of the late seventeenth and early eighteenth centuries, then 1832 would have to do." His second answer points to the "consistently hazy" definition of the key concept, middle class (pp. 254–55).

For more detail on the role of the league in repeal, see McCord, *Anti–Corn Law League*, pp. 197–204, and pp. 208–16. He refers to "the fundamental impotence of the League" as of 1846 (p. 203). For a rich array of detail, see McCord, "Cobden and Bright." After his defeat in 1857, Cobden wrote: "The Higher classes never stood so high in relative social and political rank, as compared with the other classes, as at present. The middle class has been content with the very crumbs from their table" (p. 113).

44. Chateaubriand, while visiting with the British prime minister, Lord Liverpool, congratulated him on the solidity of the nation's institutions. Liverpool pointed to the capital outside his windows and replied: "What can be stable with these enormous cities? One insurrection in London and all is lost?" Quoted from Lorwin, "Working Class Politics," p. 341.

It is curious: Given his wide personal experience in the leading business circles of Manchester, Engels could easily have written a book on the British bourgeoisie. He did not produce even an article on the subject. He did devote some twenty pages of *The Condition of the Working Class in England* to "The Attitude of the Bourgeoisie Towards the Proletariat." Those pages, however, contain no serious analysis; they argue at length his claim of bourgeois indifference, callousness, or worse, viciousness (*MECW*, 4:562–83, *MEW*, 2:486–506). The chapter opens with a note of definition: "In speaking of the bourgeoisie I include the so-called aristocracy." Later in that chapter, in a discussion of the New Poor Law, he refers to 1833—"when the bourgeoisie had just come into power through the Reform Bill" (*MECW*, 4:562, 571, *MEW*, 2:486, 495).

45. Engels, "Special Introduction," p. 99, *MEW*, 22:303. That bourgeois triumph was not quite complete—the statement overlooks the restoration in 1815.

46. Langer, *Political and Social Upheaval*, p. 47. Gash reports another instructive example of mutual understanding between the two classes: "Even in such industrialized areas as the West Riding of Yorkshire the Earl Fitzwilliam, in the 1860s as in the 1790s, was the uncrowned king of local society and politics. The only two men from the non-gentry class who became MPs for the constituency between the first and second Reform Acts were Cobden in 1847 and 1852 and Francis Crossley, the Halifax carpet manufacturer, in 1859. This was not because the landowners had direct electoral control. It resulted from a sensible adjustment of urban and landed interests and the willingness of town liberals to accept aristocratic whig leadership when exercised with tact and responsibility" (*Aristocracy*, p. 348). For an instructive account of politics in this district, see Thompson, "Whigs and Liberals."

47. Langer, *Political and Social Upheaval*, p. 48. For more detail, see Spring, "Earl Fitzwilliam." The noble mineowners are reviewed and discussed on pp. 297–98. For a more comprehensive overview, see Spring's earlier article, "English Landed Estate." These mineowning noblemen were not exceptions to a rule nor atypical cases. Spring writes: "Not many landed estates in Durham and Northumberland . . . escaped being touched by the development of the northern coal field. . . . Much the same story can be told about the gentry in Cumberland or Lancashire or south Staffordshire. Big or small throughout the land, they sought to fatten their agricultural incomes by profits derived from the working of their minerals" ("English Landed Estate," pp. 4–5). Also of considerable interest in this connection are Spring's articles "Reflections," and "Aristocracy."

For a brief case study, see Richards, "Structural Change." For an extended review of the same experience, see Richards, *Leviathan*. For comprehensive overviews, see Spring, *English Landed Estate*, and the essays in Ward and Wilson, *Land and Industry*. For a comparative study, see Spring, *European Landed Elites*.

48. Vincent, *Formation*, p. 2n. The noble urban landlords are discussed in Spring, "Earl Fitzwilliam," p. 298, and "English Landed Estate," pp. 9–11. Lawrence Stone reports that in the seventeenth century, prior to the civil war, "the two largest urban developers in London" were Salisbury and Bedford. See his "Bourgeois Revolution," p. 282. The noble holders of urban property appear at many points in Rubinstein's important study. At the end of the nineteenth century, one striking example, "the Duke of

Westminster was said to be worth £14 [million] on his London holdings alone." See Rubinstein, *Men of Property*, esp. p. 44.

The opposite process, ennoblement of bourgeois notables, increased sharply toward the end of the nineteenth century. The new pattern dates from 1886: prior to that time, about one-tenth of the newly named peers were linked to commerce and industry; thereafter, it was nearly a third. The proportion was not large; the absolute number of bourgeois persons raised to the peerage between 1886 and 1911 was also small, 47 persons. For more detail, see Pumphrey, "Introduction of Industrialists."

49. Intermarriage would provide another indication of a merging of the two classes. Some famous marriages involved cross-continent mergers as well. Randolph Churchill, the younger brother of the eighth duke of Marlborough, married Jennie Jerome, the daughter of an American businessman. She, of course, was the mother of Winston Churchill. The ninth duke of Marlborough married Consuelo Vanderbilt, another American bourgeois. Several generations later, still another duke of Marlborough married Tina Onassis, the ex-wife of the Greek shipping magnate. For a portrait of the Vanderbilt marriage, see Balsan, *Glitter*.

Harold Macmillan, who became prime minister in 1956 after the Suez crisis, was from a bourgeois family. He was of the third generation in the family's publishing enterprise. Macmillan's father was a close friend of Lord Robert Cecil (see n. 33 above). Harold married Dorothy Cavendish, daughter of the duke of Devonshire. Her family was linked by marriage to the Cecils, the closest link involving her brother Eddy. In this case, however, the relationships were not amicable. "The Cecil clan patronised [Macmillan] and made little bones about regarding the publisher as being 'in trade', and socially rather bourgeois. . . . Politically, they became suspicious of his radical views and what they regarded as his opportunism." From Horne, *Macmillan*, 1:66–67. See also Tuchman, *Proud Tower*, pp. 40–44.

A systematic study of the marital patterns of the British nobility found that in all periods of the eighteenth and nineteenth centuries the majority of heirs married outside the nobility. In the early decades of the nineteenth century, only about four marriages in ten were in-marriages. In the last decades the level had declined to three in ten. Most of the marriages to commoners, however, were to wives whose fathers were either landed or in the armed forces. The highest percentage of marriages with business, one in ten, came late in the century. See Thomas, "Social Origins."

Aristocracy and bourgeoisie could, of course, have common interests but at the same time be separate and distinctive socially. The absence of intermarriage does point to social separation.

50. For the "Principles of Communism," see *MECW*, 6:356, *MEW*, 4:379. The piece also appears in Henderson, *Friedrich Engels*, 1:378. For Engels on Poland, see *MECW*, 6:389–90, *MEW*, 4:418.

51. Engels, "Special Introduction," pp. 102–3, *MEW*, 22:307–8.

52. Marx, "Preface" to his *Contribution to the Critique of Political Economy*, *MECW*, 29:263, *MEW*, 13:9.

53. Forster was an M.P. from 1861 and was first named to office, as under-secretary for the colonies, by Palmerston in 1865. That is to say, he came into office before the new Reform Act. Neither the *MECW* nor the *MEW* editors point out the error. See Woodward, *Age of Reform*, p. 482n. See n. 30 above for Forster's opinion of Bright and Cobden. See also McCord, "Cobden and Bright," pp. 99–103.

54. See, of course, Arnstein, "Survival"; Guttsman, *Political Elite*, chap. 5; and also Clark, *Victorian England*, esp. p. 277.

For comprehensive scholarly histories of the aristocracy, see Stone and Stone, *An Open Elite?*, and Beckett, *Aristocracy*. For a documented account of aristocratic power in the eighteenth century, see Cannon, *Aristocratic Century*, chap. 4; see also McCahill, "Peerage Creations." A useful brief summary history, including a consideration of "the last stage of aristocracy," is provided by Sampson, *Anatomy*, chap. 1. See also, for a more popular account, Perrott, *Aristocrats*.

The aristocracy-bourgeoisie dualism, it should be noted, does not adequately capture the complexity of the British class structure. Elizabeth Harman was born of a professional family; both her parents, by training, were medical doctors. Her mother was a Chamberlain, a first cousin to Neville, the problematic prime minister. That meant, in terms of background, a link with a leading bourgeois family. At Oxford, she met and later married Frank Pakenham, who was from a famous titled family. Years later, when Packenham's older brother died without issue, Frank automatically gained the title, and his wife became Lady Elizabeth Longford. That might sound like another merging of aristocratic and bourgeois class interests except for one thing—they were both ardent supporters of the Labour Party. Earlier, prior to the death of the brother, Prime Minister Attlee wanted to make Frank a peer in order to give the Labour Party strength in the House of Lords and to allow Frank to be given a cabinet position. Packenham found the implication—to be a socialist peer—rather embarrassing. But, for several reasons, he finally accepted and was appointed to be chancellor of the Duchy Lancaster and minister in charge of Germany. See Longford, *Pebbled Shore*, pp. 229–30, 248. The two belonged to another class, to the intelligentsia, a segment generally said to be independent of both aristocracy and bourgeoisie. See Annan, "Intellectual Aristocracy."

55. Engels, writing in 1872–73, discusses the German experience: "In Prussia—and Prussia is now decisive—there exists side by side with a landowning aristocracy, which is still powerful, a comparatively young and extremely cowardly bourgeoisie, which up to the present has not won either direct political domination, as in France, or more or less indirect domination [*sic*] as in England" (*The Housing Question*, *MECW*, 23:363, *MEW*, 18:358). The same orientation appears in Arno J. Mayer, *Persistence*; see, for example, pp. 84–86.

56. Stone, *Causes*, pp. 39–40.

57. Marx, "Preface," *MECW*, 29:261, *MEW*, 13:7. Marx makes the same point in another important statement. The third volume of *Capital* ends with a fragment devoted to classes. In the opening sentence Marx declares that "wage-labourers, capitalists and land-owners, constitute [the] three big classes of modern society based upon the

capitalist mode of production." See *Capital*, 3:885; *MEW*, 25:892–95. The Hexter quotations appear in his essay, "Historical Method," p. 235n. Hill sees no problem in such usage; it is a difficulty only "for purists who regard 'rural bourgeoisie' as a contradiction in terms" ("Bourgeois Revolution?," p. 113). On one occasion, in a fugitive reference, Engels wrote of "a new class of *industrial landowners*. His inconsistent treatment of the various farm segments is reviewed below in Chapter 4. On the industrial landowners, see n. 9 of that chapter.

58. "Preface," *MECW*, 29:263, *MEW*, 13:9; and, for the *Eighteenth Brumaire*, *MECW*, 11:103–5, *MEW*, 8:115–16.

59. In a 1980 discussion of "whether the English Revolution was a bourgeois revolution or not," Christopher Hill declares that the phrase "in Marxist usage does *not* mean a revolution made by or consciously willed by the bourgeoisie." He then argues, at length, the consequential position: that the outcome facilitated the development of capitalism. The major conclusions are reiterated, if anything, even more forcefully at the end of this discussion. There was, he states unequivocally, "no direct takeover of power by 'the bourgeoisie'" in the years following the civil war, and "at all points, then, I wish to disclaim the imputation of conscious will, which the opponents, but not the proponents of the idea of bourgeois revolution attribute to it." See "Bourgeois Revolution?," pp. 110, 131.

In an earlier work, however, in his initial exposition of his position, Hill expressed unequivocally the claim of a takeover: "The new class of capitalist farmers was there, thrusting its way forward, hampered by feudal survivals, without whose abolition it could not develop freely; in the revolution, in alliance with the urban bourgeoisie, it took over the State, creating the conditions within which further expansion was possible" (*English Revolution*, p. 21). The quotation, it will be noted, contains a clear statement of awareness and intention. Similar statements are found throughout that work; see pp. 9, 10, 11, 23, 26, 28, 34, 38, 39, 40, 42, 43, and 56.

Hill's revisionism involves a shift from Marx I, the principal direction, to Marx II. Revision in the face of new insight and/or new evidence is, of course, always appropriate. Hill's denial of his previous exposition of Marx I is, of course, not at all appropriate. His denial of Marx I, moreover, is flatly contradicted by the Marx-Engels quotations provided throughout this chapter. Hill refers to some of these passages but does not quote them. Many of the quotations do appear in Hill's earlier essay, "English Civil War." Hill's discussion there indicated both bourgeois takeover and conscious intent, e.g., on p. 135: "Such is the Marxist concept of bourgeois revolution, the revolution in which the feudal state is overthrown by the middle class that has grown up inside it, and a new state created as the instrument of bourgeois rule."

An important note of criticism is provided by Hexter's "Historical Method." The essay first appeared in the *Times Literary Supplement* of October 24, 1975. Hill's reply appeared there (November 7), and a scatter of other letters commented on the issues raised. Also of some interest in this connection is Quentin Skinner's review of Hill's

Milton and the English Revolution in the *New York Review of Books*, March 23, 1978, pp. 6–9.

60. Rubinstein, "Wealth." The quotations are from pp. 102–4. Rubinstein provides an Engels quotation (from 1885) declaring the Reform Bill of 1832 to have been "the victory of the whole capitalist class over the landed aristocracy." The repeal of the Corn Laws "was the victory of the manufacturing capitalist not only over the landed aristocracy, but over those sections of capitalists too whose interests were more or less bound up with the landed interest—bankers, stock-jobbers, fund-holders, etc." (p. 125).

For a more extended treatment of the subject, see Rubinstein's *Men of Property*. The work is a treasure house of documented findings. For information on the numbers and role of businessmen in Parliament, see p. 168. Most of them, he notes, were "merest lobby fodder." For evidence challenging Weber's "protestant ethic" thesis, see pp. 145–63. Some commentators have argued that the bourgeoisie bought estates and, giving up its historic mission, integrated with aristocracy (or at least sought to do so). For evidence challenging that view, see pp. 213–22.

For an overview, critique, and comment on subsequent (i.e., post-Rubinstein) discussions, see Daunton, "'Gentlemanly Capitalism.'"

61. Arnstein, "Survival," p. 256; Thompson, *English Landed Society*, pp. 327–35.

62. Moore, *Social Origins*, p. 19; Rosenberg, *Bureaucracy*, pp. 51–52; Blackbourn and Eley, *Peculiarities*, p. 59.

63. The *MECW* is the work of three editorial commissions based in Great Britain, the United States, and the USSR. The membership varies somewhat from one volume to the next. The British editors listed in vols. 6, 7, 10, and 11 are Jack Cohen, Maurice Cornforth, Maurice Dobb, E. J. Hobsbawm, Nicholas Jacobs, James Klugmann, Martin Milligan, Margaret Mynatt, and Ernst Wangermann. The United States's editors listed in these volumes are James S. Allen, Louis Diskin, Philip S. Foner, Dirk J. Struik, and William W. Weinstone. An example of the editorial procedure: Engels, in an 1847 article, referred to the French Revolution as "a glorious example to the whole world," adding that "we cannot silently pass by the fact that England, a hundred and fifty years sooner, gave that example." The editors appended this explanation: "The reference is to the English revolution of the mid-17th century which led to the eventual establishment of the bourgeois system in the country" (*MECW*, 6:399, 690).

For the other references: Blackbourn and Eley, *Peculiarities*, p. 61; Therborn, "Rule of Capital," pp. 5, 17, 26; George, "Century,"—the principal exposition appears on pp. 812–13, and an equivocal "yes, but not quite" statement appears on p. 818—"The English Revolution of 1640–60 was significantly bourgeois, but within a larger social transformation that was not consummated for at least another century"; Foucault, *Discipline and Punish*, p. 222.

A radical economics text opens with a review of "the evolution of economic institutions and ideologies," one which gives much attention to the English experience. The civil war is given only a fleeting mention—that the Christian corporate ethic was accepted up to that time. "After the Glorious Revolution of 1688," the authors announce, "the English government was dominated by the gentry and the middle-class capitalists." See Hunt and Sherman, *Economics* (1972), p. 33. That statement is modified slightly in the sixth edition of the work (1990) to read: "After the civil war of 1648–1660 [sic] and the Glorious Revolution of 1688, the English government was dominated. . . ." At another point the authors claim that "in the revolutions of 1648 and 1688, the supremacy of Parliament, or of the bourgeois middle classes, was finally established." By the early seventeenth century, the authors report, in "the modern nation-states, coalitions of monarchs and capitalists had wrested effective power from the feudal nobility in many important areas, especially those related to production and commerce" (pp. 30, 22).

A radical sociology text announces, without benefit of any supporting references, that "feudalism was finally overthrown in France and England in revolutions led by the bourgeoisie and supported by the peasants, when the bourgeoisie found that feudal restrictions got in the way of *their* own growing commercial and industrial power." See Sherman and Wood, *Sociology*, p. 393.

64. Goldstone, "Capitalist Origins." The quotations are from p. 175. Goldstone's article reviews a different line of argument, one not touched in this chapter, that of the enclosure movement. For decades the movement has been treated as part of the development of commercial farming, the protocapitalist nobility and gentry enclosing common lands to gain pasture for sheep farming and profits in the developing wool industry. The dispossessed peasantry, in the process, were forced into the proletariat. This view is argued by Marx in *Capital*, 1, pt. 8. That portrait, to summarize Goldstone's argument briefly, is not accurate.

65. See Engels's description of the Belgian case in Henderson, *Friedrich Engels*, 1:135–36.

66. For the 1830 revolution, see Rooney, *Revolt*. On the business opposition to the revolution, see pp. 49, 62, 65, 69–70, and 75.

Christopher Hill, incidentally, drawing on a Marx text, described the "Netherlands Revolt in the second half of the sixteenth century" as "the first successful bourgeois revolution on a national scale" ("English Civil War," p. 135).

Chapter 3

1. The Engels quotations are from his 1895 introduction. Since the introduction is not contained in the not-yet-complete *Collected Works*, I have quoted from Marx and Engels, *Selected Works*, 1:109–10. For the German, see *MEW*, 22:509. Quotations from *The Class Struggles in France, 1848–1850* are from *MECW*, 10:45–145. I have checked the translations there against the German version in the *MEW*, 7:9–107. For the history of the work, see *MECW*, 10:651–53 n. 63, and McLellan, *Karl Marx*, pp. 237–43.

2. The quotations are from Wilson, *Finland Station*, p. 199; McLellan, *Karl Marx*, p. 238; Rudé, introduction to Duveau's *1848*, p. x; Price, *Second Republic*, p. 5; Tucker, *Marx-Engels Reader*, p. 586; Stearns, *1848*, p. 183; and Rubel, "Karl Marx," p. 36.

3. The Marx quotation is from an article in the *Neue Rheinische Zeitung*, December 15, 1848, *MECW*, 8:161. The Furet quotation is from *Marx*, p. 3.

4. For overviews, see Cobban, *Modern France*, vol. 1; Lefebvre, *Coming of the French Revolution, French Revolution to 1793*, and *French Revolution from 1793*; Rudé, *Revolutionary Europe*; Bosher, *French Revolution*—the quotation is from p. 29; Doyle, *History*; and Schama, *Citizens*. The most important review and critique of Marxist readings of the event are in Cobban, *Social Interpretation*, and *Aspects*. For more recent overviews, see Furet, *Interpreting*, and Doyle, *Origins*—the quotation is from p. 3. For a defense of the orthodox view, see Kaplow, *New Perspectives*, pp. 1–22. J. H. Hexter, it will be remembered, referred to ad hoc changes in the definition of a key concept in order to provide the "bourgeois of convenience." For a classic example, see Kaplow, *New Perspectives*, pp. 13–14.

Many leading figures in the old regime were killed in the course of the terror. The most comprehensive review, however, reports only 8 percent of those executed were noble. The vast majority, 84 percent, belonged to the Third Estate. The majority of the victims were poor, either workers (31 percent) or peasants (28 percent). Basically they were persons seen as political enemies of the Jacobins. These findings are from Greer, *Incidence*, pp. 97, 123, 161–64.

5. For Marx on Laffitte, see *MECW*, 10:48, *MEW*, 7:12. For Laffitte's role in the revolution, see Pinkney, *Revolution of 1830*, pp. 138–40, 161. For his role in the new government, see Pinkney, 300–301. Pinkney's comment on the leaders of the revolution appears on p. 195. For his review of evidence on the composition of the new government, see chap. 9. The conclusion quoted here appears on p. 367. Another historian offers this conclusion: "To the end, the so-called bourgeois monarchy was dominated by the landed *notables*" (de Luna, *French Republic*, p. 70).

The leading work on France's upper classes during the July Monarchy is by Tudesq, *Grands notables*. There was, at one time, a general agreement that the July Monarchy brought the bourgeoisie to power. It was a view put forth by, among others, Louis Blanc and Alexis de Tocqueville, before Marx and Engels's analyses had appeared. But, as indicated, recent research has cast some doubt on the claim of a revolutionary transformation. For a brief review of the positions, see Merriman, *1830*, pp. 1–11. For more detail, see Christopher Johnson's chapter in the same volume, "Revolution of 1830." For an account of the struggle between old regime forces and the emerging bourgeoisie in Limoges, see Merriman, *French Cities*, chap. 2.

The comment on Laffitte's abilities is from Douglas Johnson, *Guizot*, p. 163. The naming of Laffitte as a move to get rid of him and an entire faction is asserted by Howarth, *Citizen King*, pp. 184–85.

Marx's opening sentence has it that Laffitte led his compère, the duke of Orleans (Louis Philippe), in triumph to the Hôtel de Ville. *MEW* (7:12) provides translations of the French term, indicating it could mean godfather or accomplice (*Gevatter, Helfershelfer*). The editors of *MECW* (10:48), varying from their usual practice, provide no translation. In the *Selected Works* version, p. 128, Laffitte "led his companion, the

Duke of Orleans." In the International Publishers edition of the work, Laffitte "led his godfather" (p. 33). Since Laffitte was the older of the two men, by six years, the godfather option is unlikely. The term can mean good companion, pal, or crony as well as the stronger possibility, confederate or accomplice.

In opposition to Marx's negative view of the finance aristocracy's bankers, one economic historian, Arthur Louis Dunham, gives a rather positive account of Laffitte; see his *Industrial Revolution*, p. 218. Laffitte lured money "out of hoards" and lent it to industry; he restored public credit after Napoleon and by converting state bonds, brought down the nation's interest rates. Laffitte was, Dunham writes, "much interested in financing the development of industry and in the last years of his life did notable work and took great risks in that field."

6. *MECW*, 10:48, *MEW*, 7:12.

7. *MECW*, 10:48–49, *MEW*, 7:12. The sources, respectively, are Stoeckl, *King of the French*; Pinkney, *Decisive Years*; Douglas Johnson, *Guizot*; and Dunham, *Industrial Revolution*, p. 437. Brief biographies of the three are contained in the name index of the *MECW*. Marx portrays Faucher as one of the leaders of the industrial bourgeoisie. He would, presumably, be a dedicated opponent of Louis Philippe and his regime. The biographical note, however, lists him as an Orleanist (10:718). The same is true of the *MEW* note (7:659). See also the biographies in *Grande Encyclopédie*, for Bastiat, 5:663–64; and for Faucher, 17:38–40.

Grandin receives a page of comment in a book which, among other things, reviews the April 1848 violence in Rouen and in nearby Elbeuf. Grandin is described as the area's "most unpopular and powerful boss." He was a "member of the dynastic opposition during the July Monarchy and a [successful] conservative candidate in the April elections." Nothing in that account suggests the important national role Marx claimed for him. See Merriman, *Agony*, p. 19.

Faucher did appear later in this history. In December 1848, Louis Napoleon chose him to be minister of public works. Shortly thereafter, he was moved to head the Ministry of the Interior.

8. *MECW*, 10:49–51, *MEW*, 7:13–14.

9. Robertson, *Revolutions of 1848*, p. 13. For a rich array of documentation, see Irene Collins, *Government*, esp. chaps. 6–8, and Ledré, *La Presse*, pp. 197–218. The most comprehensive accounts are those of Bellanger et al., *Histoire générale*, vol. 2, esp. Ledré's chapter on the July Monarchy, pp. 111–46, and Aguet, "Tirage des quotidiens." Ledré (p. 146) gives circulation figures for the major Paris dailies as of 1846. The three largest were *Le Siècle* (32,885), *Le Constitutionnel* (24,771), and *La Presse* (22,170). Each was linked to a leading member of the opposition; these were, respectively, Barrot, Thiers, and Girardin. Guizot's support came from the smaller, government-subsidized *Journal des Débats* (9,305). The February Revolution, as will be seen, was centered in *Le National* (4,280) and *La Réforme* (1,860). Two very knowledgeable historians refer to "the hostility with which [Guizot] was viewed by the vast majority of the Parisian press." See Jardin and Tudesq, *Restoration and Reaction*, p. 188. This is a translation of

their *France des notables*, 1973. The fourth largest Paris daily was *L'Epoque* (11,254). Rarely mentioned in accounts of the period, it had been exposed by Girardin as government financed; see Collingham, *July Monarchy*, p. 393.

During the reign of Louis Philippe, there were frequent newspaper calls for regicide. In what might be counted as a media effect, there were eight assassination attempts during his seventeen years on the throne.

10. See Pinkney, *Decisive Years*, chaps. 2 and 3. See also Cameron, *France*; Clapham, *Economic Development*, chap. 3 and pp. 104–7, 143–46; Clough, *France*, chap. 5; Dunham, *Industrial Revolution*, chap. 4; Jardin and Tudesq, *Restoration and Reaction*, chap. 8; Sée, *Histoire économique*, vol. 2, and his earlier work, *Vie économique*. More specialized, but also of interest in this connection is Doukas, *French Railroads*, pp. 11–32. For a comprehensive portrait, see Léon et al., *Histoire économique*, tome 3.

11. *MECW*, 10:51–52, *MEW*, 7:15–16. See Tocqueville, *Recollections*, chap. 1, and Price, *Second Republic*. It should be noted that Marx is reporting the reactions of liberal (or progressive) circles in France. Among French Catholics, the Sonderbund War and the government position would have been viewed with favor.

Another important contemporary source is Stern, *Histoire*. Stern is a pseudonym for Marie de Flavigny, comtesse d'Agoult. The first edition was published in 1850. All citations here are to the second edition published in 1862. This very detailed account makes passing references to the Palermo events. None of these, however, suggest an "electric shock" on Paris opinion (1:92, 119–20). Langer's comprehensive work gives one sentence to the January rising; he does refer to it as "the spark that set off the revolutions of 1848." See his *Political and Social Upheaval*, p. 255. Robertson makes only a passing reference to the event: "As a matter of fact, revolution did break out in Naples before it did in France in this year of 1848, forcing the Bourbon who happened to be on that southern throne to grant a constitution. Yet no one paid much attention to the Neapolitan affair" (*Revolutions of 1848*, p. 4).

Stern (vol. 1, chap. 3) provides a useful review of Louis Philippe's foreign policy, one which agrees with Marx on the basic facts and shares also the same progressive orientation (see esp. pp. 92–93). For a useful summary of the foreign affairs issues, see Jardin and Tudesq, *Restoration and Reaction*, pp. 156–67; for the economic crisis, see their chap. 9.

Stern's remarkable history was first published in 1850, the same year as Marx's *Class Struggles*. For a critical assessment of her work, see Gugenheim, *Madame d'Agoult*, pp. 149–65, and Vier, *Comtesse d'Agoult*, 3:97–118 and 4:77–99.

12. *MECW*, 10:52, *MEW*, 7:16. For a review of those efforts, see Baughman, "Banquet Campaign." All sources, of course, focus on the banquet campaign, the immediate stimulus to the uprising. For a few of the many treatments, see Duveau, *1848*, pp. 9–20; Douglas Johnson, *Guizot*, pp. 222–62; Stern, *Histoire*, vol. 1, chaps. 6, 7; Tocqueville, *Recollections*, chap. 2; and Bury and Tombs, *Thiers*, pp. 89–93. Lamartine, soon to be a leading figure in the revolutionary government, had just published his *Histoire des Girondins*, and a banquet was given to celebrate the occasion, this on July 18 in Mâcon.

It too has been seen as part of *the* banquet campaign, although Lamartine's position was, to say the least, rather ambivalent. See Fortescue, *Lamartine*, pp. 129–32. A biography of Barrot makes no reference to bourgeois connections or to business instigation of the campaign. Richard Cobden, of the Anti–Corn Law League, met with the leaders of the dynastic opposition and reviewed the methods used in their recent campaign in Britain. See Almeras, *Odilon Barrot*, p. 158, and Hinde, *Richard Cobden*, p. 172.

13. Duveau, *1848*, pp. 7, 9; Baughman, "Banquet Campaign," p. 1; Stern, *Histoire*, 1:26, 82–83. Proudhon is quoted in Namier (where more such judgments may be found), *1848*, p. 4, and Marx, *MECW*, 10:73, 82–83 and *MEW*, 7:37, 47.

The *MECW* editors provide a note saying that the dynastic opposition, headed by Barrot, "expressed the sentiments of the liberal industrial and commercial bourgeoisie" (*MECW*, 10:653). Tocqueville, of course, was "on-the-spot," a close and longtime observer of French politics. He thought Barrot had been pushed into "the business of the banquets" by his fellow politician Louis Adolphe Thiers. One of "the main leaders" of the agitation was Tocqueville's friend and collaborator Gustave de Beaumont (Tocqueville, *Recollections*, pp. 19–20). How could Tocqueville have missed Barrot's link to the industrial bourgeoisie? How could he so mistake matters, seeing the dynastic opposition as mere place men? And why should Stern, who saw Duvergier de Hauranne as the principal instigator (*Histoire*, 1:132), also have missed that connection? Marx's conclusion, as indicated, seems to have escaped most commentators. It is possible, of course, but documentary evidence is necessary to sustain the point.

14. Mark Traugott gives total annual bankruptcy figures in the capital as follows: 1845, 691; 1846, 931; 1847, 1,139. See *Armies*, p. 11.

15. *MECW*, 10:52–53, *MEW*, 7:16.

16. Tocqueville, *Recollections*, p. 57. For an extensive treatment of the events of February 22–24, see Stern, *Histoire*, vol. 1, chaps. 8–15. Another useful detailed account is that of St. John, *Three Days*; for the provocative role of the Municipal Guard, see pp. 114–18, 126–28, 160–61. For Marx's conflicting statements about the insurgent forces, see *MECW*, 10:55, 66, *MEW*, 7:19, 30.

All of the leading sources, in contrast to Marx, contain extensive accounts of the February Days. See, for example, de Luna, *French Republic*, pp. 81–90; Duveau, *1848*, pp. 5–52; and Tocqueville, *Recollections*, pp. 18–58. It is curious: the commentator so much concerned with revolution passes casually over the actual event. A similar neglect appears in Engels's account of the armed struggle in the German states a month later, *Germany*, p. 157.

There are few analyses of participation in the February Days, for reasons reviewed by Mark Traugott in his article "The Crowd." His analysis is based on an incomplete file of requests for compensation by February insurgents (or their survivors). These records, he indicates, are probably the best that will ever be available. He suggests predominant working-class involvement, but my own recalculation of the limited occupational data indicates the presence of a fair-sized nonmanual minority; about three in ten were clerks, professionals, shopkeepers, or students (table 4, p. 650). Because of the economic crisis, workers probably had greater need for that compensation, which would mean some underrepresentation of the middle class in those records. The middle class, on the other hand, may have been more aware of the opportunity for compensation and better prepared to take advantage of it.

17. *MECW*, 10:53, *MEW*, 7:16.

18. *MECW*, 10:53, *MEW*, 7:16–17; and Fortesque, *Lamartine*, pp. 11, 114–15, 121–22. For portraits of the man, see Tocqueville, *Recollections*, p. 108, and Kelly, "Lamartine." For accounts of his political position, see Gershoy, "Three French Historians," and Stern, *Histoire*, 1:74–81.

Some sense of the difficulty may be seen in an account by Engels. He classified Lamartine, on the basis of his views, as petty bourgeois. The passage reads: "Lamartine proves himself, both under a social and a political point of view, the faithful representative of the small tradesman, the inferior *bourgeoisie*, and [one] who shares in the illusion particular to this class: that he represents the working people" ("The Manifesto of M. de Lamartine," *MECW*, 6:364–65). This first appeared in *The Northern Star*, November 13, 1847.

19. Howarth, *Citizen King*, pp. 139, 166. Laffitte died in 1844. One additional fact does not fit with the conventional stereotypes. This rich banker, according to Howarth, was a patron of the "utopian socialist, Saint-Simon" (p. 162). Laffitte provided Saint-Simon with a subsidy of 10,000 francs a month for his review *L'Industrie*. Saint-Simon was also supported by Casimir Périer, by the Pereire family (also bankers), and by Vital Roux, governor of the Bank of France. See Evans, *Social Romanticism*, p. 12.

20. See Amann, *Revolution*, chap. 2, and Calman, *Ledru-Rollin*, chap. 9. The two explosions, of clubs and newspapers, were both linked to the lifting of restrictions on civil liberties. They were also mutually supporting, the clubs typically having related newspapers to advertise their positions. For major demonstrations and for the organization of elections, the clubs joined together in peak organizations.

Given Marx's faulty distinction of the two bourgeois segments, his residual definition of the industrial segment, and his neglect of the clubs, one is surprised at George Rudé's assertion that "Marx makes a precise social analysis of all the parties involved" (introduction to Duveau's *1848*, p. xi).

21. The tax was instituted by decree on March 16, with its collection to begin after the forthcoming legislative elections in April. For a detailed account, see Stern, *Histoire*, 1:452–69, and for the Garnier-Pagès account, see his *Histoire*, vol. 2, chap. 1. For further details, see Gossez, "La résistance." Briefer accounts appear in Duveau, *1848*, pp. 72–74, 187, and Price, *Second Republic*, pp. 125–26. For Marx's discussion, see *MECW*, 10:59–62, *MEW*, 7:22–25. The *MEW* (p. 22) has it that the state let itself be exploited by the *Juden der Finanz* (Jews of finance). The *MECW* has the state exploited by the *wolves of finance* (p. 59).

Many of the subsequent accounts attribute the fall of the Second Republic to Garnier-Pagès. Duveau, for example, writes that he was "a pitiable Minister of Finance, and brought about the death of the regime with his idiotic forty-five-centime tax" (*1848*,

p. 187). The focus on a single man and on his policy is unusual in modern scholarship. The decision, as Gossez notes, was collective, made by the entire government, and it was not changed after the April election, either by the new government or by the legislature. If the decision was in fact "idiotic," many others, clearly, went along with it. There is another possibility, the one argued by Garnier-Pagès, that no better options were available. Duveau reviews a single modest alternative: that in exchange for an advantage given to the Bank of France, the finance minister could have "asked for a substantial advance." In dealing with the bank, Duveau argues, drawing on a 1946 lecture by Georges Lefebvre, Garnier-Pagès "acted far too hesitantly" (p. 73).

22. *MECW*, 10:62, *MEW*, 7:26; Duveau, *1848*, p. 59; Price, *Second Republic*, pp. 185–86. The best account of the formation and composition of the Mobile Guard is that of Traugott, *Armies*, chap. 2. On the National Guard before and after February, see Amann, *Revolution*, pp. 81–88. For more detail, see Girard, *Garde nationale*, chaps. 20–22.

Marx's portrait of the Mobile Guard, as recruited from the Paris *Lumpenproletariat*, follows in nearly identical terms Engels's account in the *Neue Rheinische Zeitung* of June 29, 1848; see *MEW* 5:131–32, and *MECW* 7:142–43. He compares them to the lazzaroni, describing them as "former beggars, vagabonds, rogues, gutter-snipes and small time thieves."

23. On the National Workshops, see Duveau, *1848*, pp. 66–68; Price, *Second Republic*, pp. 105–6, 144–45, 148, 150–54; Stern, *Histoire*, 1:483–90; and Traugott, *Armies*, chaps. 4, 5. See also Christofferson, "National Workshops." Tocqueville, too, viewed the developments in Paris in late April with considerable alarm (*Recollections*, p. 98). See also McKay, *National Workshops*. McKay's detailed scholarly account is still an outstanding source on events from February to June.

Stern's account provides many useful details. Stern gives the initial pay rate as one franc and fifty centimes per day. The measure, described as "disastrous," ultimately supported vast numbers of Paris workers and, in addition, attracted an "enormous mass" of workers from outside Paris (*Histoire*, 1:484–85). On March 16, it was announced that from then on the pay would be one franc per day. This, Stern reports, was accepted without a murmur (pp. 490–91). The announcement, as shall be seen, came the day before the first of the major *journées*. For further details on wages, see McKay, *National Workshops*, pp. xv–xvii, 25–26.

24. *MECW* 10:64, *MEW*, 7:28. For other accounts of March 16 and 17, see Calman, *Ledru-Rollin*, chap. 8; Duveau, *1848*, pp. 82–84; Fortescue, *Lamartine*, pp. 158–59; McKay, *National Workshops*, pp. 34–39; Price, *Second Republic*, pp. 127–29; Stern, *Histoire*, 2:55–78; and Traugott, *Armies*, pp. 19–20. For a more detailed account, see Amann, *Revolution*, chap. 3. He accepts the crowd estimates for March 17 of 150-200,000, which would make it "the largest unofficial outpouring of the masses of any *journée* of the revolution of 1848" (p. 107). Stern points out that the protest of the National Guard units was directed against Ledru-Rollin, the interior minister and author of the new decrees (*Histoire*, 2:61). It was not "against the Provisional Government."

25. *MECW* 10:64–65, *MEW*, 7:28–29. On the April 16 events, see Calman, *Ledru-Rollin*, chap. 10; Duveau, *1848*, pp. 87–92; Fortescue, *Lamartine*, pp. 160–62; McKay, *National Workshops*, pp. 47–55; Price, *Second Republic*, pp. 131, 138 (contains the quotation); Stern, *Histoire*, 2:155–84; and Traugott, *Armies*, pp. 21–22. Again the most detailed account is in Amann, *Revolution*, pp. 173–84. Amann sees April 16 as decisive; it made clear the altered balance between the strength of the Paris revolutionaries and the authorities. Blanqui said, "Today we are defeated," and Lamartine, later, said that after the sixteenth "everything became easy for the government" (p. 172).

26. Duveau, *1848*, pp. 93–94; McKay, *National Workshops*, pp. 55–57; Stern, *Histoire*, 2:184–86; and Traugott, *Armies*, p. 39. The latter writes, "Perhaps 200,000 paraded in a steady stream that lasted over twelve hours." If so, it would have been equal to or larger than the March 17 *journée*.

27. *MECW*, 10:65, *MEW*, 7:29. For a brilliant summary account, see Fasel, "Wrong Revolution." As opposed to the helpless pawns hypothesis, he argues republican failure, the leaders of the new regime doing nothing for the peasants, or worse, antagonizing them, damaging their interests. For other accounts of the election, see Calman, *Ledru-Rollin*, chap. 11; de Luna, *French Republic*, pp. 100–106; Duveau, *1848*, pp. 95–97; Fortescue, *Lamartine*, pp. 164–75; McKay, *National Workshops*, pp. 57–61; Price, *Second Republic*, pp. 138–40; Stern, *Histoire*, 2:192–209; and Traugott, *Armies*, pp. 22–23. For a wide range of detail, this generally supporting Fasel's hypothesis, see Amann, *Revolution*, pp. 187–91. For brief accounts of the electoral arrangements, see Campbell, *Electoral Systems*, pp. 64–65. To limit the influence of rural notables, voting was by secret ballot, and it was arranged that voting take place in the largest community of the commune. For an instructive account of the voting in one rural district, see Tocqueville, *Recollections*, p. 95. For another case study, see Merriman, *Agony*, p. 10. Also of considerable interest is Cobban, "Influence of the Clergy."

The first steps toward widely based suffrage were taken at the time of the first French republic, in the 1790s. But the attempts failed, actual participation not exceeding 10 percent of those eligible. See Campbell, *Electoral Systems*, pp. 49–54; Schama, *Citizens*, pp. 581, 646; and Stern, *Histoire*, 2:192.

28. Duveau, *1848*, pp. 100–101.

29. Ibid., p. 99; Amann, *Revolution*, pp. 188–89. The inability of the clubs to deliver votes, Amann shows, was linked to faulty planning and remarkable disorganization, see his chap. 4. Stern, *Histoire*, 2:580–81 provides complete results for the Seine Department. One could run in any number of departments. Lamartine did so with success in ten constituencies containing major population centers. His total in those ten departments amounted to 1,283,501 votes (of 7,835,327), a number far ahead of any other contender. Fortescue, for good reason, refers to it as an "astonishing electoral triumph" (*Lamartine*, p. 165).

30. *MECW*, 10:67, *MEW*, 7:30. For other accounts of May 15, see Calman, *Ledru-Rollin*, chap. 13; de Luna, *French Republic*, pp. 116–18; Duveau, *1848*, pp. 115–25; McKay, *National Workshops*, pp. 67–79; Price, *Second Republic*, pp. 146–50; Stern, *Histoire*, vol. 2,

chaps. 28, 29; and Traugott, *Armies*, pp. 24–26. For a more detailed account, see Amann, *Revolution*, chap. 7, and his two articles "A *Journée*," and "Huber Enigma." Tocqueville, an eyewitness, gives a detailed account of events in the assembly that afternoon (*Recollections*, pp. 114–26).

31. McKay, *National Workshops*, chaps. 2, 3; Traugott, *Armies*, chaps. 4, 5.

32. McKay, *National Workshops*, pp. 93–104; Traugott, *Armies*, pp. 137–42. Another explanation for the improved showing, one put forth and substantiated by Amann, is that the clubs this time organized and campaigned effectively (*Revolution*, pp. 251–64).

33. Calman, *Ledru-Rollin*, chap. 14; McKay, *National Workshops*, pp. 130–35; Traugott, *Armies*, pp. 27, 143–44.

34. *MECW*, 10:67, *MEW*, 7:31. On the June Days, see Amann, *Revolution*, chap. 9; Calman, *Ledru-Rollin*, chap. 14; de Luna, *French Republic*, chap. 6; Duveau, *1848*, pp. 133–60; McKay, *National Workshops*, chap. 6; Price, *Second Republic*, chap. 4; Stern, *Histoire*, vol 2, chaps. 31–33; and Traugott, *Armies*, pp. 28–31. A brief statement published by the insurgents appears in Stern, *Histoire*, 2:595. In contrast to Marx's claim about the annihilation of the bourgeois order, it states that "en défendant la république nous défendons la *propriété* (in defending the republic we defend *property*)."

35. Cobban, *Modern France*, 2:144. See also Traugott, *Armies*, pp. 123–24, 201–2. Traugott thinks "the greater part" of the workshop members "sat out the June Days" (*Armies*, p. 124). Another commentator, Robert Bezucha, writes: "The size of the uprising alone suggests that a majority of Parisian workers remained passive, if not neutral" ("Revolution of 1848," p. 479). One consideration likely to have reduced participation was income; the National Workshops, for tactical reasons, continued payment during the June Days (McKay, *National Workshops*, pp. 147–48). For another review, see Tilly and Lees, "People of June," esp. pp. 185–86.

That maximum estimate, the 50,000, was given by Cavaignac, who had no incentive to minimize his opposition. Engels gives two estimates, first, "30,000 to 40,000 workers" (*Neue Rheinische Zeitung*, June 29, 1848, *MECW* 7:143, *MEW*, 5:132), then, "40,000 to 50,000 men at most" (*Neue Rheinische Zeitung*, July 2, 1848, *MECW*, 7:161, *MEW*, 5:149). The industrial census of the Paris Chamber of Commerce, from 1849, indicated 205,000 male workers, to which, Amann argues (*Revolution*, p. 18) should be added at least 50,000 living in the intramural suburbs. The census, he points out, ignored workers in commercial (as opposed to industrial) establishments and also did not pick up casual laborers. These figures would indicate fewer than one in five workers of the region participated as insurgents.

36. *MECW*, 10:68, *MEW*, 7:31; Duveau, *1848*, p. 156. For the de Luna passage, see *French Republic*, pp. 149–50, and for discussion of the arrests, pp. 220–22. De Luna thinks the Ménard book might have been Marx's source. For Madame d'Agoult's conclusion, see Stern, *Histoire*, 2:479. For the *Eighteenth Brumaire* claims about deportations, see *MECW*, 11:110, 119, *MEW*, 8:122, 130. The police report on the deaths is given in Stern, *Histoire*, 2:482–83; for Stern's discussion of the arrestees, see 2:511.

Engels's *Neue Rheinische Zeitung* articles, from June and July 1848, also portray bourgeois anger and vindictiveness. Both men, it will be noted, attribute this murderous wrath to the bourgeoisie, not to the army or to the Mobile or National Guard. See *MECW*, 7:138, 139, *MEW*, 5:127, 128. Engels suggests that the savagery of the repression contains a lesson for workers: the need for their use of terror.

Engels's article dealing with June 23 ends with a puzzling aside, with a brief reference to one of the clubs, the Society of the Rights of Man (*MECW*, 7:133). A few days later, Engels published two comprehensive articles reviewing the June Days. There he reports on "the rapidly improvised organisation" of the insurgents. This "plan of action" is said to have been drawn up by "Kersausie, a friend of Raspail and a former officer." A series of offensive actions are then described, ones that appear in no other accounts. The insurgents were then overwhelmed by vastly superior forces and the use of heavy weapons. The account ends with some further words about this working-class leader. "*Kersausie* was captured," Engels reports, "and by now has probably been shot. The bourgeois can kill him, but cannot take from him the fame of having been the *first to organise street-fighting*." The *MECW* editors, in a biographical note, link Kersausie to the Society of the Rights of Man, adding also that he was author of "a military plan implemented" in the June Days (*MECW*, 7:157, 164, 666, *MEW*, 5:145, 152–53, 590n). The biographical note gives his dates as 1798–1874. None of the sources reviewed here reports any such plan or any such role for Kersausie. Amann has three passing references to him, but none of them are in connection with the June Days. Both of the Marx-Engels editorial committees pass over these problems without drawing the reader's attention to the difficulties. The only editorial contribution, in the biographical footnote, vouches for the accuracy of Engels's claim. An account in the *Nouvelle Biographie Générale*, 27–28:633 has Kersausie present at the May 15 demonstration and also in that of June 13, 1849 but makes no mention of any role in the June Days.

37. *MECW*, 10:69, *MEW*, 7:33. The workshops themselves, incidentally, were not a radical innovation. There were antecedents in the *ateliers de charité* of 1789–91; see Pinkney, "Ateliers de secours." These were revived again in 1830.

For the slogans, beginning with Engels's *Neue Rheinische Zeitung* account, see *MECW*, 7:124, *MEW*, 5:112; Amann, *Revolution*, p. 296; and de Luna, *French Republic*, p. 129. For the Arago episode see de Luna, p. 140, and Stern, *Histoire*, 2:384. The last slogans are from Tilly and Lees, "People of June," p. 182 (see also p. 184). See also the accounts in Stern, *Histoire*, 2:394, 423, 595; McKay, *National Workshops*, pp. 138–40, 149–50 (who reports a "Vive Napoléon!"); and Price, *Second Republic*, pp. 161–62.

William H. Sewell, Jr., provides another maximalist declaration. For the Parisian workers, the "message" of the February revolution "was clear: Labor had finally won the day and taken its rightful place as the essential basis of the state." From February to June, he declares, "the workers of Paris did their best to construct an entire, new social order based on labor" (*Work and Revolution*, p. 244). Sewell's discussions of "the workers" are only rarely accompanied by partitive expressions.

38. The Marx quote is from *MECW*, 7:128 (original in the *Neue Rheinische Zeitung*, June 27, 1848). On the group activity and the free rider problem, see Olson, *Logic*, pp.

105–10. Price reports that "most claim to have been forced to take part"; this was the summary conclusion drawn from interrogations (*Second Republic*, pp. 157–58). For Tocqueville's account of the colleague forced to help with the barricade, see *Recollections*, pp. 138–39. It would, clearly, be easier to force passersby into barricade construction than into the firing of weapons. Another instance of forced service, in this case the provision of medical care, is reported in Gallaher, *Students of Paris*, p. 99.

39. Tilly and Lees provide the best available portrait, based on an analysis of 11,616 arrest records (those remaining after the release, within days of the rising, of some 3,000 persons). The arrests brought in all persons in and around the action with the result that many, as indicated, were later freed, this presumably for lack of compelling evidence. Information on marital status was available for only a quarter of those arrested, and 60 percent of those indicated they were married ("People of June," p. 189). No comparable figures are given for all adult male Parisians, hence assessment of that datum is difficult. At best then, these data suggest that single men were overrepresented. Of the original suspects, only 273 (2.4 percent) were women (p. 208 n. 43).

40. On the composition of the Mobile Guard, see Traugott, *Armies*, pp. 56–77. For comparison with the workshops see pp. 124–27.

41. For a detailed account of the developments and the perceptions, see Stern, *Histoire*, vol. 2, chap. 31. Many contemporaries accepted the maximalist view that the workers, the entire class, were moving to take over the government. Many later writers have pointed to the convergence, despite widely different assessments, of Marx and Tocqueville on this point. But the evidence, of the numbers and the slogans, does not support that reading. It was a remarkable, although perhaps understandable, perceptual error (or false consciousness) on the part of the bourgeoisie (and others).

Other nations faced the same economic crisis but chose different responses. For a review of the British response, see Traugott, "Crisis in France and England," and Rudé, "Why No Revolution in England?"

42. *MECW*, 10:69–71, 74, *MEW*, 7:33–34, 37–38. For accounts of events outside of Paris, see Fasel, "Urban Workers"; Merriman, *Agony*; Eugen Weber, "Second Republic"; and Latta, "Maintien de l'ordre."

Craig Calhoun, a sociologist, refers to Marx's "acute ability to see just what different sorts of people sought in crucial social transactions." As examples, he refers to *The Class Struggles in France* and *The Eighteenth Brumaire*. See his *Question of Class Struggle*, pp. 5, 241 n. 6.

43. The option of a coalition between the bourgeoisie and the feudal monarchy appears again later in the monograph (see discussion below). For Engels's treatment of the same option within the German context, see Chapter 4 below. The passages quoted are from *MECW*, 10:70, *MEW*, 7:33–34.

44. *MECW*, 10:71, *MEW*, 7:35. Although Marx here argues a close link between the class and the group (or coterie), elsewhere he has them moving in different directions. The petty bourgeoisie, as will be seen, sought debt relief and protection of property; the *Réforme* group sought democracy and defense of the revolution's progressive achievements.

45. *MECW*, 10:72, *MEW*, 7:36.

46. For an outstanding account of these events, see de Luna, *French Republic*, esp. chaps. 6 and 7. On the selection of the Executive Commission, see Calman, *Ledru-Rollin*, chap. 12; Fortescue, *Lamartine*, pp. 171–75; and McKay, *National Workshops*, pp. 64–65.

Marx portrays Cavaignac as a ruthless, even murderous agent of the bourgeoisie. The man has not been viewed with great favor in subsequent scholarly work. Much of that hostility is based on ignorance or, at best, superficial knowledge. De Luna writes, in 1969, that no qualified historian, not even in France, had made more than cursory investigation into his role in 1848. De Luna's book provides no end of surprising challenges to that routine denigration of the man and his actions.

Tocqueville provides an interesting observation about Lamartine's support of Ledru-Rollin: "It is possible that Lamartine's subterfuges and semi-connivance with the enemy, although they ruined him, saved us. The old-school Montagnards, who were kept in the government, became separated from the socialists, who were excluded. If, before our victory, they had all been united . . . as did happen afterwards, it is doubtful whether that victory would have been won" (*Recollections*, p. 112).

47. *MECW*, 10:72, *MEW*, 7:36. It is difficult under any circumstances, in a body as large as the assembly, to obtain a sense of its political tendencies. For discussion of the problems, together with a review of the very diverse estimates, see de Luna, *French Republic*, pp. 107–16. As opposed to Marx's certainty, it is instructive to note that the *National* "confessed itself ignorant of the spirit that will animate the majority" (de Luna, p. 109). On the essentially conservative character of the Constituent Assembly, see Fasel, "Election of April." In the newly elected body of nine hundred, with many members adopting protective coloration, it was easy, as Fasel shows, to be deceived about the dominant traditionalist tendencies. Tocqueville, a member of the assembly, was under no illusions about its political character (*Recollections*, pp. 96–106). Most of those elected with him, he writes, "had belonged to the old dynastic opposition" (p. 96).

48. *MECW*, 10:74–75, *MEW*, 7:39. Marx is, once again, misleading his readers. This comment about Louis Bonaparte's win in the September by-elections is the first mention of the man. But Bonapartism had made its appearance months earlier. Louis Napoleon, in fact, had been the victor in several departments in the earlier by-elections of June 4, most importantly in the Seine. For tactical reasons, however, he had declined the honor, hence the second attempt. If the man's votes represented a declaration of war on bourgeois republicanism, those signs were present prior to the June Days. See Amann, *Revolution*, pp. 262, 280–82; Price, *Second Republic*, pp. 208–9; and, for a detailed account, Euler, *Napoleon III*, pp. 453–74.

49. *MECW*, 10:77–79, *MEW*, 7:41–43. As a counter to this insistently negative portrait of the republic under Cavaignac, see de Luna, *French Republic*, chaps. 9–12.

The eighteen-member committee charged with drafting the constitution was rather diverse politically. It included two representatives from the *Montagne*, Lamennais and Considérant, and several from the center, Gustave de Beaumont and Odilon Barrot, for example. One of its members, ultimately the most famous of the group, was Alexis de Tocqueville. His account of their deliberations is markedly different, a night and day contrast, from that contained in Marx's account (*Recollections*, pp. 167–83). Tocqueville does agree with Marx's de facto position, with his account of the republic as a history of contingent policy errors. Here is his summary judgment: "There have been more mischievous revolutionaries than those of 1848, but I doubt if there have been any stupider. They did not know how to make use of universal suffrage or how to manage without it. . . . They handed themselves over to the nation while doing everything best calculated to alienate it. . . . They seemed bent on solving this insoluble problem: how to govern through the majority but against its inclinations" (*Recollections*, pp. 96–97).

50. *MECW*, 10:78, *MEW*, 7:42. The antirepublican majority among the bourgeoisie poses still another problem; Marx later declares the republic to be the "ideal form" for the contending bourgeois factions.

51. *MECW*, 10:80, *MEW*, 7:44. In the election of the Constituent Assembly, in April, the peasants "had to vote under the leadership . . . of big landowners frantic for restoration." In December, presumably, they voted with impunity against the same big landowners, against "the republic of the rich" (*MECW*, pp. 85, 80).

52. *MECW*, 10:80–81, *MEW*, 7:44–45. Marx provides a murky rationale for that working-class support of Bonaparte, attempting to make workers conscious or aware. Given the Raspail alternative, however, and given the minuscule support for his candidacy, another alternative seems likely, that the workers were as gullible as the peasants in the face of Louis Napoleon's blandishments. Marx's portrait—advanced workers and retrograde peasants—is based on his declarations about the underlying consciousness and motivations. Raspail, incidentally, was imprisoned at this point. If anything, that should have encouraged support by class-conscious workers.

The most detailed account of this election is by Tudesq, *L'Election presidentielle*. For useful reviews of the election, see Calman, *Ledru-Rollin*, chap. 17; de Luna, *French Republic*, chap. 15; Euler, *Napoleon III*, pp. 501–34; Fortescue, *Lamartine*, pp. 244–48; and Price, *Second Republic*, pp. 208–25. Stern's account (*Histoire*, 2:536–49) is very useful. Price notes that the "highest percentage support for Louis-Napoléon [in Paris] was precisely in the most popular quarters" (*Second Republic*, p. 222). Ledru-Rollin, incidentally, outpolled Raspail in all Paris arrondissements.

Lamartine, it will be remembered, was the outstanding favorite in the Constituent Assembly election of April, gaining 1,283,501 votes in the ten departments where he was successful. He was a candidate again in December, although a rather diffident one. This time he experienced a humiliating defeat, gaining only 17,914 votes from all of France. Fortescue provides some explanation. In April, when he was seen as a moderate, Lamartine gained widespread support, this including much of the conservative press. With his subsequent support of Ledru-Rollin, that wide following disappeared. See Fortescue, *Lamartine*, pp. 164–69, 244–48.

53. *MECW*, 10:82–84, *MEW*, 7:46–48. For Louis Napoleon's contacts with Barrot, see the popular biography by Simpson, *Louis Napoleon*, pp. 230, 275, and the detailed account by Euler, *Napoleon III*, pp. 313, 315, 430.

Faucher, it will be noted, although said to be a spokesman for the industrial bourgeoisie, was given no ministerial office in the three governments managing the nation's affairs from February to early December, all of them, presumably, linked to the industrial faction. Only in December was he appointed to office, at a time when, as just noted, Marx has the industrial bourgeoisie losing power.

54. *MECW*, 10:95, *MEW*, 7:58–59. For a useful account of the Party of Order, one indicating many complications of that unusual coalition, see Cox, "Liberal Legitimists." See also de Luna, *French Republic*, pp. 190, 373, 383, 385, 398–99; Tocqueville, *Recollections*, pp. 214–29; and Tudesq, *Grands notables*, 2:1140–48.

55. *MECW*, 10:95–96, *MEW*, 7:59. Other statements of the republic-as-ideal claim appear in *MECW*, 10:76, 95–96, 114, 131, 139 (which repeats the p. 114 statement).

56. See n. 55 reference above. Marx is very clear about this. The election of Napoleon, he writes, "meant an open breach with the faction of which it had had to make use, for a moment, against the revolution, but which became intolerable to it as soon as this faction sought to consolidate [its] position." The Constituent Assembly, presumably dominated by the *National* coterie, in May 1849 was "contemptuously thrown aside by the bourgeoisie, whose tool it was" (*MECW*, 10:80, 94, *MEW*, 7:45, 58).

57. *MECW*, 10:96, 69, *MEW*, 7:60, 33.

58. *MECW*, 10:96, *MEW*, 7:60.

59. *MECW*, 10:96–97, *MEW*, 7:60–61.

60. *MECW*, 10:98, *MEW*, 7:62. Throughout the work there is an equation of the urban petty bourgeoisie and the peasantry—they "were in about the same position. . . . They had more or less the same social demands to put forward" (*MECW*, 10:99, *MEW*, 7:62).

61. *MECW*, 10:99–100, 105, *MEW*, 7:63, 68; Calman, *Ledru-Rollin*, chaps. 23, 24; and Price, *Second Republic*, p. 248. See also Moss, "June 13, 1849." Moss cites *The Class Struggles* at several points, treating it as a credible source.

Marx was in Paris at this point and wrote a brief account of the June 13 events, one which differs in some details from *The Class Struggles*, for *Der Volksfreund*, June 29, 1849. See *MECW*, 9:477–79, *MEW*, 6:527–28. For further discussion of Marx's presence there, see n. 95 below.

62. *MECW*, 10:113–14, *MEW*, 7:76. On the change of ministries, see Price, *Second Republic*, p. 262. He reports a consensus on Marx's conclusion, that it represented a shift from a royalist to a Bonapartist coalition. Barrot formed two ministries under Louis Napoleon, the second just before the June 1849 *journée*. Tocqueville was foreign minister in that government. For his account, which focuses on its beginnings, see *Recollections*, pp. 190–97. See also Jardin, *Tocqueville*, chaps. 23, 24.

63. *MECW*, 10:114–15, *MEW*, 7:76–77. The implications of Fould's appointment will be discussed again below in Chapter 5.

As seen earlier, the republic was the ideal form for the competing bourgeois segments because it allowed the concealing of those differences. Here it is the republic that pushed the differences to the forefront and the monarchies that provided concealment. In the opening pages of the work, moreover, it was argued that the nefarious activities of the finance aristocracy were very much exposed, one of the principal causes of the revolution. Marx's statement about the normal fact in England differs substantially from his (and Engels's) statements reviewed in the previous chapter. The manufacturers, not high finance, dominated in those formulations.

64. *MECW*, 10:116–17, *MEW*, 7:78–79.

65. In his discussion of the manufacturers, Marx writes that "we are speaking of the reigning princes of the manufacturing interests, who formed the broad basis of the dynastic opposition under Louis Philippe" (*MECW*, 10:116, *MEW*, 7:78). The leader of the dynastic opposition was Odilon Barrot, head of Louis Napoleon's first government. The new president, as of December 1848, must also have misunderstood the realities Marx has outlined here.

66. *MECW*, 10:117–23, *MEW*, 7:79–85.

67. *MECW*, 10:125, *MEW*, 7:87–88.

68. *MECW*, 10:127, *MEW*, 7:90.

69. *MECW*, 10:128–30, *MEW*, 7:91–92.

70. *MECW*, 10:129, 131, *MEW*, 7:94.

71. *MECW*, 10:132, *MEW*, 7:95.

72. *MECW*, 10:132–33, *MEW*, 7:95.

73. *MECW*, 10:134, *MEW*, 7:97. Tilly and Lees ("People of June," p. 178) show that there was considerable violence outside of Paris in the period 1846–49. Their graph also shows "the great, violent resistance to the *coup d'état* of December 1851," almost all of that occurring outside of Paris. It was, by far, the most violent episode of the entire period. See also the important work of Margadant, *French Peasants*. On the disturbances in the countryside between February and June 1848, see Tudesq, *Grands notables*, 2:992–1024. For a detailed account showing the dynamics of the rural conflict, see Price, "Techniques of Repression." The claim of a docile and helpless peasantry is not supported in any of these sources.

74. *MECW*, 10:135, *MEW*, 7:98.

75. For a review of reactions to the crisis of the thirties, see my *Who Voted for Hitler?*, pp. 439–41.

76. *MECW*, 10:135, *MEW*, 7:98. A grisette, according to a 1951 Cassell's dictionary, is a "gay work-girl."

77. *MECW*, 10:136–38, *MEW*, 7:99–101. For the changes in the electoral law, see Campbell, *Electoral Systems*, pp. 66–67.

78. *MECW*, 10:142, 144, *MEW*, 7:105–7. Neither of the editorial groups comment on this failed prediction.

The matter is treated differently, after the fact, in the *Eighteenth Brumaire*. There he reports that the constitutional revision allowing a prolongation of the president's power "was rejected, *as was to be anticipated*" (emphasis added), *MECW*, 11:168. Other statements suggesting foreknowledge appear there on pp. 107 and 176. It is an example of what Frank Parkin has called "the Marxist science of predicting the past." See his *Marxism and Class Theory*, pp. 172–73.

79. Engels, of course, faced the same problem. Writing in January 1848, he referred to "the acknowledged tendency of modern Democrats in all countries . . . to make political power pass from the middle classes to the working classes." The latter, he declared, constitute "the immense majority of the people." That could only be the case by redefinition of "the peasantry," by turning them into "working classes" (*MECW*, 6:440, from an article in the *Northern Star*, January 8, 1848). Shortly thereafter, within a fortnight, Marx published a small catechism containing the following: "Who alone [*sic*] will accomplish the coming French revolution?—The proletariat" (*MECW*, 6:466). It appeared in the *Deutsche-Brüsseler-Zeitung*, January 16, 1848, and in *La Réforme*, January 19, 1848.

The size of the proletariat is one thing; knowing their numbers is a relatively easy matter. But knowing their outlooks, their orientations, is, under any circumstances, a much more difficult problem. But it was no problem at all for Engels. The "working men of Paris," he reports, "seldom went into the streets, without battering to pieces every thing before them. . . . [They] are accustomed to insurrection, and . . . go into a revolution just as gaily as they go to the wineshop!" ("The Reform Movement," *MECW*, 6:381).

80. For the population statistics, see Price, *Second Republic*, pp. 10–12. Price draws on the compendious work of Adna Weber, *Growth of Cities*, esp. pp. 67–80. The figures for France's largest cities are from Pouthas, *Population française*, p. 98. The *Manifesto* quotation is from *MECW*, 6:488, *MEW*, 4:466.

81. The figures cited are from Daumard, *Bourgeoisie parisienne*, p. 14. See also Price, *Second Republic*, pp. 6–8. The first quotation is from Amann, *Revolution*, pp. 18–19. The second is from Price, *Second Republic*, p. 6. Other statements on small shop and artisanal production appear there on pp. 8 and 12. See also Jardin and Tudesq, *Restoration and Reaction*, p. 380.

Many works in recent decades have contributed to the rediscovery of the artisanal character of the working class in the first half of the nineteenth century. The radicalism of the period, they note, was linked to those artisanal structures. They were organized in trades and local communities (unlike the industrial workers) and were losing position. Their insurgency was in defense of a decaying arrangement; Craig Calhoun refers to it as "reactionary radicalism." Blurring the distinction between the two working-class segments, Marx and Engels treat those insurgencies as new and progressive, as the first signs of the coming struggle. For a start, see Calhoun, *Question of Class Struggle*, chaps. 6 and 8, and, for briefer versions, his articles "Industrialization," and "Radicalism of Tradition."

82. The quotations are from the *Manifesto*, *MECW*, 6:491, *MEW*, 4:469. For the geography of the larger enterprises, see Price, *Second Republic*, p. 13. The figures in Pouthas indicate most of the population growth in the Paris region was outside the city itself. Between 1831 and 1851, the city grew by 297,000. The suburbs (the Seine Department minus the city) grew by 393,000. Between 1846 and 1851, the city showed no growth; the suburbs added 91,000. My calculations are from Pouthas, *Population Fran-*

çaise, pp. 33, 98. See also Louis Chevalier, *Formation*. In Lyons, the immediate working-class response to the revolution was Luddite; see Latta, "Maintien de l'ordre," p. 64.

83. *MECW*, 6:485, *MEW*, 4:463. Adna Weber provides an 1850 figure on steam power. For all of France, the horsepower of stationary steam engines was 66,642 (*Growth of Cities*, p. 78). That revolution, obviously, was still in an early beginning stage.

84. For a comprehensive review of available studies, see Price, *Second Republic*, chap. 2, pp. 43–44 (based on Tudesq, *Grands notables*, 1:429). Those results, it will be noted, closely parallel Rubinstein's findings for Britain discussed in Chapter 2 above. For a review of James Rothschild's fortune, see Muhlstein, *Baron James*, introduction.

Among the leading studies of the French bourgeoisie of the period are those of Daumard, *Bourgeoisie parisienne*; Lhomme, *Grande Bourgeoisie*; and Rémond, *Droites en France*.

85. The *Manifesto* describes aggressive capitalists trading throughout the world, breaking down national barriers, and basically insisting on free trade. The French capitalists and landholders advocated and successfully defended high tariffs. The free-trade movement, supported by Faucher and Bastiat, was defeated in France. Marx mentions the tariff barriers but does not discuss the implications of that fact for his basic position.

86. The ready acceptance of Marxian class categories means many subsequent analyses also failed to give separate consideration to the civil service. The turn-of-the-century revisionist struggle brought the salaried middle class, the white-collar employees, into sharp focus. Even then, however, little attention was given to the internal division, to those in public versus private employment.

87. On the journalists' role, see the sources cited in n. 16 above.

The very last episode of the regime also involved an intellectual. Emile Girardin, the editor of *La Presse*, arrived at the Tuileries toward noon on the twenty-fourth. He was the key figure pushing for the abdication. See Stern, *Histoire*, 1:231–34; Stoeckl, *King of the French*, pp. 281–83. The quotation in the text refers to and, clearly, gives at least some credence to Namier's thesis. In Lyons also, the new government was formed by intellectuals, by the editors of *Censeur*, a liberal opposition newspaper sharing the orientation of the Paris *National* (Latta, "Maintien de l'ordre," p. 62). This entire question, the role of the intellectuals, will be discussed at greater length in Chapter 5 below.

88. For some sense of the confusion and complexities involved in the planning and execution of a *journée*, one reported earlier, see Amann, "A *Journée*" and "Huber Enigma." They also give some idea of the problems involved in establishing what happened.

89. On the withdrawal of troops on the morning of the twenty-fourth and Louis Philippe's refusal of further fighting, see Collingham, *July Monarchy*, p. 410; Duveau, *1848*, pp. 36–37; Stoeckl, *King of the French*, pp. 279–81; and, Stern, *Histoire*, 1:213–25. There is some uncertainty as to the responsibility for the withdrawal order. In exile, Louis Philippe shrugged off the issue saying that "the order was in the air" (Duveau, *1848*, p. 36).

90. *MECW*, 10:135, *MEW*, 7:98.

91. The traditional food riot, on the other hand, did have a plausible logic. It was directed against "the organization of consumption," in many instances, against a government that was indifferent to (or abetting) speculation, hoarding, or price gouging. The aim, however, was not revolutionary; it was not an attempt to overthrow a government.

The railroads, ultimately, provided the means for remedying such shortages and, apart from unusual disasters, sharply reduced the incidence of food riots. They also, by speeding the movement of troops, made the repression of riots easier. See Price, "Techniques of Repression."

92. A straightforward statement of the point appears in Douglas Johnson, *Guizot*, p. 232: "The crisis of 1846 and 1847 was, in some respects, over by the time of the Revolution." Moreover, "some of the worst features of crisis . . . occurred after February 1848 and were for many observers associated with the seven weeks of social revolution rather than with the July Monarchy." See also Fasel, "French Election," p. 291, who writes: "Although there were signs of recovery in January and early February, 1848, the revolution and its attendant disorders reversed the recovery, initiating serious and widespread depression." Price, *Second Republic*, p. 123, states that "economic recovery had been well under way before the Revolution, the quickly perceived effect of which was to cause a worsening of the economic situation." Merriman reports the same effect in two provincial communities (*Agony*, pp. 7, 14). One work quotes the reports of the Paris prefect of police from February 15–18. Fear of "possible trouble over the banquet matter," he wrote, had slowed business activity. "Business has been suspended. . . . The merchants sell nothing." From Posener, *Crémieux*, pp. 141–42.

The Paris correspondent for the *Economist*, writing on February 17, reported on the forthcoming banquet: "It is feared that this manifestation will give rise to riotous proceedings, as more than 5,000 persons are said to have an intention to be present." That approaching banquet, "has thrown our speculators into great disquietude, and the public funds continue much depressed." The basic prognosis, however, was favorable: "Money is more abundant, and has a tendency towards the public funds, commerce still remaining unsafe for investments. If the banquet passes over smoothly, and we should receive no bad news from Italy, we shall certainly have a sudden and important rise in our securities" (February 19, 1848, p. 203).

Markovitch provides data on the falloff of employment in Paris between March and June 1848. The figures ranged from a low of 19 percent in foodstuffs to over 75 percent in construction and still higher, to the high eighties in various luxury trades. Markovitch, however, portrays this disaster as a continuation and accentuation of the industrial crisis that had begun earlier. See his brief essay, "Crise de 1847–1848."

93. In his 1895 introduction to *The Class Struggles*, Engels comments on this problem. He indicates that industrial prosperity "had been returning gradually since the middle of 1848 and attained full bloom in 1849 and 1850." That would mean the economic upswing began immediately after the June Days. It is not clear why Marx should have

missed these changes, since he was writing early in 1850. Engels appears to be providing an excuse with his comments that economic history can only be written "subsequently" since statistics, "a necessary auxiliary means, . . . always lag behind."

Their belated recognition of the upturn, in the final issue of the *Revue* published on November 29, 1850, was "the only essential change that had to be made." Otherwise, Engels states, "There was absolutely nothing to alter in the interpretation of events given in the earlier chapters, or in the causal connections established therein" (Marx and Engels, *Selected Works*, 1:110–11).

94. *MECW*, 10:651.

95. Some writers claim that Marx was a member of the Society of the Rights of Man, having joined, it is said, the day he arrived in Paris. McLellan reports that Marx was active in that organization and spoke, on several occasions, at its meetings (*Karl Marx*, p. 192). McLellan cites an earlier work, that of Samuel Bernstein, which makes those claims, but the supporting evidence proves rather thin. Bernstein declares that Marx spoke before the Society on March 4, but that was the day before he arrived in Paris. Bernstein himself expressed doubts as to the authenticity of "the words attributed to him." See Bernstein, "Marx in Paris." Only four Marx-Engels letters from this period survive. Although brief and obviously written in haste, Marx's letter does report his efforts on behalf of the Bund der Kommunisten; he makes no mention of the Society of the Rights of Man (*MEW*, 27:115–23). Peter Amann has demonstrated, convincingly, that it was some other Marx who spoke at the club both before and after Karl Marx's stay in Paris. See his "Karl Marx." Bernstein admits "no definite evidence to prove it," but thinks "Marx probably marched" on the seventeenth. Two organizations with which Marx was said to be affiliated joined the march, hence Bernstein infers Marx was with one of them, the Bund der Kommunisten being the most likely possibility. The question remains: why no subsequent mention of his participation? See Bernstein, "Marx in Paris," pp. 351–53.

For a detailed account on Marx and Engels's whereabouts, see Draper, *Marx-Engels Cyclopedia*, 1:30–31, 45–46. Draper does not indicate that Marx was present at Ledru-Rollin's "abortive semi-revolt." Bernard Moss is tentative about Marx's activity on that day, saying that "possibly" he was among the demonstrators ("June 13, 1849," p. 405).

96. Merriman, *Agony*, p. 217; Seigel, *Bohemian Paris*, p. 68; Wright, *France*, p. 167, also, for another recommendation, p. 169; Tilly, *From Mobilization*, p. 13. Tilly gives three paragraphs to a review of Marx's analysis (pp. 12–13). His statements have only a distant relationship to the claims contained in Marx's text.

Merriman reports that Marx "is often unfairly criticized for his lack of access to first hand knowledge or to archival materials only available fifty years after the fact." I have not found any author making such criticism. The question of information and sources available to him will be considered again in Chapter 5 below.

97. In his letter to Weydemeyer of March 5, 1852: "I do not claim to have discovered either the existence of classes in modern society or the struggle between them. Long

before me, bourgeois historians had described the historical development of this struggle between the classes" (*MECW*, 39:62, *MEW*, 28:507).

98. Louis Napoleon's coup d'état posed problems both for specific predictions made in *The Class Struggles* and for the Marxian theory generally. To deal with those problems, Marx wrote his second historical monograph, *The Eighteenth Brumaire of Louis Bonaparte*. Many of the problems indicated in this chapter are present there also. For a review of the internal consistency problems, one covering both works, see Spencer's outstanding critique, "Marx on the State."

Chapter 4

1. For general overviews, see Pinson, *Modern Germany*, chaps. 3–11; Holborn, *Modern Germany*, vols. 2, 3; Hamerow, *Restoration*; and Sheehan, *German History*. For references on the history leading up to 1848, see n. 28 below. For events leading up to the unification, see Hamerow, *Social Foundations*, both volumes. For events leading up to the unification and for subsequent decades, see Craig, *Germany*.

2. Quoted in Henderson, *Friedrich Engels*, 1:98. See also, Kluchert, *Geschichtsschreibung*, pp. 126–41. Kluchert's book covers some of the works under review here. He focuses on a different problem, that is, on the varying treatment of the link between the economic and the social-political factors in Marx and Engels's works of the period.

Engels had written earlier articles on Germany. A three-part series entitled "The State of Germany" reviewed events from 1815 to 1840 and appeared in the *Northern Star*, October 25 and November 8, 1845, and April 4, 1846 (*MECW*, 6:15–33). An article written at about the same time as the "Status Quo," one entitled "The Prussian Constitution," appeared in the same journal, March 6, 1847 (*MECW*, 6:64–71). In January 1848, he published an article entitled "The Beginning of the End in Austria" (*MECW*, 6:530–36). There were also a couple of one-page contributions.

3. *MECW*, 6:76, 78, *MEW*, 4:42, 43. In the *Collected Works* the article is entitled "The Constitutional Question in Germany." An English-language version of this work appears in Henderson, *Friedrich Engels*, 1:337–55. At some points Henderson translates Engels's term "bourgeoisie" as "middle class," elsewhere with the construction "fully fledged bourgeoisie." Where Engels refers to the bureaucracy as a "third class," Henderson translates with the phrase a "third social group."

4. *MECW*, 6:78–79, *MEW*, 4:44. That coalition of nobles and petty bourgeoisie is mentioned throughout the text. At one point (*MECW*, 6:87–88, *MEW*, 4:53), Engels says, "The bureaucracy was set up to govern petty bourgeoisie and peasants." They have such diverse and conflicting interests that they "must be kept in leading strings." Otherwise, he says, they would ruin themselves "with hundreds and thousands of lawsuits." This "necessity" for the petty bourgeoisie becomes an unacceptable fetter for the bourgeoisie. Engels refers to the petty bourgeoisie "subjecting itself" (*sich unter-*

werfen) to the bureaucracy. The petty bourgeois involvement in lower-level civil service positions, in short, does not mean their direction or domination of the administration. The bureaucracy "serves their interest" by providing "order" in what otherwise would be a very chaotic arrangement.

5. *MECW*, 6:79–80, *MEW*, 4:44–45. The petty bourgeoisie in this account differs strikingly from that described shortly thereafter in the *Manifesto*. No reactionary tendency is indicated here; there is no concern to "roll back the wheel of history." Nor is there a chance progressive option. Here process and result are simply stated: the class is bought off; a few concessions and it is conservative.

6. *MECW*, 6:80–81, *MEW*, 4:45–46.

7. Henderson's summary statement on the 1818 tariff is from his *German Industrial Power*, p. 33. The quotations in the subsequent paragraph are from pp. 30–43. For more detail, see Henderson, *Zollverein*, and Hahn, *Geschichte*. For an investigation of the situation of Rheinland businessmen of the period, see Diefendorf, *Businessmen and Politics*. His account of bourgeois orientations differs substantially from Engels's portrait. For the tariff history, see pp. 313–26.

A liberal program, Marx and Engels would have us believe, would be favored by business, by the rising bourgeoisie, and would be opposed by the aristocracy (those fetters being there, presumably, for their economic benefit). That expectation also does not appear to be accurate. The abolition of the internal obstacles combined with the barrier against outside foodstuffs should have been attractive to any capable commercial farmer, a category that would include most of the aristocracy. Henderson reports that the German experience at this point was opposite to that of Britain, "the owners of the great estates east of the Elbe were free-traders" while some of the industrialists sought greater protection (*German Industrial Power*, p. 41). For further revisionist conclusions about the *Zollverein* history, see Sheehan, *German History*, pp. 434, 501–4.

8. *MECW*, 6:81, *MEW*, 4:46–47. Henderson ("The Status Quo in Germany, 1847," in *Friedrich Engels*, 1:344) renders this last passage as "the five percent profit of the bourgeoisie."

9. *MECW*, 6:81–82, *MEW*, 4:47. In this instance, it will be noted, Engels has classified a segment of the farm population as bourgeois. The key passage reads: "The few landed gentry wise enough not to ruin themselves formed with the newly-emerging bourgeois landowners a new class of *industrial landowners*." It is a rare usage, one that does not recur in the other works considered here (see the summary in Table 3 below). The diverse usages were discussed earlier, see Chapter 2, n. 57. In Chapter 3, it will be remembered, Marx classified the "big landed proprietors," the Bourbon Legitimists (categories that would have included most of the French aristocracy), as bourgeois.

This text had little impact since, as indicated; it was not published in Engels's lifetime. It first appeared in Russian in 1929 and then in German in 1932. It first appeared in English in 1976 when two versions were published, the *MECW* and Henderson. The key passage appears to provide a textual basis for the subsequent gentry controversy (reviewed in Chapter 2 above). But the German original is *Landjunker*. In both *Cassell's* and the *Wildhagen* dictionaries, that term is translated as "country squire" rather than "gentry."

10. *MECW*, 6:82–83, *MEW*, 4:47–48. It is impossible to get all of Engels's nuance into the present text. His portrait of the petty bourgeoisie is filled with deprecating comment. A steady sharp contrast is drawn between bourgeois capacity and the hopeless incompetence of the petty bourgeois. More of the same appears later in *MECW*, pp. 88–90, *MEW*, pp. 54–56.

11. *MECW*, 6:83, *MEW*, 4:48–49.

12. Mass opinion, in later decades, is directly expressed in elections, plebiscites, and referenda, although, to be sure, the meaning of the result is often far from clear. In still later decades, mass opinion could be gauged also through polls and surveys. It is curious that many commentators readily accept free and easy conclusions such as those put forward by Engels and yet bring such heavy suspicion and criticism to bear when faced with conclusions based on polls and surveys. There is the perplexing—and unexplored—problem of epistemology there. Why do self-declared critical commentators so easily accept an obviously doubtful procedure and so systematically reject patently superior alternatives?

13. *MECW*, 6:84, *MEW*, 4:49–50.

14. *MECW*, 6:86, *MEW*, 4:51.

15. On the high levels of bourgeois consciousness, see *MECW*, 6:88. The argument of necessity appears on pp. 81, 88, 90. The discussion of fetters is found on pp. 87–91. The equivalent pages in the *MEW* are 53–54, 46, 54, 56, 52–57.

16. In the *Manifesto*, with its focus on "the final struggle," the bourgeoisie and proletariat, the major contenders, are treated as conscious cohesive entities. The petty bourgeoisie has no realistic position. Although showing some internal division (some of its members going over to the workers), that split is said to stem from personal awareness or idealism; it is not the result of quid pro quo negotiations.

For a review of later Marxist discussions in which the original class formulations shift to coalitional analysis (i.e., cryptopluralism), see Van den Berg, *Immanent Utopia*, esp. pp. 301–2, 364, 484, 486, 489.

17. Just as surprising is Engels's statement that "the petty bourgeois seldom goes bankrupt" (*MECW*, 6:89, *MEW*, 4:55).

18. Krieger, *German Revolutions*, p. xliii. Krieger's claim about the precedence of Engels's work over other contenders is a questionable one. That might be the case with respect to popular impact, but few serious historians would judge it as superior to the three-volume work of the contemporary Adolf Wolff or to the later two-volume history by Veit Valentin (cited below in n. 28).

In his introduction to a German-language edition, Richard Sperl declares the work to be not only of historical interest but also "for the solution to contemporary problems

[it] possesses incalculable value." Sperl quotes from Engels's introduction to the third German edition of Marx's *Eighteenth Brumaire of Louis Bonaparte*: "This eminent understanding of the living history of the day, this clear-sighted appreciation of events at the moment of happening, is indeed without parallel." That statement, Sperl declares, applies equally to Engels's work. See Engels, *Revolution und Konterrevolution*, p. 5. See also Kluchert, *Geschichtsschreibung*, pp. 311–34.

19. Engels, *Germany*, pp. 125–26. In a previous article, describing "German conditions" between 1815 and 1830, Engels made the same point: "The aristocracy wanted to rule, however was too weak" (*MEW*, 2:581, *Deutsche Zustände*, III, original from the *Northern Star*, February 20, 1846).

Engels's focus on feudalism in Germany in the 1840s might at first seem puzzling. The term "feudal" appears with great frequency here and in the other works under review. No definition is provided, but for most commentators, that would mean a system based on a bound farm population, on serfdom, on a legal obligation tying peasants to land owned by the nobility. The latter, in turn, were obligated to defend the peasants against foreign invasion and to provide for them in time of need. The administration of local affairs—public business and justice—was generally in the hands of the nobles.

Bondage was abolished in the German states in the first decades of the nineteenth century, in response to the French revolutionary and Napoleonic threats. Serfdom was abolished in Schleswig-Holstein in 1804. Baron vom Stein's famous edict of October 9, 1807, ended "hereditary servitude and declared land a free commodity regardless of class" for all of Prussia. Other states quickly followed. With this emancipation, the *Bauernbefreiung*, feudalism was ended—de jure.

Those edicts terminated the mutual obligation of the feudal contract. For some of those freed, the immediate result was an eviction notice; they no longer had any right to the land. For others, the large majority, the obligation of service was transformed into the obligation of rent for use of the nobleman's property. Arrangements were made by the state for eventual purchase of land, the amount varying, "as a rule from twenty to twenty-five times their annual value." Local administration in some areas, particularly east of the Elbe, remained a noble privilege. As a result, the social relationships associated with feudalism persisted for decades after the emancipation. For a brief review, see Hamerow, *Restoration*, chap. 3. The quotations are his, from p. 45. See also Berdahl, "Conservative Politics."

20. Engels, *Germany*, pp. 126–27. Engels, it will be noted, is again treating the tariff question as a zero-sum game—the bourgeoisie wins, others (specifically, the regime) lose. It is possible, of course, a key argument of economic liberalism, that there would be many winners. But that possibility—that reality, as indicated above—does not accord with Engels's "dialectical" portraiture.

21. Ibid., pp. 128–29. The *Manifesto*, as noted, defined petty bourgeoisie (or lower middle class) by example, that is, with illustrative lists of occupations. Engels's opening sentence here must be seen as an abbreviated list—that is, "the small trading and shopkeeping class." Later in the paragraph, he adds the artisans, specifically, "the tailors,

the shoemakers, the joiners." "The peasants," contained in both *Manifesto* listings of the petty bourgeoisie, are here classified separately with the farmers.

22. Ibid., pp. 129–30, 142–43. Two leading investigations of worker demands in 1848 are those of Hamerow, *Restoration*, chap. 8, and Noyes, *Organization*, chaps. 7, 8. Both indicate the backward-looking character of worker demands, especially those of journeyman. This same orientation, it will be remembered, appeared in the French context (see Chapter 3, n. 81 above).

23. Engels, *Germany*, pp. 130–31. For a brief review of the extensive agrarian violence, see Hamerow, *Restoration*, pp. 107–11. He describes the insurrection in the countryside as "the most serious rural uprising in Germany since the days of the Reformation. . . . The suppressed resentment of generations unloosed a wave of looting and burning" (p. 107). See also Jordan, *Entstehung*, pp. 117–29.

24. Engels, *Germany*, pp. 131, 133, 137.

25. Ibid., pp. 143, 148.

26. The opening paragraphs of that text contribute to the misreading. The second sentence, elaborating on the well-known opening statement, lists a series of categorical polar opposites: "Freeman and slave, patrician and plebeian, lord and serf, guild master and journeyman, in a word, oppressor and oppressed." The following paragraph does recognize some complication, with its reference to "a manifold gradation of social rank" in the earlier epochs. It does not, however, say anything about coalitions as the key formations in that previous "history of class struggles."

The phrase "in a word" in the above passage, it will be noted, is followed by three words. That phrase is an inappropriate translation of the word *kurz* (short) of the original text (*MEW*, 4:462).

27. Diefendorf, *Businessmen and Politics*, pp. 340, 341, 351, 352–53. The argument of the monarchy as the agent of economic progress, as the enthusiastic supporter of economic liberalism, is an old one. Similarly, the argument of cooperation, of agreement between monarchy and bourgeoisie, is also one long since established in the historical literature. For a comprehensive review, see Kocka, "Preussischer Staat." East German historians, Kocka notes, are reluctant to concede these points. They focus on *instances* of conflict, thus allowing support for their claims of opposed interests, of the supposedly reluctant concessions. Much of that work focuses on the 1840s, admittedly a period of reaction, thus neglecting the more progressive experience of the twenties and thirties.

The *haute* bourgeoisie did not change course during the revolution, suddenly fearing a mass uprising but, from the beginning, was antirevolutionary. That conclusion has long since been established in biographical studies of the leading bourgeois figures. For a useful review, see Dorpalen, "Die Revolution," esp. pp. 333–35, and his *German History*, pp. 192–218.

28. Engels, *Germany*, p. 157. For accounts of the struggle in Berlin, see Langer, *Political and Social Upheaval*, pp. 387–400, and Robertson, *Revolutions of 1848*, pp. 115–31. Two leading sources are Valentin, *Geschichte*, vol. 1, chap. 6, and Wolff, *Revolutions-Chronik*, vol. 1, containing a detailed day-by-day account of the March events.

29. Engels, *Germany*, p. 185. Engels has it that the military was emboldened by the defeat of the workers in Paris during the June Days. That too is a claim requiring confirmation.

30. Ibid., pp. 163, 124. His treatment of the representatives to the Frankfurt Assembly is the same; they too are attacked for cowardice, for pusillanimity.

31. Diefendorf, *Businessmen and Politics*, pp. 353–54. It would be easy to pass off Engels's performance as an individual foible, as the reaction of one disappointed commentator. But, remarkably enough, the notion of the failed revolution, the belief that the bourgeoisie had not done its task properly, came to be *the* central line of analysis for discussion of modern Germany. It is a viewpoint (discussed earlier in Chapter 2) that is shared by Marxists and liberals. For a review, citations, and critique, see the essay by Eley, "The British Model," sections 1 and 2, esp. pp. 40–43, 66–67.

32. Engels, *Germany*, pp. 167–68 and 124.

33. Again I have quoted from the Krieger edition (see n. 18 above). He has used the English translation by Moissaye J. Olgin done for the International Publishers in 1926. Two translation errors, one minor, one major, appear in this version. The German bourgeoisie is said to have developed a "remarkable trait" (p. 5). In the original it is a "remarkable cowardice" (*merkwürdige Feigheit*), *MEW*, 16:395. In 1866, one is told that "Austria, retaining all its provinces, subjugated, directly and indirectly, the entire north of Prussia" (p. 5). The original has it, correctly, that "Prussia, directly or indirectly, subjugated the entire north" (p. 395). All passages cited in the present text have been checked against the *MEW* version.

34. Engels, "Preface," pp. 4–5. I have changed Olgin's "inefficient" to "incapable," that seeming a better translation of *unfähig*.

It will be noted that Engels is again making moral rather than analytical judgments—honor, blame, and in the next paragraph, cowardice. All of those judgments, moreover, are relative to *his* standard, to his concept of what the bourgeoisie *ought* to have done. All of this systematically excludes the obvious alternative—that Engels's original expectation might have been mistaken.

35. Ibid., pp. 5–7. "The main evil" appears as *die Hauptschikane* in the German original, that is, "the main chicanery."

36. Ibid., p. 7. Engels's statement here is directly opposite to Marx's conclusion in the *Eighteenth Brumaire*. Marx has it that Louis Bonaparte and the army simply took power from the bourgeoisie; that class did not transfer it to the usurper, as if for safekeeping. Marx summarized matters simply; the coup of December 2, 1851, meant "end of the parliamentary regime and of bourgeois rule. Victory of Bonaparte" (*MECW*, 11:181, *MEW*, 8:193).

Engels's dating of bourgeois rule in France—from 1849—is curious. If more than a careless error, it would mean that the bourgeoisie ruled only after Cavaignac, after the accession of Louis Bonaparte as president. If intended, Engels's reading would differ significantly from Marx's account of February 1848. The *MEW* editors make no comment on the matter.

37. Engels, "Preface," pp. 7–8.

38. Ibid., pp. 8–9.

39. Ibid., pp. 9–10.

40. Ibid., p. 11 (emphasis added).

41. Ibid., pp. 12–15. The "Junker dominance" of this translation derives from an even stronger original, *Junkerherrschaft*—that is, Junker *rule*. For an understanding of "Bonapartist monarchy," Engels refers readers to his 1872 publication, "The Housing Question." The basic condition of modern Bonapartism, he reports there, is "an equilibrium between the bourgeoisie and proletariat." In monarchies, whether of the old absolutist or modern Bonapartist variety, "the real governmental authority lies in the hands of a special caste of army officers and state officials" (*MECW*, 23:363, *MEW*, 18:258).

42. Engels, "Addendum," p. 15. Engels's claim about the lack of chauvinism among German workers is flagrantly contrary to fact. Bebel and Liebknecht abstained on the war credit vote and came under heavy attack from Lassalleans and from within their own party. See Armstrong, "Social Democrats"; Maehl, *August Bebel*, pp. 73–77; and Dominick, *Wilhelm Liebknecht*, pp. 188–99. Some of that opposition came from Marx and Engels; see Engels's summary letter to Marx, August 15, 1870, *MEW*, 33:39–41, and Marx's letter, August 17, 1870, *MEW*, 33:43–44. For an example of "national chauvinism," we have Engels's enthusiastic comment about "our soldiers," the "splendid fellows" who, against machine guns and breech-loaders, had taken an entrenched French position with bayonets (letter to Marx, August 5, 1870, *MEW*, 33:30).

43. Engels, "Addendum," pp. 16–17.

44. Ibid., p. 18. The Olgin translation reads, to wrest "one seat after another." Correction has been made, following the *MEW* version (18:517) to read "one city," etc.

45. See Morgan, *German Social Democrats*, pp. 192–99, and Dominick, *Wilhelm Liebknecht*, pp. 163–71, the quotation is from p. 170. For further discussion, see Hammen, "Agrarian Question"; Hertz-Eichenrode, "Karl Marx"; and Maehl, "Agrarian Policy."

46. Percentages are calculated from data contained in Hoffmann, *Wachstum*, pp. 204–5. The figures given here are for the territory embraced by the later Germany (that of 1871–1917) but without Alsace and Lorraine (see p. 2 for the details).

47. Engels, *Germany*, p. 124. On the role of individuals, one might, as an exercise of imagination, ask if things would have turned out differently if Frederick the Great had been in command at Jena in 1806. One knowledgeable expert, Napoleon Bonaparte, certainly thought so.

Leopold von Ranke, described as the father of scientific history, was easily the most important academic historian in Germany in the nineteenth century. The historian's task, as he saw it, was to report the past "as it really was" (*wie es eigentlich gewesen ist*). That meant the elimination of philosophical and theoretical considerations. As one writer put it, Ranke was "determined to hold strictly to the facts of history, to preach no sermon, to point no moral, to adorn no tale, but to tell the simple historic truth." His principal methodological innovation was the demand for reliance on documentary evidence and for critical assessment of those sources. History in his hands, not too surprisingly, came to be a narration of unique events, accounts filled with flukes, accidents, and happenstance. Marx's attitude toward Ranke was, to say the least, very negative. For a summary portrait of Ranke's orientation and influence, see Iggers, *German Conception*, chap. 4. On Marx's attitude, see Padover, *Karl Marx*, pp. 72–73.

48. The procedure appears first in "The Status Quo," p. 44. The "Addendum" follows the same route—only with a detour. It discusses the monarchy, specifying a modern, Bonapartist variety of the species, treating it as a special transitional case. See n. 41 above.

49. For a more differentiated portrait of the bureaucracy, see Sheehan, *German History*, pp. 517–23. Nowadays, one has evidence on these questions; one is not reduced to a priori speculation and guesswork. For a useful review, see Putnam, *Comparative Study*, pp. 92–103.

50. The same questions arise in connection with a still-later regime, that of Adolf Hitler. See Burin, "Bureaucracy and National Socialism," for an early general consideration. For a time at least there was some question as to whether the Holocaust reflected leadership directives or a bureaucratic impulse. The best recent work on the subject leaves little doubt as to the centrality of Hitler's role. See Fleming, *Hitler*.

51. The comments in this paragraph overlook another problem posed by the terms "short" and "long." Marx and Engels saw the entire capitalist epoch as a short-term event, one that would end with the next economic crisis.

52. Engels's strong voluntarism stands in sharp contrast to the determinism argued in his later works (see the discussion in Chapter 1 above). The positions are clearly contradictory. The commitment to determinism, however, in no way inhibited Engels, or Marx for that matter, from arguments and plans for strategic interventions. The arguments of the anti-Engels writers are doubly selective: they omit both Engels's voluntarism and Marx's determinism.

Chapter 5

1. The initial conclusion, the tripartite class structure, is based on the Marx-Engels procedure present in the works reviewed here, beginning with the *Manifesto*. Another conclusion, another tripartite division, appears elsewhere in Marx's writing, but that variant usage is not developed in his or in Engels's analyses. See Chapter 2, n. 56 above.

The Engels quotation is from his *Condition of the Working Class in England* (1845). That is my translation from the German version; see *MEW*, 2:349. The *MECW* translation (4:418) differs somewhat from mine, as does the version by Henderson and Chaloner, pp. 137–38. The differences are matters of nuance and style.

2. Aristophanes is one of the few who mocked the pretension. In *The Clouds*, he brings Socrates on stage "suspended in a contrivance like the gondola of a balloon." The philosopher explains that he is "walking upon air and attacking the mystery of the sun"

(p. 121). The notion of a *freischwebende* intelligentsia is discussed at some length in Mannheim, *Ideology and Utopia*, pp. 136–46. The concept appears to have originated with Mannheim's mentor, Alfred Weber, the noted Heidelberg economist and sociologist. The notion, to be sure, is most favorably received by literary-political intellectuals, by essayists given to data-free speculation. Serious social scientific researchers, on the whole, do not give it credence.

3. For an extended discussion of this immanentism, see Van den Berg, *Immanent Utopia*.

Outside of Marxist circles one does, of course, find other readings. One explanation for the rise of Hitler and his party in Germany is cultural, arguing an independent contribution made by an assortment of intellectuals, writers, artists, and so forth. See, for example, Mosse, *Crisis*. For a brief review and critique of that argument, see my *Who Voted for Hitler?*, pp. 621, 628–29. The autonomy thesis, however, is a minority position. The more frequent, dominant position sees the intellectual (or artist) "in relation to his times," as if formed by and the inevitable product of those times.

4. Engels, *Germany*. See p. 134 for his discussion of Prussia and, for Austria, pp. 155–56.

5. Muhlstein, *Baron James*, pp. 177–79. Muhlstein's source is Feydeau, *Mémoires*, pp. 159–61. The grounds for alarm were certainly real. Solomon Rothschild, James's brother, lost his Suresnes chateau, which was pillaged, vandalized, and burned to the ground. A mob set fire to James's chateau at Puteaux. James told the assembled members of his Paris household to offer no resistance if attacked. His wife and daughter were sent to London.

6. Corti, *House of Rothschild*, p. 240. Goudchaux, a friend of Rothschild, was financial editor of the *National*. Corti refers to Rothschild's "Orléanist sympathies" but notes also his "opportunist nature" which facilitated his development of "a conciliatory understanding" with the new regime. James was quickly on good terms with Goudchaux's successor, Garnier-Pagès, and was a frequent visitor. Again the contact provided him with useful information as to the government's intentions (p. 249). See also, Gille, *Maison Rothschild*, 2:27–53. Garnier-Pagès mentions his Bourse connection in his *Histoire*, 3:122. Rothschild's 50,000-franc contribution is mentioned on p. 121. On the same page, contributions of 211,500 francs by a dozen leading bankers are reported along with a subscription of 100,000 francs by the Bank of France. The cash contribution of the dozen bankers was escorted to the Hotel de Ville by some 1,500 workers and national guardsmen.

It would be a mistake to see Crémieux as a Rothschild agent in the government. He had worked both with and against Rothschild. Very much his own man, he was an active supporter of the banquet campaigns and was directly involved in the February uprising. Previously, in the chamber he had introduced an amendment forbidding certain conflicts of interest for its members. The motion touched on the railroad interests of Rothschild and the Péreire brothers, who "did not hide their discontent." As minister of justice, Crémieux supported a wide range of innovations best described as left-liberal in character. Defeated in many struggles and under increasing attack (among others from the *National*), he resigned after only a month. See Posener, *Crémieux*, pp. 125–27, 134, 144–46, 155–61.

7. Caussidière followed a somewhat erratic course in his service as Paris police prefect, supporting the left where he could and, in general, making life difficult for the government's moderate majority. Only days after the revolution, he struck up a relationship with Rothschild. When Caussidière went into exile after the June Days, Rothschild sent him 30,000 francs along with a note saying "Pay me back in the next ten or twenty years, or whenever you can." Some years later he settled in New York where, continuing his earlier career, he became a wine and cognac merchant. James's son visited him there in 1860 and found him flourishing, having captured the city's "most aristocratic clientele" (Muhlstein, *Baron James*, p. 222 n. 36). She is quoting from Rothschild, *Casual View*, pp. 22–23. The initial contact with Rothschild is reported in Caussidière, *Mémoires*, 1:210–12. Contradicting Louis Blanc's denial, Caussidière reports that he did have the banker under surveillance (p. 211).

Rothschild's presence in the Finance Ministry negotiations, as Muhlstein indicated, was "noted by various newspapers." For more on the linkage of the revolutionary government and Rothschild, see Duveau, *1848*, p. 190. Marx must have known the basic facts of this history. He would certainly have read the newspaper reports and could easily have learned additional details from Ferdinand Flocon (editor-in-chief of *La Réforme*, a member of the provisional government, and Marx's sponsor) and from other leaders with whom he had personal contact during his stay in Paris.

Marx first moved to Paris in October 1843. Shortly thereafter, in December of that year, he met Heinrich Heine, and they quickly developed a warm friendship. The poet was a regular visitor in the Marx household, with Jenny too finding his company a source of enjoyment. Marx was expelled from France a year later and moved to Brussels. On his return for the brief stay following the revolution in 1848, he (and Engels) visited Heine several times. Because of the poet's illness, however, little significant conversation occurred.

Although they did not share political perspectives, Marx certainly enjoyed the poet's biting sardonic wit and quoted him repeatedly in later years. The religion as "opium of the people" phrase stems originally from Heine. Padover describes Heine as "one of [Marx's] favorite poets" and later as Marx's "favorite poet." Heine could have been a useful source for Marx since, for a while at least, as will be seen below, the poet was an intimate in the Rothschild household. It seems unlikely that Marx would not at some point have inquired about *the* leading member of France's bourgeoisie. See Padover, *Karl Marx*, pp. 178–79, 255, and for the quotations, 126 and 463; and Sammons, *Heinrich Heine*, pp. 260–64 (the religion-opium point appears on p. 262).

8. Muhlstein, *Baron James*, p. 193. On the Fould discussion, see *MECW*, 10:114, *MEW*, 7:76; and Corti, pp. 259–60, 268–69, 327, 332, 361, 378.

9. Muhlstein, *Baron James*, p. 188.

10. The relationships between Rothschild and those regimes were symbiotic—

mutually beneficial. The arrangements unquestionably served Rothschild's purposes well, even though in some matters he would have preferred other policies. But it was the political partners who initiated the arrangements, who made them possible. They too, in most matters, made policy; they had the last word. When Louis Napoleon chose another banker, there was nothing Rothschild could do about it. Rothschild continued to prosper after the loss of the favored position. Muhlstein estimates his fortune to have been 40 million francs under Louis Philippe and 150 million francs at his death in 1868 (*Baron James*, p. 11).

For the Palmer quotation, see *Democratic Revolution*, 2:24–25. For a review of business attitudes elsewhere at that time, see Godechot, "Business Classes." See also, for discussion of a later period, the Langer quotation in Chapter 2 above, n. 42. Joseph Schumpeter, the noted economist, wrote that "the attitudes of capitalist groups toward the policy of their nations are predominantly adaptive rather than causative, today more than ever." See his *Capitalism*, p. 55. For a portrait of business attitudes and behavior in a later context, possibly the best-documented experience of the entire modern era, see Turner, *German Big Business*.

11. Decades later, after the work of Robert Michels, after his enunciation and documented case studies of the "iron law of oligarchy," there is little excuse for the unquestioned acceptance of such claims. The reference is to Michels's *Political Parties*. For discussion of the man, the thesis, and later impact, see Linz, "Michels." For an actual study, one comparing the generally liberal attitudes of small businessmen with the markedly conservative pronouncements of organizations claiming to represent them, see my *Restraining Myths*, chaps. 2, 7. For a study of an interest group pursuing objectives at the expense of member interests, see Kwavnick, "Pressure-Group Demands."

12. Bouillon, "Démocrates-Socialistes."

13. For a review of claims and presentation of relevant evidence on both the independent and salaried lower-middle-class segments, see my *Restraining Myths*, chaps. 2, 3, and "Marginal Middle Class."

An early study of attitudes toward property rights made use of a scale with scores ranging from 32 (the absolute private property position) to 0 (absolute social property). Small merchants, the research showed, had a low average level of commitment to private property (mean: 12.1). They also had a wide dispersion of attitudes showing the least consensus of thirteen occupational categories (Alfred Winslow Jones, *Life, Liberty, and Property*, pp. 225–35, 378). This brilliant and important study is hardly ever cited in contemporary literature. The lesson: even when data exists, it is rarely brought to bear on the received claims.

A comprehensive review of data for eight countries from 1970, one inquiring about "Predictors of Political Party Preference Ranked According to Relative Strength in Additive Model," found the best predictor in six of the eight to be "parents' party," that variable in most cases holding a commanding lead over the next best predictor. In most instances church attendance and religious denomination came high on the list of predictors. Only well down on the list and making only a modest contribution did one find a familiar class variable—"occupation, head of household." The reference here is to Inglehart, *Silent Revolution*, pp. 246–69. For other useful reviews, see Rose, *Electoral Behavior*, p. 17, and Lijphart, "Religion." A key work in this connection is Lenski, *Religious Factor*. For discussion of the experience in Weimar Germany, see my article, "Hitler's Electoral Support," esp. p. 27.

It is easy to assume that things were different in the past, that class differences were larger, more important, that the workers were more radical before the considerable increases of affluence in the 1950s. It is, however, just as easy to assume that the earlier radicalism was a minority phenomenon and that the majority consisted of moderates, reformists, apathetics, plus a fair-sized segment of Tory workers. For a useful discussion, see Miliband, "Myth of the Golden Past." For evidence from nineteenth-century Britain showing a strong pattern of deference voting, see Joyce, "Factory Politics."

An extremely poor quality survey of workers in Germany of the late Weimar period found only a minority seeing "some form of Socialism" as the solution for the world's problems. Given the biases involved, the 41 percent figure found is doubtlessly an overstatement. The majorities appeared only among Communists, left socialists, and, by a small margin, Social Democratic leaders. The working-class clientele, in short, saw things differently from those vanguard segments. See Fromm, *Working Class*, pp. 93–94, 114–18. For a discussion of the study's inadequacies, see my review in *Society*.

When polls and surveys were first used for examination of questions derived from the Marxian framework, the differences in political outlooks and party choices between classes proved unexpectedly small. See, for example, Alford, *Party and Society*, and Glenn and Alston, "Cultural Distances." Marx and Engels anticipated a steady increase of the class differences; the processes of capitalism unveiled the underlying social relations, thus creating worker awareness. More recent studies, however, have found a pattern of diminishing class differences. See Dalton et al., *Electoral Change*, pp. 29–31; Lipset, *Consensus and Conflict*, p. 192; and Franklin, *Decline of Class Voting*.

14. The reactionary radicalism of the artisanal workers was discussed earlier; see Chapter 3, n. 81 above.

15. The reference is to Hamerow, *Restoration*, chap. 8. For Engels's sentence, see *Germany*, p. 130, and for discussion of it, see Chapter 4, n. 22 above.

16. A brief biography appears in *MECW*, 10:710. For more detail, see Maitron, *Dictionnaire Biographique*, pt. 1, vol. 1, pp. 84–85.

17. De Luna, *French Republic*, pp. 89, 91, 107, 219.

18. McKay, *National Workshops*, p. 7. See also Amann, *Revolution*, p. 29; Loubère, *Louis Blanc*, pp. 62, 82.

19. Langer, *Political and Social Upheaval*, p. 349; Moss, "June 13, 1849," p. 393. For an account of the agitational activities of the clubs prior to the June Days, see Stern, *Histoire*, 2:8–15, 20. Three leaders of the left, Barbès, Blanqui, and Raspail, all from middle-class backgrounds, were unable to participate in the June fighting because, like Albert, they had been arrested after the May *journée* and were incarcerated. The penalties dealt them were as harsh as those experienced by Albert.

20. For well over a century, people on the left have had occasion to discuss revolutionary tactics. A major issue has been the impact of confrontation with established authorities. Such engagement has been taken by some to be a good thing for the revolution. Direct struggle, even with defeat as a likely outcome, is thought to unveil the actual power relations; it would mobilize the indifferent. The movement goes forward, so it is claimed, remembering the blood of fallen martyrs. Although often taken as a valid conclusion, the question—whether conflict activates or enervates—has received little serious study. For a rare account, one which investigated the subsequent reactions to an infamous instance of antistrike violence, see Kornblum, *Blue Collar Community*, pp. 101, 105. His conclusion favors enervation—"In the aftermath of that conflict the union was devalued as a community institution."

We have scores of accounts dealing with antecedents, with the events leading up to a struggle or confrontation; few deal with the consequences, with the aftermath (or subsequent demobilization). There is an easy explanation: the upsurge of a social movement is inherently more interesting, more dramatic, and more exciting than the downswing. For example, one might compare Brissenden, *The IWW*, and Gambs, *The Decline*. This selective attention means that later practitioners and commentators, insofar as they depend on "the literature," will understand only the up phase of the cycle of dissent.

Those convinced that confrontations mobilize people sometimes draw another conclusion—that manipulation is justified to draw followers into a conflict. This option is rarely discussed in academic sources. The best accounts are literary—for example, Fyodor Dostoyevsky, *The Possessed*, and John Steinbeck, *In Dubious Battle*. Where such praxis fails—that is, where recognized or exposed—it too would have demobilizing or enervating effects. Subsequent passivity on the part of the victims would have an easy explanation; it would be a mistake to see it as due to false consciousness. Trotsky once claimed that "'lies and worse' are an inseparable part of the class struggle" (Diggins, *Up from Communism*, p. 38).

21. These figures are from Price, *Second Republic*, p. 11, and his *Social History*, p. 143. The English and German figures are from Flora et al., *State, Economy, and Society*, 2:497, 515, 525. The figures for England (and Wales) and France are from 1891 censuses; for Germany, from the census of 1895. For evidence on the farm-to-city migration patterns, see Blau and Duncan, *Occupational Structure*, chap. 8, and for some evidence on correlated political attitudes, see Hamilton, *Class and Politics*, chaps. 6, 8.

22. See the references in Chapter 4, n. 45 above.

23. For references on this point, see my *Who Voted for Hitler?*, p. 601 n. 25. Proof that farmers were not automatically conservative or reactionary appears in a Communist effort (led by ex-Nazis) in Schleswig-Holstein. In one village they took one third of the vote in July 1932 (pp. 450–51). Even more impressive was the experience of the Labor Party in Norway at the same time; with intelligent appeals to the farmers, that party won a large share of their votes and, simultaneously, defeated the National Socialist party of Vidkun Quisling (pp. 440–41). Sten S. Nilson has provided an important basic

discussion of the relationship of the left and the farmers in a comparison of events in Schleswig-Holstein and Norway in the early 1930s; see his "Wahlsoziologische Probleme."

24. On the importance of the religious factor in Weimar Germany, see Hamilton, *Who Voted for Hitler?*, pp. 364–85, and also "Hitler's Electoral Support." A Social Democratic attack on religion in Braunschweig after the 1918 revolution generated a strong counter-reaction, the effects of which were still felt in the early 1930s, see my "Braunschweig 1932." Another example of such misguided provocation is reported in William S. Allen, *Nazi Seizure*, pp. 45–46.

25. For a review of Berlin's history and the significance of annexation, see my *Who Voted for Hitler?*, pp. 64–65.

26. See Schoenbaum, *Hitler's Social Revolution*, chap. 5.

27. The reference to "the idiocy of rural life" is not the most appropriate approach for winning the support of farmers. Late in the century, Engels referred to the small farmer, rather disdainfully, as "a remnant of a passing means of production." Some private comments are even more damning. Engels, commenting on the peasant uprisings against Louis Napoleon's coup, has it that the usurper was being helped "by the excesses" of the peasantry. Referring to them as a "race of barbarians," he declared that they "don't give a rap for the government . . . but think only of tearing down the tax collector's or notary's house, raping his wife and killing the man himself if they can lay hands on him" (Engels to Marx, December 16, 1851, *MECW*, 38:517, *MEW*, 27:392).

Most scholars know such deprecating comments from direct reading of the texts or, indirectly, from reading in intellectual history. It seems likely, however, that many farmers would have seen those comments in a very hostile context, that is, in the propaganda of conservative farm organizations or of conservative parties. The tough comments by socialist spokesmen, in short, may well have provided useful material for the party's dedicated opponents.

28. Lipset and Bendix, *Social Mobility*, chap. 2; Blau and Duncan, *Occupational Structure*, chap. 2; Hamilton, *Class and Politics*, pp. 326–29; Featherman and Hauser, *Opportunity and Change*, chap. 3. For a recent overview, see Lipset, "Social Mobility."

29. The 1964 United States presidential election allowed a test of the conversion hypothesis. Two-thirds of the traditional middle class (well-off second-generation non-manuals) reported a vote for Barry Goldwater, a conservative Republican. In sharp contrast, two-thirds of the upwardly mobile businessmen (persons from working-class families now in the higher income nonmanual category) supported Lyndon Johnson, presumably continuing their original political socialization (Hamilton, *Restraining Myths*, pp. 72–73. In the literature of the 1950s much of the discussion of conversion versus transplantation of values focused on moves to suburbia. For a summary discussion, see Wood, *Suburbia*, chap. 5.

30. Palmer, *Twelve Who Ruled*, p. 18. The antibourgeois sentiments appear on pp. 34, 40, 68–69, 114, 145–46, 148, 154, 156, 160, 166–67, 170, 184, 186, 223, 227, 230, 312. The work, incidentally, was first published in 1941.

A word of caution: as noted repeatedly, the definitions of "bourgeois" and "bourgeoisie" vary. For Marx and Engels, the bourgeoisie is "the class of modern Capitalists, owners of the means of social production and employers of wage-labour" (*MECW*, 6: 483). An earlier tradition used the same term to mean well-to-do city-dwellers who were not members of the nobility. The intellectuals in Palmer's sentence might be bourgeois by the latter definition but, possibly, not by the former. Brief descriptions of the twelve appear in Palmer (p. 2). The most frequent occupation listed is that of lawyer. Palmer's argument is that their intellectual commitments made them different from other members of the profession (see pp. 18–20).

31. Bury and Tombs, *Thiers*, pp. 3, 6, 12, 20–21, 33, 40; Pinkney, *Revolution of 1830*, pp. 13, 47, 85, 150.

32. For details, see Bury and Tombs, *Thiers*, pp. 27–39; Pinkney, *Revolution of 1830*, chaps. 3, 4; and O'Boyle, "Image of the Journalist." O'Boyle provides a wide range of quotations to sustain the point. It would be a mistake to see the 1830 insurgency in either/or terms, that is, either intellectuals or businessmen. The problem is the neglect of, or the submergence of, the intellectuals' role in Marx's text. Feydeau, the 1848 barricade fighter mentioned early in this chapter, was once employed by Laffitte. He refers to the banker as the "célèbre philanthrope révolutionnaire" (*Mémoires*, p. 1).

Italy's most famous composer in the 1820s was Gioacchino Rossini. In 1823 and 1824, discussions were held, an agreement was reached, and a contract was signed that brought the composer to Paris. The contract was with the Ministry of the Royal Household. In the course of negotiations, the king, Louis XVIII, had received Rossini "with every sign of royal favor." That favor continued under the reign of his successor, Charles X. Rossini composed music for the new king's coronation and, in his first years in Paris, supervised performances of his most famous operas, all of these in Italian. The culmination of his career as opera composer involved three French-language operas. In October 1826, *Le Siège de Corinthe* opened to "prolonged shows of enthusiasm." The parallels to the Greek war of independence then being fought, one may assume, were not lost on the audience. The next opera, *Moïse et Pharaon, ou Le Passage de la Mer Rouge*, also a reworking of an Italian original, was "greeted with almost hysterical enthusiasm." Like its predecessor, it dealt with the liberation of an oppressed people and again, according to a leading source, the parallel was easily recognized; the opera was seen as "a laudable defense of the admired Greeks against the hated Turks."

The third and most famous of the Paris operas was *William Tell*, based on the Schiller original. Problems arose with the libretto. Two versions were rejected. A third was acceptable but much too long. A "play doctor" brought that version down to a practical size. But then Rossini recognized that a crucial scene was now too brief. Another script writer appeared at this point and, following Rossini's instructions, produced the text used in the completed opera. The writer was Armand Marrast, the revolutionary of 1830 and 1848 and cofounder of *Le National*. In 1828, he was the secretary to Alexandre-Marie Aguado, a banker, a close friend of Rossini's, and also the composer's patron and financial adviser. Critics received the opera, first performed in August 1829, with "paeans of mighty praise." The terms of Rossini's contract had been rewritten in May that year, improving the composer's already very favorable conditions, and was signed personally by Charles X. Four days after the premiere of *Tell*, the king rewarded Rossini with the Légion d'honneur. That evening, musicians and supporters honoring the composer crowded into Boulevard Montmartre before his house. Among those present were Armand Marrast and Armand Carrel, editors of the newspaper that was instrumental in bringing down the monarch the following July. Years later, Rossini told Richard Wagner that he had composed *Guillaume Tell* at Aguado's country house. For needed changes in the text and verses, he had help from Marrast and Adolphe Crémieux, later to appear as the minister of justice in the revolutionary government of 1848. Aguado died in 1842. All of Rossini's financial affairs in France were then handled by the Rothschild bank.

Those operatic achievements might point to a finance aristocracy at work to undermine an oppressive regime. It should also be noted, however, that their effort was sponsored and paid for by the leader of that regime. Carrel, Marrast, and Crémieux were later found, as we have seen, among the opponents of the Orleanist regime. There is another possibility, of course, namely that the king, the banker, and the composer did not foresee the possible consequences of their efforts. Although Rossini composed operas with revolutionary content, that does not appear to reflect his personal preferences. He was in Italy in July 1830 and again in 1848; the Italian revolutionaries were disappointed with his response. These details are from Weinstock, *Rossini*, pp. 160–61, 227, 242–43, and 291–92.

33. For an overview of Guizot's extensive intellectual productions, see Douglas Johnson, *Guizot*. A useful starting place is the index listing of his works on p. 462. On the reception of Lamartine's *Histoire des Girondins*, see Fortescue, *Lamartine*, pp. 128–32. A play by Alexandre Dumas dealing with an event from the time of the Girondins opened in Paris at about the same time. The play's chorus, Fortescue reports, "'Mourir pour la patrie', became one of the most popular revolutionary songs in 1848" (*Lamartine*, p. 129). An important exception to the generalization put forward in these paragraphs, to what might be called the rule of neglect, is Lewis Namier's *1848*.

34. The Hugo quotation is from the preface to *Hernani*, p. 73. The statement given here is a sloganlike summary of a more florid original. The Sainte-Beuve quotation is from Spitzer, *French Generation*, p. 6.

Karl Gutzkow (1811–78), one example among many, was a leading figure in the Young Germany movement and, for a while, a co-worker of Engels. In the early 1830s, Sammons reports, he declared that "the necessity of the politicization of our literature is undeniable." He "dashed off one aggressive work after another, until he succeeded in devising one that ignited the powder keg at last" (Sammons, *Heinrich Heine*, p. 207).

Engels's summary description of the tendency of the age was quoted above (see n. 4). For a comprehensive review, see Langer, *Political and Social Upheaval*, chap. 16. The "favorite theme" of romantic plays, he writes, "was the antagonism of social classes. The evils of wealth, the exploitation of the poor and weak, the seduction of the worker's virtuous sister or daughter by the heartless aristocrat—these topics were constantly harped upon. The cumulative effect of this propaganda must have been considerable" (p. 565). For a more recent account touching on some of the same themes, see James Smith Allen, *Popular French Romanticism*, esp. chap. 7, "Romanticism and Revolution."

Not all romantics were critical or revolutionary in orientation. The most striking exception was Chateaubriand. He too, however, saw the general oppositional tendency: "A generation is rising up behind us resentful of all discipline, hostile to every king, dreaming of the republic but constitutionally incapable of republican virtues. It advances, presses on us, elbows us aside. Soon it will take our place" (Spitzer, *French Generation*, p. 5). Emile Deschamps, in 1825, wrote that "the truly talented men in every epoch are always gifted with an instinct that pushes them toward the new" (p. 12). De Vigny, Balzac, Gauthier, and Flaubert were exceptions to this rule. Some writers changed position; Lamartine and Hugo, for example, began as conservatives but then moved to the left. For this earlier episode in Hugo's life see pp. 134–39.

For more general reviews of the oppositional role of intellectuals, see Lipset and Basu, "Intellectual Types," and Lepsius, "Kritik als Beruf." The basic point is also indicated in a library cross-reference card in the Institut für Soziologie, Ruprechts-Karls-Universität, Heidelberg, which read: "Intellektuelle—Siehe auch [see also] Elite, Opposition." For evidence on intellectuals in contemporary political movements, see Pinard and Hamilton, "Intellectuals" and "Leadership Roles."

35. See James Smith Allen, *Popular French Romanticism*, chaps. 5, 6, 7, on the selling and reading of romantic works in Paris. Paris had a very high literacy level as compared with the level elsewhere in the nation. Allen reports an 87 percent literacy level for Paris workers (males) in 1848 (p. 155). That potential, however, does not appear to translate into much actual access. Long work hours and marginal income levels did not allow reading. The literacy-illiteracy dichotomy, moreover, is misleading, bypassing an important reality, levels of literacy. By present-day standards, even best-selling "high" literature had a very limited audience. Walter Scott's most popular novel in France was *Ivanhoe*. Up to 1851, the total number of known copies printed was 60,000. That was for all of France over almost four decades. See Lyons, "Audience of Romanticism."

Possibly the most influential literary figure of the age was Lord Byron, the British poet. He was clearly on the left politically. As he put it, "I was born for opposition." As late as 1814, he reminded a friend of this, saying "You know I am a Jacobin." The Byronic hero, in the words of one biographer, Elizabeth Longford, "is a beacon to every subversive leader and enemy of society." Byron and the members of his literary circle were at this time "directly connected with the Whig establishment." The Byronic hero, Childe Harold, in contrast, was an outcast standing in opposition to society. Longford points out the paradox: "What sort of an outcast was he whom all society lionized?" See her *Life of Byron*, pp. 47, 66, 51, 46, 54. For a more extended review, see Abrams, *Natural Supernaturalism*; Howard Mumford Jones, *Revolution and Romanticism*; and Winegarten, *Writers and Revolution*. Engels offered an opposite claim about the readership; he declared that Shelley and Byron found most of their readers among the workers. See Demetz, *Marx, Engels und die Dichter*, p. 69.

Also of some interest in this connection is Mack Walker's discussion, "The subterfuge of liberal bureaucracy," pp. 284–98, in *German Home Towns.* That discussion appears in a chapter entitled "Undermining the Walls."

36. On Solomon Rothschild's relationship to Saphir, see Corti, *House of Rothschild,* pp. 46–49. On the first performance of *Les Huguenots* and the ball following, see p. 201. For the Rothschild-Balzac connection, see pp. 260–61. Balzac, like many other writers, had difficulties with his personal finances. Having made James's acquaintance, Corti reports, he "naturally borrowed money from him."

The easy relationships of artists, politicians, and businessmen is also reported in another account. "Under the July Monarchy and the Second Empire," it is said, "the luminaries of all facets of society gathered in his [Crémieux's] salon." An unnamed writer provides the following portrait: "Seated in his armchair, Crémieux watches his salon, whose hospitality is so much desired, where all the celebrities of the period mingle, become thronged all at once with great spirits and friendly faces. Lamartine, Hugo, Musset, reciting their verse, and Barbier, in a corner, declaiming his iambics to George Sand and Rachel. Alboni and Mario sing. Mérimée chats with Mme. de Girardin. Barryer encounters Lamennais, and Montalembert meets Proudhon, who is explaining his theories to Baron de Rothschild" (Posener, *Crémieux,* p. 172).

37. Corti, *House of Rothschild,* pp. 195–203; Sammons, *Heinrich Heine,* pp. 249–50. Heine's political views are not easily summarized. He once explained: "I am not exactly republican or monarchist. I am for liberty." For that reason, he is said to have "favored republics governed by monarchists and monarchies governed by republicans." He "professed a certain admiration for the rising communist movement" but never made any actual commitment. Part of the problem stemmed from his conception of the masses. "The people are not pretty," he wrote. "On the contrary, they are ugly. . . . I love the people, but I love them from a distance" (Kramer, *Threshold of a New World,* pp. 84, 86).

38. Grillparzer's comment appears in Corti, *House of Rothschild,* p. 203. The Heine-Rothschild relationship, understandably, cooled somewhat but was never completely broken. In 1843, Heine learned that his publisher, Campe, was about to publish a book (or pamphlet) hostile to the Rothschilds. Heine intervened, had Campe send him the manuscript, and brought it to James's attention. The planned publication was halted. The work first appeared some fifteen years later in Prague (pp. 203–4). In a late work, *Lutezia,* Heine made Rothschild "the object of more or less friendly jibes in a context of criticism of vast capitalist power." This, Sammons reports, did not "prevent Heine from begging railroad stocks from Rothschild or Rothschild from giving them" (*Heinrich Heine,* p. 325).

On several occasions Heine threatened public abuse of his opponents in order to secure some gain. In 1850, he "threatened to pillory Ferdinand Friedland in [his] memoirs if he did not make restitution for the losses incurred" in an earlier business transaction. In 1855, he used the memoirs "in a similar way to induce the banker Emile Périere to make him a gift of railroad stocks" (Sammons, *Heinrich Heine,* p. 337). When Heine's rich uncle died in 1844, his cousin Carl announced his intention of stopping the financial support. Heine launched an international campaign and after two years of contention, won the battle; the allowance was restored. In a letter to an accomplice, he outlined his basic tactic: "Public opinion is easily won for the poet—against millionaires" (pp. 278–83).

39. On the government subsidy, see Sammons, *Heinrich Heine*, pp. 223–25. The sum involved was "roughly equal to the annual salary of a French university professor." Muhlstein gives the annual income of a Parisian laborer of the period as 450 francs (*Baron James*, p. 13). Heine was a correspondent for the influential liberal newspaper, the Augsburg *Allgemeine Zeitung*. Although the subsidy appears to have begun under Thiers's government, Heine did not always defend his benefactor (Sammons, *Heinrich Heine*, p. 243). See also Kramer, *Threshold of a New World*, pp. 84–85.

At an earlier point, in 1828, Heine sought a professorial appointment in Bavaria. To secure this unlikely goal, he wanted the king to know that he was "much milder, better . . . quite different than in his earlier works." Sammons declares that "it is bluntly on the record that he attempted to sell his pen to the Bavarian court with the broadest of hints that his fierce polemical skills were at the buyer's disposal" (*Heinrich Heine*, pp. 137–38). In this case however, unlike that of Saphir, the request was refused.

40. Cate, *George Sand*. For some sense of her impact, see the preface, and for an account of her role in 1848, see chap. 33.

41. *MECW*, 39:62–65, *MEW*, 28:503–9. The statement of the first contribution, in the original, uses the verb *nachweisen* which can be translated, as here, with the English "to show." A stronger verb, "to prove," is also appropriate, as was used in the *Selected Works* version, 2:410. Weydemeyer, as indicated, published the first edition of Marx's *Eighteenth Brumaire*. It appeared in New York City, in two installments, in January and May of 1852.

42. For overviews, see Robertson, *Revolutions of 1848*, and Langer, *Political and Social Upheaval*, chaps. 10–14. For references on the absence of revolution in Britain, see Chapter 3 above, n. 41.

43. Part Three of the *Manifesto* contains the most familiar critique of the disdained utopian socialist view. See also Engels, *Socialism: Utopian and Scientific*, in Marx and Engels, *Selected Works*, 2:86–142, *MEW*, 19:181–228.

44. For accounts of their utopian efforts, see Manuel, *Saint-Simon*; Christopher H. Johnson, *Utopian Communism*; and Beecher, *Charles Fourier*.

45. Although one might not know on the basis of evidence, speculation is always possible. The logic of the case against Marxian socialism was spelled out by Bakunin in his *Statehood and Anarchy*, 1873. Long before Michels wrote, the anarchists argued that socialism would merely be one more system of oppression. Marx copied passages from Bakunin's work and commented on them, see *MEW*, 18:599–642. Some selections from those notes appear in Tucker, *Marx-Engels Reader*, pp. 542–48.

In later decades, one could draw lessons from the experience of the Marxist parties. The tendencies toward oligarchy, the need for expertise, and so forth, argued strongly against socialism as bringing a new era of freedom. It was the lesson of Robert Michels's work (see n. 11 above); Max Weber predicted that socialism would be a continuation of the ongoing tendency toward bureaucracy; see his essay "Sozialismus" (1924), or, for the English version, "Socialism" (1971). Lenin's approach to the management of the new socialist state in Russia after the revolution is remarkable for its naiveté. See Fuller on this point, *Conduct of War*, chap. 10.

When information on the failure of the Russian experiment first appeared, it was persistently rejected by intellectuals of the left. For the experience of Max Eastman, see Diggins, *Up from Communism*, pp. 30–39, and O'Neill, *Last Romantic*, chap. 7. For more comprehensive accounts, see O'Neill, *A Better World*; Hollander, *Political Pilgrims*, chap. 4; and Caute, *Fellow-Travellers*. Also of some relevance in this connection is the work of Djilas, *The New Class*.

46. The motto appears in Padover, *Karl Marx*, p. 628.

47. Santayana, *Life of Reason*, 1:284.

48. For Marx's interest in the Prometheus myth, see Prawer, *Karl Marx*. The first chapter, entitled "Prometheus," opens with a Marx quotation: "Prometheus is the foremost saint and martyr in the philosopher's calendar." It appears on the first page of Marx's doctoral dissertation, *MEW*, supplementary vol., no. 1, p. 263.

Many quotations point in the same direction as Santayana's. Hegel, for example, declared that "what experience and history teach is this—that people and governments never have learned anything from history, or acted on principles deduced from it." Coleridge is even closer: "If men could learn from history, what lessons it might teach us! But passion and party blind our eyes, and the light which experience gives is a lantern on the stern, which shines only on the waves behind us!" These quotations, of course, are bleakly pessimistic; there is no hope. The Santayana statement provides a glimmer of hope. It also provides a role for the concerned intellectual (*Oxford Dictionary*, pp. 244, 167).

49. Where did they stand in those discussions about dropping history? And, more importantly, where do they stand now on the question? Are those concerned about not remembering the past now actively working to rectify the mistake? Are they seeking to reinstitute history as a requirement? If not, then they are playing some part in condemning others, their students, to repeat the past. One might cite Euripides here: "Whoso neglects learning in his youth, / Loses the past and is dead for the future." But that would involve "blaming the victim" when, possibly, it was some anonymous authority who was responsible for that neglect. If so, then adult citizens, parents, and students made a mistake by not questioning that authority. Perhaps what we are dealing with is a complex interaction effect. As Hippocrates put it: "Life is short, the art long, opportunity fleeting, experience treacherous, judgment difficult" (Bartlett, *Familiar Quotations*, p. 703).

BIBLIOGRAPHY

Abrams, M. H. *Natural Supernaturalism: Tradition and Revolution in Romantic Literature.* New York: Norton, 1971.

Aguet, Jean-Pierre. "Le Tirage des quotidiens de Paris sous la monarchie de juillet." *Schweitzerische Zeitschrift für Geschichte* 10 (1960): 216–86.

Alford, Robert R. *Party and Society.* Chicago: Rand McNally, 1963.

Allen, James Smith. *Popular French Romanticism: Authors, Readers, and Books in the 19th Century.* Syracuse: Syracuse University Press, 1981.

Allen, William S. *The Nazi Seizure of Power.* Rev. ed. New York: Franklin Watts, 1984.

Almeras, Charles. *Odilon Barrot: Avocat et homme politique.* Paris: Zavier Mappus, 1948.

Amann, Peter H. "Karl Marx, 'Quarante-huitard' français?" *International Review of Social History* 6 (1961): 249–55.

———. "The Huber Enigma: Revolutionary or Police-Spy?" *International Review of Social History* 12 (1967): 190–203.

———. "A *Journée* in the Making: May 15, 1848." *Journal of Modern History* 42 (1970): 42–69.

———. *Revolution and Mass Democracy: The Paris Club Movement in 1848.* Princeton: Princeton University Press, 1975.

Anderson, Perry. *Lineages of the Absolutist State.* London: Verso, 1979.

Annan, N. G. "The Intellectual Aristocracy." In *Studies in Social History*, edited by J. H. Plumb, chap. 8. London: Longmans, Green, 1955.

Aristophanes. *The Acharnians, The Clouds, Lysistrata.* Translated by Alan H. Sommerstein. Harmondsworth: Penguin, 1973.

Armstrong, Sinclair W. "The Social Democrats and the Unification of Germany, 1863–71." *Journal of Modern History* 12 (1940): 485–509.

Arnstein, Walter L. "The Survival of the Victorian Aristocracy." In *The Rich, the Wellborn, and the Powerful: Elites and Upper Classes in History*, edited by Frederic Cople Jaher, pp. 203–57. Urbana: University of Illinois Press, 1973.

Ashton, Robert. *The English Civil War: Conservatism and Revolution, 1603–1649.* New York: Norton, 1979.

Avineri, Shlomo. *The Social and Political Thought of Karl Marx*. Cambridge: Cambridge University Press, 1968.

Aylmer, G. E. *Rebellion or Revolution?: England, 1640–1660*. Oxford: Oxford University Press, 1986.

Balsan, Consuelo Vanderbilt. *The Glitter and the Gold*. New York: Harper, 1952.

Bartlett, John. *Familiar Quotations*. 15th ed. Boston: Little, Brown, 1980.

Baughman, John J. "The French Banquet Campaign of 1847–48." *Journal of Modern History* 31 (1959): 1–15.

Beckett, J. V. *The Aristocracy in England, 1660–1914*. Oxford: Basil Blackwell, 1986.

Beecher, Jonathan. *Charles Fourier: The Visionary and His World*. Berkeley: University of California Press, 1986.

Bellanger, Claude, Jacques Godechot, Pierre Guiral, and Fernand Terrou, eds. *Histoire générale de la Presse Française*. Paris: Presses Universitaires de France, 1969.

Bender, Frederic L. *The Betrayal of Marx*. New York: Harper Torchbooks, 1975.

———, ed. *The Communist Manifesto*. New York: Norton, 1988.

Berdahl, Robert M. "Conservative Politics and Aristocratic Landholders in Bismarckian Germany." *Journal of Modern History* 44 (1972): 1–20.

Bernstein, Samuel. "Marx in Paris, 1848: A Neglected Chapter." *Science and Society* 3 (1939): 344–51.

Bezucha, Robert J. "The French Revolution of 1848 and the Social History of Work." *Theory and Society* 12 (1983): 455–68.

Blackbourn, David, and Geoff Eley. *The Peculiarities of German History: Bourgeois Society and Politics in Nineteenth-Century Germany*. New York: Oxford University Press, 1984.

Blake, Robert. *Disraeli*. New York: Carroll & Graf, 1966.

Blau, Peter M., and Otis Dudley Duncan. *The American Occupational Structure*. New York: Wiley, 1967.

Böhm-Bawerk, Eugen. *Karl Marx and the Close of His System*. New York: Kelley, 1949. First published in German in 1896.

Bosher, J. F. *The French Revolution*. New York: Norton, 1988.

Bouillon, Jacques. "Les Démocrates-Socialistes aux élections de 1849." *Revue française de science politique* 6 (1956): 70–95.

Bradford, Sarah. *Disraeli*. New York: Stein and Day, 1983.

Brenner, Robert. "The Civil War Politics of London's Merchant Community." *Past and Present* 58 (1973): 53–107.

Brissenden, Paul. *The IWW: A Study of American Syndicalism*. New York: Columbia University Press, 1920.

Burin, Frederic S. "Bureaucracy and National Socialism: A Reconsideration of Weberian Theory." In *Readings in Bureaucracy*, edited by Robert K. Merton et al., pp. 33–47. Glencoe, Ill.: Free Press, 1952.

Bury, J. P. T., and R. P. Tombs. *Thiers, 1797–1877: A Political Life*. London: Allen & Unwin, 1986.

Calhoun, Craig. *The Question of Class Struggle: Social Foundations of Popular Radicalism during the Industrial Revolution*. Chicago: University of Chicago Press, 1982.

———. "Industrialization and Social Radicalism: British and French Workers' Movements and the Mid-Nineteenth-Century Crisis." *Theory and Society* 12 (1983): 485–504.

———. "The Radicalism of Tradition." *American Journal of Sociology* 88 (1983): 886–914.

Calman, Alvin R. *Ledru-Rollin and the Second French Republic*. New York: Columbia University Press, 1922.

Cameron, Rondo. *France and the Economic Development of Europe, 1800–1814*. 2d ed. Chicago: Rand McNally, 1966.

Campbell, Peter. *French Electoral Systems and Elections since 1789*. Hamden, Conn.: Archon, 1965.

Cannon, John. *Aristocratic Century: The Peerage of Eighteenth-Century England*. Cambridge: Cambridge University Press, 1984.

Carver, Terrell. "Marx, Engels, and Dialectics." *Political Studies* 28 (1980): 353–63.

———. *Marx and Engels: The Intellectual Relationship*. Brighton, Sussex: Wheatsheaf Books, 1983.

———. "Marx, Engels, and Scholarship." *Political Studies* 32 (1984): 249–56.

Cate, Curtis. *George Sand: A Biography*. Boston: Houghton Mifflin, 1975.

Caussidière, Marc. *Mémoires de Caussidière*. 3d ed. 2 vols. Paris: Michel Lévy Fréres, 1849.

Caute, David. *The Fellow-Travellers: Intellectual Friends of Communism*. Rev. ed. New Haven: Yale University Press, 1988.

Chevalier, Louis. *La Formation de la population parisienne au XIXe siècle*. Paris: Presses Universitaires de France, 1950.

Chodorow, Stanley, et al. *The Mainstream of Civilization*. San Diego: Harcourt Brace Jovanovich, 1989.

Christofferson, Thomas R. "The French National Workshops of 1848: The View from the Provinces." *French Historical Studies* 11 (1980): 505–20.

Clapham, J. H. *The Economic Development of France and Germany, 1815–1914*. 4th ed. Cambridge: Cambridge University Press, 1936.

Clark, G. Kitson. *The Making of Victorian England*. London: Methuen, 1962.

Clough, Shepard B. *France: A History of National Economics, 1789–1939*. New York: Charles Scribner's Sons, 1939.

Cobban, Alfred. "The Influence of the Clergy and the 'Instituteurs Primaires' in the Election of the French Constituent Assembly, April 1848." *English Historical Review* 58 (1942): 334–44.

———. *A History of Modern France*. 3d ed. 3 vols. Harmondsworth: Penguin, 1963.

———. *The Social Interpretation of the French Revolution*. Cambridge: Cambridge University Press, 1964.

———. *Aspects of the French Revolution*. New York: George Braziller, 1968.

Collingham, H. A. C. *The July Monarchy: A Political History of France, 1830–1848.* London: Longman, 1988.

Collins, Irene. *The Government and the Newspaper Press in France, 1814–1881.* London: Oxford University Press, 1959.

Collins, Randall. *Three Sociological Traditions.* New York: Oxford University Press, 1985.

Corti, Egon Caesar. *The Reign of the House of Rothschild: 1830–1871.* New York: Gordon Press, 1974.

Cox, Marvin R. "The Liberal Legitimists and the Party of Order under the Second French Republic." *French Historical Studies* 5 (1968): 446–64.

Craig, Gordon A. *Germany: 1866–1945.* New York: Oxford University Press, 1978.

Dalton, Russell J., Scott C. Flanagan, and Paul Allen Beck, eds. *Electoral Change in Advanced Industrial Democracies: Realignment or Dealignment?* Princeton: Princeton University Press, 1984.

Daumard, Adeline. *La Bourgeoisie parisienne de 1815 à 1848.* Paris: SEVPEN, 1963.

Daunton, M. J. "'Gentlemanly Capitalism' and British Industry, 1820–1914." *Past and Present* 122 (1989): 119–58.

de Luna, Frederick A. *The French Republic under Cavaignac, 1848.* Princeton: Princeton University Press, 1969.

Demetz, Peter. *Marx, Engels und die Dichter.* Stuttgart: Deutsche Verlags-Anstalt, 1959.

Diefendorf, Jeffry M. *Businessmen and Politics in the Rhineland, 1789–1834.* Princeton: Princeton University Press, 1980.

Diggins, John P. *Up from Communism: Conservative Odysseys in American Intellectual History.* New York: Harper & Row, 1975.

Djilas, Milovan. *The New Class: An Analysis of the Communist System.* New York: Harcourt Brace Jovanovich, 1957.

Dominick, Raymond H., III. *Wilhelm Liebknecht and the Founding of the German Social Democratic Party.* Chapel Hill: University of North Carolina Press, 1982.

Dorpalen, Andreas. "Die Revolution von 1848 in der Geschichtsschreibung der DDR." *Historische Zeitschrift* 210 (1970): 324–68.

———. *German History in Marxist Perspective.* Detroit: Wayne State University Press, 1985.

Doukas, Kimon A. *The French Railroads and the State.* New York: Columbia University Press, 1945.

Doyle, William. *Origins of the French Revolution.* 2d ed. Oxford: Oxford University Press, 1988. The first edition was published in 1980.

———. *The Oxford History of the French Revolution.* Oxford: Clarendon Press, 1989.

Draper, Hal. *The Marx-Engels Cyclopedia.* 2 vols. New York: Schocken, 1985.

Dunham, Arthur Louis. *The Industrial Revolution in France, 1815–1848.* New York: Exposition Press, 1955.

Dunham, W. H., Jr., and C. T. Wood. "The Right to Rule in England: Depositions and the Kingdom's Authority, 1327–1485." *American Historical Review* 81 (1976): 738–61.

Duveau, Georges. *1848: The Making of a Revolution*. New York: Random House, 1967.

Eley, Geoff. "The British Model and the German Road: Rethinking the Course of German History before 1914." In Blackbourn and Eley, *The Peculiarities of German History*, pp. 39–155.

Eley, Geoff, and William Hunt, eds. *Reviving the English Revolution: Reflections and Elaborations on the Work of Christopher Hill*. London: Verso, 1988.

Engels, Friedrich. "Special Introduction to the English Edition" (1892) of *Socialism: Utopian and Scientific*. In Marx and Engels, *Selected Works*, 2:86–106.

———. "Addendum to Preface to the Second Edition" of *The Peasant War*. In Engels, *The German Revolutions*, pp. 12–18.

———. *The German Revolutions*. Edited by Leonard Krieger. Chicago: University of Chicago Press, 1967.

———. *Germany: Revolution and Counter-Revolution*. In Engels, *The German Revolutions*, pp. 123–240.

———. "Preface to the Second Edition" of *The Peasant War in Germany*. In Engels, *The German Revolutions*, pp. 3–13.

———. *The Condition of the Working Class in England*. Edited by W. O. Henderson and W. H. Chaloner. 2d ed. Oxford: Basil Blackwell, 1971.

———. *Revolution und Konterrevolution in Deutschland*. Edited by Richard Sperl. Frankfurt/Main: Verlag Marxistische Blätter, 1971.

Engels, Friedrich, and Paul and Laura Lafargue. *Correspondence*. 3 vols. Moscow: Foreign Languages Publishing House, 1959.

Ensor, R. C. K. *England: 1870–1914*. Oxford: Clarendon Press, 1936.

Euler, Heinrich. *Napoleon III. in seiner Zeit: Der Aufstieg*. Würzburg: A. G. Ploetz Verlag, 1961.

Evans, David Owen. *Social Romanticism in France, 1830–1848*. Oxford: Clarendon Press, 1951.

Fasel, George. "The French Election of April 23, 1848." *French Historical Studies* 5 (1968): 285–98.

———. "Urban Workers in Provincial France, February–June 1848." *International Review of Social History* 17 (1972): 661–74.

———. "The Wrong Revolution: French Republicanism in 1848." *French Historical Studies* 8 (1974): 654–77.

Featherman, David, and Robert Hauser. *Opportunity and Change*. New York: Academic Press, 1978.

Feydeau, Ernest. *Mémoires d'un coulissier*. Paris: Librairie nouvelle, 1873.

Fleming, Gerald. *Hitler and the Final Solution*. Berkeley: University of California Press, 1984.

Flora, Peter, Franz Kraus, and Winfried Pfenning. *State, Economy, and Society in Western Europe, 1815–1975*. London: Macmillan, 1987.

Fortescue, William. *Alphonse de Lamartine: A Political Biography*. New York: St. Martin's Press, 1983.

Foucault, Michel. *Discipline and Punish: The Birth of the Prison*. New York: Vintage, 1979.

Franklin, Mark N. *The Decline of Class Voting in Britain*. Oxford: Clarendon Press, 1985.

Fraser, Antonia. *Cromwell: The Lord Protector*. New York: Knopf, 1974.

Fromm, Erich. *The Working Class in Weimar Germany: A Psychological and Sociological Study*. Cambridge: Harvard University Press, 1984.

Fuller, J. F. C. *The Conduct of War*. London: Eyre & Spottiswoode, 1961.

Furet, François. *Interpreting the French Revolution*. Cambridge: Cambridge University Press, 1981.

————. *Marx and the French Revolution*. Chicago: University of Chicago Press, 1988.

Gallaher, John G. *The Students of Paris and the Revolution of 1848*. Carbondale: Southern Illinois University Press, 1980.

Gambs, John S. *The Decline of the I.W.W.* New York: Columbia University Press, 1932.

Garnier-Pagès, Louis A. *Histoire de la révolution de 1848*. 2d ed. 8 vols. Paris: Pagnerre, 1866.

Gash, Norman. *Aristocracy and People: Britain, 1815–1865*. Cambridge: Harvard University Press, 1979.

George, C. H. "A Century of Marxist Historical Writing about the English: A Critical Retrospect." *Social Science Quarterly* 64 (1983): 811–25.

Gershoy, Leo. "Three French Historians and the Revolution of 1848." *Journal of the History of Ideas* 12 (1951): 131–46.

Gille, Bertrand. *Histoire da la Maison Rothschild*. 2 vols. Geneva: Libraire Droz, 1967.

Girard, Louis. *La Garde nationale: 1814–1871*. Paris: Librairie Plon, 1964.

Glenn, Norval D., and Jon P. Alston. "Cultural Distances among Occupational Categories." *American Sociological Review* 33 (1968): 365–82.

Godechot, Jacques. "The Business Classes and the Revolution outside of France." *American Historical Review* 64 (1958): 1–13.

Goldstone, Jack A. "Capitalist Origins of the English Revolution: Chasing a Chimera." *Theory and Society* 12 (1983): 143–80.

————. "State Breakdown in the English Revolution: A New Synthesis." *American Journal of Sociology* 92 (1986): 257–322.

————. "East and West in the Seventeenth Century: Political Crises in Stuart England, Ottoman Turkey, and Ming China." *Comparative Studies in Society and History* 30 (1988): 103–42.

Gossez, R. "La Résistance à l'impôt: Les quarante-cinq centimes." In *Bibliothèque de la révolution de 1848*, 15:89–131. Nancy: George Thomas, 1953.

Gottheil, Fred M. *Marx's Economic Predictions*. Evanston, Ill.: Northwestern University Press, 1966.

Gouldner, Alvin. *The Two Marxisms: Contradictions and Anomalies in the Development of Theory*. New York: Seabury Press, 1980.

Grande Encyclopédie. Paris: La Société Anonyme de la Grande Encyclopédie, 1886–1902.

Greer, Donald. *The Incidence of the Terror during the French Revolution: A Statistical Interpretation*. Cambridge, Mass.: Harvard University Press, 1935.

Gugenheim, Suzanne. *Madame d'Agoult et la pensée européenne de son époque*. Florence: Biblioteca dell' "Archivum Romanicum," 1937.

Guttsman, W. L. *The British Political Elite*. New York: Basic Books, 1963.

Hahn, Hans-Werner. *Geschichte des Deutschen Zollvereins*. Göttingen: Vandenhoeck & Ruprecht, 1984.

Hamerow, Theodore S. *Restoration, Revolution, Reaction: Economics and Politics in Germany*. Princeton: Princeton University Press, 1958.

———. *The Social Foundations of German Unification, 1858–1871: Ideas and Institutions*. Princeton: Princeton University Press, 1969.

———. *The Social Foundations of German Unification, 1858–1871: Struggles and Accomplishments*. Princeton: Princeton University Press, 1971.

Hamilton, Richard F. "The Marginal Middle Class: A Reconsideration." *American Sociological Review* 31 (1966): 192–99.

———. *Class and Politics in the United States*. New York: Wiley, 1972.

———. *Restraining Myths*. New York: Sage-Halsted-Wiley, 1975.

———. *Who Voted for Hitler?* Princeton: Princeton University Press, 1982.

———. "Braunschweig 1932: Further Evidence on the Support for National Socialism." *Central European History* 17 (1984): 3–36.

———. "Hitler's Electoral Support: Recent Findings and Theoretical Implications." *Canadian Journal of Sociology* 11 (1986): 1–34.

———. Review of Erich Fromm. *The Working Class in Weimar Germany* in *Society* 23, no. 3 (March/April 1986): 82–85.

Hammen, Oscar J. "Alienation, Communism, and Revolution in the Marx-Engels *Briefwechsel*." *Journal of the History of Ideas* 33 (1972): 77–100.

———. "Marx and the Agrarian Question." *American Historical Review* 77 (1972): 679–704.

Haswell, Jack. *James II: Soldier and Sailor*. London: Hamish Hamilton, 1972.

Heilbroner, Robert L. *Marxism: For and Against*. New York: Norton, 1980.

Henderson, W. O. *The Zollverein*. Cambridge: Cambridge University Press, 1939.

———. *The Rise of German Industrial Power, 1834–1914*. Berkeley: University of California Press, 1975.

———. *The Life of Friedrich Engels*. 2 vols. London: Frank Cass, 1976.

Hertz-Eichenrode, Dieter. "Karl Marx über das Bauerntum und die Bündnisfrage." *International Review of Social History* 11 (1966): 383–402.

Hexter, J. H. *Reappraisals in History*. London: Longmans, Green, 1961.

———. "The Historical Method of Christopher Hill." Chap. 5 of his *On Historians*. Cambridge, Mass.: Harvard University Press, 1979.

Hill, Christopher. "The English Civil War Interpreted by Marx and Engels." *Science and Society* 12 (1948): 130–56.

———. *The English Revolution, 1640*. 3d ed. London: Lawrence and Wishart, 1955. The work first appeared in 1940.

———. *God's Englishman: Oliver Cromwell and the English Revolution*. New York: Dial Press, 1970.

———. "A Bourgeois Revolution?" In Pocock, *Three British Revolutions*, chap. 2.

Hinde, Wendy. *Richard Cobden: A Victorian Outsider*. New Haven: Yale University Press, 1987.

Hoffmann, Walter G. *Das Wachstum der deutschen Wirtschaft seit der Mitte des 19. Jahrhunderts*. Berlin: Springer Verlag, 1965.

Holborn, Hajo. *A History of Modern Germany*. 3 vols. Princeton: Princeton University Press, 1964.

Hollander, Paul. *Political Pilgrims*. New York: Oxford University Press, 1981.

Horne, Alistair. *Harold Macmillan*. 2 vols. New York: Viking, 1989.

Horowitz, Irving Louis, and Bernadette Hayes. "For Marx/Against Engels: Dialectics Revisited." *Social Praxis* 7 (1980): 59–75.

Howarth, T. E. B. *Citizen King: The Life of Louis-Philippe, King of the French*. London: Eyre & Spottiswoode, 1961.

Howell, Roger. "The Structure of Urban Politics in the English Civil War." *Albion* 11 (1979): 111–27.

———. "Neutralism, Conservatism and Political Alignment in the English Revolution: The Case of the Towns, 1642–9." In Morrill, *Reactions to the English Civil War*, chap. 3.

Hugo, Victor. Preface to *Hernani, ou l'Honneur Castillan*. Edited by David Owen Evans. London: Thomas Nelson, 1936.

Hunt, E. K., and Howard J. Sherman. *Economics: An Introduction to Traditional and Radical Views*. New York: Harper & Row, 1972, 1990.

Iggers, George G. *The German Conception of History*. Middletown, Conn.: Wesleyan University Press, 1968.

Inglehart, Ronald. *The Silent Revolution: Changing Values and Political Styles among Western Publics*. Princeton: Princeton University Press, 1977.

Institut für Marxismus-Leninismus. *Marx, Engels, Lenin, Stalin zur deutschen Geschichte*. 2 vols. Berlin: Dietz Verlag, 1953.

Jardin, André. *Tocqueville: A Biography*. New York: Farrar Straus Giroux, 1988.

Jardin, André, and André-Jean Tudesq. *Restoration and Reaction, 1815–1848*. Cambridge: Cambridge University Press, 1983.

Johnson, Christopher H. *Utopian Communism in France: Cabet and the Icarians, 1839–*

1851. Ithaca: Cornell University Press, 1974.

———. "The Revolution of 1830 in French Economic History." In Merriman, *1830 in France*.

Johnson, Douglas. *Guizot: Aspects of French History, 1787–1874*. London: Routledge & Kegan Paul, 1963.

Jones, Alfred Winslow. *Life, Liberty, and Property*. Philadelphia: Lippincott, 1941.

Jones, Howard Mumford. *Revolution and Romanticism*. Cambridge, Mass.: Harvard University Press, 1974.

Jones, J. R. *The Revolution of 1688 in England*. London: Weidenfeld & Nicolson, 1972.

———, ed. *The Restored Monarchy, 1660–1688*. London: Macmillan, 1979.

Jordan, Erich. *Die Entstehung der konservativen Partei und die preussischen Agrarverhältnisse von 1848*. Munich: Dunker und Humblot, 1914.

Joyce, Patrick. "The Factory Politics of Lancashire in the Later Nineteenth Century." *Historical Journal* 18 (1975): 525–53.

Kaplow, Jeffry, ed. *New Perspectives on the French Revolution: Readings in Historical Sociology*. New York: Wiley, 1965.

Kelly, George Armstrong. "Alphonse de Lamartine: The Poet in Politics." *Daedelus* 116 (1987): 157–80.

Kennedy, A. L. *Salisbury, 1830–1903: Portrait of a Statesman*. London: John Murray, 1953.

Kline, George L. "The Myth of Marx's Materialism." *Annals of Scholarship* 3 (1984): 1–38.

Kluchert, Gerhard. *Geschichtsschreibung und Revolution: Die historischen Schriften von Karl Marx und Friedrich Engels, 1846 bis 1852*. Stuttgart: Friedrich Frommann, 1985.

Kocka, Jürgen. "Preussischer Staat und Modernisierung im Vormärz: Marxistisch-leninistische Interpretationen und ihre Probleme." In *Sozialgeschichte Heute*, edited by Hans-Ulrich Wehler, pp. 211–27. Göttingen: Vandenhoeck & Rupprecht, 1974.

Kolakowski, Leszek. *Main Currents of Marxism*. 3 vols. New York: Oxford University Press, 1978.

Kornblum, William. *Blue Collar Community*. Chicago: University of Chicago Press, 1974.

Kramer, Lloyd S. *Threshold of a New World: Intellectuals and the Exile Experience in Paris, 1830–1848*. Ithaca: Cornell University Press, 1988.

Krieger, Leonard, ed. *The German Revolutions*. Chicago: University of Chicago Press, 1967.

Kwavnick, David. "Pressure-Group Demands and Organizational Objectives: The CNTU, the Lapalme Affair, and National Bargaining Units." *Canadian Journal of Political Science* 6 (1973): 582–601.

Langer, William L. *Political and Social Upheaval, 1832–1852*. New York: Harper & Row, 1969.

Latta, Claude. "Le Maintien de l'ordre à Lyon (février–juillet 1848)." In *Maintien de l'ordre et polices en France et en Europe au XIXe siècle*, edited by Philippe Vigier et al., pp. 61–85. Paris: Créaphis, 1987.

Ledré, Charles. *La Presse à l'assaut de la monarchie, 1815–1848*. Paris: A. Colin, 1960.

Lefebvre, Georges. *The Coming of the French Revolution*. Princeton: Princeton University Press, 1947.

———. *The French Revolution from Its Origins to 1793*. London: Routledge & Kegan Paul, 1962.

———. *The French Revolution: From 1793 to 1799*. London: Routledge & Kegan Paul, 1964.

Lenski, Gerhard. *The Religious Factor*. Garden City, N.Y.: Doubleday, 1961.

Léon, Pierre, et al., eds. *Histoire économique et sociale de la France*. 2 vols. Paris: Presses Universitaires de France, 1976.

Lepsius, M. Rainer. "Kritik als Beruf: Zur Soziologie der Intellektuellen." *Kölner Zeitschrift für Soziologie und Sozialpsychologie* 16 (1964): 75–91.

Levine, Norman. *The Tragic Deception: Marx Contra Engels*. Santa Barbara, Calif.: Clio Books, 1975.

———. "The Engelsian Inversion." *Studies in Soviet Thought* 25 (1983): 307–21.

———. "Lenin's Utopianism." *Studies in Soviet Thought* 30 (1985): 95–107.

Lhomme, Jean. *La Grande Bourgeoisie au pouvoir (1830–1880)*. Paris: Presses Universitaires de France, 1960.

Lichtheim, George. *Marxism: An Historical and Critical Study*. New York: Praeger, 1961.

Lijphart, Arend. "Religion vs. Linguistic vs. Class Voting: The 'Crucial Experiment' of Camparing, Belgium, Canada, South Africa, and Switzerland." *American Political Science Review* 73 (1979): 442–58.

Lindsay, A. D. *Karl Marx's Capital: An Introductory Essay*. London: Oxford University Press, 1925.

Linz, Juan J. "Michels, Robert." In *International Encyclopedia of the Social Sciences*, 10:265–72. New York: Macmillan–Free Press, 1968.

Lipset, Seymour Martin. "Social Mobility in Industrial Societies." *Public Opinion* 5 (June/July 1982): 41–44.

———. *Consensus and Conflict: Essays in Political Sociology*. New Brunswick, N.J.: Transaction Books, 1985.

Lipset, Seymour Martin, and Asoke Basu. "Intellectual Types and Political Roles." In *The Idea of Social Structure*, edited by Lewis Coser, pp. 433–70. New York: Harcourt Brace Jovanovich, 1975.

Lipset, Seymour Martin, and Reinhard Bendix. *Social Mobility in Industrial Society*. Berkeley: University of California Press, 1959.

Longford, Elizabeth. *The Life of Byron*. Boston: Little, Brown, 1976.

———. *The Pebbled Shore*. London: Weidenfeld and Nicolson, 1986.

Lorwin, Val. "Working Class Politics and Economic Development in Western Europe." *American Historical Review* 63 (1958): 338–51.

Loubère, Leo. *Louis Blanc: His Life and His Contribution to the Rise of French Jacobin Socialism*. Evanston, Ill.: Northwestern University Press, 1961.

Lyons, Martyn. "The Audience of Romanticism: Walter Scott in France, 1815–51." *European History Quarterly* 14 (1984): 21–46.

McCahill, Michael W. "Peerage Creations and the Changing Character of the British Nobility, 1750–1830." *English Historical Review* 96 (1981): 259–84.

McCord, Norman. *The Anti–Corn Law League, 1838–1846*. London: Unwin University Books, 1958.

————. "Cobden and Bright in Politics." In *Ideas and Institutions of Victorian Britain*, edited by Robert Robson, chap. 4. New York: Barnes & Noble, 1967.

McInnes, Angus. "When Was the English Revolution?" *History* 67 (1982): 377–92.

McKay, Donald C. *The National Workshops: A Study in the French Revolution of 1848*. Cambridge, Mass.: Harvard University Press, 1933.

McLellan, David. *Karl Marx: His Life & Thought*. London: Macmillan, 1973.

Maehl, William Harvey. *August Bebel: Shadow Emperor of the German Workers*. Philadelphia: American Philosophical Society, 1980.

————. "German Social Democratic Agrarian Policy, 1890–1895, Reconsidered." *Central European History* 13 (1980): 121–57.

Magnus, Philip. *Gladstone: A Biography*. London: John Murray, 1954.

Maitron, Jean, ed. *Dictionnaire Biographique du Mouvement Ouvrier Français*. Paris: Les Editions Ouvrières, 1964.

Mannheim, Karl. *Ideology and Utopia*. New York: Harcourt, Brace, 1949.

Manuel, Frank E. *The New World of Henri Saint-Simon*. Cambridge, Mass.: Harvard University Press, 1956.

Margadant, Ted W. *French Peasants in Revolt: The Insurrection of 1851*. Princeton: Princeton University Press, 1979.

Markovitch, T. J. "La Crise de 1847–1848 dans les Industries Parisiennes." *Revue d'Histoire économique et sociale* 43 (1965): 256–60.

Marx, Karl. *Capital: A Critique of Political Economy*. 3 vols. New York: International Publishers, 1967.

Marx, Karl, and Friedrich Engels. *Selected Works*. 2 vols. Moscow: Foreign Languages Publishing House, 1951.

————. *On Britain*. 2d ed. Moscow: Foreign Languages Publishing House, 1962.

————. *Werke*. 42 vols. plus supplements. Berlin: Dietz Verlag, 1964.

————. *Collected Works*. New York: International Publishers, 1975.

Mayer, Arno J. *The Persistence of the Old Regime*. New York: Pantheon Books, 1981.

Mayer, Gustav. *Friedrich Engels: Eine Biographie*. 2d ed. 2 vols. The Hague: Martinus Nijhoff, 1934.

Merriman, John M., ed. *1830 in France*. New York: New Viewpoints, 1975.

————. *The Agony of the Republic: The Repression of the Left in Revolutionary France, 1848–1851*. New Haven: Yale University Press, 1978.

————, ed. *French Cities in the Nineteenth Century*. London: Hutchinson, 1982.

Michels, Robert. *Political Parties: A Sociological Study of the Oligarchical Tendencies of Modern Democracy*. Glencoe, Ill.: Free Press, 1949. First published in German in 1911 and in English in 1915.

Miliband, Ralph. "Socialism and the Myth of the Golden Past." In *The Socialist Register: 1964*, edited by Ralph Miliband and John Saville, pp. 92–103. New York: Monthly Review Press, 1964.

Miller, John. *James II: A Study in Kingship*. Hove, East Sussex: Wayland, 1977.

Moore, Barrington. *Social Origins of Dictatorship and Democracy: Lord and Peasant in the Making of the Modern World*. Boston: Beacon Press, 1966.

Morgan, Roger. *The German Social Democrats and the First International, 1864–1872*. Cambridge: Cambridge University Press, 1965.

Morrill, John, ed. *Reactions to the English Civil War*. New York: St. Martin's, 1983.

Moss, Bernard H. "June 13, 1849: The Abortive Uprising of French Radicalism." *French Historical Studies* 13 (1984): 390–414.

Mosse, George L. *The Crisis of German Ideology: Intellectual Origins of the Third Reich*. New York: Grosset & Dunlap, 1964.

Muhlstein, Anke. *Baron James: The Rise of the French Rothschilds*. New York: Vendome, 1982.

Namier, Lewis. *1848: The Revolution of the Intellectuals*. London: Oxford University Press, 1946.

Nilson, Sten S. "Wahlsoziologische Probleme des Nationalsozialismus." *Zeitschrift für die gesamte Staatswissenschaft* 110 (1954): 295–311.

Nouvelle Biographie Générale. Paris: Firmin Dido, 1966.

Noyes, P. H. *Organization and Revolution: Working-Class Associations in the German Revolutions of 1848–1849*. Princeton: Princeton University Press, 1966.

O'Boyle, Lenore. "The Image of the Journalist in France, Germany, and England, 1815–1848." *Comparative Studies in Society and History* 10 (1968): 290–317.

Olson, Mancur. *The Logic of Collective Action*. Cambridge: Harvard University Press, 1965.

O'Neill, William L. *The Last Romantic: A Life of Max Eastman*. New York: Oxford University Press, 1978.

———. *A Better World: The Great Schism: Stalinism and the American Intellectuals*. New York: Simon and Schuster, 1982.

Oxford Dictionary of Quotations. 3d ed. New York: Oxford University Press, 1979.

Padover, Saul K. *Karl Marx: An Intimate Biography*. New York: McGraw-Hill, 1978.

Palmer, Robert R. *The Age of the Democratic Revolution*. Princeton: Princeton University Press, 1964.

———. *Twelve Who Ruled: The Year of the Terror in the French Revolution*. Princeton: Princeton University Press, 1969.

Parkin, Frank. *Marxism and Class Theory: A Bourgeois Critique*. London: Tavistock, 1979.

Paul, R. S. *The Lord Protector: Religion and Politics in the Life of Oliver Cromwell*. London: Lutterworth Press, 1955.

Pearl, Valerie. *London and the Outbreak of the Puritan Revolution: City Government and National Politics, 1625–1643*. Oxford: Oxford University Press.

Percy, Eustace. *Some Memories*. London: Eyre & Spottiswoode, 1958.

Perrott, Roy. *The Aristocrats: A Portrait of Britain's Nobility and Their Way of Life Today*. New York: Macmillan, 1968.

Pinard, Maurice, and Richard F. Hamilton. "Intellectuals and the Leadership of Social Movements: Some Comparative Perspectives." In *Research in Social Movements, Conflict and Change*, 11:73–107. Greenwich, Conn.: JAI Press, 1989.

———. "The Leadership Roles of Intellectuals in Traditional Parties: Canadian and Comparative Perspectives." In *Canadian Parties in Transition*, edited by Alain G. Gagnon and B. Tanguay, chap. 12. Toronto: Methuen, 1989.

Pinkney, David H. "Les Ateliers de secours à Paris (1830–1831): Précurseurs des ateliers nationaux de 1848." *Revue d'histoire moderne et contemporaine* 12 (1965): 65–70.

———. *The French Revolution of 1830*. Princeton: Princeton University Press, 1972.

———. *Decisive Years in France, 1840–1847*. Princeton: Princeton University Press, 1986.

Pinson, Koppel S. *Modern Germany: Its History and Civilization*. 2d ed. New York: Macmillan, 1966.

Pocock, J. G. A., ed. *Three British Revolutions: 1641, 1688, 1776*. Princeton: Princeton University Press, 1980.

Posener, S. *Adolphe Crémieux: A Biography*. Philadelphia: Jewish Publication Society of America, 1941.

Pouthas, Charles H. *La Population française pendant la première moitié du XIXe siècle*. Paris: Presses Universitaires de France, 1956.

Prawer, S. S. *Karl Marx and World Literature*. Oxford: Clarendon Press, 1976.

Price, Roger. *The French Second Republic: A Social History*. London: B. T. Batsford, 1972.

———, ed. *Revolution and Reaction: 1848 and the Second French Republic*. London: Croom Helm, 1975.

———. "Techniques of Repression: The Control of Popular Protest in Mid-Nineteenth-Century France." *Historical Journal* 25 (1982): 859–87.

———. *A Social History of Nineteenth-Century France*. London: Hutchinson, 1987.

Pumphrey, Ralph E. "The Introduction of Industrialists into the British Peerage: A Study in Adaption of a Social Institution." *American Historical Review* 65 (1959): 1–16.

Putnam, Robert D. *The Comparative Study of Political Elites*. Englewood Cliffs, N.J.: Prentice-Hall, 1976.

Rémond, René. *Les Droites en France*. 4th ed. Paris: Aubier Montaigne, 1982.

Richards, Eric. *The Leviathan of Wealth: The Sutherland Fortune in the Industrial Revolution*. London: Routledge & Kegan Paul, 1973.

————. "Structural Change in a Regional Economy: Sutherland and the Industrial Revolution, 1780–1830." *Economic History Review* 26 (1973): 63–75.

Richardson, R. C. *The Debate on the English Revolution Revised*. London: Routledge, 1988.

Ridley, Jasper. *Lord Palmerston*. New York: Dutton, 1971.

Roberts, Clayton. "The Constitutional Significance of the Financial Settlement of 1690." *The Historical Journal* 20 (1977): 59–76.

Robertson, Priscilla. *Revolutions of 1848: A Social History*. Princeton: Princeton University Press, 1952.

Rooney, John W., Jr. *Revolt in the Netherlands: Brussels—1830*. Lawrence, Kans.: Coronado Press, 1982.

Roots, Ivan. *The Great Rebellion: 1642–1660*. London: Batsford, 1966.

Rose, Richard, ed. *Electoral Behavior: A Comparative Handbook*. New York: Free Press, 1974.

Rosenberg, Hans. *Bureaucracy, Aristocracy and Autocracy: The Prussian Experience, 1660–1815*. Cambridge, Mass.: Harvard University Press, 1958.

Rothschild, Salomon de. *A Casual View of America*. Translated and edited by Sigmund Diamond. Stanford: Stanford University Press, 1961.

Rubel, Maximilien. "Karl Marx." In *International Encyclopedia of the Social Sciences*, 10:34–40. New York: Macmillan and the Free Press, 1968.

Rubinstein, W. D. "Wealth, Elites and the Class Structure of Modern Britain." *Past and Present* 76 (1977): 99–126.

————. *Men of Property: The Very Wealthy in Britain Since the Industrial Revolution*. New Brunswick, N.J.: Rutgers University Press, 1981.

Rudé, George. *Revolutionary Europe, 1795–1815*. Glasgow: Fontana/Collins, 1964.

————. Introduction to Duveau, *1848: The Making of a Revolution*.

————. "Why Was There No Revolution in England in 1830 or 1848?" In *Studien über die Revolution*, edited by Manfred Kossok, pp. 231–44. Berlin: Akademie Verlag, 1969.

Sammons, Jeffrey L. *Heinrich Heine: A Modern Biography*. Princeton: Princeton University Press, 1979.

Sampson, Anthony. *Anatomy of Britain Today*. London: Hodder and Stoughton, 1965.

Santayana, George. *The Life of Reason*. 2 vols. New York: Scribner's, 1911.

Schama, Simon. *Citizens: A Chronicle of the French Revolution*. New York: Knopf, 1989.

Schoenbaum, David. *Hitler's Social Revolution: Class and Status in Nazi Germany, 1933–1939*. Garden City, N.Y.: Doubleday Anchor Books, 1967.

Schumpeter, Joseph. *Capitalism, Socialism and Democracy*. New York: Harper Torchbooks, 1962.

Sée, Henri. *La Vie économique de la France sous la monarchie censitaire (1815–1848)*. 2 vols. Paris: Alcan, 1927.

———. *Histoire économique de la France*. Paris: A. Colin, 1942.

Seigel, Jerrold. *Bohemian Paris: Culture, Politics, and the Boundaries of Bourgeois Life, 1830–1930*. New York: Viking, 1986.

Sewell, William, Jr. *Work and Revolution in France: The Language of Labor from the Old Regime to 1848*. Cambridge: Cambridge University Press, 1980.

Shannon, Richard. *The Crisis of Imperialism, 1865–1915*. London: Hart Davis, MacGibbon, 1974.

Sheehan, James J. *German History, 1770–1866*. Oxford: Clarendon Press, 1989.

Sherman, Howard J., and James L. Wood. *Sociology: Traditional and Radical Perspectives*. 2d ed. New York: Harper & Row, 1989.

Simpson, F. A. *The Rise of Louis Napoleon*. London: Frank Cass, 1968.

Speck, W. A. *Reluctant Revolutionaries: Englishmen and the Revolution of 1688*. Oxford: Oxford University Press, 1988.

Spencer, Martin E. "Marx on the State: The Events in France between 1848–1850." *Theory and Society* 7 (1979): 167–98.

Spitzer, Alan B. *The French Generation of 1820*. Princeton: Princeton University Press, 1987.

Spring, David. "The English Landed Estate in the Age of Coal and Iron: 1830–1880." *Journal of Economic History* 11 (1951): 3–24.

———. "Earl Fitzwilliam and the Corn Laws." *American Historical Review* 59 (1953–54): 287–304.

———. "Some Reflections on Social History in the Nineteenth Century: The Role of the Aristocracy in the Late Nineteenth Century." *Victorian Studies* 4 (1960): 55–64.

———. "Aristocracy, Social Structure, and Religion in the Early Victorian Period." *Victorian Studies* 6 (1963): 263–80.

———. *The English Landed Estate in the Nineteenth Century: Its Administration*. Baltimore: Johns Hopkins University Press, 1963.

———. *European Landed Elites in the Nineteenth Century*. Baltimore: Johns Hopkins University Press, 1977.

St. John, Percy B. *Three Days of February 1848: An Eye-Witness of the Whole Revolution*. 2d ed. London: Richard Bentley, 1848.

Stanley, John L., and Ernest Zimmermann. "On the Alleged Differences between Marx and Engels." *Political Studies* 32 (1984): 226–48.

Stearns, Peter. *1848: The Revolutionary Tide in Europe*. New York: Norton, 1974.

Stern, Daniel. *Histoire de la révolution de 1848*. 2d ed. 2 vols. Paris: Charpentier, 1862. Stern is the pseudonym of Marie de Flavigny, comtesse d'Agoult.

Stoeckl, Agnes de. *King of the French: A Portrait of Louis Philippe 1773–1850*. London: John Murray, 1957.

Stone, Lawrence. *The Causes of the English Revolution, 1529–1642*. New York: Harper Torchbooks, 1972.

———. "The Results of the English Revolutions of the Seventeenth Century." In Pocock, *Three British Revolutions*, chap. 1.

———. "The Bourgeois Revolution of Seventeenth-Century England Revisited." In Eley and Hunt, *Reviving the English Revolution*. The article first appeared in *Past and Present* 109 (1985): 44–54.

Stone, Lawrence, and Jeanne C. Fawtier Stone. *An Open Elite?: England, 1540–1880*. Oxford: Clarendon Press, 1984.

Taine, Hippolyte. *Notes on England*. London: Thames and Hudson, 1957.

Therborn, Gören. "The Rule of Capital and the Rise of Democracy." *New Left Review* 103 (May–June 1977): 5, 17, 26.

Thomas, David. "The Social Origins of Marriage Partners of the British Peerage in the Eighteenth and Nineteenth Centuries." *Population Studies* 26 (1972): 99–111.

Thompson, F. M. L. "Whigs and Liberals in the West Riding, 1830–1860." *English Historical Review* 74 (1959): 214–39.

———. *English Landed Society in the Nineteenth Century*. London: Routledge & Kegan Paul, 1963.

Tilly, Charles. *From Mobilization to Revolution*. Reading, Mass.: Addison-Wesley, 1978.

Tilly, Charles, and Lynn H. Lees. "The People of June, 1848." In Price, *Revolution and Reaction*, pp. 170–209.

Tocqueville, Alexis de. *Journeys to England and Ireland*. New Haven: Yale University Press, 1958.

———. *Recollections*. Garden City, N.Y.: Doubleday, 1970.

Traugott, Mark. "The Mid-Nineteenth-Century Crisis in France and England." *Theory and Society* 12 (1983): 455–68.

———. *Armies of the Poor: Determinants of Working-Class Participation in the Parisian Insurrection of June 1848*. Princeton: Princeton University Press, 1985.

———. "The Crowd in the French Revolution of February, 1848." *The American Historical Review* 93 (1988): 638–52.

Trevelyan, George Macaulay. *The English Revolution, 1688–1689*. London: Oxford University Press, 1938.

Tuchman, Barbara. *The Proud Tower: A Portrait of the World before the War, 1890–1914*. New York: Macmillan, 1966.

Tucker, Robert C., ed. *The Marx-Engels Reader*. 2d ed. New York: Norton, 1978.

Tudesq, André-Jean. *Les grands notables en France (1840–1849): Etude historique d'une psychologie sociale*. 2 vols. Paris: Presses Universitaires de France, 1964.

———. *L'Election presidentielle de Louis-Napoléon Bonaparte*. Paris: A. Colin, 1965.

Turner, Henry A. *German Big Business and the Rise of Hitler*. New York: Oxford University Press, 1985.

Valentin, Veit. *Geschichte der deutschen Revolution von 1848–1849*. 2 vols. Cologne: Kiepenheuer und Witsch, 1977. First published in 1930.

Van den Berg, Axel. *The Immanent Utopia: From Marxism on the State to the State of Marxism*. Princeton: Princeton University Press, 1988.

Vier, Jacques. *La Comtesse d'Agoult et son temps*. 4 vols. Paris: A. Colin, 1961.

Vincent, John. *The Formation of the Liberal Party, 1857–1868*. London: Constable, 1966.

Walker, Mack. *German Home Towns: Community, State, and General Estate, 1648–1871*. Ithaca: Cornell University Press, 1971.

Ward, J. T., and R. G. Wilson, eds. *Land and Industry: The Landed Estate and the Industrial Revolution*. Newton Abbot, Devon: David & Charles, 1971.

Weber, Adna. *The Growth of Cities in the Nineteenth Century*. Ithaca: Cornell University Press, 1963. Originally published in 1899.

Weber, Eugen. "The Second Republic, Politics, and the Peasant." *French Historical Studies* 11 (1980): 520–50.

Weber, Max. "Socialism." In *Max Weber: The Interpretation of Social Reality*, edited by J. E. T. Eldridge, pp. 191–219. New York: Scribner's, 1971.

———. "Sozialismus." In his *Gesammelte Aufsätze zur Soziologie und Sozialpolitik*, pp. 492–518. Tübingen: J. C. B. Mohr–Paul Siebeck, 1924.

Weinstock, Herbert. *Rossini: A Biography*. New York: Knopf, 1968.

Welty, Gordon. "Marx, Engels, and 'Anti-Dühring.'" *Political Studies* 31 (1983): 284–94.

Wilson, Edmund. *To the Finland Station: A Study in the Writing and Acting of History*. Garden City, N.Y.: Doubleday Anchor Books, 1953.

Winegarten, Renée. *Writers and Revolution: The Fatal Lure of Action*. New York: Franklin Watts, 1974.

Wolff, Adolf. *Berliner Revolutions-Chronik*. Vaduz, Liechtenstein: Topos Verlag, 1979. First published 1851–54.

Wood, Robert C. *Suburbia: Its People and Their Politics*. Boston: Houghton Mifflin, 1959.

Woodward, Llewellyn. *The Age of Reform, 1815–1870*. Oxford: Clarendon Press, 1962.

Wright, Gordon. *France in Modern Times*. Chicago: Rand McNally, 1960.

INDEX

287